Work Stress and Coping in the Era of Globalization

Work Stress and Coping in the Era of Globalization

Rabi S. Bhagat
University of Memphis

James C. Segovis
Bryant University

Terry A. Nelson
University of Memphis

Routledge
Taylor & Francis Group
New York   London

Routledge
Taylor & Francis Group
711 Third Avenue
New York, NY 10017

Routledge
Taylor & Francis Group
27 Church Road
Hove, East Sussex BN3 2FA

© 2012 by Taylor & Francis Group, LLC
Routledge is an imprint of Taylor & Francis Group, an Informa business

Printed in the United States of America on acid-free paper
Version Date: 20120314

International Standard Book Number: 978-0-8058-4846-5 (Hardback) 978-0-8058-4847-2 (Paperback)

Library of Congress Cataloging-in-Publication Data

Bhagat, Rabi S., 1950-
    Work stress and coping in the era of globalization / Rabi S. Bhagat, James C. Segovis, Terry A. Nelson.
        p. cm.
    Includes bibliographical references and index.
    ISBN 978-0-8058-4846-5 (hardcover : alk. paper) -- ISBN 978-0-8058-4847-2 (pbk. : alk. paper)
    1. Job stress. 2. Stress (Psychology) 3. Organizational behavior. I. Segovis, James C. II. Nelson, Terry A. III. Title.

HF5548.85.B486 2012
158.7'2--dc23   2012010216

Visit the Taylor & Francis Web site at
http://www.taylorandfrancis.com

and the Psychology Press Web site at
http://www.psypress.com

To my family, Ebha, Priyanka, Monika, and Tim, my son-in-law. These four significant individuals in my life have encouraged me for the past several years to complete this book.

To Dr. Srinath Bellur, Dr. R. Chandrasekaran, Dr. Vijay Marathe, Dr. Jagdish N. Sheth, and Dr. Dipak Jain for their support and inspiration during Spring 2011 when I had to deal with my own stresses.

To my students at the University of Texas–Dallas and the University of Memphis for providing me with numerous insights into the role of work and life stresses.

Rabi S. Bhagat

To my loving wife of 40 years, Elizabeth Segovis, who has supported me unconditionally during the many challenges while writing this book.

To the memory of my mother, Helen Bogani Segovis, who opened my life to the excitement of reading and the discovery of new worlds.

James C. Segovis

To the memory of my mother, Barbara Jean Nelson, who instilled in me the love of learning.

To my dad, Ray Wallace Nelson, who supported and encouraged me throughout this project.

To Thomas F. Stafford, who has supported me in numerous ways.

Terry A. Nelson

Contents

Foreword

Coping With the Changing Nature of Work Today

In the 1970s, we had the industrial relations conflicts between management and the unions; in the 1980s, we had the "enterprise and entrepreneurial" culture; and in the 1990s and through the first half of the first decade of this century, we have had "globalization and economic growth" that has been unprecedented, with the emerging economies of China, India, Brazil, and Russia. The stresses and strains endured by many in the workplace have been unrelenting, even though the sources of these may have been different over this time period. The issues behind the stress epidemic have been numerous, from the advent of new technology that has sped the pace of work-life to massive competition from the emerging countries, to the global nature of business which has meant that many are now globe-trotters, to the political issues surrounding energy supply and governance. Technology has also meant that there is now more electronic overload, with less person-to-person contact and more virtual relationships. The consequence of this is that people are not communicating as much with one another. As President Ronald Reagan once quipped, "I've always believed that a lot of the troubles in the world would disappear if we were talking to each other instead of about each other!"

Another facet of this is that jobs in most countries are no longer for life. Most developed and developing cultures have created different psychological contracts with their employees. These almost-one-sided contracts demand commitment, long hours, and heavier workloads, but without any job security. This is particularly the case now, when we have experienced the recession and post-recession period, where companies are trying to survive and compete in a low economic growth world, and where the public sector in most countries has been substantially downsized; all in all, a more "lean and mean" era for all employers and employees. Employees in many companies are now considered disposable assets that are used when needed and downsized when not. This has meant that we have a two-tier workforce: those who lived under the old order of relative job security, less mobility, and greater loyalty by the employer; and those who understand the changing dynamics of the workplace and don't expect "jobs for life," are more mobile, and less loyal. The stresses and strains on these two groups may be significantly different, but the one thing they have in common is they both need to develop coping strategies to deal with this changing nature of work. Though Leonardo da Vinci lived long ago, his recommendation is still valid: "Every now and then go away and have a little relaxation. To remain constantly at work will diminish your judgment. Go some distance away, because work will be in perspective and a lack of harmony is more readily seen."

This book is a very important contribution to the literature of the field of health and well-being in the workplace because it highlights the primary issues of stress and coping in the context of this new globalized world. We must be optimistic that we can change things, and this book takes the first step in helping us systematically think through this process and create the environment for positive change. As George Bernard Shaw wrote in his play, *Mrs. Warren's Profession*, "People are always blaming their circumstances for what they are. I don't believe in circumstances. The people who get on in this world are the people who get up and look for the circumstances they want, and if they don't find them, make them!" This is our challenge.

Cary L. Cooper
Lancaster University

Cary L. Cooper, CBE, is distinguished professor of organizational psychology and health at Lancaster University Management School, Lancaster University, England, and Chair of the Academy of Social Sciences (a body of over 40 learned societies in the social sciences comprising over 86,000 social scientists).

Preface

Since the early studies on work-related stresses in the 1960s, there has been an explosion of research into the determinants and consequences of work stress and coping. When combined with research on the social psychological aspects of stress and coping in nonwork contexts, there has been a remarkable growth. In addition, we live in an age of globalization that has introduced enormous changes in the nature of society and the workplace in particular. Although the pros and cons of globalization have continued to be addressed in economics, economic sociology, and cross-national studies, there has been little research on the effects of globalization on work organizations and their employees. Scholars have addressed the issues relating to why globalization works (Wolf, 2004) and discontents with globalization (Stiglitz, 2003), but relatively little is known regarding the positive and negative consequences of globalization on people in organizations, especially across national borders and cultures.

This book is about the phenomenon of work stress and coping in the era of globalization. It has been noted that although we are living longer, we may be suffering more. This has been called an age of anxiety, reflected in significant increases in the use of antidepressant drugs such as Prozac in the United States (Wurtzel, 2000). Anxiety disorders, one of the two most common symptoms of stress, affects one in every six people in the United States and one in every five in the United Kingdom (Cooper & Quick, 1999). The situation has continued to worsen, particularly in the United States, as noted by Fareed Zakaria (2011). Rapid growth of the global economy coupled with major technological changes in the workplace and the structure of modern families are largely responsible for significant increases in work stress in the Western and non-Western world.

The tables are turning; the economies of several non-Western countries including the BRIC (Brazil, Russia, India, and China) are becoming prominent. The gulf between the rich and the poor has increased substantially in most of the globalizing nations and more so in the United States, which still continues to be the largest economy in the world. The unemployment rate is approximately 10% in the United States and as high as 21% in some of the suburbs of the Midwestern states since the beginning of the recession in 2008. It is ironic that these states were largely responsible for the tremendous growth of industrial production in the 1960s, which made America the most prosperous nation after the Second World War. However, the times are different as the United States enters the new millennium. Globalization-related pressures, which have created major restructuring of the workplace, have been responsible for increasing various types of work- and nonwork-related stresses for individuals.

We write this book to address this phenomenon of work stress and coping in the era of globalization. While a great deal of research has been conducted on the causes and consequences of globalization and work stress and coping, there has not been any systematic attempt to create a body of knowledge that integrates these two areas of inquiries.

In terms of organization of the book, Chapter 1 deals with the issues of globalization. We discuss the economic rationale for the evolution of globalization and the nature of the global marketplace including the role of the BRIC countries. In Chapter 2, we discuss organizational and human consequences of globalization. Chapter 3 presents the theoretical perspectives on work stress and coping from a Western perspective. Western researchers such as Robert Kahn and his associates at the University of Michigan were the first to pay attention to this phenomenon in the early 1960s. Management of work stress and its effectiveness is discussed in Chapter 4. In Chapter 5, we present some of the major approaches for understanding work stress and coping from a non-Western perspective. Theoretical non-Western perspectives on work stress and coping-related issues have been relatively recent in its origin. However, one needs to seriously take into account research insights from non-Western and collectivistic countries given the growing importance of these countries in the global marketplace. We present multicultural perspectives on work stress and coping in Chapter 6. Ethnic differences on how stress is experienced and coped with are also addressed in this chapter. Multiculturalism has become important not only in the United States but in the European Union, Australia, New Zealand, and other countries as well. It has significant implications for understanding work stress and coping for ethnic and cultural minorities. In Chapter 7, we discuss the role of employee assistance programs (EAPs)—an institutional approach for managing dysfunctional consequences of work stress and enhancing coping skills. A cross-cultural perspective is adopted to examine the significance of EAPs across nations and cultures. Methodological issues are presented in Chapter 8, including recent innovations in methodology and use of qualitative techniques. In the final chapter, we present our concluding thoughts. Emergent theoretical and applied issues are presented with implications for developing theory, research, and practice.

The idea of this book was conceived by the first author about a decade ago. Numerous developments in the global economy and the world of work have taken place since then. He remembered many exciting discussions he used to have with his former student, Jim Segovis, in the mid-eighties when he was in the process of coediting *The Human Stress and Cognition in Organizations* (1985) with Terry A. Beehr. Jim joined the writing endeavor 3 years ago, and then Terry Nelson, a current and promising doctoral student who was a senior vice president of First Tennessee Bank in Memphis, joined in the effort in 2009. We have spent many hours discussing the theoretical and applied issues concerning work stress and coping in the current era of globalization. Our goal is to provide an enriched and comprehensive understanding of the topics that lie at the crossroads of globalization and work stress and coping. It helps to focus our efforts on the future of work stress research, where it is going, and the role that organizational stress researchers can play in understanding and managing work stress. It is hoped that this book will provide a springboard for future research into the role of this important phenomenon for scholars, PhD students, and human resources practitioners in the world of work.

Rabi S. Bhagat
James C. Segovis
Terry A. Nelson

References

Beehr, T. A., & Bhagat, R. S. (1985). *Human stress and cognition in organizations: An integrated perspective.* New York: Wiley.
Cooper, C. L., & Quick, J. C. (1999). *Fast facts: Stress and strain [Clinical monograph].* Oxford, England: Health Press.
Stiglitz, J. E. (2003). *Globalization and its discontents.* New York: W.W. Norton & Company.
Wolf, M. (2004). *Why globalization works.* New Haven, CT: Yale University Press.
Wurtzel, E. (2000). *Prozac nation.* New York: Quartet Books.
Zakaria, F. (2011, March 4). Yes, America is in decline. *Time Magazine.*

Acknowledgments

The authors wish to express their sincere appreciation to Anne Duffy whose role as the editor of this book has been significant from the very beginning. She provided valuable suggestions at different stages in the preparation of the manuscript. Appreciation is also expressed to the reviewers for their suggestions during the preparation of the manuscript. The authors also thank Robert Vickrey for his tireless help during the final stages of the preparation of the manuscript. Kulraj Singh, a new doctoral student, also provided timely assistance.

The first author expresses his gratitude to Harry Triandis and Manuel London for their many years of encouragement while completing this project.

The second author wishes to acknowledge the support of his children, Colin, Ian, and Courtney, during the writing process of this book. He also acknowledges his colleagues Dr. Lori A. Coakley, Dr. Kenneth Sousa, and Dr. William O'Hara for their encouragement throughout the writing of this book.

The third author wishes to acknowledge the support of her siblings, Anthony, Paula, and Keithen, and their spouses for their encouragement. She also acknowledges encouragement from friends Tracy, Dondi, Charlotte, Althea, Susan, Diana, Karen, and Rachida.

Author Biographies

Rabi S. Bhagat, PhD, is a professor of organizational behavior and international management in the Fogelman College of Business at the University of Memphis. He is a fellow of the Society for Industrial & Organizational Psychology (SIOP), American Psychological Association (APA), Association for Psychological Science (APS), International Association for Analytical Psychology (IAAP),  and the International Academy for Intercultural Research (IAIR). He has coedited the *Cambridge Handbook of Culture, Organizations, and Work; Handbook of Intercultural Training, Human Stress, and Cognition in Organizations;* and *Work Stress: Health Care Systems in the Workplace.* He has published widely in leading journals in the field and continues to be interested in the areas of work stress and coping across national borders and cultures. He has presented research papers and seminars in over 30 countries and maintains an active interest in cross-cultural issues in work stress and coping-related issues.

James C. Segovis, PhD, is the executive-in-residence in the College of Business at Bryant University, where he has won several teaching awards. Previous to this position, Segovis served as director of the John H. Chafee Center for International Business at Bryant University overseeing academic and business international initiatives. In addition, he has published in leading academic journals, such as the *Journal of Management Studies, Journal of Applied Psychology,* and *Small Group Behavior.* He also has been  an invited speaker at several international universities. Before joining Bryant University, he was a national senior education and training director at the Federal Home Loan Bank System and U.S. Treasury during the national financial crisis of the 1980s.

Terry A. Nelson is a doctoral student in the Fogelman College of Business and Economics at the University of Memphis. She has published in the *International Journal of Cross Cultural Management* and *IEEE Engineering Management Review*. A former senior vice president with First Tennessee Bank in Memphis, Tennessee, she remains interested in exploring effects of work stress on employees and their families. She has over 17 years of managerial experience.

Chapter 1

An Introduction to Globalization: Organizational and Human Consequences

Merriam-Webster's new international dictionary included the term *globalization* in 1961. According to the dictionary, *globalization* as a term was being used from 1951. Its earliest meaning and the most widely understood connotation was on the spread of the global economy to regional economics around the world. It involves deepening of relationships and broadening interdependence among people of dissimilar nations and cultures. The term can mean many different things to different people, but in its essence it focuses on the integration of various countries to international trade and free flow of capital, information, and people across countries and political boundaries. Making efficient use of cheaper foreign labor markets is also a major objective in the process of the economic facet of globalization.

The process of growing relationships and economic interdependence among people across dissimilar nations and cultures is much older than 1951, having occurred throughout recorded human history and before. The term *globalization* not only is being used by university professors, professional managers of multinational and global corporations (i.e., MNCs), and government officials but also is in daily use throughout the world. It has been referred to as *mondialisation* in French, *globalisierung* in German, or *Quan qui hua* in Chinese. Various news articles, television programs, and best-selling books such as *The Lexus and the Olive Tree* (Friedman, 1999), *The World Is Flat* (Friedman, 2005), and *The World is Curved* (Smick, 2008) use the term *globalization* on a regular basis to refer to the growing interconnectedness of the various economies of the world. Ohmae (1995) refers to globalization as the absence of national borders and barriers to trade among nations. It has also been described as a shift in traditional patterns of international production, investment, and flow of capital, goods, information, and people among dissimilar nations. Scholars of international management and global strategy propose that the process of globalization is a set of practices that facilitate economic transactions among various countries. Based on their ideas, we define globalization as follows:

> Globalization is a process whereby worldwide interconnections in vir-
> tually every sphere of activity are growing. Some of these interconnec-
> tions lead to integration/unit worldwide; others do not. Together global
> interconnections and the relationships they forge represent a histori-
> cally unprecedented process that is rapidly reshaping the context for
> many activities. The result is blurred boundaries within and between
> organizations, nations, and global interests. (Parker, 2005, p. 5)

This book is about globalization and how it affects work organizations that are either actively participating or are seeking to actively participate in the global marketplace. Multinational and global organizations employ workers in their worldwide subsidiaries and export their products and services to consumers in both developed and developing countries. From the perspective of economic trade, when global corporations invest in developing countries it creates jobs and improves income levels. Scholars are in general agreement that globalization is essential for economic development and uplifting the standards of living in developing and emergent economies such as the BRIC countries (Brazil, Russia, India, and China).

In the process of developing worldwide connections, multinational and global companies develop various kinds of links and relationships on a regular basis—involving people who work in them, governmental and nongovernmental agencies and organizations, and social and political institutions. Over 180 countries are members of the World Trade Organization (WTO), and the increasing levels of economic interdependence among a large number of them (including multinational corporations) is a major aspect of globalization. Multiple relations interconnect different types of economic, political, social, and cultural environments of different societies that affect people and social institutions in myriad ways. Examples of globalization are the evolution of similar types of preferences for music, cell phone designs, and video games. Emergence of identical or nearly identical tastes in music preferences among young adults is a good example of how globalization affects people and societies uniformly in various dissimilar geographical and cultural locales.

Worldwide spread of common economic interests is growing on a continuous basis. This happens because we live in a world where the infrastructure of global communication connects our lives regardless of the physical distance involved. Globalization refers to a state of the world that involves networks of interdependence among organizations of different types and from industry sectors and located at various geographical regions. The linkages occur because of flows and influences of capital and goods, information and ideas, people, and forces as well as environmentally and biologically relevant substances (e.g., pollutants or pathogens) that are relevant for the physical climate of the globe. Processes of *globalization* and *deglobalization* refer to the increase or decline of the worldwide spread of mainly economic activities. However, other aspects of globalization are critical for the study of work and organizational stress and coping.

Interdependence and globalization are both multidimensional phenomena that should be studied from economic as well as other aspects. Important facets need to be considered for a complete discussion of the nature of globalization and its affect on multinational and global companies.

Facets of Globalization

■ *Economic globalization* involves exchange of capital, goods, and services over networks involving long distance relationships among various organizations located in different parts of the globe. It also involves the movement of information and data to facilitate market exchanges. Worldwide coordination of the processes that are linked to these flows such as developing organizational and institutional linkages among various low-wage production facilities in, for example, Asia or Latin America for generating goods and services for the more developed markets in the United States, Japan, and Western Europe is also considered an important facet of the economic globalization. The globalization of production, which has been promoted by MNCs though assisted by financial institutions and governments in developed countries, is a good example of this facet of globalization. The invention and diffusion of new technologies not only for advancing agricultural production but also for high-tech electronic and biochemical products and services is another good example that has major consequences for the second facet of globalization dealing with social and cultural consequences.

■ *Social and cultural globalization* involves the exchange of ideas and information and the people who carry ideas and information with them. Examples include transfer of scientific knowledge and technologies across national and cultural boundaries. Diffusion of practices, values, and institutional procedures of an advanced and globalized society to other nations is also considered social and cultural globalization. Imitation of Western societies' (e.g., United States, United Kingdom, France) dominant values, practices, and institutions by other non-Western countries is referred to as the isomorphic tendency of this facet of globalization. Such isomorphic tendencies in shaping the future developments in societies that are dissimilar from the West are vigorously debated both in theory and practice (Sassen, 1998). At a most profound level, globalization involving social, political, and cultural processes not only has the potential to influence the beliefs, attitudes, and values of people in dissimilar national contexts who may favor different forms of social and political organizations but also often succeeds in transforming these societies. These societies were relatively resistant to such changes in the past; however, with the promise of benefits of globalization (e.g., of the positive economic consequences), they have begun to appreciate the value of globalization.

Especially with the development of the Internet and computer-mediated technologies, the flow of ideas that have the potential either to change or to succeed in changing the beliefs and values of dissimilar societies takes place independently of economic globalization. It is important to note that the distinction of the aforementioned two facets of globalization is somewhat arbitrary. Economic globalization carries with it the potential for social, political, and cultural globalization and vice versa. The eleven countries and regions that have enjoyed the highest rate of economic growth in the process of globalizing their economies between 1980 and 2010 are China, India, Brazil, Singapore, South Korea, Vietnam, Taiwan, Oman, Malaysia, Thailand, and Indonesia. Coupled with an average growth rate of 5% to 9%, they have also experienced both major and minor social and cultural changes and transformations. It is necessary to point out that this second facet of globalization also has implications for fostering or slowing down the process of economic globalization.

Globalization: A Brief History

Since 1945, the United States has been the world's dominant economic power. Even during the cold war (1945–1991), its economy was far more advanced than and more than twice as large as that of the Soviet Union. In addition, the United

States has been the prime mover and supporter in the creation of a large number of multinational and global institutions such as the United Nations (UN), International Monetary Fund (IMF), and World Bank. In terms of sponsoring and benefiting from the economic aspect of globalization, the United States has been the most important global power and authority. The collapse of the Soviet Union in 1991 largely enhanced America's already established preeminent economic position. The demise of its main adversary—the USSR—also resulted in the spread of both economic and political forms of globalization to territories and countries of the former Soviet Union bloc. The opening of the markets of the previous Soviet bloc countries such as Poland, the Czech Republic, Slovakia, and Hungary resulted in the further spread of globalization. Patterns associated with the U.S. type of globalization became the norm and were widely shared by a vast majority of the countries in Western and Eastern Europe, Asia, Latin America, Africa, and Australia. Even in the heyday of the British Empire in the nineteenth century, the United States enjoyed a wide reach of its economic sphere of influence. The dollar became the world's preferred currency, and most global trade for the past 60 years has been conducted in U.S. dollars. Most countries including the People's Republic of China (PRC) and Russia hold their reserves in it. The global position of the United States in terms of its military remains unsurpassed in every part of the world. Its global position in economics remained mostly unparalleled until the rapid growth of China during the past two decades.

The preeminent role up until 1945 was held by the countries of Western Europe, especially Britain, France, and Germany, and previously to a much lesser extent by Spain, Portugal, and The Netherlands. From the beginning of the industrial revolution in the late eighteenth century until the mid-twentieth century, European countries were shaping the economic developments of much of the nations in Asia, Latin America, Africa, and other parts of the world. The engine of Europe's dynamism was "industrialization," and it expanded its economic influence to various globalizing countries by expanding its colonial reach. Even as Europe's position began to decline after World War I and more definitely after 1945, the rise of the United States as a global economic power continued with the same momentum of globalization with one exception: It was not a colonial power and has not been one in its history. However, the culture of the U.S. society has been largely a product of various Western European cultures with some influences from various countries of Africa. For over two centuries (i.e., 1800s and 1900s), Western civilization and culture has dominated much of the world.

However, we are now witnessing a historic change that, though still in its relatively early stages, is bound to transform the world. The developed world, that for over a century largely meant the West (namely, the United States, Canada, Western Europe, Australia, and New Zealand) plus Japan, is now being challenged in terms of its economic size by the developing world ("Playing Leapfrog", 2006). In 2001, the developed countries' accounted for over 50% of the world's gross domestic product (GDP) compared with 60% in 1973. In other words, in a span of slightly over 25 years, the developed countries' share of the global GDP declined by 10%. Scholars of globalization note that it will take a long time for even the most advanced country among the developing countries to acquire the necessary economic and technological sophistication of the developed countries. However, because of the developing countries' collective share of the world's population, their economic growth has been higher than that of the developed world, and their rise is resulting in a significant shift in the nature of globalization—particularly of the economic and cultural facets. Figures 1.1 and 1.2 depict the projected size of the national economies of the world in 2025 and in 2050. These predictions were made by Goldman Sachs, a global investment bank located in New York City, and are largely regarded as fairly accurate estimates of the changing economic contexts of the world. According to these predictions, the three largest economies in the world by 2050 will be China followed by a closely matched United States and India; the next four in order of importance will be Brazil, Mexico, Russia, and Indonesia.

It is interesting to note that only two Western European countries (the United Kingdom and Germany) have been projected to be among the top 10 economically important countries in 2050, according to one Goldman Sachs study (2009). The rank of the United Kingdom will be ninth, and Germany will be the tenth. Of the present G-7 countries, only 4 will appear in the top 10. PricewaterhouseCoopers (PwC), a global accounting firm headquartered in

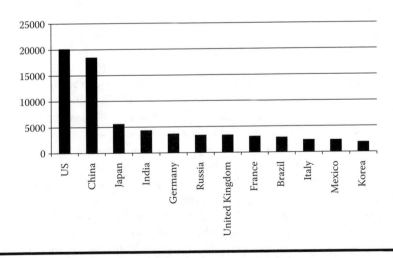

Figure 1.1   Projected GDP size in 2025 (in 2006). (Adapted from *Global Economic Paper No. 153*, Goldman Sachs, March 28, 2007.)

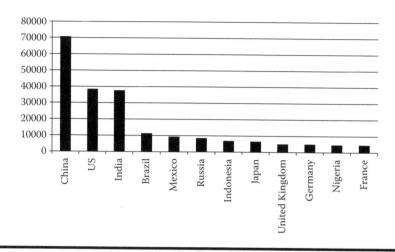

Figure 1.2 Projected GDP size in 2050 (in 2006). (Adapted from *Global Economics Paper No. 153*, Goldman Sachs, March 28, 2007.)

New York, predicts that the Brazilian economy will be larger than Japan's and that the Russian, Mexican, and Indonesian economies will each be larger than the German, French, and U.K. economies by 2050. If these predictions or something similar to these predictions take place 40 years from today, the world will look like a very different place indeed.

The implications of this new world have not been fully explored in research on human stress and cognition in multinational and global corporations of today. It is our objective to provide a detailed analysis of how this new world of work is evolving in the era of globalization. However, before we describe some of the new challenges that are emerging as a result of increased competition among globalized countries of the West and emerging economies from Asia, Eastern Europe, and Latin America (i.e., the BRIC economies), it is necessary to understand the process of measuring globalization that may evolve in different countries of the world. A growing number of companies from emerging markets are beginning to appear in the Fortune 500 ranking of the world's biggest firms. A total of 62 companies from the BRIC economies of Brazil, Russia, India, and China are currently in the 2008 listing of the Fortune 500 companies. The number of companies from the BRIC economies in this listing was 31 in 2003, which means in a period of 5 years there has been a 100% increase of the number of companies from the non-Western countries to appear in the Fortune 500 ranking of the world's largest companies. *Globalization* is no longer just synonymous with *Americanization* or *Westernization*. With an increasing number of emerging-market companies acquiring established large businesses and brands from the developed countries in the Western Europe and the United States, the process

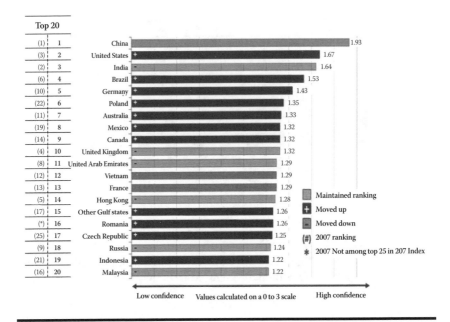

Figure 1.3 Top 20—Foreign Direct Confidence Index, 2007. (Reprinted from *Investing in a Rebound: The 2010 A.T. Kearney FDI Confidence Index®*. Copyright 2010, A.T. Kearney, Inc. All rights reserved. With permission.)

of globalization and the accompanying changes that occur in the organizational contexts of both the acquired and the acquiring companies tends both to be complex and to occur in both directions in nature. This issue has major consequences for examining non-Western and multicultural perspectives on work stress and coping (these are discussed in Chapters 2, 5, and 6). Organizational and corporate cultures of acquired companies (including joint ventures, mergers, and alliances) begin to change in line with the expectations of the ethos and values of the acquiring companies from the emergent economies. For example, a software company from the Eastern United States acquired by Wipro Inc. or Tata Consulting Company might begin to reflect the companies' corporate values and standards of India. It is also true that acquiring companies from the non-Western countries (i.e., BRIC economies) begin to learn and incorporate some of the practices of the Western companies that they acquire. In 2008, Budweiser, America's favorite beer, was bought by a Belgian–Brazilian conglomerate and is no longer run by U.S. managers. While there has not been a major change in the sales and marketing practices of Budweiser, there is evidence that different types of management and organizational practices have been instituted in the various plants of Budweiser in the United States and elsewhere (Cendrowicz, 2008). In addition, several of the U.S. leading investment firms avoided bankruptcies by seeking assistance from sovereign-wealth firms (i.e., state-owned investment firms) of various Arab Kingdoms such as the United Arab Emirates and from the Chinese government. It is often noted that if the Chinese companies decided to sell their holdings of the U.S. treasury notes, there will be a major financial collapse of the global economic system. This collapse would be more severe than the financial meltdown experienced by the United States and other Western economies in late 2008. The point is that MNCs from the BRIC economies and other non-Western countries are providing many opportunities for investment and strategic alliances throughout the world. In the process, they are establishing themselves as new competitors to reckon with in the twenty-first century.

Measuring Globalization

Most researchers approach the global measurement issue by examining the extent to which the world is actually becoming more interdependent primarily in economic terms. The global domestic product (GD) reflects a composite of several indicators consisting of historical rates of growth of trade, imports and exports, capital flows, and international labor migration patterns. Even though international trade has existed over thousands of years, the world was less globalized a century ago than is the case today. An increasing number of countries have become important players in increasing the rate of growth of world trade. Three historical factors largely account for this trend:

1. Decolonization of many countries following World War II (e.g., India, Malaysia, countries in sub-Saharan parts of Africa)
2. The collapse of Soviet Union along the east–west division of countries in 1999
3. The rapid economic growth of some of the economies in Southeast Asia

There is evidence that recent growth in international trade has been largely regional because of lower transportation costs. It is cheaper to transport capital goods between the United States and Canada than between the United States and China. The evolution of economic blocks and agreements among the countries located in close geographical proximity—for example, the North American Free Trade Agreement (NAFTA) in North America, the Association of Southeast Asian Nations (ASEAN) in Southeast Asia, and Mercosur in South America—also facilitates regional trade. New developments in institutional structures (i.e., legal regulations and systems, labor market conditions, business customs, cultural norms and values) are beginning to facilitate the growth in international trade on an ongoing basis in the twenty-first century. In addition to measures that reflect high degrees of economic globalization among countries, there are indicators of political exchanges and engagements, reflected in the number of consulates, embassies, and connective technologies such as easy access to Internet and other forms of computer-mediated technologies. Direct contact through relatively cheaper means of international transportation (i.e., lower air fares to travel long distances) and international telephone calls are also important indicators of economic and political aspects of globalization. The point is that as different countries come in contact with each other through increasing involvement of international business and trade, they will begin to experience both energizing and unsettling experiences resulting from exchange of innovative ideas, information, and new forms of knowledge.

Martens and Zywietz (2006) examined both economic and noneconomic indicators for comparing the degree of globalization that different countries have experienced in recent decades. In addition to economic measures of globalization, indicators of political aspects of globalization (i.e., political engagement with a larger number of countries), easier access to the Internet and information processing technologies, and international telephone facilities are included in this measurement of globalization. The results show that a country's relative rank in terms of how globalized it is may be higher on one dimension, such as economic, but not on other dimensions, such as political, social, or cultural.

Emerging Realities for Multinational and Global Organizations

Competition among multinational and global corporations has now evolved to a new unprecedented level. This competition is characterized by networks of international linkages involving countries, both governmental and nongovernmental institutions and organizations, and people in the interdependent global marketplace. Economic integration results from the lessening of trade barriers and the increase flow of capital, goods, technology, knowledge, and labor among various developed countries and emerging markets. Ohmae (1995) argued that the invisible hand of global competition is being energized by an increasingly borderless world. Worldwide technological advancements, the rise of economies in the BRIC countries, and the increase of multinational and global corporations from these and other non-Western countries have had major implications for the structuring of work and work organizations around the world. The playing field has been leveled among countries—what Friedman (2005) calls the *flattening of the world*.

The general concept of globalization has been that business expands from the developed to the developing and emerging economies. However, the concept has been expanded to include transnational business transactions. It is no longer a one-way process largely characterized by the flow of capital, goods, knowledge, information, and people from the developed economies of North America, Western Europe, and Australia to the countries in Asia, Latin America, and Africa. The new reality in the global marketplace is that the businesses in different parts of the world are competing with every other business in the same industry sector and often in related industries as well. However, with this new reality, Ghemawat (2007) argued that the world is in a state of "semi-globalization" and will remain so for decades to come. It has also been suggested (Smick, 2008) that the global economic and financial system is indeed curved and does not foster the flattening of the global marketplace as was discussed in the worldwide best-selling book *The World Is Flat* (Friedman, 2005). In fact, the world is only partially globalized, with about 10% of the world's population being affected by developments in various facets of globalization on an ongoing basis. The remaining 90% of the world's population remains relatively unaffected by the growth of globalization but experiences some of its indirect effects (Keohane, 2002).

Despite these observations, it is amply clear that all facets of globalization (i.e., economic, social, and cultural) have led to a strong interconnectedness among various countries, companies, and people located in dissimilar countries and cultures. The rise of the BRIC economies in particular has driven up the volume of world trade by 133% during the last 15 years or so, to over $54 trillion. With the continuous growth increase of international trade among developing countries and emerging markets of the world, there has been an increased pressure on multinational and global corporations to improve their global competitiveness. Firms from any country are relatively free to compete with firms both in the domestic and in the international context. Domestic competitors generally compete on price and sales volume of resources and services, and it is relatively easier to predict the course of future competition originating from domestic than from international competitors. Competition among multinational and global companies in the twenty-first century is clearly borderless in nature, with most global companies producing and selling more of their brands and services in foreign markets than in their home markets. Avon, for example, estimates that it employs about 5 million sales representatives globally and that a large share of its sale revenues comes from China. It hired about 400,000 sales representatives in 2006, largely in response to demand in the emerging markets of the world particularly from China. Nestle of Switzerland employs 50% of its sales representatives outside of its home market. This is not surprising given the relatively small size of the Swiss market. The Coca-Cola company of the United States receives 80% of its sales revenue from its international operations. The Tata Group, a global conglomerate originating in India, has operations in 85 countries and has made a number of acquisitions (such as Jaguar of the United Kingdom from Ford Motor Company) of large firms around the world.

Investment by multinational and global companies around the world means that globalization benefits developing economies through the transfer of financial-, technological-, and knowledge-based management resources. Development of local partners and allies in various parts of the world also enables the developing countries and the emerging economies to start on the path of being self-sufficient and improving operations in their manufacturing plants and outsourcing operations. Companies that operate globally are becoming increasingly detached from their home country context. Toyota of Japan likes to be known as a global company and not as a Japanese conglomerate manufacturing cars for the automobile markets of the world. It is the largest automobile company in Japan, and it is ranked very highly in the Fortune 500 ranking of global companies. The senior management team of Toyota, though largely composed of Japanese nationals, has a significant number of foreign-born managers.

The current chief executive officer (CEO) and president of the Sony Corporation of Japan, the largest electronic company in the world, is a British national—something that was unexpected for a Japanese global corporation to initiate and accept. Multinational and global corporations that like to remain globally competitive and expand their transnational operations to other countries need to cultivate a global mind-set in their senior managers (Bhagat, Triandis, Baliga, Billing, & Davis, 2007). Companies with large numbers of executives with global mind-sets possess sophisticated information and knowledge of the realities in the world markets. Managers in these firms have considerable experience in operating subsidiaries in various parts of the world and in the process have developed greater insights. They design new organizational structures (e.g., network, decentralized, and virtual) and workplaces (e.g., teamwork across cultures, telecommuting, and working with various forms of electronic media) that are better suited to deal with fluctuating realities of the global marketplace.

Developing cultural sensitivities in working with others from dissimilar cultures is also of crucial importance. Many multinational and global companies are increasingly becoming known to function like stateless corporations, where work is outsourced to global locations wherever it is most efficient. This results in only the essential strategic core of the corporation functioning from the home country context. Senior managers make their decisions from important locations that are strategically vital for competing in the global marketplace. Increased use of computer-mediated technologies, teleconferences, and other advanced information processing technologies are emphasized on a 24/7 basis. The pressures to compete with companies from different parts of the world can be rather intense for both small and large multinational and global companies— sometimes leading to significant declines in market share, consumer loyalty, and stock performance.

Let us examine the current situation with General Motors (GM) headquartered in the United States. GM used to be the largest global company in the early 1960s. In 2009, it had to declare bankruptcy, and the U.S. government, with the leadership of President Barack Obama, bailed the company out. Significant changes in the leadership roles of GM followed, accompanied by considerable downsizing of the scope and operations in the global market. Unthinkable as it was in the early' 60s, the behemoth GM no longer exists as the largest global company. The largest automobile company became Toyota Inc. of Japan in 2010, as noted earlier. We also noted that Toyota Inc. would rather be known as a global company and not necessarily as a large Japanese company. Numerous examples such as this are found in the popular business press and periodicals. Consider another example: the decline of IBM from being the largest manufacturer of mainframe computers to its current status as a business process solution company. The 1980s and 1990s were fraught with intense competition from both domestic (e.g., Apple, Hewlett Packard, and Dell) and international companies (e.g., Sony Inc., Fujitsu, Toshiba of Japan, and Siemens of Germany) in the high-technology sector.

A parallel situation exists for small and medium enterprises (SMEs). Small and medium-sized companies are also affected by both economic and social facets of globalization. In numerous ways, these companies, much like their large counterparts, play vital roles in contributing to their national economies through the process of job creation and the development of new product, services, and technologies. They aid the national economic objectives of boosting exports of the developing countries and emergent economies. In the process, they facilitate growth and development of global mind-sets and new organizational structures and workplaces. The vast majority (over 90%) of businesses that engage in international transactions reflect this pattern in their organizations. They typically employ fewer than 500 to 1,000 employees. They market their products and services in accordance with the fluctuating demands in the global marketplace. Competition from abroad and especially from increasing entrepreneurial activities from MNCs in both developed and developing economies affects the nature and quality of products and services on a worldwide scale. For example, U.S.-based travel-related and financial services company American Express is facing strong competition from Eurocard, Alliance Card, and other global financial services companies. Fierce competition for customers among these companies results in the streamlining of global operations and better services. The implications of these market forces for the design of work and organizations are being discussed and presented in both academic and practitioners circles.

While SMEs are likely to be more vulnerable from global competition in their respective industry sectors, the pressures to innovate build rapidly. This situation is particularly true for high-technology and biomedical firms. Managers and workers in these SMEs are also likely to experience considerable pressure to improve competitiveness of their operations to survive and prosper. Whereas large multinational and global corporations have the benefits of research and development (R&D) laboratories in producing innovative products and therefore maintaining their competitiveness, SMEs do not. Thus, they are likely to be much more adversely affected unless entrepreneurial and technological initiatives are undertaken. As a result, the employees of SMEs at all levels are likely to experience considerable organizational pressures and work stress stemming from the global marketplace. In the next section, we discuss the nature of these changes that are occurring in the world of work as a result of rapid advances in globalization.

Emerging Realities for Work

Global competition creates new challenges for organizations including design of new forms of work and increased use of technology and computer-mediated methods for accomplishing business transactions. The pressures from both continuous and discontinuous changes in the global marketplace create work stress and expose workers at various levels of the organization to health risks, both psychological and physical. These risks not only are present for high-level executives at the headquarters of the MNCs but also tend to be pervasive in scope. Managers and workers in the worldwide subsidiaries are also subjected to risks that arise on a continuous basis. Risk associated with occupational obsolescence, layoffs, job losses, and pressures to transfer to culturally dissimilar foreign locations are common place. Continuous pressures to perform at a high rate and dealing with both continuous and discontinuous changes are prerequisites to working effectively in the era of globalization.

WORK STRESS IN CHINA IN THE 21ST CENTURY

A survey by Regus (a U.S. based provider of workplace solutions) polled 11,000 companies in 13 countries in 2009. It finds that 58% of the companies have experienced a significant elevation in work stress experienced by their employees at all levels. This has continued since 2007. Of particular interest, nearly 9 of 10 Chinese workers are working under tremendous pressures as Chinese companies begin to increase their exports to the West.

It is interesting that the smallest increase in work stress was reported by German and Dutch workers. However, in

the Chinese context, the pressure for performance to produce at a high rate continues to mount. Hans Leijten, the
regional vice-president for the East Asian operations of the
Regus group, notes that Chinese workers are confronted
with high pressures to produce as Chinese companies meet
demands for the global market place along with the possible uncertainty of being laid off due to downturn in the
global economy from September 2008. Forty-two percent
(42%) of Chinese workers reported that they were stressed
from the pressures they experienced with increasing focus
on profitability and market share by the top management.
Twenty-eight percent (28%) said that attempting to maintain
excellent levels of customer service is the main reason for
many sleepless nights.

Another survey from Horizon Research group reported
that increased work stress due to pressures from globalization affected those in the 24 – 30 year age group. In addition,
work stresses were perceived to be higher in subsidiaries of
foreign multinational and global companies, and less so in
public sector organizations.

Some individuals are beginning to sacrifice their leisure
time activities and hobbies in order to work harder in the
current era of economic downturn. There is massive competition within the work force – a phenomenon not known
to Chinese workers before China joined the World Trade
Organization.

Adapted from Zhuoqiong, W., Chinadaily.com, 2009.

It is no longer the case that only employees from companies based in the
United States and Western Europe experience work stresses and learn to cope with
them. Unexpected changes from the complex and fluctuating demands of the
global marketplace are indeed stressful for individuals in all countries that are globalized or are globalizing rapidly. MNCs outsource work and nonessential business processes to various non-Western countries (e.g., India, Philippines, Mexico,
and Poland). Employees from these countries experience significant work stresses
because of working in call centers, business process operations, and manufacturing
plants. Coupled with these common examples are numerous other managerial and
nonmanagerial roles that are loaded with discontinuous demands and pressures.
The pace of change in work lives leading to work stress and poor health is certainly
present on a large scale in U.S. and Western European MNCs, but other parts

of the world are not immune (Chang & Spector, 2011; Macik-Frey, Quick, & Nelson, 2007; Quick, Cooper, Nelson, Quick, & Gavin, 2003). While individuals welcome some changes in their work lives and can deal with them comfortably, it is difficult and indeed quite stressful to deal with changes on an ongoing basis—especially changes that are rather abrupt, are discontinuous, and have the potential to cause obsolescence, layoffs, and underemployment. Individuals experience changes as a threat and respond with well-learned mechanisms that are often inappropriate and dysfunctional (Staw, Sandelands, & Dutton, 1981). When appraised as a threat, changes induced by the need to compete on a continuous basis in the global marketplace carry with them the fear of impending loss and experience of stress both on a short- and long-term basis.

Conclusion

In this chapter, we described the nature of globalization in some detail. The economic literature concerning the rise of non-Western and BRIC economies were also reviewed. Throughout our discussions, we noted that globalization is largely responsible for improving economic growth rates of many countries that belong to the World Trade Organization. Two different facets of globalization—economic and social–cultural—were presented, and their effects on MNCs discussed. Research and practical examples reviewed in this chapter illustrate that globalization-related pressures induce both continuous and discontinuous changes in organizations that operate across nations and cultures. In addition, work lives are affected in all types of organizations in industries that compete in the global marketplace. It has been suggested that work stresses increase in these organizations and result in health risks for employees at all levels. In the next chapter, we present a detailed examination of the organizational and human consequences of work stress in the current era of globalization.

References

Bhagat, R. S., Triandis, H. C., Baliga, B. R., Billing, T. K., & Davis, C. A. (2007). On becoming a global manager: A closer look at the opportunities and constraints in the 21st century. In M. Javidan, R. M. Steers, & M. A. Hitt (Eds.), *The global mindset* (pp. 191–213). San Diego, CA: JAI Press.

Cendrowicz, L. (2008). Bud brewer braced for change. *Time*. Retrieved from http://www.time.com/time/business/article/0,8599,1822811,00.html

Chang, C., & Spector, P.E. (2011). Cross-cultural occupational health psychology. In J. C. Quick & L. E. Tetrick (Eds.), *Handbook of occupational health psychology* (pp. 119–138). Washington, DC: American Psychological Association.

Friedman, T. L. (1999). *The Lexus and the olive tree.* New York: Simon & Schuster.
Friedman, T. L. (2005). *The world is flat: A brief history of the twenty-first century.* New York: Farrar, Straus and Giroux.
Ghemawat, P. (2007). *Redefining global strategy: Crossing borders in a world where differences still matter.* Boston, MA: Harvard Business School Press.
Goldman Sachs. (2007, April 28). *Global economic paper no. 153.* Retrieved April 10, 2011, from http://www.scribd.com: http://www.scribd.com/doc/29410667/Goldman-Sachs-Report-the-N11-More-Than-an-Acronym
Keohane, R. (2002). *Power and governance in a partially globalized world.* New York: Routledge.
Macik-Frey, M., Quick, J. C., & Nelson, D. L. (2007). Advances in occupational health: From a stressful beginning to a positive future. *Journal of Management, 33*(6), 809–840.
Martens, P., & Zywietz, D. (2006). Rethinking globalization: A modified globalization index. *Journal of International Development, 18*: 331–350.
Ohmae, K. (1995). *The end of the nation state: The rise of regional economies.* New York: Free Press.
Parker, B. (2005). Evolution and revolution: From international business to globalization. In S. R. Clegg, C. Hardy, & W. R. Nord (Eds.), *Handbook of organization studies* (pp. 484–506). London: Sage.
Playing leapfrog. (2006, September 16). *The Economist, 380,* 28–30.
Quick, J. C., Cooper, C. L., Nelson, D. L., Quick, J. D., & Gavin, J. H. (2003). Stress, health, and well-being at work. In J. Greenberg (Ed.), *Organizational behavior: The state of the science* (2nd ed.). Mahwah, NJ: Lawrence Erlbaum Associates.
Sassen, S. (1998). *Globalization and its discontents: Essays on the new mobility of people and money.* New York: The New Press.
Smick, D. M. (2008). *The world is curved: Hidden dangers to the global economy.* New York: Penguin Group (USA).
Staw, B. M., Sandelands, L., & Dutton, J. (1981). Threat rigidity effects in organizational behavior. *Administrative Science Quarterly, 26,* 501–524.
Zhuoqiong, W. (2009, November 24). Pressure builds on employees. Accessed October 18, 2011 from www.chinadaily.com.cn/bizchina/2009=11/24/content-9029382.htm

Chapter 2

Organizational and Human Consequences: A Detailed Examination

As discussed in Chapter 1, globalization involves high degrees of interconnectedness among regional economies in various parts of the world. One of the major consequences of globalization involves the development of new types of work arrangements and work organizations, not only in the advanced Western countries but also in the developing and emerging economies. Another major consequence concerns the employees of multinational and global organizations who have to be increasingly concerned with and adapt to evolving technologies.

Globalization is altering the historical pattern of relationships of people in many domains: economic, political, social, cultural, environmental, and technological. Inda and Rosaldo (2002) refer to this as the intensification of global interconnectedness, suggesting an environment filled with constant movement and fusion of dissimilar economies and cultures, and development of multiple institutional linkages and inexorable interactions. It is characterized by the freedom of goods, technology, capital, and labor migrating back and forth across national boundaries. While these tangible components are quickly considered customary aspects of globalization, the significance of importation and exportation of cultures that occurs during this process receives less recognition.

Exhibit 2.1

On Work and Health in Developing and Industrialized Countries

■ About 75% of the world's labor force (which counts about 2400 million people) lives and works in developing countries.

■ 20% to 50% of workers in industrialized countries may be subject to hazardous exposures at work, and this rate is expected to be higher in the developing and newly industrialized countries.

■ An equal number of working people report psychological overload at work resulting in stress symptoms.

■ 50% of workers in industrialized countries judge their work to be "mentally demanding."

■ More than 80% of the workforce consists of small and medium enterprises (SMEs). In developing countries it is estimated to be even more, and the largest workforce is to be found in the informal sector. Small and medium enterprises, in particular, as well as the informal sector have poor access to occupational health and safety services and other external support. They often lack knowledge about occupational health in general.

■ Poor occupational health and reduced working capacity of workers may cause economic loss up to 10% to 20% of the gross national product (GNP) of a country. Globally occupational deaths, diseases, and illnesses account for an estimated loss of 4% of the gross domestic product.

(Source: Adapted from World Health Organization (WHO), *Global Strategy on Occupational Health for All: The Way to Health at Work*, 1995. Retrieved from http://www.who.int/occupational_health/en/oehstrategy.pdf)

Over 63,000 multinational and global corporations and their 821,000 foreign subsidiaries operate in distinct geographical and cultural locals of the world. Over 90 million people work in multinational corporations (MNCs) either directly in the subsidiaries including call centers and outsourced operations or indirectly in providing commodities, manufactured goods, and services. As a consequence of growing global transactions across nations of the world, the importance of examining the cultural underpinnings of how these individuals experience work stress and learn to cope with their dysfunctional consequences becomes more important every year.

People, organizations, communities, and nations around the world are being affected by economic, technological, political, and environmental developments that take place in different geographic locales—some close and others far away. Increased global competition, fluctuating interest rates, rapid introduction of new technologies, and related economic, and social and cultural consequences lead to both positive and negative outcomes. One of the major negative consequences of globalization is concerned with the increases in work and organizational stresses—this is the primary focus of our book.

The implications for work stress, resilience, and coping with changes induced by distinct facets of globalization (i.e., economic, and social and cultural) are already profound in the beginning of the twenty-first century and will assume more importance in future decades. Global competition induces organizational restructuring, which in turn creates adverse conditions at work. Individuals at all levels may begin to lose their sense of self-confidence as they grapple with the issues of ambiguities and uncertainties that characterize routine and nonroutine aspects of their work lives. The sheer number and severity of stressful life events occurring in the domain of work and nonwork tend to increase as globalization begins to connect the activities of their work organizations with supply and demand networks of other organizations located in dissimilar contexts and cultures. This chapter prepares us for developing better insights into work stress and coping, and the consequences of globalization for organizations and individuals in dissimilar nations and cultures.

Organizational Consequences

There are many organizational consequences of globalization, including the following:

1. Phenomenal rate of growth in mergers and acquisitions
2. Complexities in coordinating worldwide operations
3. Relentless pressures to innovate
4. Dealing with new workplace realities and organizational structures
5. Evolution of new managerial roles
6. Changing patterns of psychological contract and employee attitudes
7. Managing work–life balance

Mergers and Acquisitions

The rate of international mergers and acquisitions has increased since the early 1980s. These mergers, acquisitions, and downsizing events generally result in a fearful, suspicion, and cynical workforce. Mergers and acquisitions typically do not create pleasant experiences and become even more difficult to deal with when accompanied by technological changes, business process reengineering and reorganization efforts, governmental regulations pertaining to antitrust activities, the delayering and whittling of middle managers, and other methods of corporate rationalization. Fear of job loss after a merger or acquisition was the number one factor among worries and anxieties reported by 54% of the senior managers in the 1,000 largest U.S. companies—many of which operate in the global marketplace. The second most common factor, burnout, was reported by

26% of these executives (Robert Half International, 1991; Shirom, 2011). These kinds of stressful experiences not only occur in the case of hostile takeovers but also are common among managers of companies that are likely to experience mergers and acquisitions whether domestic or cross-border. Instead of managing crises that arise during times of mergers and acquisitions, senior managers tend to experience threats, to become less accessible to their colleagues and subordinates, and to either cut off or limit lines of communication. A large number of personnel experiencing mergers and acquisitions experience considerable uncertainties because they are uninformed about the changes taking place in their place of work as well as in their own job descriptions.

Complexities in Coordinating Worldwide Operations

The early 1990s were characterized by an economic slowdown, planned closings, budget reductions, layoffs, and plant closings. The last few years have been witnessing the same situation once again. Major austerity programs have affected the operation of both private and public organizations, resulting in an emphasis on balanced budgets and strong fiscal responsibilities. Organizations are becoming "leaner and meaner" (Gilmore & Hirschhorn, 1983; Levine, 1980) as they compete globally and face the challenges of coordinating worldwide operations. Although over one third of Fortune global 1,000 companies have downsized their workforces by about 10% each year from the 1980s, they did not do so because they were losing money. The key economic drivers were increased global competition and technological changes (e.g., robots, computers, and information processing technologies) that lowered labor costs and increased productivity. These drivers have become increasingly salient in recent times.

Blue-collar workers in manufacturing were downsized at a rate much faster than managers and white-collar workers (accounting for about 50% of the job losses in the 1990s). However, the downsizing that continued as a strategy to increase profitability and lower labor costs began to affect the white-collar workers as well. In the past decade, white-collar workers have become as vulnerable as blue-collar workers, and past performance is not necessarily a guarantee of continued employment. If a division or department is being downsized because of the future strategic objectives of the company, then both blue- and white-collar employees will be downsized, that is, laid off or terminated. During the past few years, the downsizing of the automobile companies in Michigan has caused the unemployment rate in the state to increase up to 22% in some areas—a rate that is the highest recorded by the U.S. Labor Department since it started recording unemployment statistics in the 1940s. The major factor responsible for downsizing is overhead cost. As long as overhead costs remain uncompetitive with their domestic and international rivals, a company has little competitive choice but to downsize various departments and the workforce. The stresses experienced by downsized workers tend to be quite severe and unsettling because of the loss of self-esteem and the pressures to find another job with comparable income.

Relentless Pressures to Innovate

Companies from the United States, the United Kingdom, Canada, and Asia are confronted with increasing pressures from the global marketplace to innovate. Innovation can take place at the level of developing new products and services or in designing new forms of work arrangements (e.g., globally distributed work teams), both of which have major consequences for organizations. We live in an Information Age defined by the Internet. Its impact on the connections a multinational and global company makes across borders and cultures has been phenomenal. It was inconceivable 30 years ago to think of a manager working in Dallas corresponding with colleagues in Bangalore, Shanghai, and Dublin, not on a sporadic basis but in real time and continuously. It has been noted that global organizations that survive the challenging realities of the marketplace do so by engaging in creative processes of technology and knowledge creation (Davenport & Prusak, 1998; Hamel, 1999).

GOOGLE GOES TO INDIA

Cricket, anyone? Google has come to India with its usual generous life style perks of free food, relaxed atmosphere, and stock options. The difference is its Indian flavor.

Past the lobby decorated with lava lamps and the cubicles adorned with cricket jerseys, a computer programmer sits in front of two flat-screen monitors while coding. Another programmer is relaxed in a beanbag chair working on a laptop while in a corner a turbaned Sikh is ensconced in a massage chair with his eyes closed enjoying the pulsating kneading up and down his back. Intermingled among the cubicles are a foosball tables, billiards, darts, a chessboard, and board games. A tent-shrouded chair sports a sign proclaiming, FORTUNES TOLD HERE. Cans of Pringles, bags of *chaat* (fried snacks), and a large assortment of candy bars are located conveniently in the midst. "The key here is we are not just Google, but Indian," says Prasad Ram, who heads the research center.

Google is purposely strategizing to lure back Indian talent that helped fuel the dot-com boom in the United States by replicating its Silicon Valley workplace indulgences. This is not your usual concept of outsourcing where companies seek cheap labor with few benefits. Rather, it can be seen as brain drain in reverse. Google selected Bangalore as its first research and development (R&D) site located outside of the United States, says Sukhinder Sing Cassidy, "because so many Googlers who are Indian want to move back to India and participate in India's growth."

The United States is issuing half the H-18 visa for skilled high-tech workers that it did in 1999, and fewer foreign students are coming to study at American universities. At one time, Indians thought it was more prestigious to get a U.S. education and work in California, but that is no longer the case.

Google has jumped on board with the trend, as are many other companies in India. What is unique about Google is the cool factor. Its online lure, "We're hiring," is seen by everyone who uses Google's search engine—which has been estimated as 75% of India's 25 million regular Internet users, much more than Yahoo and the local portal Rediff, according to online research firm JuxtConsult.

Those who work at Google talk about the halo effect of working for Google. Supposedly landing a job at Google will increase marriage prospects in a culture where title and income are critical to prearranged marriages. On average, Google pays about three times the annual salary of a tech services company in India. Based on experience, that equated to $13,000 to $30,000 a year, according to industry watchers, who say Google engineers with 5 years' experience make approximately $40,000, and those who are innovative enough to have developed a patent can make up to $100,000 plus stock options, taxi service to and from work, and health insurance that includes the employee's parents. With this in mind there is not a lack for applications. Human resources director Manoj Varghese says they receive "thousands and thousands of job applications a month and they have had only one defection to another company so far." This is very unusual considering attrition rates for tech workers average 12% to 20% a quarter.

So is Bangalore an innovation hotbed? The main driver of innovation during the dot-com boom was Silicon Valley's diversity, the convergence of people from different cultures and nationalities. One-third of Silicon Valley's engineers were born outside of the United States. According to management theory, a diversified group of people will be more creative because of the greater variety of ideas, perspectives, and approaches to problem solving. So Google's R&D center in India has the potential to produce greater innovations than its research centers in China, Korea, Japan, and Australia where populations are more homogenous. So far, this theory has worked; Google Finance, Google's first innovation, was conceived in a foreign R&D center.

Adapted from Prasso, S., & Tippu, S., *Fortune*, 156(9), 2007, pp. 160–166.

Dealing With New Workplace Realities and Organizational Structures

The major restructuring of work and work organizations has been taking place on a scale not seen since the industrial revolution of the early 1800s. With rapid innovations in technologies and global competition, modern workplaces are being transformed in terms of the restructuring of managerial roles, the nature of psychological contract between the employee and organization, and the number of working hours. Smaller, networked organizations are evolving not only in the Western world but also in the developing companies and emergent economies (Grantham, 2000). Organizational stress researchers from different parts of the world are reporting that the amount of work that managers are expected to perform at all levels of organizations has been increasing every decade with no signs of relief. Fewer individuals are being required to do more without any expectation of increases in pay and other benefits. Moreover, the sense of job insecurity is a hallmark of twenty-first-century work organizations, and it is a constant companion of all employees regardless of their position in the organizational hierarchy. Gone are the days when "blue-collar blues" characterized the workers at lower levels of the organization. "White-collar woes" are becoming just as common in all globalized economies due to sudden and turbulent changes in the nature of demands coming from the global marketplace (Heckscher, 1995).

Evolution of New Managerial Roles

As noted earlier, the nature of managerial work has been undergoing profound changes in the advanced and globalizing countries of the world. No doubt the nature and speed of these changes are more intense in the G-7 countries, but they are spreading to other countries in the G-20 network. Cooper (1998), in a survey of managerial work, found that the demands being placed on managers are increasing over time and that a majority had minimal training to cope with such pressures and changes. The major findings of the Cooper survey are as follows:

- 82% of the managers felt that they were suffering from excessive amounts of information overload.
- 76% reported that they were being increasingly dependent on use of social and interpersonal skills more than using the authority associated with their positions.
- 60% reported that they were spending far more time dealing with the various dilemmas associated with organizational politics and strategies of upward influence.
- 60% thought that their jobs were becoming increasingly fragmented and that they had less uninterrupted time to focus on and complete an important task which may be of long-term significance.

Observations such as these and other reports published in various business and trade magazines clearly depict that *role overload* (too much work to do in a given span of time), *role conflict* (conflicting expectations in the performance of one's role), and *underuse of valued skills* (when individuals do not get to use their important occupational skills in performing tasks associated with their work role) have been increasing since the 1980s.

CHURNING AT THE TOP

Corporate chief executive officers (CEOs) are being hired and fired at a rate never seen before, and more are expected to meet this fate as the economic slowdown continues. The question arises: Why is it proving hard to find good leaders these days?

An article authored by Warren Bennis and James O'Toole (2000), two American academics, theorized about a phenomenon they expressed as CEO churning. The rate of corporate bosses being hired and fired was unprecedented, they contended. As of February 2001, data gathered and evaluated by Challenger, Gray & Christmas, an outplacement firm based in Chicago, showed that 119 CEOs had left their positions at American companies. That was 37%

more than the previous year. More CEOs are expected to be displaced during this economic slowdown. Stakeholders (i.e., investors and boards of directors) will become less tolerant with CEOs and executive bosses who are not producing results.

Bennis and O'Toole argue that there is another reason for this phenomenon besides the economic slowdown: The position of the CEO has become more demanding. As companies shift their strategies, the stresses placed on the person in the top position are resulting in an increase of executives being displaced or choosing to resign. Furthermore, the flattening of the corporation has increased the span of control of executives. They now have eight to nine people reporting to them, whereas in the past they may have had four or five. Simultaneously, globalization has forced executives to travel more abroad to monitor their subsidiaries. These additional types of stresses are exacerbating the churning situation.

The CEO of Kimberly-Clark, Wayne Sanders, attempted to decrease his stress by delegating more of his travel to another top executive. He informed the Wall Street Journal that he realized during a 2-week trip to Asia that he was in trouble. At 1 o'clock in the morning, unable to sleep and fatigued, he found himself munching on a Snickers bar and thinking, "I'm in trouble."

The wave of mergers and acquisitions has also increased the churn. The expectation of a merger is to combine two companies so that they work together amicably, but usually one of the top executives of the two companies is left by the wayside without a position. Immediately after a merger agreement is very stressful for CEOs and is sometimes the last straw, prompting them to resign.

Adapted from *The Economist*, 358(8213), 2001, pp. 67–69.

The modern workplace is characterized by changing scenarios in the roles that groups, teams, and individuals perform. The nature of changes with which an organization has to cope is a direct function of the nature of its involvement in the global marketplace. The theoretical significance of these types of stresses is discussed in Chapter 3.

Changing Patterns of Psychological Contracts and Employee Attitudes

Many multinational and global companies outsource some of their key business functions to organizations located in low-labor-cost countries and employ individuals on contingent, short-term, or part-time contracts. The development of the contingent workforce, temporary personnel, and others on a part-time basis has profound implications for changing the nature of the psychological contract that employees have with their organizations (Rosseau, 1995). The number of individuals in part-time jobs has nearly doubled during the 1990s, and the trend is continuing (Quick, Cooper, Nelson, Quick, & Gavin, 2003). The trend seems to be to cut labor and employee costs as much as possible by employing as few individuals as are needed on a purely cost-benefit analysis basis. Organizations with only a small cadre of full-time permanent employees working from a conventional office in the urban or the suburban parts of cities are becoming common. These organizations tend to keep core competencies in-house and to buy the skills that are likely to become quickly obsolete by hiring individuals on a contract basis. These individuals generally work from home or are linked to the company by means of computer-mediated communication and telecommuting. The clear trend is to hire individuals on short-term contracts to do specific tasks or carryout specific projects for the company. Collectively these developments leave little room for considering the role of the psychological contract in the employment equation. In other words, individuals are being asked to exchange their skills or expertise for a specific amount of compensation and are being given the clear and unambiguous signal that their psychological expectations regarding other skills not stipulated or written into the contract do not matter. What is being emphasized is a reality of exchange of labor and valued skills for a price determined by the supply and demand factors in the labor market. In the United Kingdom, for example, there are growing perceptions that more people are working on short-term contracts and do not have permanent full-time jobs. Most of the growth of part-time jobs takes place in small organizations employing fewer than 500 people. The majority of these employees have children at home and find the idea of working at home part-time or on a freelance basis desirable. While work of a routine nature can be successfully subcontracted to employees who are not attached to the workplace by their physical presence, the psychological contract that is essential for developing commitment to the work roles is often absent in such employment relationships (Heckscher, 1995). Heckscher's observations were important in 1995 and seem to be applicable to these part-time, freelance, and telecommuting workers. Additional research needs to be conducted to compare reactions to increased pressures to perform by these employees with their full-time colleagues.

The changing workplace in the current era of globalization precipitates a significant transformation of employee attitudes, commitment, and related affective and behavioral intentions toward their work organization. As noted earlier, this process of transformation is not limited to the organizations in the Western world. There have been significant changes in the attitudes, work norms, expectations, and work-related values of employees in countries of Southern Europe (e.g., Italy, Spain, Greece, and Portugal), Western Europe (e.g., Ireland, the United Kingdom, and France), South Asia (e.g., India and Sri Lanka), East Asia (e.g., China, South Korea, and Japan), and South America (e.g., Brazil, Chile, and Argentina). (See Steers, Sanchez-Runde, and Lee [2009] and Cleveland, McCarthy, and Himelright [2008] for a review of the changing attitudes and motivation of individuals in the current era of globalization.) A longitudinal study conducted in the United Kingdom from 1996 to 2000 found that persistent levels of change characterize the nature of managerial work (Worrall & Cooper, 2000). When organizational changes induced by globalization-related demands are poorly managed, the stresses of managers and other employees increase. In more than 40% of situations, managers who have been adversely affected by the restructuring of their organizations felt that they were not given a rationale for the restructuring. Only in 20% of the situations were they made aware of the real reasons for restructuring. In most privately held companies, managers felt that the restructuring was being done to accomplish some goals pursued by the board of directors and stockholders for the company as opposed to something that was done with their cooperation and understanding. Therefore, it is not surprising that there were intense feelings of insecurity, powerlessness, and alienation during organizational restructuring and changes. Individuals' organizational commitment was also low and decreased along with their sense of job security from the onset of organizational restructuring—over 64% felt lower levels of commitment to their organizations. It should be clear that the negative impact of restructuring on work stress, job satisfaction, and morale is high. From numerous studies, it is becoming increasingly clear that the changing nature of the workplace is responsible for inducing a variety of stressful reactions at all levels of the organization.

Managing Work–Life Balance

A clear impact of participation in the global marketplace is reflected in the increasing number of hours that individuals work. Working hours have been increasing since the 1980s, not only in the Western countries but also in the context of the East and Southeast Asian economies. Juliet Schor (1992) reported that Americans worked the greatest number of hours (1,949 per year), followed by the Japanese, more than any other country among the G-20 nations. In fact, it can be noted that the more globalized the country and work organizations are, the longer the workdays become. Countries that are hardly globalized (e.g., Bolivia, Ecuador, Mongolia, and countries in sub-Saharan Africa) have a lower per capita income and other material benefits. However, the number of working hours is much less compared with those in the globalized and emerging economies (i.e., the BRIC countries). Since 2000, 40% of managers from the United Kingdom work longer than 50 hours a week. Managers at higher levels of the organization tended to work considerably longer hours than those below them. A total of 62% of senior executives work over 50 hour per week compared with 25% of junior managers. There is a strong disconnect between the number of hours that managers supposedly have written in their employment contract and how many they really have to work, especially during times of coping with pressures of a global marketplace. It is interesting to note that managers of public-sector organizations and government bureaucracies work less compared with those in private-sector organizations. This is a natural consequence due to pressures experienced from competing with rivals in the domestic and international marketplace. Public-sector organizations and government bureaucracies tend to have stable environments and tend to benefit from some level of protection from their national governments. Therefore, they do not require their managers to work as hard or as long as private-sector organizations. This trend is true in both globalizing and emerging economies.

Pressures to work long hours necessitate that one has to learn to manage the work–life balance (the delicate relationship between work and nonwork life). Issues concerning work–life balance have emerged as a major topic of research and practice in the past 2 decades (see Pitt-Catsouphes, Kossek, & Sweet, 2006). The importance of work in relation to personal life has been increasing since the 1970s, and it increases as one moves up the corporate ladder. In other words, the higher individuals advance in their careers and the more decision-making and responsibility they assume, the more work "looms large" in their lives. Employees are quite aware of the adverse effects of working long hours at the expense of developing nurturing relationships in their personal lives. A total of 65% of managers think that the amount of work they do has an adverse effect on their psychological, emotional, and physical health, and about 70% think that spending long hours on the job leads to poor relationships with their spouse or significant other (Quick et al., 2003).

Human Consequences

Along with organizational consequences, there are many human consequences of living in the era of global change. These consequences are directly related to the effects of globalization at the level of the organization and the society;

however, in order to provide a clear theoretical distinction, we call them human consequences because they strongly manifest themselves at a microlevel with implications for individuals and their families. They include

1. Adapting to new patterns of culture at work and in the society
2. Continuous upgrading of skills and abilities
3. Working in cross-cultural work teams
4. Dealing with new demographic realities

Adapting to New Patterns of Culture at Work and in Society

Globalization introduces rapid changes in patterns of consumption and the spread of global brand goods and services across dissimilar cultures. It leads to the growth of the consumer class in developing nations and emergent economies and creating similar patterns of material desires and lifestyles (Wolf, 2004). The new consumer class consists of individuals and families who use telephones, televisions, and the Internet and are influenced by the culture and ideas that are transmitted via these media (*The Worldwatch Institute Annual Report 2004*, n.d.). There has been substantial growth in the consumer class in countries such as China, India, Brazil, Mexico, and South Africa, and the patterns of consumption tend to converge with those of the Western countries such as the United States, Canada, and the United Kingdom. The supermarkets in the globalizing countries now carry many global brands (e.g., Coca-Cola, Sprite, 7UP) leading to "McDonaldization of consumer culture" (Ritzer, 1998). Such changes in the patterns of consumption in non-Western countries lead to slow transformation of cultural values and practices. In some sectors of the economy, the process tends to be slow, whereas in others the transformation process is rapid. The worldwide spread of economic activities increases the tendency to emphasize rationality and reliance on science and technology. As developing countries and emerging nations take steps toward becoming more globalized, they begin to use Western countries as references not only in the governance of economic and political affairs but also in the regulation of lives at work and nonwork. Corporate cultures of organizations are becoming more results oriented, driven more by profit as opposed to concern for employees. Values of consumerism, individualism, competition, and efficiency gradually replace traditional values of nonmaterialism, collectivism, and cooperation in the workplace. Human consequences of such changes are profound.

A curious new breed of professional workers, called the creative class (Florida, 2005), has emerged. In describing their work habits, Deborah Blumenthal (1979) wrote, "Tucked away discretely in corners of living rooms, behind bedroom doors, in basements, attics, garages, and even bureau drawers, home offices have become the primary place of work for thousands...." Until around 1987, the type of work one could do at home was fairly limited. Today's creative classes, to cope with the changing pressures at work, are working with iPhones, iPads, Blackberries, and Android smartphones and tablets that are connected to the Internet continuously. The negatives of such work patterns have only intensified since Blumenthal's analysis in 1979: They are characterized by the complete lack of separation between work and nonwork lives, the lack of face-to-face interaction with colleagues, and the dogging sense that work is expected to be done at all hours. The need to work-work-work has penetrated our sense of collective well-being. Reports of executives buying expensive gifts for children but not having time to spend with them during the holidays are found in newspapers and business periodicals all over the world. A new era has evolved where one may enjoy working on a software problem for the company and find it more rewarding than helping children with schoolwork or a spouse with household chores. New computer-mediated technologies such as Skype often substitute for personal interaction and allow one to rationalize staying in the office to complete projects. Numerous careers are being characterized by what Korman and Korman (1980) called the "career success/personal failure syndrome." This syndrome, which connotes high levels of accomplishment accompanied by divorce, marital conflict, and related symptoms of family strain, has become rather commonplace in the largest global economy of the world (the United States) and is spreading to other emergent economies.

With more multinational and global organizations expanding their worldwide operations and using such management techniques as outsourcing, offshoring, and temporary work teams to improve efficiency, serious consequences for work stress and employee health have developed. Corporate and work cultures of rapidly globalizing companies are becoming less employee centered, and psychological contracts, implied at the time of recruitment, lose significance rather rapidly (Cappelli, 1999). Fluctuating market demands of the global marketplace make it necessary for many organizations to develop new patterns of employment contracts that in our view are largely responsible for the evolution of stressful experiences for the employees and their families.

HOW TO EMBRACE CHANGE

Between 2005 and 2006 more than 1 million jobs left the U.S., Europe, and Japan, as well as over one-quarter of a million service jobs to overseas countries. For the first time in history, Asian companies are producing more than their European counterparts. However, the success of globalization has brought political uncertainties in Southeast Asia, a continuous need to export to Western Markets, and pressures to grow rapidly economically.

The fast pace of globalization has brought with it major discontents. Movements against immigration and a growing resistance to change are occurring in just about all continents. There seems to be a rise of nationalistic movements in the form of "economic patriotism" in Europe and Latin America. An example of this protectionist mode can be seen in how the European single market philosophy with its free movement of goods, people, and capital has been threatened. Yet in the last few months, France sought ways to block Italian utility takeovers, Italy warned against Dutch banking acquisition, Spain held up German energy bids, and Poland fought Italian financial service merger attempts. World trade deals are becoming elusive with rich countries' protectionism criticized for standing in the way of poor countries' development.

The paradox of globalization is that even winners can be the losers. The benefits of globalization result in considerably lower prices for everyday consumer goods. Televisions, cameras, and mobile phones are now accessible to millions of households in the developing world. However, a nonbenefit speculated by the citizens of the richest countries is the transfer of jobs offshore increasing their unemployment. They tend to ignore or dismiss the fact that cheaper products and services from newly emerging and developing countries spurs increased competition, innovation, and productivity for both developed nations and the emerging markets of developing nations. As America's history has shown, open markets and competition works in building robust economies. Isolationism and protectionism are not the answers. There needs to be a conversation about globalization's benefits and risks. Why? By lowering our market barriers, we can attain the prize of a 50% increase in world trade. By increasing productivity and investing in innovation, Britain alone could create 100,000 jobs from energy conservation to micro generation.

If nations leave their displaced feeling stressed and hopeless, there will be more backlashes and protectionism against economic globalization. Yet these actions are self-defeating. But if they expand the opportunities to include new skills, new jobs, and investments in strengthening communities, citizens will be more receptive to seeing the positive aspects of globalization.

Adapted from Brown, G., *Newsweek*, 147(24), 2006, p. 69.

Job insecurity, higher work pace, long and fluctuating working hours, low control over job content and processes, and low wages add further stresses and occupational hazards (Smith & Carayon, 2011). Incompetent styles of management, sexual harassment of working women, poor working conditions, inappropriate and unfair labor relations practices, discrimination in hiring and advancement policies, and insufficient training are all negative aspects found in work environments that individuals confront routinely in different countries. To be sure, working conditions are generally much better in advanced globalized countries of the West but not so in globalizing and emergent economies (such as the BRIC countries). In their rush to improve economic growth, national governments and work organizations of globalizing countries have paid insufficient attention to the occupational health psychology and physical well-being of workers in the sectors that are particular vulnerable.

Continuous Upgrading of Skills and Abilities

Globalization results in relentless pressures to innovate and continually upgrade occupational skills and abilities at all levels of the organization. It also severely weakens the participation and earnings potential of older workers. Massive restructuring processes in both economic and occupational structures of globalizing countries create discrepancies between those who have the right kinds of skills and talents as needed in the marketplace and those who do not. More often than not, those who do not have the right skills suffer from working in roles that are underpaid, do not get access to appropriate forms of training, and continue to lag behind in terms of their economic success and psychological well-being (see Grantham, 2000; Hofacker, 2010). Upgrading political skills in managing relationships at work has also been found to relate to work effectiveness (Ferris, Davidson, & Perrewé, 2005). The issue of making sense of the political reality in one's work group and organization was almost never raised and discussed in the organizational literature in the 1970s, but now it has become an important topic and many researchers claim that a lack of political skills and abilities can create a stressful experience in one's work life (Ferris et al., 2005).

Working in Cross-Cultural Work Teams

Geographically distributed work teams are composed of members of the same organization (or sometimes different organizations) from different countries of the world. More often than not, they differ in terms of their national and cultural origins and in terms of their work habits and work ethics. It is not easy to work with the members of a geographically distributed work team (Stanko & Gibson, 2009). Consider the case of a financial services manager of American Express in the New York City headquarters who has to correspond with his Japanese or Chinese counterpart by using both the telephone and computer-mediated communication. This manager has to wake up in the early hours of the morning to coordinate his work with those located in the Asian time zones (i.e., typically 9 to 10 hours ahead of U.S. Eastern Standard time). Along with difficulties of coordinating across time zones, one has to make sense of working in the context of multicultural work teams (Burke, Priest, Upshaw, Salas, & Pierce, 2008) and manage the challenges of dealing with cultural diversities that characterize virtual work teams (Stanko & Gibson, 2009).

Dealing With New Demographic Realities

The economic and cultural realities of the rapid growth of global linkages lead to significant changes in the composition of not only the working population but also the population of the globalizing societies. Huntington (2004) provides a detailed portrayal of the new demographic realities in U.S. society. Similar developments also characterize the population distributions of Western Europe, Australia, and New Zealand. In particular, the large cities of the world, which are the global headquarters of large multinational and global organizations, are increasingly more populated. The working population in multinational and global companies is increasingly composed of immigrants and culturally dissimilar individuals from different nations. Global cities such as London, Paris, Sydney, and Sao Paolo have become highly heterogeneous in terms of the composition of workers that come from distinct national, ethnic, racial, and religious groups. Consider the current demographic situation in New York City: It has over 30% foreign-born workers. Given the nature of cultural diversity that characterize cities such as Toronto and New York it is quite conceivable that a native New Yorker might feel more comfortable, working in another global city such as Sydney or Berlin compared with working in Memphis, Tennessee, or Paris, Texas, which have remained relatively static in terms of cultural composition.

There is growing evidence that immigrant workers from the former Communist Bloc countries, such as Poland, Hungary, and Romania, have distinct patterns of work motivation and ethics that are difficult for Western colleagues and supervisors to understand and work with. The point is that learning to deal with the challenges of growing heterogeneity in terms of gender, age, racial, ethnic, and cultural background is important. In Chapter 6 we present a more detailed discussion of these multicultural perspectives that emerge in different immigrant populations in appraising the experiences of work stress and coping.

Consequences of Globalization From a Cultural Perspective

Globalization involves increasingly frequent encounters with organizations, individuals, and situations whose national and cultural backgrounds differ considerably. Learning to appreciate the exact nature and consequences of globalization at the level of the organization and the individual necessarily involves a comprehensive understanding of cultural differences. We define *culture* as a multifaceted construct that is composed of the totality of knowledge, beliefs, attitudes, norms, and values of a group of people who speak the same language and are located in the same geographical context of the world. Culture is a collection of habits, beliefs, practices, arguments, and values that regulates and guides human life in various geographical regions of the world. Culture transmits practical solutions to everyday problems—like how to avoid painful interpersonal and social interactions and how to form successful family structures. Perhaps one of the most important roles that culture plays is to educate and train our emotions such as feelings of joy, pride, pain, accomplishment, grief, shame, and guilt.

Different cultures of the world emphasize distinctive narratives, holidays, symbols, and works of art that contain implicit and explicit messages about how we ought to feel, respond, and make sense of our social environment. Brooks (2011) examines the following behaviors and patterns as examples of sustained cultural differences:

1. Plays and movies produced in Germany are three times as likely to have unhappy and tragic endings as plays from the United States and India.
2. Members of Western societies are surprised that in India love is not a precondition for marriage (where over half the population have arranged marriages).
3. A total of 65% of Japanese are afraid of saying or articulating the wrong thing in social situation compared with just 25% of Americans.
4. In the United Kingdom couples rarely touch each other in public, whereas in France more physical touching is common; in Paris over 110 touches were observed in coffee houses in an hour of having coffee (Keltner, 2009). In the Latino culture of San Juan, Puerto Rico, the number of touches between a couple during an hour of coffee was close to 180.
5. Cultural differences are also observed in the various regions of the United States. In the American South, where a culture of honor is dominant, words like *gun* are found in the names of cities (e.g., Gun Point, Florida); however, in the Northern states words like *joy* and *ville* are more common (Joy, Illinois; Louisville, Kentucky; Danville, Indiana).

The culture of a country or a region of the world (e.g., Japan, East Asia) is not a recipe book that creates uniformity. Each culture has its own internal debates, unresolved issues, and persistent tensions. Consider the case of race relations in the United States—this issue is still debated strongly in both private and public circles. Each culture provides a historical emphasis on maintaining continuity of unresolved conflicts that pass from generation to generation. Despite the logic of industrialism, which claimed that culture of ruling elites and managers of industrializing countries would converge (see Karsh & Cole, 1968), much of the current evidence suggests that cultures of the globalizing countries have not converged. In fact, they seem to be growing in different directions. To be sure, some work and organizational practices are becoming common on a world-wide basis—that is, the practice of downsizing, having fewer employees at the company headquarters, and developing virtual work teams. However, these practices are being moderated by strong cultural preferences (Leung, Bhagat, Buchan, Erez, & Gibson, 2005).

Consider the case of merit pay that is common in the United States linking compensation directly to corporate financial performance. Other cultures believe that compensation should be based on group effort and that equality is more important than personal contribution. Despite attempts by an American multinational corporation to emphasize individually based bonus systems in a Danish subsidiary, the practice repeatedly failed. The Danish employees rejected the proposal because it favored equity over equality in compensating individuals and work groups. They felt that all employees should receive equal cash bonuses instead of a bonus based on a percentage of salary (Schneider, Wittenberg-Cox, & Hansen, 1991). People living in Japan have a culture in common that is different from people in Canada. Asian countries are generally quite different in terms of the kinds of knowledge, belief, and value systems that they emphasize compared with Anglo societies such as the United Kingdom, Australia, Canada, and New Zealand.

Cultures do not exist simply as static differences. Instead, cultures compete with one another for establishing better and worse ways of getting things done and accomplishing cherished goals for future generations. They pursue the objectives of social, economic, and technological growth at the organizational and societal levels, not from the standpoint of some objective observers but from the standpoint of people within the culture who act as guides in developing practices and value systems. Haitians and Dominicans share the island of Hispaniola, but Dominicans have a gross domestic product (GDP) that is roughly four times the GDP of Haitians. Life expectancy is 18 years longer in the Dominican Republic than in Haiti, and the literacy rate is 33% higher. In New York City, Jews and Italians have lived in the lower East Side of Manhattan since the turn of the twentieth century; however, it was the Jewish people who achieved greater economic and career-related success compared with their Italian counterparts.

During the past 3 decades there have been growing reports about Chinese American children doing far better than Latino and African American children in elementary, middle, and high schools. They take more demanding courses (e.g., college advanced placement [AP] courses) compared with children from other ethnic groups. A total of 50% of Asian Americans graduate from college compared with 34% of native-born mainstream Americans between the ages of 25 and 29 (Thernstrom & Thernstrom, 2003). Asian Americans have a life expectancy of 87 year compared with 79 years for Whites and 73 years for African Americans. It is interesting to note that in the northern state of Michigan, Asian American life expectancy is around 90 despite all of the economic hardships that are present in this region of the United States (see Brooks, 2011, for details.)

Certain cultures are better adapted for absorbing technological advances and become increasingly modern. Lawrence Harrison (2006) reports that people in progress-prone cultures start with the assumption that they can play major roles in shaping their destiny while people in progress-resistant cultures believe that they are not able to control events that occur in their lives and are largely fatalistic in their outlook. He found that people in progress-prone cultures live to work, whereas those in progress-resistant cultures work to live (Harrison, 2006). People in progress-prone cultures are likely to trust others, to be more competitive and optimistic, to emphasize education, and to value punctuality. The social mechanism for controlling people in these cultures is to make them internalize guilt so that they are more likely to hold themselves responsible. In contrast, people in progress-resistant cultures are likely to be distrustful of others, to externalize guilt, and to blame others for their failures and misfortunes.

We advance the notion that progress-prone cultures are likely to deal with the organizational and human consequences of globalization better than progress-resistant cultures. The Scandinavian countries and the Western European countries are good examples of progress-prone cultures. While they have experienced considerable difficulties in dealing with many of the dilemmas that are associated with globalization, they are largely successful; however, countries of the Middle East, North Africa, sub-Saharan Africa, and much of Central America and Asia have not benefited much from advances in globalization. Admittedly, these countries lack adequate infrastructures, institutions, and educational systems that make their citizens appreciate the benefits that accompany globalization and in the process reject xenophobia. Still, they are not able to differentiate between the positive consequences of globalization from the dysfunctional ones. Historical and cultural backgrounds are largely responsible for this state of affairs. For us to better appreciate the role of international differences in how nations deal with the organizational and human consequences of globalization, it is necessary to understand the theoretical underpinnings of cultural variations.

Theoretical Frameworks

Culture is a multifaceted construct that is hard to define in a concrete fashion. It has been defined as a totality of knowledge, beliefs, values, attitudes, norms, and mores of a social group whose members speak the same language (Triandis, 1994, 1995). Kroeber and Parsons (1958) define *culture* in contrast with *society* as consisting of transmitted and created patterns of values, ideas, and symbols that are essential for shaping human thoughts and behaviors necessary for survival of the group. For six decades since the classic work of Kluckhohn and Strodtbeck (1961), culture has been understood in terms of six basic orientations:

1. Relation to nature
2. Basic human nature
3. Temporal orientation
4. Space orientation
5. Activity orientation
6. Relationships among people

The two dimensions that are most relevant in determining which countries are likely to be progress-prone or progress-resistant are temporal orientation and relationships among people. The extent to which individuals are socialized to emphasize the past, present, or future is called the *temporal focus of human activity*. Progress-prone cultures are likely to be more concerned with economic activities and events that take place in the present and are likely to take place in the future. They are less concerned with the accomplishments of the past generations. Cultures of the United States and Western Europe are largely progress-prone, whereas those of the Middle East, Central and sub-Saharan Africa, Central Asia, and some parts of Central and South America are largely progress-resistant.

The second dimension reflects the extent to which the culture of the country emphasizes individualistic, group-oriented, or hierarchy-focused ways of relating to one another. Cultures emphasizing individualistic orientation socialize their members to relate to each other in terms of their personal characteristics and achievements—for example, "I am an honor student," "I am a star athlete," "I am honest and fair-minded." In the United States, Canada, and most parts of the Western world, people relate to each other largely one to one; however, in group-oriented societies, people relate to each other in terms of emphasizing the needs of the group to which they belong. The emphasis is on equality, harmony, unity, and loyalty to group objectives; for example, the Japanese make decisions by referring to group consensus and do not depend on decisions made solely based on individual criteria or needs. Hierarchical societies value group relationships but emphasize the awareness of the status or rank of the individual with whom one is relating—for example, "I am a plant manager; I have the power to hire you." Venezuela, Colombia, Mexico, the Philippines, China, and India are largely hierarchical societies.

Perhaps the most important theoretical framework of value in analyzing the consequences of economic globalization on societies, organizations, institutions, social groups, and individuals is based on the work of Geert Hofstede (1980, 1991, 2001). He defines *culture* as the collective programming of the mind that distinguishes one group or category from another (Hofstede, 1991). Culture is to a society what memory is to an individual (Triandis, 1994, 1995, 1998). It consists of standard operating procedures, unstated assumptions, and implicit ways of perceiving, evaluating, and acting for a group of people who live in the same historical period in the same geographical region of the world. The shared outlook and the commonality of thought result in an acceptance of common codes of conduct and expectations that influence and control a large majority of belief, norms, attitudes, and values. People are born into a given culture (e.g., Japanese, Chinese, American, Brazilian), and they gradually experience the subtle and overt internalizing effects of their national cultures through various social institutions such as family, school systems, work organizations, national media, and governmental agencies. Over time, cultures evolve as societies adapt to changes in their internal and external environments. Internal environments consist of political systems, customs, and traditions, whereas external environments consist of the ecological setting of the society. Economic globalization typically occurs as the more developed countries interact with the internal and external environments of the globalizing countries. This process leads to changes and sometimes often radical transformations of the dominant values and patterns of thinking in the less developed country.

To better appreciate the role of cultural variations, it becomes necessary to discuss the dimensions of culture as proposed and validated by Hofstede (1980, 2001). This framework has been found to be effective in explaining the role of cultural variations in various organizational, group-level, and individual-level phenomena (Hofstede, 2001). Throughout the 1970s, Hofstede researched paper-and-pencil survey results from 72 subsidiaries of the IBM Corporation. Based on over 140,000 responses, he was able to identify five dimensions on which countries of the world diverge:

Power distance: the extent to which positions of status and privilege are expected to be distributed unequally. In high power distance societies, centralized authority prevails and designates procedures for the less powerful members to follow and abide by.

Uncertainty avoidance: the degree to which members of a society are socialized to avoid situations characterized by a lack of clarity and to avoid the resulting anxieties that accompany such situations. Citizens of countries that are high in uncertainty avoidance feel easily threatened by ambiguous and uncertain situations.

Individualism–collectivism: the extent to which individuals are supposed to be responsible for their own thoughts, feelings, and behaviors. Individualistic countries socialize their members to pursue their individual goals and objectives and not be highly concerned with the goals of the collective or group to which they belong. Collectivism refers to a social pattern where members of a group are highly interdependent and individuals are socialized to prefer group-based goals and objectives. Work organizations of the West are largely individualistic in their orientation, whereas those of the East are largely collectivistic. Salespeople in the United States, the United Kingdom, France, and Australia like to take pride in their individual accomplishments for selling more than others. In contrast, sales people in Japan, China, South Korea, and Venezuela are socialized to take pride in the accomplishments of their sales group.

Masculinity–femininity: the degree to which gender roles are defined. Masculinity pertains to those societies where gender roles are clearly more distinct. Men are supposed to be assertive, tough, and focused on material success, whereas women are supposed to be modest, tender, nonmaterialistic, and concerned with raising children. Feminine cultures are those in which gender roles overlap and both men and women are expected to perform in similar fashions in their work and nonwork roles. In countries such as Sweden, Denmark, Norway (i.e., the Nordic countries), and the Netherlands, husbands are allowed paternity leave to take care of their newborn children. Such a practice is unlikely to develop even in the most advanced economies of the world, (i.e., the United States, China, Japan, India, and Germany). In masculine cultures, success and the achievement of wealth are highly emphasized, whereas in feminine cultures the quality of life is the dominant value. In Scandinavian countries, the values of cooperation and the security of all members are considered more important than pure materialistic success.

Long- versus short-term orientation: the importance that different societies place on time. The efficient use of time is emphasized in Germany, Switzerland, the United States, the United Kingdom, Canada, and most other Western economies. However, in many Latin American countries (e.g., Brazil, Mexico, Columbia), time is not considered to be limited and valuable but an inexhaustible resource. Waiting in line to mail a letter or to get a driver's license renewed is considered to be more frustrating by a majority of Americans, Germans, and Swiss than by members of many Latin American and Central and South Asian countries.

These five dimensions of cultures embrace wide-ranging phenomena that occur on a routine and nonroutine basis in various countries of the world. In societies characterized by high individualism, such as the United States, Canada, Australia, the United Kingdom, and France, people learn to deal with new and unforeseen situations in work and societal contexts without experiencing a great deal of stress and anxiety. A positive attitude toward experiencing novelty is emphasized resulting in a relatively quicker embrace of new forms of products, services, and work arrangements (e.g., virtual work and working across cultures). Economic globalization is likely to generate fewer destabilizing effects at both the organizational and individual levels in countries that are highly individualistic and where the temporal focus of activity is on the future. In contrast, collectivistic societies are not as likely to socialize their members in accepting the uncertainties and novelties that accompany economic globalization. In addition, if the temporal focus is largely on the past, then progress-resistant patterns develop in the collective milieu. The need to conform and be accepted by the social groups or collectives makes it difficult for many collectivistic societies to engage in learning those patterns of thinking and acting that are likely to be helpful in adapting to new forms of products, services, and work arrangements. The process of globalization inevitably precipitates various forms of conflicts at different levels of the work organizations, institutions, and society. Since conflicts and debates concerning competing values, ideas, and preferences are generally avoided in collectivistic cultures in favor of maintaining group-generated consensus and harmony, these societies are likely to be affected negatively by globalization to a greater extent than individualistic cultures.

In many ways, the language of the country influences the evolution of cultural patterns. Cross-cultural researchers find striking similarities and contrasts in learning a new language and in learning a new culture. Table 2.1 presents the parallel principles of second language and second culture learning based on Guthrie (1975). Just as the first language greatly influences the way we learn the content and verbal intonation patterns of the second language, values inherent in one's native culture continue to influence and may even distort the learning of a new culture. Learning to function effectively in the era of globalization makes it necessary for citizens of globalizing countries to learn the languages of the more advanced countries (e.g., English, Japanese, French) and learn to make

Table 2.1 Parallel Principles of Second Language and Second Culture Learning

Language	*Culture*
1. First language is acquired early and fixed by the age of 5.	1. Native culture acquired early, relatively fixed by the age of 5.
2. Language of the country of settlement is more easily learned by children of immigrants.	2. New cultural values, norms, and orientation are learned more easily by youngsters than by adults over 30.
3. First language structures habits of thinking.	3. The first culture of the immigrants determines habits and values.
4. A new language has a new set of pitch levels that immigrants must learn, and an accent remains that reveals the nature of the first language.	4. The adopted culture has a new range of nonverbal and expressive patterns of communication that immigrants must learn to communicate more fluently.
5. In times of experiencing severe stressful events or frustrations, one is likely to revert to using one's first language in expressing the felt psychological strain.	5. First culture of the immigrants introduces errors and distortions in the interpretation of the second culture.
6. One can best express one's deepest feelings of affection, love, or disgust in one's first language.	6. One can best express one's deepest values in overt behavior patterns that reflect long-term significance of one's first culture. It is more difficult to learn a new way of expressing deep feelings of love or affection or disgust than adopting a new style of clothing.
7. One ponders one's deepest cultural conflicts and dilemmas in terms of the words and concepts of one's first language.	7. One's first culture determines one's profound emotions and values.

Source: Adapted from Guthrie, G. M. In R. W. Brislin, S. Bochner, and W. J. Lonner (Eds.), *Cross-Cultural Perspectives on Learning*, New York, Sage, 1975, pp. 95–116.

adaptations in both the internal and external environments of their countries. Closer ties between the language of the globalizing country with that of the globalized country make it easier for the process of cultural transformation to occur. In other words, countries that emphasize the learning of the language of the dominant globalizing nations (in most cases, it is English—the language of the United States, Canada, the United Kingdom) are better able to embrace various aspects of economic and cultural globalization.

Conclusion

In this chapter, we have discussed the organizational and human consequences of economic globalization. While economists (e.g., Wolf, 2004) have presented a strong case for globalizing different countries of the world noting that it benefits a large majority of people in poorer countries, we take the perspective that adverse consequences of globalization occur in both globalized and globalizing countries. These consequences are experienced by work organizations and their employees. Six consequences were examined at the organizational level and four at the individual level. To develop better insights into how various nations of the world might interpret and subsequently experience these outcomes, we present theoretical frameworks for understanding cultural differences. It is argued that while progress-prone cultures are likely to be better equipped to grapple with the complexities of changes that accompany the process of economic globalization compared with progress-resistant cultures, the fact remains that globalization does have adverse consequences whose implications for work stress and coping need to be carefully analyzed. In the next chapter, we discuss the theoretical frameworks that are developed primarily in Western contexts to understand the dynamics of work stress and coping.

References

Bennis, W., & O Toole, J. (2000). Don't hire the wrong CEO. *Harvard Business Review, 78*(3),170–176.

Blumenthal, D. (1979, July 15). At work they are at home. *New York Times*.

Brooks, D. (2011). *The social animal*. New York: Random House.

Brown, G. (2006, June 12). How to embrace change. *Newsweek, 147*(24), p. 69.

Burke, C. S., Priest, H. A., Upshaw, C. L., Salas, E., & Pierce, L. (2008). A sensemaking approach to understanding multicultural teams: An initial framework. In D. L. Stone & E. F. Stone-Romero (Eds.), *The influence of culture on human resource management processes and practices* (pp. 269–306). New York: Taylor & Francis.

Cappelli, P. (1999). *The new deal at work: Managing the market-based employment relationship*. Boston, MA: Harvard Business School Press.

Churning at the top. (2001, March 17). *The Economist, 358*(8213), 67–69.

Cleveland, J., McCarthy, A., & Himelright, J. (2008). Work and family concerns and practices: A cross-national and cultural comparison of Ireland and the United States. In D. Stone & G. Stone-Romero (Eds.), *The influence of culture on human resource management processes and practices.* New York: Lawrence Erlbaum Associates.

Cooper, C. L. (Ed.). (1998). *Theories of organizational stress.* Oxford: Oxford University Press.

Davenport, T. H., & Prusak, L. (1998). *Working knowledge: How organizations manage what they know.* Boston, MA: Harvard Business School Press.

Ferris, G. R., Davidson, S. L., & Perrewé, P. L. (2005). *Political skills at work.* Boston, MA: Davis–Black.

Florida, R. (2005). *The flight of the creative class.* New York: HarperCollins.

Gilmore, T., & Hirschhorn, L. (1983). Management challenges under conditions of retrenchment. *Human Resource Management, 22*(4), 341–357.

Grantham, C. (2000). *The future of work: The promise of the new digital work society.* New York: McGraw-Hill.

Guthrie, G. M. (1975). A behavioral analysis of culture learning. In R. W. Brislin, S. Bochner, & W. J. Lonner (Eds.), *Cross-cultural perspectives on learning* (pp. 95–116). New York: Sage.

Hamel, G. (1999). Strategy as revolution. *Harvard Business Review* , 69–82.

Harrison, L. (2006). *The central liberal truth.* Oxford: Oxford University Press.

Heckscher, C. (1995). *White-collar blues: Management loyalties in an age of corporate restructuring.* New York: Basic Books.

Hofacker, D. (2010). *Older workers in a globalizing world.* Cheltenham, UK: Edward Elgar.

Hofstede, G. (1980). *Culture's consequences: International differences in work-related values.* Beverley Hills, CA: Sage.

Hofstede, G. (1991). *Cultures and organizations: Software of the mind.* London: McGraw-Hill.

Hofstede, G. (2001). *Cultvre's consequences: Comparing values, behaviors, institutions, and organizations across nations* (2nd ed.). Thousand Oaks, CA: Sage.

Huntington, S. P. (2004). *Who we are: The challenges to America's national identity.* New York: Simon & Schuster.

Inda, J., & Rosaldo, R. (2002). Introduction: A world in motion. In J. Inda & R. Rosaldo (Eds.), *The anthropology of globalization: A reader* (pp. 1–34). Oxford: Blackwell.

Karsh, B., & Cole, R. (1968). Industrialization and the convergence hypothesis: Some aspects of contemporary Japan. *Journal of Social Issues, 24*(4), 45–64.

Keltner, D. (2009). *Born to be good: The science of a meaningful life.* New York: W. W. Norton & Co.

Kluckhohn, F. R., & Strodtbeck, F. L. (1961). *Variations in value orientations.* Evanston, IL: Row Publishing.

Korman, A. K., & Korman, R. W. (1980). *Career success/personal failure.* Englewood Cliffs, NJ: Prentice-Hall.

Kroeber, A. L., & Parsons, T. (1958). The concepts of culture and of social system. *American Sociological Review, 23*, 582–583.

Leung, K. S., Bhagat, R. S., Buchan, N. R., Erez, M., & Gibson, C. (2005). Culture and international business: Recent advances and future directions. *Journal of International Business Studies, 36,* 357–378.

Levine, C. H. (Ed.). (1980). *Managing fiscal stress: The crisis in the public sector.* Chatham, NJ: Chatham House Publishers, Inc.

Pitt-Catsouphes, M., Kossek, E. E., & Sweet, S. (2006). *The work and family handbook: Multi-disciplinary perspectives and approaches.* Mahwah, NJ: LEA Publishers.

Prasso, S., & Tippu, S. (2007, October 29). Google goes to India. *Fortune, 156*(9), 160–166.

Quick, J. C., Cooper, C. L., Nelson, D. L., Quick, J. D., & Gavin, J. H. (2003). Stress, health, and well-being at work. In *Organizational behavior: The state of the science* (pp. 53–89). London: LEA.

Ritzer, G. (1998). *The McDonaldization thesis: Explorations and extensions.* London: Sage Publications.

Robert Half International. (1991). *A survey of executives' greatest anxieties.* New York: Robert Half International.

Rosseau, D. M. (1995). *Psychological contracts in organizations: Understanding written and unwritten agreements.* Thousand Oaks, CA: Sage Publications.

Schneider, S. C., Wittenberg-Cox, A., & Hansen, L. (1991). *Honeywell Europe.* Fontainebleu, France: INSEAD.

Schor, J. (1992). *The overworked American: The unexpected decline of leisure.* New York: Basic Books.

Shirom, A. (2011). Job-related burnout: A review of the major research foci and challenges. In J. C. Quick & L. E. Tetrick (Eds.), *Handbook of occupational health psychology* (pp. 245–265). Washington, DC: American Psychological Association.

Smith, M. J., & Carayon, P. (2011). Controlling occupational safety and health hazards. In J. C. Quick & L. Tetrick (Eds.), *Handbook of occupational health psychology* (pp. 75–92). Washington, DC: American Psychological Association.

Stanko, T. L., & Gibson, C. B. (2009). The role of cultural elements in virtual teams. In R. S. Bhagat & R. M. Steers (Eds.), *Cambridge handbook of culture, organizations, and work* (pp. 272–304). New York: Cambridge University Press.

Steers, R. M., Sanchez-Runde, C., & Lee, S. M. (2009). Cultural drivers of work behavior: Personal values, motivation, and job attitudes. In R. S. Bhagat & R. M. Steers (Eds.), *Cambridge handbook of cultures, organizations, and work.* Cambridge: Cambridge University Press.

Thernstrom, A., & Thernstrom, S. (2003). *No excuses: Closing the racial gap in learning.* New York: Simon & Schuster.

Triandis, H. C. (1994). Cross-cultural industrial and organizational psychology. In H. C. Triandis, M. D. Dunnette, & L. M. Hough (Eds.), *Handbook of industrial and organizational psychology* (2nd ed., Vol. 4, pp. 103–172). Palo Alto, CA: Consulting Psychologists Press, Inc.

Triandis, H. C. (1995). *Individualism and collectivism.* Boulder, CO: Westview Press.

Triandis, H. C. (1998). Vertical and horizontal individualism and collectivism: Theory and research implications for international comparative management. In J. L. Cheng & R. B. Peterson (Eds.), *Advances in international and comparative management* (pp. 7–35). Greenwich, CT: JAI Press.

Wolf, M. (2004). *Why globalization works.* New Haven, CT: Yale University Press.
Worldwatch Institute Annual Report 2004. (n.d.). Retrieved April 26, 2011 from http://www.worldwatch.org/system/files/Annual_Report-2004.pdf
World Health Organization (WHO). (1995). Global Strategy on occupational health for all: The way to health at work. Retrieved March 2010 from www.who.int/occupational_health/en/oehstrategy.pdf
Worrall, L., & Cooper, C. L. (2000). *Quality of working life survey.* London: Institute of Management.

Chapter 3

Work Stress and Coping From the Western Perspective

Globalization has created considerable economic prosperity throughout the world in both Western and non-Western countries. However, as discussed in Chapter 2, globalization has its discontents (Stiglitz, 2003) and has resulted in many dysfunctional social, organizational, and cultural consequences. A recent survey by Regus Management Group of 11,000 companies in 13 countries found a 58% increase in work and organizational stress from 2007 to 2009. Chinese workers, in particular, reported an 86% increase in the amount of work stress that they experienced during this 2-year period (The Regus Group, 2009). Anecdotal and qualitative evidence from call centers in India describes accounts of long work hours coupled with excessive demands from supervisors and fast-paced repetitive jobs at low wages. The rate of turnover among female call center employees had reached 45% to 50% in 2005 ("Busy Signals," 2005). There have been some improvements in turnover rate since then; however, increased global competition by these Indian companies has resulted in considerable elevation of work and organizational stress. The phenomenon of *karoshi*—excessive overworking—is no longer confined to Japan but has spread to China, South Korea, Vietnam, Singapore, and India with its adverse consequences. This kind of unrelenting work pressure resulted in a young software engineer dying at his desk after putting in a succession of 13-hour days ("Japanese Employees Are Working Themselves to Death," 2009).

Similar reports on how increases in work stress and pressures for coping with new types of technologies and structures in both globalized and emerging economies are available from trade and business publications. Global competition is creating a new organizational reality that has considerable implications for health and well-being (Macik-Frey, Quick, Quick, & Nelson, 2009; Quick, Cooper, Nelson, Quick, & Gavin, 2003). Given these developments, it is necessary to understand the underpinnings and applicability of the theories and models of work stress and coping developed in the United States and Western Europe since 1965.

Definitions

The term *stress* has been in the English language for a very long time and has its origins in Latin meaning "to injure or constrain a person from normal functioning." Stressful experiences and events, whether they originate in the domain work or nonwork, are of great significance to individuals in all countries regardless of national and cultural differences. A large percentage of our daily conversations often focus on stressful experiences at work and in the family context. Work-related issues concerning pressures such as long working hours during economic downturns, demanding and abrasive supervisors, and unreasonable deadlines to complete a task tend to occupy our attention. Similarly, nonwork-related issues such as marital conflict, car accidents, children's school problems, major illnesses, everyday hassles, missed appointments, and bureaucratic inconveniences are other examples of stressful experiences which compound the difficulties of our lives.

If the term *stress* is understood to refer to external events, what type of events should we discuss? Should researchers primarily concern themselves with stressful experiences of work overload and of being unemployed, or should they also look at positive events such as being promoted at work, significant pay raises, and exciting overseas work assignments? In this book we refer to *stressors* as stress-producing events or conditions in the work environment (Beehr, 1998; Beehr & McGrath, 1992, 1996; Cooper, Dewe, & O'Driscoll, 2001; McGrath & Beehr, 1990). *Strains* are individual responses to stressors that have adverse psychological, physiological, and behavioral outcomes. And the term *stress* is an all-encompassing term describing situations in which both stressors and strains are present and the individual appraises stressors that may or may not result in adverse consequences. There are four categories of approaches for understanding, intervening in, and preventing occupational and work stress: medical, counseling and clinical psychology, engineering psychology, and organizational behavior and organizational psychology. The first approach focuses on the effects of stressors on the physical well-being of the employees and treating them by physiological and biochemical means. The use of antidepressants, such as Prozac and Zoloft, is a good example of the medical approach to managing occupational stress and anxiety. The second approach, counseling and clinical psychology, is concerned with the effects of stressors in the psychological and sociocultural environment in the work organization and deals with the management of psychological strain (e.g., work-related anxiety or depression) by treating the individual through various therapeutic and psychiatric techniques. The third approach, engineering psychology, is concerned with the effects of stressors in the physical work environment (e.g., crowded work stations in call centers, open layout of offices, ergonomic features) and with various aspects of work performance and work adjustment processes. Attempts are made to alleviate stressful experiences by reengineering and redesigning of workplaces and also by instituting various training programs. The fourth approach, organizational behavior and organizational psychology, is concerned with identifying stressors in the immediate work environment (e.g., role conflict, excessive work load, interpersonal conflict) and their effects on psychological strains and organizationally valued outcomes. This approach focuses on managing work stress by intervening in the immediate organizational context and recommending strategies for enriching the content of jobs as well as related contextual conditions that are stressful (e.g., rapid technological changes, occupational obsolescence).

In this book, we are primarily concerned with the theoretical issues, concepts, and models of work stress developed in the paradigmatic tradition of organizational behavior and organizational psychology. A major theme that has guided research in this area focuses on experience of stress as a transaction between employees and their immediate work experience.

Theoretical Models of Stress

Most of the important models of stress developed in the United States and Western European counties are described in this section starting with the classic work by Robert Kahn and his colleagues at the University of Michigan in 1964 (Kahn, Wolfe, Quinn, Snoek, & Rosenthal, 1964).

The Role Stress Model

Roles describe patterns of expectations that impinge on individuals in the work organization (Kahn et al., 1964). The process through which work roles create the experience of stress was the primary focus of Kahn and his colleagues (see

Beehr & Glazer, 2005; Kahn & Byosiere, 1992, for detailed reviews). *Role conflict* was the first facet of role stress that was investigated, and it concerns two or more sets of incompatible work demands. *Role ambiguity*, the next facet, deals with the lack of specificity or predictability in the responsibilities or duties that are associated with one's work role. The third facet of role stress is *role overload*, which is a more common form of work stress and is a function of too much work to do with high time pressures and a lack of appropriate resources to meet one's commitments and responsibilities associated with the role. Historically, there has been substantial support for the predictive efficacy of this model—with role conflict and ambiguities being the two most frequently studied aspects of work stress in both Western and non-Western research on organizational stress. The average correlation between role stressors and psychological strains has been reported in the range of 0.43 to 0.48 (Jackson & Schuler, 1985; Sauter, Murphy, & Hurrell, 1990). This model can be viewed under the rubric of a stimulus-based model of stress (Goodwell, Wolf, & Rogers, 1986), and the rationale of this approach is that some external forces impinge on employees in a manner that disrupts their equilibrium resulting in the experience of psychological strains, which complicate performance in work role and related adjustment processes.

Several criticisms are directed at the stimulus–response model. The most important criticism is that the role stress model reflects on the static interaction between individuals and their environment and provides us little information regarding the transaction or the process that is involved. In an attempt to explore the range of situations and responses that are stress producing, little attention has been paid to the inherent properties of the situations and events that occur in the workplace and how they are uniquely appraised by individuals. The next criticism is that there has been little conceptual differentiation between chronic (i.e., ongoing and routine) and episodic (i.e., periodic and infrequent) types of job stresses. Having to deal with an abrasive supervisor on a daily basis is an example of chronic job stress, but having to be temporarily transferred to a different work environment (e.g., an overseas assignment) is an episodic job stress. It could be argued that although the three aspects of role stresses (role ambiguity, role conflict, and role overload) help us capture the essence of ongoing stresses on individuals, we are not in a position to assess the impact of more severe, unsettling, and long-lasting effects of stressful events such as layoffs, unexpected job transfers, and marital dissolution.

The Transactional Model of Work Stress

The next model was developed by McGrath (1976), who proposed stress as a function of work events where the demands of an encounter and its outcomes are linked through three processes: cognitive appraisal, decision making, and performance. *Cognitive appraisal* is concerned with how the demand is perceived (called perceived demand). The second, *decision making*, concerns the selection of a response on the part of individuals, and the third, *performance of the act,* involves the process of managing the encounter by engaging in a single or a series of actions. In McGrath's formulation:

> Experienced stress = f (perceived demand of the encounter – perceived ability to meet the challenges and constraints associated with the demand) × (perceived consequences for not being able to meet the perceived demand associated with the encounter).

According to this model an imbalance or misfit occurs as a result of the individual's appraisal of the events and emphasizes the perceived consequences of not meeting the demands. If individuals are assigned to complete a project within a week and they realize that it is beyond their ability to do so and at the same time there are real adverse consequences for not meeting the demand, then stressful experiences result. McGrath's (1976) theoretical analysis was instrumental in further developments in the field, although as a model, its generalizability to non-Western economies and cultures remains largely unexplored.

The Stress at Work Model

Cooper and Marshall (1976) and Marshall and Cooper (1979) contributed to the *Person–Environment* (P–E) fit model theory of organizational stress by identifying five major categories:

- Pressures intrinsic to the job or work role
- Nature of interconnectedness with the roles of coworkers and others in the work organization
- Nature of interpersonal relationships at work
- Career development–related concerns and limitations
- Organizational climate and structure

Pressures intrinsic to the job include difficult working situations characterized by time pressures and role overload. Lack of clear expectations and descriptions regarding an employee's responsibilities contributes to role ambiguity and role conflict. Interpersonal relationships can also be quite stressful when one has to work with abrasive supervisors, unfriendly coworkers, and uncooperative subordinates. Career development–related difficulties are stressful because they create job insecurity and a lack of appropriate opportunities for advancement in the organization. In some organizations, the structural- and climate-related issues make it considerably difficult for employees to be recognized for their contributions.

Lack of participation in decision making is also stressful and is often a function of ineffective bureaucratic processes and organizational structures. The Stress at Work Model takes into account the personal characteristics of the employees and the spillover effects of work stress on nonwork situations and family problems. In doing this, this model provides a more comprehensive understanding of the antecedents and consequences of job stress on work- and nonwork-related outcomes.

Demand–Control Model

WORK STRESS IS A MAJOR RISK FACTOR IN SUBSEQUENT CARDIOVASCULAR DISEASES AND HEART ATTACKS

A Canadian study on work stress published in the prestigious Journal of the American Medical Association (JAMA) reports that work stress maybe as hazardous to employees' cardiovascular health as smoking, high cholesterol, and other conventional risk factors like obesity and sedentary lifestyle (Aboa-Eboule et al., 2007). A majority of employees who suffer cardiovascular diseases (CHD) and heart attacks return to their normal duties in their work organizations. The research was conducted with 972 individuals between 35 and 59 years old who returned to work after the first heart attack and followed them for an average of six years. Those in high stress jobs were about 2–3 times as likely as those in low stress jobs to suffer a heart attack and be hospitalized for angina related pain which leads to heart attack.

Michel Vezina, a researcher at the University of Laval in Quebec and a senior researcher of the study, notes that for senior managers who hold pressure packed positions, increases in job stress may precipitate heart attacks especially when they work intensely to meet deadlines. Two characteristics define a high stress job, according to this Canadian research team from the University of Laval. One is the demand to do more tasks with fewer resources and under continuous pressure of deadlines. The second is the individual's lack of control over the pace of work and lack of authority to make decisions. These conditions generally reflect the condition of workers at lower levels of the organization and have been shown to have detrimental effects on health and longevity—according to Whitehall Study of British civil-service workers.

Research at Mayo Clinic in Rochester, Minnesota has also shown that job strain is the leading factor for cardiovascular diseases and heart attacks. Randal Thomas, a cardiologist associated with this research, notes that "fight or flight" tendencies associated with stressful work experiences triggers the release of high levels of adrenaline which under chronic conditions damage the heart. Dr. Vezina and his colleagues at the University of Laval are studying coping strategies that may reduce stress for individuals in high pressured situations. Encouraging a collaborative rather than a competitive work environment tends to have positive effects on employee health across all levels of the organizations. In addition, exercise, meditation, and a supportive social network and family are most helpful according to the Canadian study.

Adapted from Winslow, R., *The Wall Street Journal,* **2007, p. D4.**

Karasek's (1979) Demand–Control Model makes specific predictions regarding objective demands of the work environment and the decision latitude of employees in meeting these demands (Karasek & Theorell, 1990). According to this model, the combination of an active job with a relatively little decision latitude contributes to job strain, lower productivity, and greater risk of health-related problems (Theorell & Karasek, 1996). This model recognizes the important role of job-related support from supervisors and coworkers (Karasek, Triantis, & Chaudhry, 1982). Highly demanding jobs (e.g., air traffic controllers, stock market analysts working in volatile economic times) that are characterized by low levels of decision latitude (lower levels of autonomy as to when and where the job-related duties and responsibilities need to be performed) and low levels of social support carry the highest risk of creating stress and illness. This model was developed in the context of comparing job demands and strains in Sweden and the United States in 1979. The concept of job-related decision latitude is an important moderator that was proposed in this model. Extensive research has been and still continues to be conducted with this model (Cooper et al., 2001). However, the model's applicability has not been tested in non-Western countries and cultures.

WORK STRESS IN CALL CENTER OPERATIONS IN UNITED KINGDOM

The city of Manchester, which is located in Northwestern England, was the first city in the era of industrial renaissance.

It was called the wonder of the era and the first port of call for 19th century pilgrims were the cotton mills located in the city. People came from different parts of Europe: some to express marvel at the invention of steam powered locomotives whereas others were horrified at the poor working conditions and open sewers that flowed through the surrounding slums where workers lived. Friedrich Engels came from Germany and start developing a new theory of class conflict. The industrial spirit of Manchester continued for a century or so except people talked about the cotton mills as dark satanic mills.

These days with the growth of call centers, the agony of satanic mills are being talked about again. These call centers, according to a report in The Economist (2001), have been drawing attention from German, Portuguese, Japanese multinational and global organizations. Call centers are well established in the U.S. Companies, such as American Express, Citicorp, Delta Airlines, United Airlines, and others, have set up call centers in countries like Ireland, Poland, and India. British companies are the leaders of call center operations in Europe with over 5,200 call centers in the U.K., according to Data-monitor, a research company. Over 400,000 Britons have full-time jobs in the call center industry – twice as many as the total number during the renaissance days in Manchester.

The industry has expanded due to the rapid growth of service sector operations in the U.K. Call centers are filling the void created by the current period of economic meltdown. Much of the industry is concentrated in Scotland and in Northwestern England. An interesting development of the call center operations is that supervisors often bully their operators so that they spend less time away from their phones taking a break or going to the toilet. Called "customer service representatives" (CSRS), these call center operators work at a intense and relentless speed and are expected to handle over 20 calls per hour and in some cases 2 calls per minute. Some of the major stresses and hassles experienced by these operators are high levels of electronic monitoring undertaken by their supervisors, fewer trips to the toilet, and a lack of a reasonable number of breaks. The international trade unions of call center employees are preparing hundreds of legal claims due to loss of hearing caused by "acoustic shock," the sudden loud noises employees receive in their headsets.

These difficulties could have been perceived as tolerable if the wages were competitive. However, that is not the case in these call centers. The average salary is about £8,000 lower than the average wages in other industries in the U.K. The managers of call centers note that although the pay is not great, shift working offers the kind of flexibility that young students and single mothers need. Today's call centers are over 67% female and 70% are between the ages 16 – 35. In some call centers, over 50% of the employees are single mothers.

Despite these difficulties, the real stresses that call centers are going to face is from fierce competition from new operations in India which happen to be set up by the call center managers from Britain. This is being done due to labor cost related advantages that Indian call centers offer. Taken together, the employees of call centers in the Northwestern England and Scotland are bracing for major stressful experiences in their work and non-work lives in the current era of intense global competition.

Adapted from *The Economist*, 359(8219), 2001.

The Uncertainty Model of Work Stress

Beehr and Bhagat (1985) examined the nature of typical work stressors and concluded that the experience of uncertainty is likely to be the most common response of employees before psychological and behavioral strains develop. This theory proposes that experienced stress is a multiplicative function of uncertainty, importance, and duration: $S = Uc \times I \times D$ (see Figure 3.1). This model assumes a proactive person and proposes that people try to perform certain behaviors as a starting point for understanding the impact of various types of work stressors. The four commonly studied stressors of role ambiguity, role conflict, role overload, and underuse of skills can be analyzed in terms of the uncertainty theory of work stress (Beehr, 1995, 1998; Beehr & Bhagat, 1985). Experience of role conflict takes place when two or more sets of expectations impinge on individuals in the sense that meeting one set of expectations makes

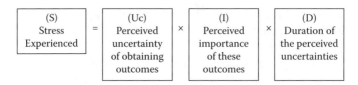

Figure 3.1 The uncertainty theory of work stress.

it difficult or impossible to meet the other. In this case, the employees experience uncertainty regarding how to direct their efforts to have adequate job performance. Employees whose occupational skills and abilities are underused are likely to experience uncertainties because such situations make it almost impossible to achieve the intrinsic rewards and satisfaction associated with successful job performance. Role ambiguity, as a job stressor, occurs when one experiences uncertainty in terms of being able to see clear connections between the linkages of effort and performance and then their performance to valued organizational rewards—both intrinsic and extrinsic. This model has inspired a significant body of research; however, one of its primary contributions lies in terms of highlighting the role of *duration* as a major component in the experience of work stress (Beehr, 1995, 1998; Beehr & Bhagat, 1985). The longer individuals have to deal with or to manage a stressful situation, the more stress they are likely to experience. The multiplicative function, as proposed in this formulation, has been validated in Western research. However, the validity and applicability of this model to non-Western contexts have yet to be systematically studied.

The Cybernetic Model

The Cybernetic Model of work stress incorporates the importance of personal goals and feedback loops as central features of the stress process (Cummings & Cooper, 1979, 1998; Edwards, 1998). According to this framework, individuals monitor the discrepancy between a preferred or reference state and the perceived work conditions. A perceived discrepancy results in psychological strains that motivate actions to reduce the discrepancy by changing or adapting to the immediate work environment in some meaningful way. For example, a discrepancy between preferred and perceived level of work load leads to an attempt to reduce the work load or to adapt to this new level. The coping action is then initiated by the new comparison of the discrepancy between preferred and actual workload levels (Edwards, 1998). The notion of a cybernetic feedback cycle assumes that individuals seek a steady state of balance (i.e., homeostasis) between the preferred state of being and the actual work environment. When the homeostasis is disrupted, individuals begin to engage in necessary coping activities to restore the balance. According to Edwards (1998), who provides a comprehensive review of the cybernetic view of work stress, feedback cycles involving transactions between individuals and the environment are most important.

Although not as well researched as the previous models of work stress, the major predictions of the cybernetic model have received some empirical support. Elsass and Veiga (1997) found that desired control accounts for significant additional variance in job strain–related experiences after controlling for both job autonomy and desired level of participation. Stronger support is demonstrated in the work of Ter Doest, Maes, Gebhardt, and Koelewijn (2006), who found that personal efforts to facilitate desired goals accounted for additional variance in four organizationally valued outcomes (job satisfaction, personal accomplishment, emotional exhaustion, and psychological symptoms).

The Challenge–Hindrance Model

Based on Lazarus's sociocognitive model (Folkman & Moskowitz, 2004; Lazarus & Folkman, 1984), stressors are conceptualized as either *challenges* or *hindrances*. When stressors are appraised as challenging, positive emotions are likely to be evoked, and active coping strategies including the problem-solving mode of coping are engaged. Examples of challenging stressors include job and role demands and time pressure to complete an important project. LePine, Podsakoff, and LePine (2005) noted that challenge stressors are likely to be associated with high levels of motivation and therefore facilitate better performance. Individuals are likely to believe in a stronger association between effort and expectancy when they encounter a challenging stressor in their work situations. Experiences of hindrance stressors (e.g., limited technical support, daily hassles, persistent role ambiguities, strong interpersonal conflicts and harassment on the job, and organizational politics) are appraised as threatening and generally evoke negative emotions. Coping with hindrance stressors is normally accomplished by engaging in emotion-focused and passive styles of coping. Hindrance stressors do not motivate individuals toward higher levels of role performance because efforts directed at coping with them are unlikely to be successful or to bring valued rewards. What kind of valued reward can individuals expect to get by coping with sexual harassment and workplace bullying?

This model emphasizes the importance of primary appraisal in the experience of stress and resulting distress or psychological strain. We must note that this framework deemphasizes the importance of individual differences in the perception of both challenge and hindrance stressors—that is, some stressors will be appraised as challenging whereas others will be appraised as hindrances regardless of the differences in demographics and personalities. Some support exists for this model of stress since it was proposed in 2005; however, the findings are not consistent. There is a need for recognizing individual differences, especially relating to how individuals selectively emphasize certain aspects of their job environments at the expense of others due to their ethnic or cultural background.

The Conservation of Resource Model

The Conservation of Resources Model proposes that individuals seek to obtain, retain, protect, and restore resources that are fundamental to normal functioning and existence. Resources describe a wide range of objects (e.g., need for safety, shelter), personal characteristics (e.g., self-efficacy, need for achievement or affiliation), conditions (e.g., status in the organization, personal and occupational reputation), or energies (e.g., knowledge, convictions) that are important for adaptive functioning (Hobfoll, 1989, 2001). Resources are valued in their own right because they can help employees obtain other personally or organizationally valued resources. Psychological strains and feelings of distress result from the potential or real threat of the loss of resources or failure to obtain ample amounts of resources. Individuals strive to develop surplus resources that are fundamental to sustaining higher levels of subjective and objective levels of well-being. Stressors are perceived to be negative because they can potentially, as well as in real terms, deplete the resources that individuals possess. A meta-analysis by Lee and Ashforth (1996) found support for the basic propositions of the conservation of resources theory. They found that five out of eight work-related demands were strongly related to the experience of strain because they were directed at lowering the amount of resources that individuals had.

Even though this theory has not been widely validated in Western organizational stress research, it has unique elements for understanding the nature and evolution of work stress and their consequences across ethnic, racial, and cultural divides.

Toward an Integrative Model

A careful review of much of the research and theory on work stress and coping reveals that there is considerable overlap of theoretical constructs and approaches. All of the models presented in this chapter have some features in common. Few examples provide radically different approaches that result in considerably different types of predictions or outcomes of stressful experiences in the workplace. The complexity of stress processes means that different approaches have tended to emphasize some aspects of the process more strongly than others. For example, role theories of work stress (Kahn & Byosiere, 1992; Kahn et al., 1964) emphasize the demands of the work environment in terms of how they influence the performance of various aspects of the work role. In contrast, transactional theories emphasize the appraisal process and are more appropriate to analyze the process of job-related burnout and the consequences of long-term stressful experiences. Especially as the world of work transforms itself in the current era of globalization, it is necessary to incorporate the significance of broader classes of work- and nonwork-related phenomena that reflects the complexity of stress–strain relationships. In Figure 3.2 we depict a comprehensive model of work stress based on the theoretical integration proposed by Griffin and Clarke (2011). This framework provides a broader picture of the relationship between the various subcomponents of stress and outcomes.

The framework highlights two central processes of work stress:

1. The nature of transactions between individuals and their environment
2. The dynamic processes that unfold in the short-term and long-term

The transactional approach describes how individuals appraise and respond to the specific conditions in the workplace that are likely to be perceived as demanding, uncertain, and perhaps of long duration and therefore stressful. The transactional focus of this model is the central element of many important stress models, particularly the Sociocognitive Model (Lazarus & Folkman, 1984) and

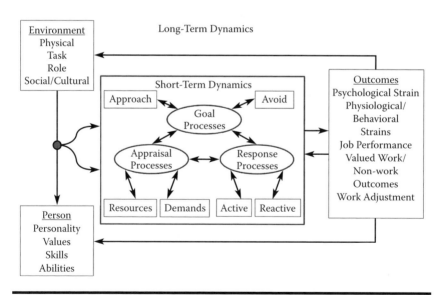

Figure 3.2 An integrative framework of work stress incorporating short- and long-term dynamics. (Adapted from Griffin, M.A., & Clarke, S., in S. Zedeck (Ed.), *APA Handbook of Industrial and Organizational Psychology*, APA, Washington, DC, 2011.)

Figure 3.3 Environmental influences on work stress and coping-related processes.

the Challenge–Hindrance Model (LePine et al., 2005). These models specify the process of appraisal of the environmental conditions. The discrepancy between the preferred state of functioning and the perceived state of the job conditions is the main motivation behind the responses that the individual selects. Role theory and the Demand–Control Model focus on specific characteristics of work, and their importance is reflected in the appraisal process as depicted in Figure 3.2. This model proposes that the process of experiencing and coping with stress is dynamic because the transaction between the person and the environment unfolds over time through a process of mutual influence. It incorporates this notion by noting the importance of short-term cycle of cognitive appraisal, preferred state and goals, and action within a longer cycle of interaction. The longer cycle shows that the experience of various outcomes of the stress process has significant implications for modifying the various attributes of the person (i.e. personality, values, skills, and abilities) and the environment (i.e. physical, task, role, social/cultural). Previous theories of work stress have sought to specify both short- and long-term consequences of stressful experiences at work (Beehr & Franz, 1986) but have not dealt with them simultaneously as should be the case. See details regarding this Integrative Model of Stress in Griffin and Clarke (2011).

Moderators of Stressor–Strain Relationships

The models discussed describe the basic processes involved in the development of psychological, physiological, and behavioral strains and their effects on individually and organizationally valued outcomes. However, the direct relationship between stressors and their effects on an individual and the organization are influenced by variables called moderators of stress–strain relationships in organizational research. A moderator is defined as a variable that influences the direction and the strength of the relationship between an independent or predictor variable and a dependent or criterion variable (Baron & Kenny, 1986; Schwab, 2005). A moderator is therefore a third source of influence on the strength of relationship between two variables. Moderator effects are typically assessed by the interaction between the predictor variable and the moderator in a hierarchical regression where the predictor and the moderator are entered first, followed by the interaction term, which is a multiplicative term of the predictor and the moderator. Research on moderating effects on the relationship between different types of work and organizational stresses and outcomes have characterized much of the advances in research in the Western traditions for the past four decades since the 1980s. We classify the moderators in terms of whether they facilitate or hinder individual vulnerability or one's predisposition toward experiencing psychological strain. Also we include nonwork-related factors as well as organizational interventions–based techniques as moderators of the relationship between work stress and outcomes.

Moderators That Facilitate Individual Resilience

Coping with stressful work experiences and life events is one of the fundamental issues related to quality of life. Everyone experiences stress and psychological strain (Cooper et al., 2001; Kohn, Lafreniere, & Gurevich, 1991). If psychological strains (including feelings of anxiety, distress, and alienation) are left unmanaged, they can become detrimental to subjective and physiological well-being. The fact that people cannot function for a long period of time without some type of intervention on their part was realized before 1970. Lazarus (1999, p. 102) noted that the basic idea behind coping was not new and that the process of how humans cope with stress has been studied from three theoretical perspectives. The early approach had a strong psychodynamic perspective emphasizing the concept of defense as a means of dealing with externally imposed demands and threats. This idea was later developed to suggest that individuals learn an idiosyncratic or preferred mode of coping in managing work and nonwork stresses. The second approach focused on styles of coping as personality traits and how some dispositions were shown to consistently play effective roles in shaping coping-related thoughts and actions. Lazarus and his colleagues (Folkman & Moskowitz, 2004; Lazarus, 1999; Lazarus & Folkman, 1984) developed the concepts of coping styles to reflect stable patterns of behaviors that may operate across various stressful experiences whether they originate in the domain of work or nonwork. The conceptual overlap between personality and coping styles continues to be debated with strong evidence in favor of broad dimensions of personality being selectively associated with preferred ways of coping (David & Suls, 1999). There is also growing evidence how coping with various stressful encounters and dilemmas of life is influenced by cultural-specific beliefs and values regarding coping strategies (discussed in detail in Chapter 5). With additional psychological inquiry into the basic processes involved in coping, research began to shift its emphasis from *styles* or *personality traits* toward coping as a *process*. This perspective highlights the importance of changes in actions related to managing or coping with stress over time; individuals undergo both primary and secondary types of cognitive appraisals and learn to cope with the encounters by employing selective patterns of thoughts, actions, and behaviors. Folkman and Moskowitz (2004) note that it was Lazarus's formulation that expanded the boundaries of coping beyond the trait or style perspective to include a broader range of cognitive and behavioral responses that individuals use and learn to use to manage psychological strains. What Lazarus and his colleagues proposed was an emphasis on the central role of *cognitive appraisal*. Primary appraisal takes place when individuals learn about the stressful circumstances and begin to view and analyze the importance of the encounter or life event in terms of whether it is irrelevant, benign, harmful, threatening, or challenging in nature. Individuals' sense of immediate well-being is determined largely by the accuracy of primary appraisals. However, secondary appraisal, which occurs after individuals have had an opportunity to reflect on the nature and severity of the stressful encounter, is more important in determining the question of what can be done. These two appraisals are interdependent, and secondary appraisal is not necessarily less important than primary appraisal in determining both short- and long-term dynamics of the coping process. Following the work of Lazarus (1991) and Lazarus and Folkman (1984), coping has been defined in terms of actions that individuals undertake to deal with the various dimensions of a stressful event that may have either short- or long-term consequences for subjective well-being. Some scholars have noted that just because coping has been widely defined in this way, it does not necessarily mean that research following this definition has been consistent. Hobfoll, Schwarzer, and Chon (1996) suggest the need for considering qualifiers, such as effort and consciousness, in the coping process. Personal strategies constructed in the midst of dealing with a stressful encounter should be incorporated to capture the broader significance of the process of coping. Perhaps the most important distinguishing characteristic of coping is the amount of effort (e.g., personal, interpersonal, and social support related) that individuals have to apply to deal with the possible adverse consequences of stressful encounters. There are some unanswered questions regarding how to conceptualize and measure coping in populations that are largely collectivistic in cultural orientation (we discuss some of these strategies in Chapters 5 and 6).

Coping

The moderating role of coping has been of considerable interest to researchers in the area of work and organizational stress for the past three decades. The most common approach to the study of work-related coping has been to develop a taxonomy of coping that classifies and describes coping styles and strategies that are broadly applicable to almost all work- and organization-related situations. The most important approach in categorizing coping has been proposed by Lazarus and Folkman (1984) and defines two broad categories of coping styles and strategies: *problem focused* and *emotion focused*. Problem-focused coping is defined as attempts to deal with the demands of stressful encounters by engaging in a series of purposeful actions to modify or eliminate the sources of work stress. Emotion-focused coping, on the other hand, involves cognitive efforts to lessen emotional distress that often results from demands and uncertainties inherent in stressful encounters on the job. Both of these coping strategies are organized around the *self* and treat individuals as the central point of reference in the stress and coping process (Hobfoll, 1998). Coping styles that have been investigated in Western research on work and organizational stress are discussed in Dewe and Cooper (2007) and Dewe, O'Driscoll, and Cooper (2010). We provide some of the examples of coping styles and efforts that have been investigated in work stress research:

1. *Direct action* to solve problems
2. *Optimistic comparison* of one's situation compared with one's past situation and related to those of peers in the work group and organization
3. *Selective inattention* to unpleasant aspects of stressful encounters and more focused attention to positive aspects of the situation
4. *A conscious restriction of expectations* regarding job satisfaction and a focus on monetary rewards from one's employment

Except for direct action, which is problem focused, the remaining three coping efforts and styles are largely emotion focused in nature because they do not involve actions to change unpleasant and demanding aspects of one's job situation. The coping efforts of optimistic comparison, selective ignoring, and restrictive expectations are aimed at modifying the perception and appraisal of the stressful situation or event and at selectively emphasizing some aspects of one's experience more than others. Optimistic comparison involves making several types of comparisons that enhance the ability to cope with stressful situations.

One may choose to judge the current situation as an improvement over what one has experienced in the past. The situation could also be appraised as being less problematic than the jobs of others. In addition, one may appraise the future to be considerably better than the present, minimizing the importance of current stressors as being either temporary in nature or relatively less harmful for one's subjective well-being. Optimistic comparison with the future and past is conceptually separable from comparisons of one's stressful experiences of those of one's peers. However, the psychological process involved in such comparisons are fairly similar, and therefore these strategies are grouped under the broad category of emotion-focused coping, which has some relevance for determining the types of problem-focused strategies that one may engage in the future.

Selective inattention is concerned with the extent to which individuals can appraise a work situation so that some specific problems that might have appeared as being stressful in the past may now be regarded as relatively unimportant and therefore less stressful. Several strategies might be involved as an amalgam in this situation, such as finding counterbalancing advantages in the situation or being highly focused in specific duties of the work role in such a fashion so that stressful encounters begin to recede from one's awareness or begin to assume much less importance. Trying to emphasize the importance of the quality of one's family and personal life as opposed to dealing with a stressful situation in a continuous fashion is also an important feature of selective inattention–related coping strategies.

Conscious restriction of expectations for achieving job satisfaction is also an important coping style. It focuses on lessening the importance of work-related experiences in favor of intrinsic aspects of the job such as opportunities for self-realization and self-absorption and extrinsic aspects of the job including monetary compensation and opportunities for social interactions on the job. This coping style seeks to shift the criterion of a "good job" from being stressful to one that provides fair extrinsic rewards such as pay and opportunities for placement in a desirable location. However, in doing so one accepts unsatisfying occupational and organizational conditions as being inevitable in nature. There is an element of *fatalism* in employing this coping strategy to deal with stressful aspects of organizational life—especially those that are routine in character and cannot be successfully dealt with even by performing adequately in one's work role for a long time.

This classification was developed by Menaghan and Merves (1984) and has been quite valuable in our thinking regarding the effects of work stress and coping across racial, ethnic, and cultural divides. However, the point to be made here is that coping styles have been regarded as important moderators (and sometimes mediators) of work stress and outcomes for over 20 years. The important findings from this line of inquiry have been summarized and updated by Cooper et al. (2001), Dewe and Cooper (2007), and Dewe et al. (2010).

Self-Esteem/Self-Efficacy

A second group of moderating influences deals with the role of self-esteem and self-efficacy. These are not identical constructs; however, both play similar moderating roles such that their effects are difficult to distinguish (Semmer, 1996). Ganster and Schaubroeck (1995) noted that certain personality or dispositional variables may insulate individuals from adverse consequences of work stress by evoking *behavioral plasticity,* which refers to the extent one is likely to be affected by external stressful situations or events. Brockner (1988) suggests that individuals with high self-esteem are less vulnerable to environmental events than their low self-esteem counterparts. Persons with low self-esteem are more likely to experience uncertainties concerning appropriateness and applicability of their thoughts and emotions during a stressful experience. They tend to rely on more external social cues and are more likely to seek social approval as well as to conform to others' social expectations. These tendencies lead to self-critique and allow negative feedback from their occupational functions to generalize into other aspects of their lives, thus predisposing them toward experiencing stress.

Support for the plasticity hypothesis is found in Mossholder, Bedeian, and Armenakis (1981) and Pierce, Gardner, Dunham, and Cummings (1993). Mossholder et al. (1981) found that nurses with high self-esteem did not report low levels of job satisfaction despite the experiences of role ambiguity and role conflict. In addition, their job performance was not adversely affected. However, nurses with low self-esteem reported lower levels of job satisfaction under identical situations and also had lower levels of job performance. Ganster and Schaubroeck (1995) suggest that high levels of self-esteem influence the choice of coping strategies because individuals with high self-esteem are more confident in their ability to influence their immediate work environment. The moderating effect of self-esteem on the relationship between work stress and physiological (i.e., health-related) outcomes remains unclear at this point.

Studies on the moderating role of self-efficacy found that it has an important role in reducing cardiovascular and other negative health-related outcomes of ongoing job-related strains. Researchers have found that when people are confident in their job-related abilities, they become increasingly effective in exercising their control or job decision latitude in active and demanding jobs; however, they found that high control or decision discretion combined with high job demands can have adverse health consequences particularly among individuals who are low on job-related self-efficacy (Karasek, 1979; Schaubroeck & Merritt, 1997). The distinction has been made between individual-focused self-efficacy, which is concerned with whether individuals are capable of managing stressful encounters on the job, and collective self-efficacies, which deal with individuals' assessments of their group's collective ability to deal with similar situations. Jex and Gundanowski (1992) found that in some situations individual self-efficacies did not either mediate or moderate the relationship between stressor and strain; however, efficacies of the group taken as a collective did. The number of hours worked (especially overtime work) as a stressor had lower effects on job satisfaction, anxiety, and turnover intentions when collective efficacies of the work group were high. While additional research regarding the moderating or mediating role of self-efficacy needs to be conducted, research to date strongly supports the behavioral plasticity hypothesis—that is, the belief in one's self—functions as an effective buffer in stressful situations, particularly stresses arising from role-related pressures and expectations.

Locus of Control

The next moderator that has received some attention is *locus of control* (LOC) and particularly work-specific locus of control. LOC differs from perceived control over the work environment in that the former refers to a generalized expectancy regarding the sense of control over life situations and events and is a dispositional construct following the classic work of Julian Rotter (1966), whereas perceive control of a work situation is a function of the objective conditions at work and widely varies across job situations and one's life span. Elder workers may have high work-specific locus of control but may perceive their job environment to be difficult to control because of lower levels of physical and mental coordination. Perrewé and Ganster (1989) found that employees with high external locus of control (those who believe that events in life occur without a great deal of control on their part) experienced less anxiety and distress as a result of lower perceived control over their work environment when compared with those with higher internal locus of control. It signifies the importance of isomorphism in the moderating effects of locus of control; that is, individuals with higher predispositions toward external locus of control are less affected by lack of perceived control over their work environment than those who have higher internal levels of locus of control. However, the overall evidence concerning the effectiveness of the moderating role of locus of control remains mixed (see Cohen & Edwards, 1989; Semmer, 1996; Spector et al., 2002).

Hardiness

The fourth moderating variable that has received much attention is the concept of *psychological hardiness,* which falls under the category of personal resilience. Kobasa (1979) and her colleagues (Kobasa, Maddi, & Kahn, 1982) found that hardy persons reported fewer illnesses and higher levels of subjective well-being compared with their colleagues who were less hardy or low in hardiness. *Hardiness* is defined as a personality characteristic that is composed of high levels of commitment or involvement in day-to-day activities, high levels of perceived control over the hassles of daily lives and life events, along with the tendencies to view unexpected changes taking place in lives as a set of *challenges* rather than as *threats* to personal well-being. Gentry and Kobasa (1984) noted that hardiness moderates the unhealthy effects of stress and prevents strains that are immediate precursors to psychological and physiological illnesses. Except for one classic study conducted by Kobasa with executives of Illinois Bell Telephone Company in 1979, research on the moderating effects of this construct has been relatively rare. Research indicates that hardy employees tend to have adaptive cognitions concerning the role of stressors and are likely to experience lower levels of physiological and physiological arousal when confronting stressful experiences (Allred & Smith, 1989). It is sufficient to note at this point that the concept of hardiness and its hypothesized moderating effect on the relationship between work stress and psychological strain in particular tend to have intuitive appeal among researchers from dissimilar countries and cultures. The best way to think about this construct is to examine it not as a global construct but in terms of its specific components, as has been demonstrated in the works of Hull, Van Treuren, and Virnelli (1987) and Roth, Weibe, Fillingim, and Shay (1989). A more sophisticated approach to measuring this important construct, one that is grounded in rigorous psychological theory regarding how people confront and cope with the difficult circumstances in life, will be more fruitful in future research. Given the long-term significance of hardiness for coping with work and organizational stresses in the rapidly globalizing world, one wishes that more research had been conducted in this area.

Positive Affect

Another type of moderating effect that has received increasing attention is *positive affect* (PA), which is a state of pleasurable engagement individuals experience while engaging with their work. It reflects the extent to which people feel enthusiastic, active, and alert (Watson, Clark, & Tellegen, 1988). Conceptually, it is distinct from the concept of negative affect, which had its origin in the work stress research of George and Brief (1992). Individuals with higher positive affect generally perceive a glass to be half full and not necessarily half empty—they look for opportunities as opposed to feeling bogged down by negative cues and information stemming from their jobs and work context (Mittal & Ross, 1998). They are better at processing complex information more accurately than those who tend to be high on negative affect (Staw & Barsade, 1993). Individuals with high positive affect are able to make better decisions, engage in creative problem solving, and have diagnostic reasoning (Estrada, Isen, & Young, 1994, 1998; Isen, Rosenzweig, & Young, 1991). Overall, findings concerning the moderating role of positive affect reveal that it can be considered an important variable in future research on job stress across dissimilar nations and cultures.

Optimism/Optimistic Outlook

Another class of moderating influence that has much potential for international research is concerned with the *role of optimism* or an *optimistic outlook* toward life. It reflects the conviction that the future generally holds a preferred set of outcomes regardless of the ability to influence the course of these outcomes (Marshall & Lang, 1990). It is better to conceptualize this moderator in terms of its superordinate status, and it may indeed be a reflection of a constellation of a number of positive personality predispositions; it affects the process of primary appraisal in a positive way and assists in the process of choosing effective forms of coping as applicable to the situation (Chang, 1998; Cooper et. al., 2001). Like the previous construct of positive affect, not a great deal is known regarding the generalizability of optimism across dissimilar nations and cultures. Overall, it appears clear that when measured accurately optimism is found to positively influence satisfaction with work and nonwork aspects of life and also to moderate the relationship between work stress and psychological strains (Scheier & Carver, 1992). We suggest that more research needs to be conducted on this moderating variable not only in the Western contexts but also in other non-Western cultures of the world.

Moderators Reflecting Individual Vulnerabilities

As was discussed in the previous section, some personality and cognitive characteristics predispose individuals toward experiencing lower levels of psychological and physiological strains while encountering stressful experiences or stressful events on the job. However, other characteristics have the opposite effect; that is, they accentuate the predisposition toward experiencing higher levels of strains.

Negative Affect

First among of these constructs, the moderating role of *negative affect* (NA) has been studied in the work stress literature. It reflects a relatively stable predisposition to highlight negative emotional states more strongly than positive states. Individuals who are high on this personal predisposition tend to have a lower sense of self-esteem and a negative worldview (Watson & Clark, 1984; Watson & Pennebaker, 1989). It has been suggested that they are more sensitive to stressful experiences and tend to be responsible for generating negative experiences in their coworkers (Spector, Zapf, Chen, & Frese, 2000). In addition, they are likely to report more job strains (Watson & Pennebaker, 1989). It seems to be the case that persons with higher levels of negative affect may inflate the significance of selective cues regarding possible encounters with various types of role stress (Brief, Burke, George, Robinson, & Webster, 1988; Cooper et. al., 2001;

Parkes, 1990). In general, the etiology of negative affect in the development of hypertension and cardiovascular diseases is yet to be determined (Costa & McCrae, 1985; Landsbergis et al., 2002).

Types A, B, and D

The next class of moderating influences that predispose individuals toward experiencing higher levels of strain deals with behavioral patterns known as *Type A* personalities. Starting over 50 years ago, Friedman and Rosenman (1959, 1974) suggested that certain individuals have a higher predisposition toward experiencing coronary heart diseases (CHD). These individuals demonstrate high levels of time urgency, aggressiveness, competitiveness, and career-related aspiration (Friedman & Booth-Kewley, 1987). Collectively, these attributes develop a "hard-charging" predisposition in individuals in that they tend to be highly impatient and become easily irritable when even minor obstacles block their ability to achieve their preferred goals and objectives in the workplace. Over time these kinds of behavioral propensities result in higher incidences of poor cardiovascular health (Landsbergis et al., 2001). In addition, they seem to lack emotional intelligence and are often not able to relate well with others at work (Cooper et al., 2001). In contrast, individuals characterized by the *Type B* related personality syndrome act in a distinctively different fashion when compared with Type A individuals; that is, they are less troubled by time urgency, tend to be less competitive, and avoid confrontations. Despite the initial significant promise for this line of work, the research findings are somewhat mixed, and a number of methodological issues remain (Cooper et al., 2001; George, 1992; Williams, 2001).

Another personality characteristic that seems to be receiving attention in recent research is concerned with the notion of the *Type D* personality, which is characterized by a tendency to experience emotions but suppress expression in the presence of others (Sher, 2005). Type D individuals suffer from relatively higher levels of emotional distress and are found to be more vulnerable to experience cardiac problems and related health concerns (Denollet, Pedersen, Vrints, & Conraads, 2006; Pedersen et al., 2004; Whitehead, Perkins-Porras, Strike, Magid, & Steptoe, 2007; Williams et al., 2008). The moderating influence of this construct has not been extensively researched in the work stress literature (see De Fruyt & Denollet, 2002; Oginska-Bulik, 2006 for notable exceptions). Given the significance of this personality syndrome in occupational health, additional research needs to be conducted in the area of work and organizational stress.

Cynicism

Finally, we discuss the moderating role of cynicism—a construct whose role as a moderating variable in work stress and organizational stress research has received hardly any attention. *Cynicism* is a predisposition that reflects a negative tendency involving disillusionment, distrust, and frustration with one's peers and work organization (Anderson & Bateman, 1997). Its moderating role on the relationship between job stress and valued work outcomes has been studied by Shirom (2003) and Brandes and Das (2006) and has been found to be associated with burnout. It seems to be a complex constellation of traits that may prevent or facilitate the experience of depression that often results while encountering difficult, stressful situations in one's occupation and work. It prevents employees from experiencing organizational commitment, and therefore they do not invest as much psychological energy and effort in their work roles as their noncynical counterparts. This strategy of calculative involvement with their organization prevents job-related dissatisfaction and depression when appropriate rewards are not forthcoming. However, the excessive tendency to be cynical about their role and future in their work role and personal life predisposes them from experiencing opportunities for future growth and development (Brandes & Das, 2006). As with the constructs of negative affect and Type D personality syndrome, more theory and research is needed concerning the effects of cynicism on coping with work stresses.

Social Support and Organizational Intervention-Related Moderators

Since the 1980s, research on stress in general and work stress in particular has been concerned with the moderating effects of support that individuals receive from their social network. Social support received from family, peers, supervisors, and other significant members in the work organization can enhance affective experiences on the job. However, there is some debate concerning how the effects of social support as it relates to the experience of work stress—does it have a direct or a moderating effect? While work-related social support has been found to have direct effect on lowering the experience of psychological strains, much of the research in the past three decades has been concerned with the moderating influences of different facets of social support. House (1981) differentiated among four types of support that individuals are likely to receive in the context of their work role in the organization:

1. *Informational support*: receiving information that helps individuals in dealing with work-related problems and in the interpretation of job-related duties and responsibilities
2. *Emotional support:* showing a personal understanding of individuals' work-related difficulties and stressful experiences—expressing sympathy at times of need

3. *Appraisal support:* providing individuals with feedback regarding their job-related performance and duties so that they can not only guide them but also enhance their self-esteem
4. *Instrumental support:* providing concrete help in performing various task-related duties and responsibilities

The first two types of social support have provided much of the impetus behind research on the moderating role of support on work stress—psychological strain relationships. While social support has been analyzed in terms of its role as a moderator and mediator, it is the moderator role that has been looked at in terms of its *stress-buffering* effects. This hypothesis proposes that the relationship between work stress and various types of strains differs according to the kind of support that a person receives. People receiving all four types of social support are likely to experience lower levels of psychological strains compared with those who receive little or none. The role of social support as a moderator across nations and cultures has been analyzed from a multicultural perspective (Wong, Wong, & Lonner, 2006). However, the results are not sufficiently integrated with the mainstream findings and applications in both Western and non-Western contexts. What we seem to know for sure is that members of collectivistic cultures are much more sensitive to social cues and contextual information regarding the availability of social support in their work context. In a study of Israeli managers and social service professionals, the importance of the different sources of social support was found to vary based on gender. Job-related social support was a better moderator for men than for women, who preferred to receive social support from their families and friends (Etzion, 1984). Research on the role of social support in collectivistic work contexts will be of significant value in advancing the frontiers on research on work stress and coping in the current era of globalization.

Last but not necessarily the least in its importance, one should look at the moderating role of the availability of counseling on the job, employee assistance programs, and related human resources training programs that are directed at managing the adverse effects of role overload, role conflict, role ambiguity, and work–family-related conflicts, which are increasing as globalization spreads in various non-Western cultures of the world. In Chapters 6 and 7, we discuss the roles of multicultural issues in managing work stress and employee assistance programs (EAPs).

Stressful Life Events and Daily Hassles

How a researcher measures work stress depends on the type of research question and also the way the nature of stress is conceptualized. Researchers who define *stress* in terms of *environmental demands* study extremely stressful work situations (e.g., working in emergency rooms, psychiatric wards, and hospices;

police and surveillance work, and combat situations in war) or individual life events (e.g., death of a spouse, major car accident causing long-lasting physical injuries, major legal problems, death of respected supervisor or coworker). These events are stressful because they require persons undergoing these life events to make significant changes and adaptations in their interpersonal and social interactions in both the short- and long-term; that is, they require a considerable amount of social readjustment. The pioneering work of Holmes and Rahe (1967) and Dohrenwend and Dohrenwend (1974) on the stressful effects of life events created a large body of findings on the effects of major stressful life events on adjustment and performance of individuals in their work and nonwork roles. The Social Readjustment Rating Scale (SRRS) was developed by Holmes and Rahe to measure the collective impact of the major life events that individuals might encountered during the previous year in their life. The death of a spouse was rated as the most stressful event one can experience in life, whereas a minor violation with the law (e.g., receiving a speeding ticket for a traffic violation) was considered the least stressful. Individuals were asked to identify the number of life event changes that they encountered during the previous year and the degree of psychological and physiological strains experienced. These two types of strains were directly associated with the number and severity of critical life event changes that they had experienced during the previous 12 months of their life. Research on life event changes has been rare in the work stress literature. One major exception is the study by Bhagat, McQuaid, Lindholm, and Segovis (1985), who investigated the effects of total life stress (calculated by adding the scores associated with critical life event changes from work and nonwork domains). Using a modified version of the life events questionnaire developed by Johnson and Sarason (1978), they found that total life stress was predictive of a number of organizationally valued outcomes and withdrawal tendencies from the job. More research on the effects of stressful life events on job performance and work adjustment processes is sorely needed. The experience of and coping with stressful life events is a function of cultural background. Sudden changes in job-related duties and responsibilities, having to deal with a culturally dissimilar environment in a foreign context, and the experience of psychological trauma due to negative experiences of a respected or beloved coworker or supervisor are all examples of life inducing changes that may occur in one's work life. There is considerable blurring of work and nonwork roles, duties, and responsibilities in the current era of globalization among cultures that traditionally emphasized a strict separation of work and nonwork roles (as discussed in Chapter 2). Stressful life events occurring in the domain of work have strong potential to affect important outcomes in the nonwork domain and vice versa. In Chapter 5 we will discuss the significance of conducting more research on the role of multicultural perspectives on work stress and coping.

Another line of research on work stress emphasizes the transaction between the person and the work environment. These researchers are interested in studying the effects of everyday stressors such as role stresses that we discussed earlier. However, another class of stressful experiences may result from the continuous experiences of daily hassles that individuals may encounter in their work role in the organization. A *hassle* is an event of short duration that is usually minor in nature and is embedded in the larger context of an ongoing stressful life event or work stress. *Daily hassles* are defined as minor irritations experienced in the course of performing one's role-related duties and responsibilities. Computer malfunctions, having to deal with a coworker who wastes individuals' time on the job, difficulties finding a parking space, and having to walk a long distance from the parking garage to the place of work are not major life events by any means but can exacerbate chronic difficulties experienced on a daily basis. The severity of a daily hassle is directly related to the psychological and sociocultural context of a life event. Consider the following example: Waiting to meet one's boss who is late to appointments some of the time may constitute a minor hassle on the job; however, if the boss tends to be persistently late in meeting with his subordinates, then it can be a daily hassle. This kind of daily hassle can develop into a major job-related stressful event. It can precipitate a major confrontation in the work group—perhaps leading to one or several important employees' leaving to work for another work group or work organization.

Burnout on the Job

The phenomenon of burnout, which was first identified by Bradley (1969) and later refined by Freudenberger (1974), deals with the extreme type of psychological strains that are experienced by human service professionals such as nurses, police officers, social workers, school teachers, and psychiatric counselors. A large number of research studies have been conducted in the area of job burnout during the past 30 years primarily among human service professionals. It is a major topic of research in the area of counseling and consulting psychology, but because of its growing role in the areas of various service professions today, we provide an overview of research involving burnout. Burnout has been defined as a chronic job situation that tends to produce severe emotional exhaustion. Burnout results due to chronic and excessive pressures that one encounters in one's work role without much hope for positive emotional experiences.

BREAKING POINT FOR A HARVARD UNIVERSITY PRESIDENT

It is difficult for us to imagine that presidents of Harvard University in Cambridge, Massachusetts (i.e., the most prestigious university in the world) to experience a complete breaking point. But a breaking point did happen for Harvard President Neil Rudenstine on a November morning in 1994. He overslept one morning when he was in the midst of a $1 million a day fundraising campaign. Oversleeping may not be monumental event for most senior academics or executives. However, for this zealous perfectionist Renaissance scholar, it was burnout. While at his previous job as provost of Princeton, he demonstrated a passion for overseeing even the smallest details of such activities as fundraising, meeting with football boosters, dormitory issues, and other university matters. He also had the habit of composing dozens of handwritten notes late into the night. This habit continued after he became the president of Harvard University to the point that he fretted over banquet menus and other activities which senior administrators of universities would typically delegate to their assistants or staff. He was even concerned about the benefits of either $10 or $15 co-payments that Harvard professors had to pay their primary care physicians. His work days were over 12 hours long, his sleep habits became sporadic, and after three years of nonstop toil in this hypermetabolic work habit, Dr. Rudenstine hit the breaking point in November 1994. Two weeks before the symptoms of exhaustion consumed him, he told reporters that his waking hours were always preoccupied with never finished tasks. Dr. Rudenstine stated, "My sense was that I was super exhausted." After consulting his doctor, he took a 3-month sabbatical from his hectic life at Harvard. He read Lewis Thomas, listened to classical music, and worked with his wife on a Caribbean beach. His symptoms of exhaustion and burnout were pretty much gone and he returned to his post as the President of Harvard in March 1995, promising to delegate more, take more long walks, obsess less with unfinished tasks, and even learn to use a dictaphone.

Adapted from Hancock, L., & Rosenberg, D., *Newsweek* 125(10), 1995, p. 56.

The job burnout research reported by Cherniss (1980), Leiter and Maslach (1988), Maslach (1993), and Hobfoll and Shirom (1993) shows that job-related stress is associated with great personal costs for employee well-being and organizational effectiveness. Chronic role stresses that are not easily solved are causes of absenteeism, turnover, lower productivity, and poor personal health and well-being. Cardiovascular and coronary heart diseases, drug and alcohol abuse, and job-related accidents are also related to the experience of burnout on the job. There is evidence that job-related burnout is correlated with feelings of depersonalization and emotional exhaustion in a sample of school teachers from Fort Worth, Texas (Bhagat, Allie, & Ford, 1995). (An extensive review of job-related burnout may be found in Shirom, 2003.) It is sufficient to note that burnout seems to be more pervasive in advanced globalized countries where the distinctions between work and nonwork are beginning to disappear. Research on burnout still has to uncover the specific types of sociocultural contexts in which work exerts the most influence. A wide variety of situational factors and coping resources, such as access to different types of social support, job decision latitude, and personal factors such as hardiness and optimism, are likely to exert selective influences in the experience of burnout. It is clear that more research needs to be conducted on various types of moderating and mediating influences of work stress–burnout relationships in dissimilar nations and cultures as globalization expands.

An Appraisal of the Western Theories of Work Stress

In this section we outline and discuss the major theoretical models that have guided research on work stress and coping in the Western countries (i.e., the United States and the United Kingdom). The classic studies on work stress were pioneered by Robert Kahn and his colleagues (1964). The transactional model of work stress developed by Lazarus and his colleague (1966, 1984) has been instrumental in probing into the nature of work stress even though there is no explicit theoretical model of work stress called the Lazarus and Folkman model of work stress and coping. We also discuss the role of various moderating influences that either enhance or hinder individuals in experiencing psychological, physiological, and behavioral strains.

Undoubtedly, research on work stress and coping has been a major area of inquiry in both organizational behavior and occupational health psychology since the pioneering studies by Robert Kahn and his associates in the 1960s. Research findings have been helpful in designing various types of stress management programs and intervention strategies including employee assistance programs. These findings have been primarily applied to work settings in the Western countries of the world where the issues of work and organizational stress and quality of work life have been important concerns since the 1970s. However, there is a growing need to expand the range of issues that need to be considered to grasp the realities of work stress in the current era of globalization.

Table 3.1 Moderators of Work Stress and Valued Outcomes

Individual Resilience	Individual Vulnerability	Work and Nonwork Related
Coping styles and resources	Negative affect	Work-related social support
Self-esteem	Type A personality	Nonwork-related social support (family, friends, and significant others)
Work-specific locus of control	Type D personality	Access to counseling, employee assistance programs (EAP), and related self-development programs
Hardiness	Cynicism	
Positive affect		
Optimism		

In Table 3.1 we list some of the topical themes that have began to emerge as significant areas of inquiries. Research conducted in the Western mode has been predominantly concerned with the stressful consequences of factors that are intrinsic to work and the organization. Issues of role overload, role ambiguities, person–environment fit, sexual harassment on the job, and abrasive personalities have been studied. Stressful consequences that arise at the interface of work and family have been receiving increasing attention in recent years, but clearly more needs to be done as we begin to further explore the effects of work and organizational restructuring on the well-being of the family.

Environmental influences from the domain of nonwork, cultural contexts of work organizations, and society need to be considered in developing a comprehensive understanding of how work stresses develop in the current era of globalization. In addition, the stressful consequences of economic, social, and cultural globalization (see Chapter 2 for a detailed review of these issues) should also be considered. As we mentioned earlier, a large majority of the Western studies have been primarily concerned with stressful experiences that originate from factors that are intrinsic to one's work, work group, and organization. Issues dealing with boundary-less work, effects of telecommuting, gender and career issues in work–family conflicts, and ethnic and cultural differences have not received the kind of attention that they should as globalization connects people and organizations across dissimilar nations and cultures. Cultural issues become increasingly important as we begin to seek better understanding into the experience of work stress of immigrants in Western countries—a large majority of whom originate from non-Western countries.

In Table 3.2, we provide a new classification of research on work stress and coping. Issues of work–family conflicts, boundary-less work, telecommuting, national and cultural variations in the experience and operation of work stress

Table 3.2 A New Classification of Research in the Domain of Work Stress and Coping

Domain	Themes
Factors intrinsic to work and organization	Role overload, role conflict, role ambiguities
	Person–environment fit, coping with job stresses, lack of social support at work
	Underuse of skills, occupational obsolescence, job loss and its consequences
	Sexual harassment, workplace bullying, abrasive personalities
Work–family issues	Work–family conflicts, daily hassles
	Boundary-less work, telecommuting
	Gender and career issues in work–family conflicts
Social and cultural context	National and cultural variations in work stress, coping, and social support
	Ethnic differences in work stress and coping
	Acculturation-related stresses and coping
Economic, social, and cultural aspects of globalization	New rules of work and working
	Rapid technological changes including increased use of Internet and computer-mediated communication
	Globally distributed work teams, virtual teams, and organizations
	Aging and demographic-related changes
	New types of organizational structures and related changes (e.g., joint ventures, mergers and acquisitions, vertical to network-based organizations)

and coping, and rapid technological changes will become increasingly important as dissimilar countries and cultures become integrated in the global economy. We seem to know a considerable amount, but not as much on the role of factors listed under the domains of work–family issues, social and cultural variations, and economic, social, and cultural aspects of globalization.

Where Do We Go From Here?

Areas where more research needs to be conducted are listed in the following sections.

Work–Family Interface

Although conflict between work and family has been a major source of stressors for many employees prior to 1970, this issue has begun to generate substantial interest during recent years. There has been a significant increase in the families in which all of the adults work for pay (Bianchi & Raley, 2003; Jacobs & Gerson, 2001). In 1970 about 36% of married couples between the ages 18 and 64 were composed of two earners, but this figure rose to over 70% in 2008. This trend, while not as common in non-Western countries, is slowly emerging in the Eastern and developing world. The proportion of single parents who are employed increased from 53% in 1970 to over 71% in 2010. These demographic changes in the United States, Western Europe, and other parts of the globalizing world have major consequences in the development of new patterns of work stress. The implications for coping are also likely to be quite different from the ones that have been studied in the context of work stress. In addition, work- and organizational-related changes that occur as a result of global competition create pressures for more working hours, which intensify work–family conflict.

Incorporating Ethnic, Social, and Cultural Variations

As globalization expands across nations and cultures, people of dissimilar values, practices, habits, and norms come in contact as customers, employees, and managers, and in other roles. Cross-cultural and cross-national research on work stress is of growing importance in this era of globalization. For example, Japanese managers of the subsidiary of a large global company such as Toyota Incorporated located in the United States need to understand the role of work and societal cultures to develop better human resources practices. Similarly, managers from U.S. global national companies need to develop better insights into the importance of culture, religion, and local values and mores in managing call centers and outsourcing operations in India, where cultural patterns differ considerably from those of the United States. Research on cultural variations that are applicable to various nations and cultures has grown tremendously since Hofstede's classic study in the 1980s (Hofstede, 1980). It is important for work stress researchers to incorporate the insights from these theoretical models in advancing the role of ethnic, societal, and cultural variations in work stress and coping-related processes.

Incorporating the Consequences of Economic, Social, and Cultural Aspects of Globalization

Last but not least, researchers and practitioners should also be concerned with stressful effects of various facets of economic, social, and cultural globalization. We provide a detailed examination of how economic and social aspects of globalization are altering the demographics and organizational landscapes across nations and cultures. Such changes require new types of coping and adaptational skills. For example, immigrants from collectivistic cultures (e.g., China, Brazil, India) might need to learn more individualistic styles (e.g., United States, United Kingdom, Canada, and Australia) of coping as they migrate for better jobs and economic opportunities. The role of large ethnic minorities such as Hispanic Americans, African Americans, and Asian Americans also need to be reexamined for enhancing their participation in the global world. The idea of integrating large minority populations is not necessarily unique to the U.S. experience. It is becoming increasingly important for countries of the European Union, Australia, New Zealand, and Canada. The relevance of multicultural perspectives on work stress and coping is discussed in Chapter 6.

Conclusion

In this chapter, we have presented the models of work stress that have been developed in the United States and other Western European countries since the 1960s. An integrative model that incorporates both short- and long-term dynamics was also presented. The role of various moderating influences on the relationship between work stress and various organizational and individually valued outcomes was discussed. Research conducted in the Western tradition has indeed been quite robust and valuable in the design of various stress management methods including employee assistance programs. However, the role of other factors that are growing in importance and should be considered in a comprehensive understanding of the evolving patterns of work stress and coping in the current era of globalization is not being given sufficient attention. We provided a new classification of research on work stress and coping and discussed the importance of more research in the area of work–family interface, social and cultural variations, and economic and cultural facets of globalization.

In the next chapter, we will discuss the process of managing work stress and evaluate the effectiveness of various techniques in the Western tradition.

References

Aboa-Eboule, C., Brisson, C., Maunsell, E., Masse, B., Bourbonnais, R., Vezina, M., Milot, A., Theroux, P., & Dagenais, G. R. (2007). Job strain and risk of acute recurrent coronary heart disease events. *The Journal of the American Medical Association, 298*, 1652–1660.

Allred, K. D., & Smith, T. W. (1989). The Hardy personality: Cognitive and physiological. *Journal of Personality and Social Psychology, 56*(2), 257–266.

Anderson, L. M., & Bateman, T. S. (1997). Cynicism in the workplace: Some causes and effects. *Journal of Organizational Behavior, 18*, 449–469.

The Asians are coming, again. (2001, April, 28). *The Economist, 359*(8219). Retrieved March 12, 2012, from http://www.economist.com/node/593132/print.

Baron, R. M., & Kenny, D. A. (1986). The moderator-mediator variable distinction in social psychological research: Conceptual, strategic, and statistical considerations. *Journal of Personality and Social Psychology, 51*(6), 1173–1182.

Beehr, T. A. (1995). *Psychological stress in the workplace*. London: Routledge.

Beehr, T. A. (1998). Research on occupational stress: An unfinished enterprise. *Personnel Psychology, 51*, 835–841.

Beehr, T. A., & Bhagat, R. S. (1985). *Human stress and cognition in organizations: An integrated perspective*. New York: John Wiley & Sons.

Beehr, T. A., & Franz, T. M. (1986). The current debate about the meaning of job stress. *Journal of Occupational Behavior, 8*(2), 5–18.

Beehr, T. A., & Glazer, S. (2005). Consistency of implications of three role stressors across four countries. *Journal of Organizational Behavior, 26*(5), 467–487.

Beehr, T. A., & McGrath, J. E. (1992). Social support, occupational stress, and anxiety. *Anxiety, Stress & Coping, 5*, 7–19.

Beehr, T. A., & McGrath, J. E. (1996). The methodology of research on coping: Conceptual, strategic, and operational level issues. In M. Zeidner & N. Endler (Eds.), *Handbook of coping: Theory, research and applications* (pp. 1–10). Wiley.

Bhagat, R. S., Allie, S. M., & Ford, D. L. (1995). Coping with stressful events: An empirical analysis. In R. Crandall & P. L. Perrewé (Eds.), *Occupational stress: A handbook. Series in health psychology and behavioral medicine* (pp. 93–112). Philadelphia, PA: Taylor & Francis.

Bhagat, R. S., McQuaid, S. J., Lindholm, H., & Segovis, J. (1985). Total life stress: A multimethod validation of the construct and its effect on organizationally valued outcomes and withdrawal behaviors. *Journal of Applied Psychology, 70*, 202–214.

Bianchi, S. M., & Raley, S. (2003). Time allocation in families. In S. M. Bianchi, L. M. Casper, & R. B. King (Eds.), *Work, family, health, and well-being* (pp. 21–42). Mahwah, NJ: Lawrence Erlbaum Associates.

Bradley, H. B. (1969). Community-based treatment for young adult offenders. *Crime and Delinquency, 15*, 359–370.

Brandes, P., & Das, D. (2006). Behavioral cynicism at work: Construct issues and performance implications. In P. L. Perrewé & D. C. Ganster (Eds.), *Research in occupational stress and well being* (Vol. 5, pp. 233–266). Amsterdam: Elseiver JAI.

Brief, A. P., Burke, M. J., George, J. M., Robinson, B., & Webster, J. (1988). Should negative affectivity remain an unmeasured variable on the study of job stress. *Journal of Applied Psychology, 73*, 193–198.

Brockner, J. (1988). *Self-esteem at work: Research, theory and practice.* Lexington, MA: Lexington Books.

"Busy signals." (2005, September 8). *The Economist, 376.* Retrieved February 17, 2012, from http://www.economist.com/node/4379034

Chang, E. C. (1998). Dispositional optimism and primary and secondary appraisal of a stressor: Controlling for confounding influences and relations to coping and psychological and physical adjustment. *Journal of Personality and Social Psychology, 74*, 1109–1120.

Cherniss, C. (1980). *Professional burnout in human service organizations.* New York: Praeger.

Cohen, S., & Edwards, J. R. (1989). Personality characteristics as moderators of the relationship between stress and disorder. In R. W. Neufeld (Ed.), *Advances in the investigation of psychological stress* (pp. 235–283). New York: John Wiley & Sons.

Cooper, C. L., Dewe, P. J., & O'Driscoll, M. (2001). *Organizational stress: A review and critique of theory, research, and applications.* Thousand Oaks, CA: Sage.

Cooper, C. L., & Marshall, J. (1976). Occupational sources of stress: A review of the literature relating to coronary heart disease and mental ill-health. *Journal of Occupational Psychology, 49*, 11–28.

Costa, P. T., & McCrae, R. R. (1985). *The NEO Personality Inventory manual.* Odessa, FL: Psychological Assessment Resources.

Cummings, T. G., & Cooper, C. L. (1979). A cybernetic framework for studying occupational stress. *Human Relations, 32*, 395–418.

Cummings, T. G., & Cooper, C. L. (1998). A cybernetic theory of occupational stress. In C. L. Cooper (Ed.), *Theories of organizational stress* (pp. 101–121). Oxford, England: Oxford University Press.

David, J., & Suls, J. (1999). Coping efforts in daily life: Role of big five traits and problem appraisal. *Journal of Personality, 67*, 119–140.

De Fruyt, F., & Denollet, L. (2002). Type D personality: A five-factor model perspective. *Psychology and Health, 17*(5), 671–683.

Denollet, J., Pedersen, S. S., Vrints, C. J., & Conraads, V. M. (2006). Usefulness of type D personality in predicting five-year cardiac events above and beyond concurrent symptoms of stress in patients with coronary heart disease. *American Journal of Cardiology, 97*, 970–973.

Dewe, P., & Cooper, C. L. (2007). Coping research and measurement in the context of work related stress. In G. P. Hodgkinson & J. K. Ford (Eds.), *International review of industrial and organizational psychology* (Vol. 22, pp. 141–191). Chichester, UK: Wiley.

Dewe, P. J., O'Driscoll, M. P., & Cooper, C. L. (2010). *Coping with work stress: A review and critique.* Oxford: John Wiley & Sons.

Dohrenwend, B. P., & Dohrenwend, B. S. (Eds.). (1974). *Stressful life events.* New York: John Wiley & Sons.

Edwards, J. R. (1998). Cybernetic theory of stress, coping, and well-being: Review and extension to work and family. In C. L. Cooper (Ed.), *Theories of organizational stress* (pp. 122–152). Oxford: Oxford University Press.

Elsass, P., & Veiga, J. (1997). Job control and job strain: A test of three models. *Journal of Occupational Health Psychology, 2*(3), 195–211.

Estrada, C. A., Isen, A. M., & Young, M. (1994). Positive affect influences creative problem solving and reported source of practice satisfaction in physicians. *Motivation and Emotion, 18,* 285–299.

Estrada, C. A., Isen, A. M., & Young, M. J. (1998). Positive affect facilitates integration of information and decreases anchoring in reason among physicians. *Organizational Behavior and Human Decision Processes, 72,* 117–135.

Etzion, D. (1984). Moderating effect of social support on the stress–burnout relationship. *Journal of Applied Psychology, 69,* 615–622.

Folkman, R. S., & Moskowitz, J. T. (2004). Coping: Pitfalls and promise. *Annual Review of Psychology, 55,* 745–774.

Freudenberger, H. J. (1974). Job burnout. *Journal of Social Issues, 30,* 159–165.

Friedman, H., & Booth-Kewley, S. (1987). The "disease-prone" personality: A meta-analytic view of the construct. *American Psychologist, 42,* 539–555.

Friedman, M., & Rosenman, R. H. (1959). Association of specific overt behavior patterns with blood and cardiovascular findings: Blood cholesterol level, blood clotting time, incidence of arcus senilis and clinical coronary artery disease. *Journal of the American Medical Association, 169,* 1286–1296.

Friedman, M., & Rosenman, R. H. (1974). *Type A behavior and your heart.* New York: Knopf.

Ganster, D. C., & Schaubroeck, J. (1995). The moderating effect of self-esteem on the work stress–employee health relationship. In R. Crandall, & P. L. Perrewé (Eds.), *Occupational stress: A handbook* (pp. 167–177). Washington, DC: Taylor & Francis.

Gentry, W. D., & Kobasa, S. C. (1984). Social and psychological resources mediating stress-illness relationships in humans. In W. D. Gentry (Ed.), *Handbook of behavioural medicine* (pp. 87–116). New York: Guilford Press.

George, J. (1992). The role of personality in organizational life: Issues and evidence. *Journal of Management, 18,* 185–213.

George, J. M., & Brief, A. P. (1992). Feeling good—doing good: A conceptual analysis of the mood at work—organizational spontaneity relationship. *Psychological Bulletin, 112,* 310–329.

Goodwell, H., Wolf, S., & Rogers, F. B. (1986). Historical perspective. In S. Wolf & A. J. Finnstone (Eds.), *Occupational stress, health, and performance at work.* Littleton, MA: PSG, Inc.

Griffin, M. A., & Clarke, S. (2011). Stress and well-being at work. In S. Zedeck (Ed.), *APA handbook of industrial and organizational psychology* (Vol. 3, pp. 359–397). Washington, DC: American Psychological Association.

Hancock, L., & Rosenberg, D. (1995, March 6). Breaking point. *Newsweek, 125*(10), 56.

Hobfoll, S. E. (1989). Conservation of resources: A new attempt at conceptualizing stress. *American Psychologist, 44*, 513–524.

Hobfall, S. E. (1998). *Stress, culture, and community: The psychology and philosophy of stress.* New York: Plenum.

Hobfoll, S. E. (2001). The influence of culture, community, and the nested-self in the stress process: Advancing conservation of resources theory. *Applied Psychology:An International Review*, 337–421.

Hobfoll, S. E., Schwarzer, R., & Chon, K. K. (1996). Disentangling the stress labyrinth: Interpreting the term stress as it is studied in health context. *Japanese Journal of Health Psychology, 4*, 1–22.

Hobfoll, S. E., & Shirom, A. (1993). Stress and burnout in work organizations. In R. T. Golembiewski (Ed.), *Handbook of organization behavior* (pp. 41–61). New York: Marcel Dekker.

Hofstede, G. (1980). *Culture's consequences: International differences in work-related values.* Beverly Hills, CA: Sage.

Holmes, T. H., & Rahe, R. H. (1967). The Social Readjustment Rating Scale. *Journal of Psychosomatic Research, 11*(2), 213–218.

House, J. (1981). *Work stress and social support.* Reading, MA: Addison–Wesley Publishing Company.

Hull, J. G., Van Treuren, R. R., & Virnelli, S. (1987). Hardiness and health: A critique and alternative approach. *Journal of Personality and Social Psychology, 53*, 518–530.

Isen, A. M., Rosenzweig, A. S., & Young, M. J. (1991). The influence of positive affect on clinical problem solving. *Medical Decision Making, 11*, 221–227.

Jackson, S. E., & Schuler, R. S. (1985). A meta-analysis and conceptual critique of research on role ambiguity and role conflict in work settings. *Organizational Behavior & Human Decision Processes, 36*, 16–78.

Jacobs, J. A., & Gerson, K. (2001). Overworked individuals and overworked families? Explaining trends in work, leisure, and family time. *Work and Occupation, 28*, 40–63.

Japanese employees are working themselves to death. (2007, December 19). *The Economist.* Retrieved February 17, 2012, from http://www.economist.com/node/10329261/print

Jex, S. M., & Gudanowski, D. M. (1992). Efficacy beliefs and work stress: An exploratory study. *Journal of Organizational Behavior, 13*, 509–517.

Johnson, J. H., & Sarason, I. G. (1978). Life stress, depression and anxiety: Internal-external control as a moderator variable. *Journal of Psychosomatic Research, 22*, 205–208.

Kahn, R. L., & Byosiere, P. (1992). Stress in organizations. In M. Dunnette & L. Hough (Eds.), *Handbook of industrial and organizational psychology* (2nd ed., Vol. 3, pp. 571–650). Palo Alto, CA: Consulting Psychologists Press.

Kahn, R. L., Wolfe, D. M., Quinn, R. P., Snoek, J., & Rosenthal, R. A. (1964). *Organizational stress: Studies in role conflict and ambiguity.* New York: Wiley.

Karasek, R. (1979). Job decision latitude, job demands and mental strain: Implications for job redesign. *Administrative Science Quarterly, 24*, 285–308.

Karasek, R., & Theorell, T. (1990). *Healthy work: Stress, productivity, and the reconstruction of working life.* New York: Basic Books.

Karasek, R., Triantis, K., & Chaudhry, S. (1982). Co-worker and supervisor support as moderators of association between task characteristics and mental strain. *Journal of Occupational Behavior, 3*, 147–160.

Kobasa, S. C. (1979). Stressful life events, personality, and health: An inquiry into hardiness. *Journal of Personality and Social Psychology, 37*, 1–11.

Kobasa, S. C., Maddi, S. R., & Kahn, S. (1982). Hardiness and health: A prospective study. *Journal of Personality and Social Psychology, 42*, 168–177.

Kohn, P. M., Lafreniere, K. D., & Gurevich, M. (1991). Hassles, health, and personality. *Journal of Personality and Social Psychology, 61*, 478–482.

Landsbergis, P. A., Schnall, P. L., Belkic, K., Baker, D., Schwartz, J. E., & Pickering, T. G. (2001). Work stress and cardiovascular disease. *Work: A Journal of Assessment and Prevention, 17*, 191–208.

Landsbergis, P. A., Schnall, P. L., Belkic, K. A., Baker, D., Schwartz, J. E., & Pickering, T. G. (2002). Workplace and cardiovascular disease: Relevance and potential role for occupational health psychology. In J. C. Quick & L. E. Tetrick (Eds.), *Handbook of occupational health psychology* (Vol. 2, pp. 243–264). Washington, DC: American Psychological Association.

Lazarus, R. S. (1966). *Psychological stress and the coping process.* New York: McGraw-Hill.

Lazarus, R. S. (1991). *Emotion and adaptation.* New York: Oxford University Press.

Lazarus, R. S. (1999). *Stress and emotion: A new synthesis.* New York: Springer.

Lazarus, R. S., & Folkman, S. (1984). *Stress, appraisal, and coping.* New York: Springer.

Lee, R. T., & Ashforth, B. E. (1996). A meta-analytic examination of the correlates of the three dimensions of job burnout. *Journal of Applied Psychology, 81*(2), 122–133.

Leiter, M. P., & Maslach, C. (1988). The impact of interpersonal environment on burnout and organizational commitment. *Journal of Organizational Behavior, 9*, 297–308.

LePine, J. A., Podsakoff, N. P., & LePine, M. A. (2005). A meta-analytic test of the challenge stressor-hindrance stressor framework: An explanation for inconsistent relationships among stressors and performance. *Academy of Management Journal, 48*, 764–775.

Macik-Frey, M., Quick, J. D., Quick, J. C., & Nelson, D. L. (2009). Occupational health psychology: From preventive medicine to psychologically healthy workplace. In A.-S. G. Antoniou, C. L. Cooper, G. P. Chrousos, C. D. Spielberger, & M. W. Eysenck (Eds.), *Handbook of managerial behaviour and occupational health* (pp. 3–19). Cheltenham, UK: Edward Elgar Publishing.

Marshall, G. N., & Lang, E. L. (1990). Optimism, self-mastery, and symptoms of depression in women professionals. *Journal of Personality and Social Psychology, 59*, 132–139.

Marshall, J., & Cooper, C. C. (1979). Work experiences of middle and senior managers: The pressure and satisfaction. *International Management Review, 19*, 81–96.

Maslach, C. (1993). Burnout: A multidimensional perspective. In W. B. Schaufeli, C. Maslach, & T. Marek (Eds.), *Professional burnout: Recent developments in theory and research* (pp. 19–32). Washington, DC: Taylor & Francis.

McGrath, J. E. (1976). Stress and behavior in organizations. In M. Dunnette (Ed.), *Handbook of industrial organizational psychology* (pp. 1351–1395). Chicago: Rand McNally Co., Inc.

McGrath, J. E., & Beehr, T. A. (1990). Time and the stress process: Some temporal issues in the conceptualization and measurement of stress. *Stress Medicine, 6,* 93–104.

Menaghan, E. G., & Merves, E. S. (1984). Coping with occupational problems: The limits of individual efforts. *Journal of Health and Social Behavior, 25,* 406–423.

Mittal, V., & Ross, W. T. (1998). The impact of positive and negative affect and issue framing on issue interpretation and risk taking. *Organizational Behavior and Human Decision Processes, 76*(3), 298–324.

Mossholder, K. W., Bedeian, A. G., & Armenakis, A. A. (1981). Role perceptions, satisfaction, and performance: Moderating effects of self-esteem and organizational level. *Organizational Behavior and Human Performance, 28,* 224–234.

Oginska-Bulik, N. (2006). Occupational stress and its consequences in healthcare professionals: The role of type D personality. *International Journal of Occupational Medicine and Environmental Health, 19*(2), 113–122.

Parkes, K. K. (1990). Coping, negative affectivity and the work environment: Additive and interactive predictors of mental health. *Journal of Applied Psychology, 75,* 399–409.

Pedersen, S. S., Lemos, P. A., van Vooren, P. R., Liu, T. K., Daemen, J., Erdman, R. A., et al. (2004). Type D personality predicts death or myocardial infarction after bare metal stent or sirolimus-eluting stent implantation: A Rapamycin-Eluting stent evaluated at Rotterdam Cardiology Hospital (RESEARCH) registry substudy. *Journal of the American College of Cardiology, 44*(5), 997–1001.

Perrewé, P. L., & Ganster, D. C. (1989). The impact of job demands and behavioral control on experienced job stress. *Journal of Organizational Behavior, 10,* 213–229.

Pierce, J. L., Gardner, D. G., Dunham, R. B., & Cummings, L. L. (1993). Moderation by organization-based self-esteem of role condition-employee response relationships. *Academy of Management Journal, 36*(2), 271–288.

Quick, J. C., Cooper, C. L., Nelson, D. L., Quick, J. D., & Gavin, J. H. (2003). Stress, health, and well-being at work. In J. Greenberg (Ed.), *Organizational behavior: The state of the science* (pp. 53–89). London: LEA.

The Regus Group. (2009, November). Stress out? A study of trends in workplace stress across the globe. Retrieved February 17, 2012, from http://www.regus.co.uk/images/Stress%20full%20report_Final_Designed_tcm7-21560.pdf

Roth, D. L., Weibe, D. J., Fillingim, R. B., & Shay, K. A. (1989). Life events, fitness, hardiness, and health: A simultaneous analysis of proposed stress-resistance effects. *Journal of Personality and Social Psychology, 57,* 136–142.

Rotter, J. B. (1966). Generalized expectancies for internal versus external control of reinforcement. *Psychological Monographs, 80*(1), 1–28.

Sauter, S. L., Murphy, L. R., & Hurrell, J. J. (1990). Prevention of work-related psychological disorders: A national strategy proposed by the National Institute for Occupational Safety and Health (NIOSH). *American Psychologist, 45*(10), 1146–1158.

Schaubroeck, J., & Merritt, D. (1997). Divergent effects of job control on coping with work stressors: The key role of self-efficacy. *Academy of Management Journal, 40,* 738–754.

Scheier, M. F., & Carver, C. S. (1992). Effects of optimism on psychological and physical well-being: Theoretical overview and empirical update. *Cognitive Therapy and Research, 16,* 201–228.

Schwab, D. P. (2005). *Research methods for organizational studies* (2nd ed.). Lawrence Erlbaum.

Semmer, N. K. (1996). Individual differences, work stress, and health. In M. J. Schabracq, J. A. Winnubst, & C. L. Cooper (Eds.), *Handbook of work and health psychology* (pp. 83–120). Chichester, UK: Wiley.

Sher, L. (2005). Type D personality: The heart, stress, and cortisol. *QJM: An International Journal of Medicine, 98*, 323–329.

Shirom, A. (2003). Job-related burnout. In J. C. Quick & L. E. Tetrick (Eds.), *Handbook of occupational health psychology* (pp. 245–265). Washington, DC: American Psychological Association.

Special report: South Africa, The price of freedom. (2010, June 5). *The Economist, 395*, 3–4.

Spector, P. E., Cooper, C. L., Sanchez, J. I., O'Driscoll, M., Sparks, K., Bernin, P., et al. (2002). Locus of control and well-being at work: How generalizable are Western findings? *Academy of Management Journal, 45*, 453–466.

Spector, P. E., Zapf, D., Chen, P. Y., & Frese, M. (2000). Why negative affectivity should not be controlled in job stress research: Don't throw out the baby with the bath water. *Journal of Organizational Behavior, 21*, 79–95.

Staw, B. M., & Barsade, S. G. (1993). Affect and managerial performance: A test of the sadder-but-wiser vs. happier-and-smarter hypotheses. *Administrative Science Quarterly, 38*, 304–331.

Stiglitz, J. E. (2003). *Globalization and its discontents.* New York: W.W. Norton & Company.

Ter Doest, L. T., Maes, S., Gebhardt, W., & Koelewijn, H. (2006). Personal goal facilitation through work: Implications for employee satisfaction and wellbeing. *Applied Psychology: An International Review, 55*(2), 192–219.

Theorell, T., & Karasek, R. (1996). Current issues relating to job strain and cardiovascular disease research. *Journal of Occupational Health Psychology, 1*, 9–26.

Watson, D., & Clark, L. A. (1984). Negative affectivity: The disposition to experience aversive emotional states. *Psychological Bulletin, 96*, 465–490.

Watson, D., Clark, L. A., & Tellegen, A. (1988). Development and validation of brief measures of positive and negative affect: The PANAS scale. *Journal of Personality and Social Psychology, 54*, 1063–1070.

Watson, D., & Pennebaker, J. W. (1989). Health complaints, stress, and distress: Exploring the central role of negative affectivity. *Psychological Review, 96*, 234–254.

Whitehead, D. L., Perkins-Porras, L., Strike, P. C., Magid, K., & Steptoe, A. (2007). Cortisol awakening response is elevated in acute coronary syndrome patients with Type D personality. *Journal of Psychosomatic Research, 62*, 419–425.

Williams, L., O'Connor, R. C., Howard, S., Hughes, B. M., Johnston, D. W., Hay, J. L., et al. (2008). Type-D personality mechanisms of effect: The role of health-related behavior and social support. *Journal of Psychosomatic Research, 64*(1), 63–69.

Williams, R. B. (2001). Hostility: Effects on health and the potential for successful behavioral approaches to prevention and treatment. In A. Baum, T. A. Revenson, & J. E. Singer (Eds.), *Handbook of health psychology* (pp. 661–668). Mahwah, New Jersey: Erlbaum.

Winslow, R. (2007, October 10). Work stress is a major risk factor in subsequent cardiovascular diseases and heart attacks. *The Wall Street Journal* (Eastern edition), D4.

Wong, P. T. P., Wong, L. C. J., & Lonner, W. J. (2006). (P. T. P. Wong & L. C. J. Wong, Eds.). In *Handbook of multicultural perspectives on stress and coping.* New York: Springer.

Chapter 4

Management of Work Stress: An Appraisal

As the recent financial crisis hit the United States, Great Britain, and Germany, its reverberations could be felt worldwide. In Singapore stress levels were reported to be 69%; only Japan, with 71%, was higher (Hooi, 2009). Longer hours, no bonuses, fewer employees, and shrinking resources all contributed to these strains as people faced extreme cost-cutting measures and downsizing. Even when employees went home, many Singapore white-collar workers put in another 30 minutes or more of work, according to 65% of the survey's respondents, against the 57% global average. In other countries, job pressures continued to mount. There was a cutthroat competition to keep what one had in terms of their financial success and societal status. In China, 51% of the Chinese respondents surveyed by the Hudson Group reported higher levels of work stress than in the previous year (Lawrence, 2008). The industrialization of China and its mass population migrations from the north to the south within the country has come at a heavy price. A full 26 million Chinese have reported clinical depression; each year 2 million people attempt suicide ("Coping With Stress", 2006). Given these stark statistics, it is not surprising to see Asian executives and managers willing to try any coping measure that will help them. In addition to their traditional stress management methods, they have turned to Western psychotherapy and pop psychology for advice, even though many of these methods are questionable (Lawrence, 2008; Lilienfeld, Lynn, Ruscio, & Beyerstein, 2010). Psychoanalysis with the patient lying on the couch has become popular. Seminars titled "Stress Management in the New World of Work" are being advertised in Hong Kong, where participants learn about Type A and B personalities, along with suggestions for physical and mental distractions, such as tai chi, sports, fishing, reading, music, and meditation (Shi, 2007). Within India, meditation workshops have become big business. There are spiritual shops successfully offering "health and wealth kits" (Gentleman, 2005). Adopting Western marketing techniques, spiritual gurus aggressively push their teachings, such as the "Art of Living," through public sessions, books, and CDs. As in Western countries, spiritual gurus can also be found on television; they even consult with personnel divisions of major companies. Spirituality and materialism have now become convenient business partners.

If Western stress management practices are spreading to the rest of the world, whether from pop or clinical sources, the question arises as to what these non-Western countries should expect. What are the Western conceptions of managing work stress? How effective are these strategies? Moreover, what ideas from non-Western nations and cultures can be useful in helping individuals cope effectively with job and personal life stressors? Fortunately, the stress management literature has been rich in its development. The recent *Handbook of Occupational Health Psychology* by Quick and Tetrick (2010), as one example, offers a comprehensive view of this research. A number of workplace stress management interventions can be taken to protect the health of individuals (Quick, Quick, & Nelson, 1998). The goals of each of these types of interventions are to mitigate individuals' susceptibility to stressors, prevent their onset, and ameliorate the advanced damage caused by stressors in restoring a person to health. In this chapter, we will look in more depth at the current preventive strategies that accomplish these goals at the organizational, team-group, and individual levels of analysis. Next, we will discuss the challenges or limitations these historical stress management methods and research perspectives present. Finally, a transformational model of stress and coping will be presented based on the emerging literature on transactional coping, religious and spiritual coping, and positive organizational psychology that will form a more holistic understanding of the potential of Western generated stress management research within a global context.

BAD STRESS RELIEF PRACTICES

Destructotherapy has emerged as the latest stress management fad on the global stage. In China's major electronics firm, the Foxconn Corporation, workers are encouraged to take out their aggressions on punching bags. In Jianguomen, residents can go to stress-busting rooms where they can hit inflatable dolls or throw inflatable balls to relieve their frustrations. Instead of dolls and balls, reports from Spain indicate that individuals are taking sledgehammers to junked cars and household items following the beat of a rock band. The basic idea is that people can transfer their angry feelings toward others or displace their daily frustrations onto some type of object. As a result, the person has a *catharsis,* alleviating the problem. The method sounds logical. Unfortunately, the *catharsis hypothesis* does not work. This is an old idea that science debunked long ago as an effective treatment of stress. In controlled scientific experiments, individuals' aggression and anger actually increased after pounding nails while being insulted or playing violent video games. Moreover, psychologists Scott O. Lilienfeld, Steven Jay Lynn, John Ruscio, and Barry L. Beyerstein (2010) gave the *catharsis hypothesis* a dubious place of honor in their book *50 Great Myths of Popular Psychology: Shattering Widespread Misconceptions About Human Behavior.*

It is dangerous to use bad science as a guide to solve real organizational problems. Foxxconn's response to its highly publicized number of suicides was to create a room with punching bags rather than to uncover the conditions that fostered these tragedies. As Patrick Mattimore (2010), a reporter, observed, "Perhaps if companies like Foxconn are worried about employees leaping to their deaths from office buildings, they would be better to build suicide barriers outside *windows* rather than aggression rooms inside them."

Adapted from Mattimore, P., Chinadaily.com.cn, 2010.

Stress Management Interventions

Stress management interventions have been categorized as *primary, secondary,* or *tertiary* (Barling, Kelloway, & Frone, 2005; Quick, Quick, Nelson, & Hurrell, 1997; Quick et al., 1998). Primary interventions focus on people who are not presently at risk. They are preventive in nature and aim at decreasing the number or the intensity of stressors (Cooper, Dewe, & O'Driscoll, 2001). They get at the potential sources of problems before they occur by eliminating the potential damaging causes of the stressors before their onset. Primary strategies target an organization's structures, work conditions, and social systems. Examples of these interventions are job redesign, decision-process changes, and restructuring workloads. Secondary interventions, on the other hand, aim at modifying individuals' responses to stressors. They target people who are likely to be at risk from potential stress-related illnesses (Tetrick & Quick, 2003). This is similar to an early warning system that promptly identifies and corrects the problem before it begins to progress much farther. The assumption is that a manager may not be able to remove or decrease a stressor; so instead the manager changes the focus to altering individuals' responses or changing their behavior. Stress management training, wellness programs, and information-sharing enhancements are different examples of secondary interventions. As one can see, these types of programs are more reactive and somewhat preventive in nature. Tertiary interventions also center on individuals, but they are past the "at-risk" status and are exhibiting actual health difficulties. The underlining emphasis for this approach is on the treatment of persons' stress-related problems or symptoms, since they have already occurred. Tertiary interventions concentrate on "damage control," whereas secondary interventions focus on potential "damage limitation" (Cooper, Dewe, & O'Driscoll, 2003). At this third juncture, people must learn how to cope more effectively with their physical maladies or poor mental health issues. Employee assistance programs (EAPs), massage therapy, and relaxation exercises are examples of tertiary intervention approaches. A summary of all three stress management interventions can be found in Table 4.1, which provides a comprehensive set of examples for each category.

Primary Interventions

A number of primary interventions have been used to directly attack the sources of stress by redesigning jobs, organizational structures, and social systems (Cooper et al., 2001; Elkin & Rosch, 1990; Hurrell, 2005; Semmer, 2011). All of these strategies have been shown by research to have ameliorating effects. Employees gain greater control of their environment either by directly eliminating the source of the stressor itself, gaining increased control from more resource support or by making the situation more manageable. In two major reviews, Semmer (2003, 2011) concluded that changes in work conditions, workload, time pressure, ergonomics, task characteristics, role clarity, and interpersonal ties have the potential to improve workers' health, well-being, and job satisfaction as well as reduce employee absenteeism. This is especially true of sociotechnical interventions in the redesign of work procedures, workloads, work processes, and work schedules (Hurrell, 2005; Kelloway, Hurrell, & Day, 2008). This can happen as simply as by reducing role conflict and ambiguity through goal setting (Quick, 1979) or with more complex interventions

Table 4.1   Stress Management Interventions

Type	Primary Intervention Strategies	Secondary Intervention Strategies	Tertiary Intervention Strategies
Goal	*Preventive*	*Preventive–Reactive*	*Reactive*
Purpose	*Modify and reduce stressors by changing and organization's work conditions, task characteristics, systems, or structures*	*Change the way individuals respond to work stressors to prevent negative health consequences by raising awareness of the causes of these effects and helping people to develop more healthy and adaptive response strategies*	*Focus on helping individuals cope with the consequences of work stressors and treat the effects of their distress*
Examples of Intervention	• Redesign of reward distributions to be more equitable • Use of employee participative management programs • Reorganization of lines of authority • Changes in decision-making processes in making relevant decisions • Restructuring organizational units • Sociotechnical interventions: Redesign of job tasks, job functions, job processes, and work schedules	• Wellness programs • Team building • Cognitive-behavioral skills training • Stress management training • Communication and information sharing programs • Meditation training • Physical fitness programs • Relaxation training	• Employee assistance programs • Counseling • Medical care • Self-hypnosis and autogenic training • Meditation practices • Mental imaging • Physical exercise • Massage therapy

(Continued)

Table 4.1 (Continued)   Stress Management Interventions

Type	Primary Intervention Strategies	Secondary Intervention Strategies	Tertiary Intervention Strategies
Goal	Preventive	Preventive–Reactive	Reactive
Purpose	Modify and reduce stressors by changing and organization's work conditions, task characteristics, systems, or structures	Change the way individuals respond to work stressors to prevent negative health consequences by raising awareness of the causes of these effects and helping people to develop more healthy and adaptive response strategies	Focus on helping individuals cope with the consequences of work stressors and treat the effects of their distress
Examples of Intervention	• Implementation of job enrichment–job enlargement programs • Improved ergonomic designs, work loads • Changes in job roles and their clarity • Reduced time pressures • Changes in climate social support and constructive feedback • Creating goal-setting programs	• Muscle-relaxation training • Spiritual and faith practices	• Relaxation techniques • Progressive relaxation techniques • Breath focus • Spiritual and faith practices

Source: Adapted from Cooper, C. L., Dewe, P. J., & O'Driscoll, M. P., *Organizational Stress: A Review and Critique of Theory, Research, and Applications*, Thousand Oaks, CA, Sage Publications, Inc., 2001; Quillian-Wolever, R. E., & Wolever, M. E., in J. C. Quick & L. E. Tetrick (Eds.), *Handbook of Occupational Health Psychology*, Washington, DC: American Psychological Association, 2003, pp. 355–375; Quick, J. D., Quick, J. C., & Nelson, D. L., in C. L. Cooper (Ed.), *Theories of Organizational Stress*, New York, NY, Oxford Press, 1998, pp. 245–268.

Note: Organized by ascending order of the estimated difficulty to implement the activity.

employing multiple strategies—job enrichment, training, ergonomic–technical changes, and schedule modifications (Lourijsen, Houtman, Kompier, & Grudemann, 1999). Unfortunately, though, the results of primary interventions have been found in studies to be short-lived and difficult to predict (Semmer, 2003, 2011). Sometimes some variables were affected and others were not; some symptoms would improve while other indicators of individual well-being would not; sometimes there was a positive trend but statistically significant levels occurred in only a few of the studies; and in other studies there might be a drop in absenteeism but it was not related to the stressfulness of the work (Semmer, 2003, 2011; Spector, 1997).

This pattern of inconsistent and mixed results in managing stress can also be found in another popular type of organizational intervention—employee participation programs or participatory action research interventions (Heaney, 2011; Hurrell, 2005). These psychosocial types of approaches, such as problem-solving committees and "health circles," attempt to provide workers the ability to significantly influence decision making at the worker–team level or at a greater organizational context. Groups meet for a series of sessions by a facilitator. Problems and any safety risks are evaluated by the group during the sessions to make operational recommendations to change these conditions. Representative participation approaches are extremely popular in Western Europe, especially in Germany (Aust & Ducki, 2004; Semmer, 2003, 2011). Within the United States, employee participation programs have been usually used to create organizational change, to generate employee satisfaction, and to promote workplace health (Argyris, 1993; Hackman & Wageman, 1995; Heaney, 2003; Lawler, 1992). The results of these employee participation interventions, though, have been highly variable (Cotton, Vollrath, Froggatt, Lengnick-Hall, & Jennings, 1988; Klein, Ralls, Smith-Major, & Douglas, 2000). Greater employee participation does offer employees increased control and mastery of their workplace. Flextime, choosing how to complete tasks, increased group autonomy, clarifying roles, information and communication sharing, and employee representative committees have all been shown to lower emotional distress and psychological strain from workplace stressors as well as decrease absences due to sickness (Aust & Ducki, 2004; Burke, 1993; Cooper et al., 2001; Cotton, Dollard, & de Jorge, 2003; Mikkelsen, Saksvik, & Landsbergis, 2000; Pierce & Newstrom, 1983; Schweiger & DeNisi, 1991; Wall & Clegg, 1981). However, there have also been studies showing negligible gains or negative results for different groups of workers in problem-solving groups (Landsbergis & Vivona-Vaughn, 1995; Semmer, 2011). Overall, changes in health indicators have been mixed.

In summarizing the research on the effectiveness of organizational interventions, Semmer (2011) states, "… 'sometimes, for some people, and on some measures,' and the main issue then becomes determining what can be expected when" (p. 307). Many studies suffer from a number of method, measurement, and design issues that prevent a clear picture of what is occurring and emerging. For example, different dimensions of work have specific relationships with different aspects of well-being. This indicates the need for researchers to carefully select and match their study's measures (Warr, 2007). At times absenteeism has been reduced, but this may have been the result of "Hawthorne effects" as well as other issues (Semmer, 2011; Spector, 1997). Job enrichment does seem to work, but it also creates a trade-off: Job satisfaction increases in these types of studies, yet there also exist increases in perceived work stress measures because of increased demands (Morgeson & Champion, 2003; Semmer, 2011). In addition, one has to carefully judge the quality of a study's implementation of the organizational intervention that was promised (Kompier & Kristensen, 2000; Semmer, 2011). Less than positive results may stem from a number of factors, such as the lack of a full implementation of the program, a limit in its duration, or an insufficient inclusion of employees in directly participating in decision making (Heaney, 2011). Were the facilitators trained? Were the circle meetings run effectively? Were the company's supervisors supportive? Were there other organizational pressures or crises that distracted management's attention from the program and diverted resources to other pressing work activities? Recently, Dollard, Le Blanc, and Cotton (2008) attempted to create a more systematic approach to address these problematic historical issues. They insisted that participatory research stress intervention programs must exhibit four qualities to be successful: active participation by the involvement of key stakeholders, collaboration between researchers and clients, employee empowerment to encourage a "voice" in a climate of participation and collaboration, and increased local knowledge used by workers to find viable solutions in charging the organization. If these characteristics become implemented, the participatory action research programs should significantly reduce the risk of stress producing factors in the workplace.

THEORY INTO PRACTICE IN COMBATING JOB STRESS

GlaxoSmithKline PLC has taken a different approach to job stress within its company. It has created a "team-resilience" program. When Jim Zisek, a Glaxo manager, signed up for this program, he listened to the concerns of his team of technical publishers about their sources of job stress. They felt overwhelmed from the rapidly changing deadlines, extremely heavy workloads, and a sense of isolation. Compounding this problem, each team member reported to a different manager. Zisek decided after the meeting to promote Mary Beth Chandler as the new manager of the team, a newly created position, to lead the publishers. This enabled her to shift assignments to create a better balance in workloads among the members to meet their different deadlines. Also, she had the authority to build more collaboration among team members and more accountability within the unit to meet the firm's standards.

Why did Glaxo and other employers implement these types of innovative stress management programs? It was to battle the increasing costs of job-related stressors that have taken a toll on companies. Researchers estimate the costs of this distress and burnout to be in the hundreds of billions of dollars each year, stemming from the impact of increased absenteeism, higher medical costs, and lower productivity. In Glaxo's case, they estimate that its team-based approach between 2003 and 2006 decreased its mental-health absences by 29% and its work-related mental illnesses affecting employees by 60%. The reduced absences in the United States saved the company $1.4 million over the 4-year period.

Adapted from Mamberto, C., *Wall Street Journal,* Eastern Edition, 2007, p. B6.

Secondary Interventions

Secondary interventions tend to be successful in aiding the modification of individuals' reactions to potential stressors as a preventive measure or as a reactive response to actual stressors (Cooper et al., 2001). These types of programs build individual self-awareness of the potential physical, emotional, mental, and behavioral responses that could occur from the stressors present in one's personal and work lives. They offer a model that emphasizes the fit between a person and the environment as well as one's transactions with the environment. However, this type of approach has an implicit assumption that it is the responsibility of the person to make choices that make this fit happen satisfactorily (Quillian-Wolever & Wolever, 2003). Examples of these types of programs are anger management, cognitive-behavioral therapy, stress inoculation training, and corporate "wellness" programs. These programs give participants the skills to cope with their environments whether they are perceived as difficult or challenging. The participants also build and practice skills in relaxation, cognitive behavioral therapy, problem solving, and guided self-dialogue instruction. With each of these approaches, individuals are challenged during exercise sessions to cope with particular stressful situations in a gradually increasing manner while remaining in a safe, controlled environment. It appears that these types of structured secondary interventions do have a positive effect in reducing psychological strain or perceived stress (Cartwright & Cooper, 2005; Cecil & Foreman, 1990; Cooper et al., 2001; Ganster, Mayes, Sime, & Tharp, 1982). The training does strengthen people's confidence in becoming more resilient. Similar results have also been found with two-way information sharing programs during mergers where a "realistic merger preview" helped employees understand how the merger would unfold; it created a two-way communication mechanism for employees and management to discuss any questions or reactions that concerned the employees (Schweiger & DeNisi, 1991). Unfortunately, though, these effects are effective primarily at the individual rather than the organization level (Briner & Reynolds, 1999), and they are not sufficiently robust or consistent from one group to another (Ganster et. al., 1982). Also, they are more short-term in their impact. Corporate "wellness" programs reflect these same research trends. They are popular and raise awareness, but overall there exists only mixed evidence as to their overall success (Kelloway et al., 2008).

Tertiary Interventions

Tertiary interventions are the most recognized and prevalent coping strategies within Western society. They can be found in our popular self-help literature at our airport book stores and local bookstore magazine racks. These types of stress interventions have a strong research foundation of support. The regular practice of physical exercise, massage therapy, relaxation techniques, meditation practices, self-hypnosis, breath mindfulness, and mental imaging appears to offer individuals some significant results for counteracting the negative physiological and psychological effects of chronic stress in improving their immune system functioning (Cartwright & Cooper, 2005; Quillian-Wolever & Wolever, 2003). Also many of these interventions, such as physical exercise, meditation, and relaxation-type methods as well as mental imaging techniques can serve as secondary interventions due to their robust prophylactic effects on people's physical systems. In addition to these commonly mentioned methods, another successful coping strategy is cognitive reframing in which the person learns to appraise and interpret events as challenges or neutral events rather than stressors (Ellis & Harper, 1975; Seligman, 1991; Taylor, 1983; Taylor & Brown, 1988, 1994). People using these methods have been shown to rethink their belief systems in a way that mitigates an event's stressful impact. Disclosure strategies offer another interesting way to reduce their negative emotions to a stressor (Francis & Pennebaker, 1992; Pennebaker, 1993, 1997). In these approaches, people disclose their private thoughts, feelings, and reactions about their problems through journal writing or talking with someone confidentially about them. These private disclosures counteract the tendency of persons to actively inhibit their thoughts and emotions. Inhibiting these thoughts and emotions unfortunately causes them to become stressors themselves and negatively affect immune functioning, cardiovascular system, and brain chemistry (Quillian-Wolever & Wolever, 2003).

Despite the many positive aspects of these individual tertiary-type methods, they work only if someone has the self-discipline to implement them and practice them regularly on an ongoing basis. This is the challenge. As with diets, there are a number of available sound methods, but many individuals seem to use them only for short periods of time. Many New Year's resolutions have been broken each year by people attempting to lose "those few pounds" by starting a new diet or exercise program. They stop because these attempts require fundamental changes in lifestyle, a strong commitment to their goals, and the self-discipline to persevere despite any setbacks. Moreover, as with secondary interventions, individually oriented strategies do not attack the root systemic causes of work stress in the organization. Eventually they become short-lived in their success. At best, they become a way for people to learn how to adjust to their life's problems and daily workplace difficulties (Cooper et al., 2001). Yet they could be a powerful tool if they could be implemented in conjunction with rigorous systemwide organizational interventions.

Along with these individual methods, organizations have in recent years created EAPs to aid employees. EAPs will be discussed in much greater detail in Chapter 7, especially in terms of their cross-cultural applicability. However, an overview of their efficacy as a tertiary stress management tactic needs to be addressed at this point. Though EAPs are implemented by organizations, they are really by design tertiary interventions that focus on individuals' helping themselves deal with "emotional damage control" or assisting in the treatment of stressful physical and psychological dysfunctions. EAPs are organized to provide employees suffering from personal- or work-based problems with direct services to support them while they remain contributing workers on the job. The services either help them to solve their dysfunctional work problem or enable them to restore their personal lives to some level of functioning so they do not interfere with their work performance (Berridge & Cooper, 1993; Cooper et al., 2003). The programs are confidential in nature with the services in most cases outsourced to professional external providers. Usually the services focus primarily on personal stress management, crisis interventions, family counseling, or drug and alcohol abuse issues. Though EAPs are valued as an enlightened approach, their effectiveness has been mixed in their accomplishments. Employees who have received counseling services have reported better psychological well-being, self-esteem, and overall mental health (Cooper & Cartwright, 1994). Other research studies report greater job attendance, quality of life, and job performance (Bhagat, Steverson, & Segovis, 2007; Cooper et al., 2003, 2011; MacDonald, Lothian, & Wells, 1997; MacDonald, Wells, Lothian, & Shain, 2000). Unfortunately, EAP studies also suffer from a number of methodological issues that make any assessment of this approach extremely difficult (Bhagat, Steverson, & Segovis, 2008: Cooper et al., 2003). A number of other studies report that these gains are short-lived and dissipate within 6 months (Cartwright & Cooper, 2005; Cooper et al., 2001; Hurrell, 2005; Whatmore, Cartwright, & Cooper, 1999). Overall though, EAPs still can make a positive impact on workers' lives and help the organization's productivity (Cooper, Dewe, & O'Driscoll, 2011).

Stress Interventions Strength

As a review of Table 4.1 shows, a manager has a comprehensive array of nearly 30 potential stress management interventions from which to choose to prevent and combat the costly occupational health consequences of a globalized economy. In fact, it is impressive what Western organizational science has learned over the past 100 years. Researchers have built an in-depth foundation of knowledge in understanding a number of psychosocial factors that create stressful organizational contexts, employee emotional and physical strain, and ultimately poor physical and mental health outcomes. Despite a number of methodological issues that surround the studies that have been conducted on stress management interventions, the general trend of these findings indicates a somewhat positive view of their impact. In Western organizations primary, secondary, and tertiary type interventions have shown the ability to improve organizational productivity and nurture employee health. This result is especially true if one views the interventions as working in collaboration with each other to manage stress rather than as an either–or proposition. As an illustration, person-oriented strategies tend to bolster a person's sense of self-efficacy and consolidate one's personal resources as individuals become more autonomous in managing their workplace stressors. This process takes place while the work-oriented strategies develop and take hold in altering the organization's work conditions (Munz, Kohler, & Greenberg, 2001; Semmer, 2011). When these two types of processes combine, there emerges a gestalt of a more positive work climate for the employees.

Finally, the success of any intervention depends on the motivations of the organization's leadership or the individual employees. Primary, secondary, and tertiary interventions have been listed in Table 4.1 by the estimated level of difficulty in accomplishing their objectives. As one moves up each section of the list, the intervention becomes more demanding in their required level of change. The individuals or organizations face more obstacles stemming from a greater level of complexity in changing the organization's structure or individuals' essential way of living. In both cases, they face extremely difficult challenges. In terms of organizational interventions, this explains why person-oriented strategies have found greater success than work-oriented ones (Richardson & Rothstein, 2008; Semmer, 2011; van der Klink, Blonk, Schene, & van Dijk, 2001). Work-oriented strategies usually entail more complex interactions and political considerations in changing work conditions. Person-oriented organizational strategies can foster more "small win" tactics that focus on more simple problems, require fewer resources, and attract less resistance (Weick, 1984). Beyond these implementation challenges, though, a number of additional serious conceptual problems still exist that limit our current understandings of Western stress management interventions approaches. These challenges will be explained in the next section.

Challenges of Western Stress Management Approaches

As the previous section has illustrated, a number of stress management interventions have emerged from organizational stress researchers and management practitioners of Western nations. Also as this review has demonstrated, many of the primary, secondary, and tertiary interventions have shown positive impacts in preventing, reducing, or mitigating the deleterious effects of stressors from the workplace. However, these historical stress management approaches, as well as the stress models covered in Chapter 3, have significant limitations that constrain our understanding of stress management and coping even before we analyze their cross-cultural implications. First, stress management interventions have been dominated by an individualistic perspective that disguises how organizational control processes significantly hinder the impact of primary organizational intervention methods. Second, stress management intervention research has focused primarily on distress rather than balancing it with more investigations on the role of eustress. Third, Western stress researchers seem to have understated or ignored the critical role that religion and spirituality have played in many people's lives as potential coping strategies. As we will see in later chapters on multicultural perspectives of work stress and coping, religious and spiritual coping strategies play a significant role in non-Western nations. Fourth, the stress management model of interventions appears to have a narrow understanding of individual coping in terms of how people actually cope and the number of stress management alternatives they can use. The field as a whole has underestimated the number of coping strategies individuals bring to bear on organizational stressors in managing their experience of distress. Finally, there exists a need to capture a more integrative, holistic perspective of stress interventions. A holistic approach would integrate the role of religion and spirituality with positive psychology, but in addition it would incorporate a medical perspective as well as including more nontraditional approaches to stress management. These forms of coping with stressful life events are more prevalent in the stress management literature than has been historically recognized.

Overemphasis on the Role of the Individual

Western stress management approaches reflect a highly individualistic perspective. They overemphasize the role of the individual in managing stressful events rather than taking a more critical view of the dominance of organizational control processes in the creation of stressors and the hindrance of effective stress management interventions. In the previous chapter's review of work stress and coping models, ten distinct personality and cognitive moderators were identified that have been investigated through numerous studies over a period of many years. Whether the focus is on the Type A personality or a person possessing the traits of optimism and hardiness, the attention remains on the individual's inherent characteristics in becoming susceptible to stress illnesses. The person is not viewed as only one variable in the stress–coping process. Stress occurs within a dynamic, complex environment with changing resource demands. Lazarus (1991, 1999) argues that the stress experience must be considered in transactional terms. It results from the transaction between the individual and the environment that must be considered as a single analytic unit instead of two causal entities. Each plays a role but only in an integrated fashion. This transactional model emphasizes the person and the environment developing a reciprocal, bidirectional relationship that evolves over time to form a new person–environment situation. This new person–environment event is then reappraised as to whether it is taxing or exceeding the resources of the person as stressful (Folkman & Lazarus, 1988). This process changes as the person and the environment's characteristics continually act and respond together as within some type of dance. Unfortunately, this perspective seems to become lost as many of the work stress management models are analyzed. Individuals remain the locus of activity without considering the overpowering role that the organization plays in the stress management process.

When you are up to your ears in alligators, it is hard to remember that your job was to drain the swamp. This popular expression from the southern part of the United States reminds us that if you want to solve your problems, you must focus on their root causes, not their symptoms. Unfortunately, most stress management intervention programs have not followed this advice well enough. Ideally, primary interventions offer the greatest potential impact for organizational health since they remove or reduce systemic stressors and their sources within an organization (Cartwright & Cooper, 2002). However, there has been less use of primary organizational interventions versus those of a secondary or tertiary nature (Cooper et al., 2001), and they have had very mixed outcomes in terms of their effectiveness when they were attempted (Briner & Reynolds, 1999; Ivancevich, Matteson, Freedmen, & Phillips, 1990; Newman & Beehr, 1979). The most common interventions are of the secondary type, where individual persons are the main target (Dewe, 1994). An analysis by Kahn and Byosiere (1992) can illustrate this point. In their review of 27 prevention and intervention studies in organizational stress, only two studies were primary organizational interventions. The rest were secondary interventions or some combination of secondary and tertiary approaches. Though there have been many more organizational level intervention studies since Kahn & Byosiere's original review, this pattern of primary, secondary, and tertiary stress management interventions still appears to hold (Semmer, 2011). Even when worksite interventions are implemented, the attention still remains on employees' appraisals of their work situation and their health instead of the work conditions, organizational practices, supervisory behavior, and peer relationships that may have contributed to those appraisals (Harenstam, 2008; Heaney, 2011).

What we can see within these stress intervention results is a strong preference in our society for order rather than fundamental change. As Burrell and Morgan (1979) demonstrated in their landmark review of Western sociological and organizational theories, most research theories have been dominated by the assumptions of "regulation" with an emphasis on stability, integration, and consensus rather than a view of the importance of "radical change" with an emphasis on transformation, structural conflict resolution, and emancipation. Organizations want persons and the environment to fit without challenging their basic structural premises or human resource philosophies that may create the sources of their employees' stress. This perspective is usually further reinforced by management attribution fallacies. These attributions ascribe the causes of strain to employees' individual traits or behavior rather than to the organization's processes. The responsibility for stress management then becomes a worker's problem instead of management's primary concern. The workers have the "deficiency" (e.g., a lack of resilience, effort, or training). Moreover, this perspective may be becoming even more entrenched with the fear of potential lawsuits by employees over who is legally responsible for the stress-related illnesses of employees in determining compensatory damages (Dewe, 1994).

One workplace case example clearly illustrates the pervasiveness of this type of approach and its unfortunate consequences. In one progressive, high-powered, nationally known law firm, the partners had hired a full-time trained nurse in their main office as a paralegal aide. Among her responsibilities, this person was expected to conduct stress management programs and teach CPR techniques as well as educate the firm's entire staff on how to use a heart defibrillator machine. These machines were placed on each floor of the firm's main office and in their other offices around the country. When one of the authors of this book asked this paralegal aide, who was a friend, why management did not begin to address the fundamental issues in their environment that created the need for this type of training and technology, such as reducing the unreasonable pace and pressure of 80 hour work weeks or hiring more legal personnel, this person just laughed. This story is not atypical of many high achievement–performance organizations in competitive environments, such as law, accounting, and high-technology firms. Intel, for example, during one severe recession, instituted the "125% Solution," where employees "voluntarily" worked 2 extra hours per day for 6 months without pay on top of their already demanding schedules (Malone, 1995). Interestingly, the person who reported this management tactic had recently suffered a near fatal heart attack. Instead of changing the work conditions, the individual decided it was best, given the circumstances, to learn how to cope with this type of environment to survive. Usually, these types of professional firms have an "Up or Out" philosophy where midlevel managers or professionals compete for a limited number of executive or partner positions. Rather than leaving, people stay due to their Western values of achievement and their desire for financial success. They are "hooked" in a game where they will invest considerable time and effort to reach their goal despite the heavy workloads and competitive pressures for survival within the company.

Even when an organization wishes to address its stressful environments, other factors emerge as barriers to prevent primary organizational intervention programs, such as participatory worksite health programs or team health circles. Examples of these participation barriers are the lack of top-management support, the fear of loss of power by frontline supervisors, an increased workload for supervisors, and a lack of resources and management support, as well as a history of labor-management distrust (Heaney, 2003, 2011). This labor distrust is not surprising given the number of barriers that exist. In fact in most participatory interventions, there occurs little movement in job control for the workers from management as the strategy originally anticipated (Egan, Bambra, Thomas, Petticrew, Whitehead, & Thomson, 2007; Semmer, 2011). These barriers to successful implementation illustrate the dominance of an organization philosophy of control, regulation, and stability. Because of this, these stress interventions will paradoxically increase the levels of worker and management stress. If any meaningful change is to take place in our workplace situations, there has to be a shift in the organization's fundamental philosophies to worker autonomy and participatory decision making for it to occur. When this happens and higher-level management commits itself to letting employees have a significant influence in decision making in their jobs, it works well (Heaney, 2003; Powell, 1995). As Conti, Angelis, Cooper, Faragher, and Gill (2006) discovered in their major study of 1,391 workers at 21 sites, stress levels were significantly related to the type of management decisions made regarding the design and operation of Lean Production (LP) systems. What they found was that management could have implemented a number of strategies to support workers at a more fundamental level. Unfortunately, this did not occur and it rarely happens in other situations since the focus by management appears to be more on maximizing employee production.

Whether the causes stem from an organizational control mind-set, value system, or emergent barriers, the reality exists for employees that most stressful situations at work are beyond their immediate control. It is critical that organizational executives realize this fact and understand its fundamental costs to the institution in terms of job burnout, absenteeism, employee hospitalizations, insurance costs, and organizational productivity (Jex & Crossley, 2005; Quillian-Wolever & Wolever, 2003; Warr, 2007). Concerted efforts by top management can ensure that primary interventions, such as sociotechnical, workload, and work-procedure interventions, would be highly successful in their impact and ultimately bottom-line results (Hurrell, 2005).

Moving From a Distress Perspective

In Selye's (1976) conceptualization of stress, the stress experience exists as two forms: eustress and distress. Eustress comprises the pleasant or curative experiences generated from challenging or positive appraisals of a situation by an individual. In contrast, distress consists of unpleasant or disease-producing responses based on taxing or threatening situations that exceed a person's perceived capacity to manage them. Up to this point in the evolution of the stress literature, the Western research has focused primarily on distress responses. There are several notable exceptions to this trend, such as the works of Quick et al. (1997), Edwards and Cooper (1988), Salovey, Rothman, Detweiler, and Steward (2000), Simmons (2000), Simmons and Nelson (2001), and Nelson and Simmons (2003, 2011). However, these studies pale in comparison with the vast number of works studying the negative or destructive effects of workplace stress.

To illustrate this problem, we will look at the role of humor—a positive emotional state—in coping and managing symptoms. Jokes and comedies are a staple of our daily lives. They are prevalent on television, websites, or nightclubs.

People come to work with their favorite current joke or send it by email to friends as part of a chain mail. Also, bestsellers, such as Norman Cousins's *Anatomy of an Illness* (1979) or the *Chicken Soup for the Soul* (Canfield, Hansen, & Bergman, 1993) series, have shown how people can laugh themselves back to health. However, when you look at several of the major historical handbooks on stress, you will rarely find the mention of humor (Barling et al., 2005; Cooper & Payne, 1988; Lazarus, 1999; Lazarus & Folkman, 1984; Monat & Lazarus, 1991; Monat, Lazarus, & Reevy, 2007). This is not to say that there are no studies of humor and stress management. Lefcourt (2001) points to a small body of emerging research literature that highlights humor's role in reappraising situations, signaling others of your humanness, obtaining social support, and creating an emotional–physical release. Other studies have also demonstrated humor's value in helping us manage our physical and emotional well-being (Kess, 2001; Kuiper, Martin, & Olinger, 1993; Martin, 2001; Nezu, Nezu, & Blissett, 1988). Given these numerous benefits, it is surprising that a larger body of work has not been created.

In our earlier review of Western stress research in the previous chapter, the moderating roles of individual optimism, hope, and positive affect were shown to positively affect one's satisfaction, well-being, and personal adjustment (Scheier & Carver, 1992; Snyder, Sympson, Ybasco, Borders, Babyak, & Higgins, 1996; Staw & Barsade, 1993). In addition, researchers have also postulated that the positive trait of "zest" plays a significant role in our lives. Zest reflects a person's stance toward life in terms of their anticipation, energy, and excitement (Peterson, Park, Hall, & Seligman, 2009). Individuals who possess this disposition have higher psychological well-being and ultimately improved job performance and reduced job turnover (Peterson et al., 2009; Wright & Bonett, 2007). Related to this personal attribute is the positive trait of "vigor." As conceptualized by Shirom (2003, 2007), vigor is seen to have three components: physical strength, emotional energy, and cognitive aliveness. Physical strength is determined by individuals' perception of their physical ability; the dimension of emotional energy centers on one's attitude toward expressing emotions, such as sympathy and empathy, to significant others; and cognitive aliveness reflects persons' emotional conception of cognitive alertness and mental agility. Individuals with high levels of vigor have in general increased positive experiences of work and the increased ability to recover more quickly over the course of several days (Shraga & Shirom, 2009; Sonnentag & Niessen, 2008). They have also been more proactive in influencing their work environment. Moreover, it appears that vigor creates positive spillover effects between individuals' workplace and home life. Besides these positive traits of zest and vigor, two recent studies further highlight the power of eustress and positive affect in moderating our stress levels. Davidson, Mostofsky, and Whang (2010) found in a 10-year prospective study of 1,739 adults that the individual predisposition of positive affect was associated with a lower risk of coronary heart disease (CHD). In a second study, Segerstrom and Sephton (2010) investigated the effect that optimistic expectancies had on 124 first-year law students' immune systems. This longitudinal study found that a positive relationship existed between measures of optimism and positive affect with cell-mediated immunity (CMI). Overall, these studies support that positive emotional states foster a stronger self-concept, which leads eventually to improved physical health (Nelson & Simmons, 2011; Salovey et al., 2000).

How eustress works can be seen in one exploratory qualitative field study of midlevel managers in a high-pressured banking regulatory environment (Segovis, 1990). Despite the extremely long hours, ridiculous pressure, numerous job changes, and intense daily challenges, participants felt alive, fulfilled, and excited. Based on the participants' self-reports from a series of longitudinal interviews, the researcher discovered that eustress consisted of four defining properties: purpose, challenge, control, and variety. Each of these dimensions combined to offer a person a sense of enjoyment and exhilaration. These feelings existed despite working around the clock and at times in 48-hour stretches.

In a eustress experience there is a feeling of accomplishment or a sense of purpose. What the work participants were doing had a high centrality to the organization. People saw their efforts in terms of a mission. In this particular study's circumstances, the middle managers were finding ways to catch bank owners and financial executives who were committing highly illegal savings and loan activities that threatened the safety and soundness of the financial industry and the very existence of the federal financial insurance fund. Second, these eustress situations contained a high level of challenge. They called forth considerable labors by the participants similar to pursuing a great quest. People recognized that they were overcoming overwhelming odds. The third distinguishing quality of eustress was a high sense of control. Participants in the study possessed a clear goal and the autonomy to pursue it. This situation allowed individuals the freedom to operate and make critical decisions; this is similar to what Karasek (1979) found in decision latitude research. Finally, there existed a high amount of variety in people's tasks. Their situations presented unique regulatory twists. People could let their imaginations run wild by creatively attacking the problems and generating their solutions.

This suggestive finding offers an analogous situation to the concept of job enrichment (Hackman, Oldham, Janson, & Purdy, 1975; Dunham, 1980). Though not exactly conceptually the same, the characteristics of purpose, challenge, autonomy, and variety create eustress's critical energizing psychological states of meaningfulness, belonging, manageability, responsibility, and knowledge of one's accomplishments. The job characteristics in this situation generated engagement and vigor, especially with high-growth need individuals. Rather than just surviving the pressured events, people transcended them to thrive on the challenges contained within them. In fact as the participants described their experiences, they appeared to be "savoring" their high-pressured situations one more time to make the positive, energizing feelings last. They enjoyed dwelling and reminiscing on them with satisfaction which in itself provided further eustress experiences (Peterson, 2006; Simmons & Nelson, 2007).

Nelson and Simmons (2003), as well as more recently Quick, Macik-Frey, and Cooper (2007), proposed that we begin to follow a holistic model of stress in future stress research. A holistic approach moves away from an exclusive focus on pathology or damage repair. We would begin looking at both eustress, where we savor an event, and distress, where we learn to mitigate the effects of workplace stressors. This follows the evolving movement of positive psychology or health psychology. Positive psychology is a major shift in our conceptualization of stress away from focusing on individuals' weaknesses and suffering and more on people's capacities to learn how to flourish within challenging environments (Nelson & Simmons, 2003; Seligman & Csikszentmihalyi, 2000). Macik-Frey, Quick, and Nelson (2007) state this case more strongly:

> First, the general notion of health in the traditional, medical sense will be obsolete. Issues such as absenteeism, burnout, strain, depression, cardiovascular disease, despair, and withdrawal will be replaced with engagement, purpose, thriving, hope, vigor, and optimism. (p. 832)

We will move from a deficit view of health as illness to a holistic view of a self-actualized person. Organizations would become places that actually design their systems to achieve this goal. From the authors' perspective, a healthy worker is a more productive worker. We know this is true from eustress and distress research outcomes. Now, it is clear that the time has come for a more inclusive, integrated approach based on the two sides of stress as Selye (1976) originally envisioned.

Limited Role of Religion and Spirituality

In reviewing the organizational stress literature, it is evident that little attention has been placed on the role of religion and spirituality. There have been some recent notable exceptions in health research (Plante & Sherman, 2001), workplace experiences (Ashmos & Duchon, 2000; Duchon & Plowman, 2005; Grant, O'Neil, & Stephens, 2004; Mitroff & Denton, 1999), and coping (Chen, 2006; Gall et al., 2005; Klaassen, McDonald, & James, 2006; Pargament, Poloma, & Tarakeshwar, 2001). This overall finding is not surprising considering the philosophical positivistic roots of Western science that permeate stress research with its emphasis on empirical research methods (Giddens, 1979; Kuhn, 1996; Popper, 2002) In addition, a traditional Western societal perspective places a greater emphasis on a secular worldview. Progress has become mainly defined more as material success rather than in spiritual or religious terms. One's work performance within a Western cultural context is seen as the driving force of one's existence. It emphasizes the values of earnings, recognition, career advancement, and challenge rather than values related to the quality of one's life or the role a community plays in determining one's sense of meaning (Hofstede, 2001; Hofstede & Hofstede, 2005). However, this viewpoint ignores the strong value many individuals place on religion and spirituality within Western society as well as in other cultures.

This spiritual yearning can be seen in the popular best-selling works of psychiatrist M. Scott Peck's *The Road Less Traveled* (1978), theologian Harold Kushner's *When Bad Things Happened to Good People* (1981), or New Age author Eckhart Tolle's *A New Earth* (2005). For many people within Western countries and especially in other parts of the world, it is one's spiritual life that has the greater value. According to the Gallup International Millennium Survey conducted in 1999, 87% of the respondents in 60 countries (57,000 adults) representing 1.2 billion citizens said that they belong to a religious denomination (Carballo, 1999). In North America and Western Europe, these figures are 91% and 88%, respectively. However, religion presents a complex picture. Religion, as defined as an organized belief system, is not the same as spirituality, an inner longing for meaning and community (Duchon & Plowman, 2005). As one can see in the declining attendances of traditional mainline Catholic and Protestant churches in the United States and Western Europe, only 32% worldwide reported attending religious services regularly—47% in North America and 20% in Western Europe. Yet, if you ask a different question—*How important is God in your life?*—you get a very different answer. Nearly 7 of 10 people report that though they belong to some religious faith their beliefs are not expressed through established institutional worship services but by creating a personal relationship with God. A total of 91% of the respondents in North America reported that they believe in a "personal God" or some sort of "spiritual life force." In Western Europe, the figure is less, 71%, but it is still substantial. This compares with 75% worldwide. Therefore, religious and spiritual beliefs are very important to people. They worship God or a spiritual life force through a variety of methods, including meditation and prayer, to maintain this very personal connection (Figure 4.1 and Table 4.2).

From what we know of stress from the research, strong religious and spiritual beliefs should provide individuals with a strong coping mechanism for buffering them from the effects of stress. First, regular meditation practice has led to

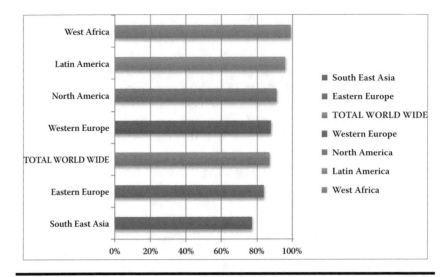

Figure 4.1 World-wide religious denomination membership. Based on a survey of 57,000 adults in 60 countries. (Adapted from Carballo, M., Gallup International Millennium Survey, 1999. Retrieved from http://www.gallup-international.com/ContentFiles/millennium15.asp.)

Table 4.2 North American Versus Western Europe Spiritual Beliefs Survey

Which of These Statements Comes Closest to Your Beliefs?			
Belief Statements	Total	North America	Western Europe
There is a personal God.	45%	62%	35%
There is some sort of spirit or life force.	30%	29%	36%
I don't really think there is any sort of spirit, God, or life force.	8%	2%	15%
I don't know what to think/NA.	17%	7%	15%

Source: Adapted from Carballo, M., Gallup International Millennium Survey, 1999. Retrieved from http://www.gallup-international.com/ContentFiles/millennium15.asp.

positive physical and psychological outcomes as well as positive behavior changes outside meditation (Freeman, 2001; Kabat-Zinn, 1990; Murphy, 1996; Quillian-Wolever & Wolever, 2003). Religious and spiritual beliefs also provide individuals with a strong sense of meaning and purpose in their lives (Bond, 2004; Tweed & Conway, 2006). This enables them to combat the uncertainty within a stressful environment, especially under adversity (Klaassen et al., 2006; Siegel & Schrimshaw, 2002). Spiritual coping brings them comfort through closeness to their God. It gives people a sense of perceived control and mastery to gain a sense of coherence of what is happening around them. This is true even though this perceived control may be illusory or vicarious in nature (Antonovsky, 1979, 1987; Rothbaum, Weisz, & Snyder, 1982; Taylor, 1983, 1989; Taylor & Brown, 1988, 1994; Taylor, Kemeny, Reed, Bower, & Gruenewald, 2000). It allows people to cognitively reframe events to regulate their emotions by improving their outlook and uplifting their moods (Beck, Rush, Shaw & Emery, 1979; Burns, 1989; Ellis & Harper, 1975; Friedman & Ulmer, 1984; Seligman, 1991). In addition, people's religious beliefs enable them to gain intimacy with others in a faith community as they share their struggles and triumphs (Klaassen et al., 2006). Finally, spiritual coping strategies can even help individuals transform their fundamental character, in terms of their personal visions, purpose, beliefs, and values, so they achieve a state of *metanoia*, that is, a turning around of one's viewpoint and self-concept in a completely new direction.

As an example of the role of spiritual beliefs in coping, it may be useful to contrast a Western perspective of stress with a Buddhist view of the human condition. Chen (2006) notes: "In the West, stress is originally an engineering concept referring to the external pressure exerted on some structure or material. Therefore, psychological stressors typically refer to events external to the individual. In contrast, Buddhism locates the primary source of stress and suffering within individuals—it is the psychological mechanism of craving and aversion and the ignorance about its workings that are responsible for most of our troubles and difficulties in life" (p. 75). Coping then in a Buddhist framework sees stress less as a reaction than an internal struggle that requires one to transform from within oneself in coping with what is stressing one. Suffering then requires mental discipline and enlightenment to attain the goals of compassion and serenity as seen through the teachings of the Four Noble Truths of Buddha.

A further illustration of this contrast to Western secularized coping approaches can be seen from the role of Hinduism within India in confronting a tragic illness. In a study of religious coping among 58 Indian family caregivers of cancer patients, it was found that their Hindu belief of accepting one's Karma and duty was a vital resource in facing their difficult burdens. The disease could be reframed as part of a "Benevolent God's plan" (i.e., God is in control) or an opportunity to affirm their spiritual connection to a larger force (Thombre,

Sherman, & Simonton, 2010). These results were also found in other studies of Indian cancer caregivers (Mehrotra & Sukumar, 2007) as well as with Western caregivers of children with disabilities (Newton & McIntosh, 2010).

This type of religious forbearance or acceptance is similar to the concept of *fatalistic voluntarism* found in Buddhism and Taoism. Fatalistic voluntarism is a life stance that reflects a harmonious attitude toward nature. A person will flow with the demands of nature and fate as one does in swimming with the current of a strong stream (Chui & Chan, 2007). This view of *fatalistic voluntarism,* though, possesses a strong distinctive quality in contrast to a Western perspective where a person passively accepts his or her fate (Lee, 1995). Instead of remaining just passive, a fatalistic voluntary-oriented individual will endure life's challenges to build their strengths to await future opportunities for action (Chui & Chan, 2007; Hsu, Chen, Wang, & Sun, 2008). This form of optimism offers people hope and confidence to proactively ride out life's vicissitudes for a better day.

As has been demonstrated in this section, religious and spiritual beliefs can be a valuable cognitive tool for many individuals in managing their psychological health and daily productivity. These results have even been substantiated through multiple cross-cultural and multifaith studies (Klaassen et al., 2006). If we are to build a more comprehensive understanding of stress and coping, we need to expand our use of coping measures that tap religious coping strategies in all types of organization stress research. This would be especially true of investigations of African and Asian populations (Ustey, Adams, & Bolden, 2000; Yeh, Arora, & Wu, 2006). It is hoped that in future reviews of stress and coping that there would even exist a category for the topic of religion in the "Subject Indexes" of many research books on organizational stress as well as more articles in the major academic management and organization journals. The formation of the "Management, Spirituality, and Religion Interest Group" in the Academy of Management was an important step in this direction.

THE ROLE OF RELIGION AND SPIRITUALITY IN MANAGING STRESS IN CHINA

In recent years, a growing number of young and well-educated Chinese have found Buddhism as a source of inner peace in China's evolving pressured pace. Even though Buddhism came to China 2,000 years ago, it has experienced an amazing revival among entrepreneurs and corporate professionals. He Jian, a 32-year-old meteorologist from Yunnan, typifies this resurgence. After studying the mainstream faiths of Catholicism, Islam, and Protestantism, as well as Mormonism, Jian discovered Buddhism as the right spiritual path to enlightenment for him. He found comfort in the fact that it does not attempt to convert or indoctrinate him. "It's more like a philosophy about living than a religion. It teaches you how to find inner peace in a frantic life," Jian said. "It spoke to me directly."

Currently, Buddhism has 100 million followers based on an estimate by Zhang Fenglei who serves as the director of the Religious Studies Centre at China's prestigious Renmin University. As the country's largest religion, it now attracts members from all segments of society and age groups. It is especially attractive to successful business people. Individuals find its emphasis on meditation and ethical living calming. It gives them a moral center to balance their busy lives. They especially appreciate its philosophy of infinite compassion as a source of spiritual nurturance for self-healing.

The central reason for Buddhism's growth stems from the Chinese's government's tolerance to religion in general. Based on an East China Normal University Poll, 31.4% of its mainland population, 16 years or older, indicated they were religious believers. The government leaders appear to value this growth as aiding their ability to govern. With the decline of a communist ideology and ethic as the ruling rationale and the welcoming of market capitalism, observers suggest that there has emerged a void in moral beliefs and societal standards. The current social unrest further highlights this need as perceived by government officials. They hope religion fills this void.

Adapted from Shi, C. T., *South China Morning Post,* Hong Kong Edition, 2007, p. 5.

Narrow Understanding of Coping

The very words *symptom management* used in our stress literature implicitly frames our attention as to how to handle our stress. We should focus on our symptoms rather than on what causes them. It is not surprising then that when we look at a review of organizational stress management interventions, only a small subset of them, *primary interventions*, are assumed to be effective in removing stressors. Examples of these approaches would be job redesign, employee decision-making participation, role restructuring, and organizational restructuring (Cooper et al., 2001). The *secondary* and *tertiary interventions* are focused on either mitigating individuals' reactions to the stressors or minimizing the damaging consequences of the stressors. Examples of these approaches include stress management training, wellness programs, counseling, massage therapy, and relaxation techniques (see Table 4.1). No one would argue that any of these programs would be helpful for bringing relief for our symptoms of distress and strain, even though they are temporary. For a long time, Japanese culture has encouraged office workers to partake of a hot soak in a tub followed by a dry sauna and then an *akasuri* treatment or *red rub*—a deep rubbing of the skin with a rough cloth (Tracey, 1995). However, these approaches, no matter how beneficial, are limited in their scope and effectiveness as individuals' primary coping approaches.

In reality we are much more proactive in reacting and handling stressful life events. For most individuals, there exists an active "flow of adaptive commerce" between the person and the environment to manage a situation (Lazarus & Folkman, 1984). This is a bidirectional, transactional process where each actor (person and environment) pushes and pulls against the other. It is more than just emotion-focused or problem-focused coping approaches as suggested in the stress literature. People engage in a wide variety of strategies to manage themselves and their environmental contexts. As Table 4.3 shows, individuals employed approximately 25 different types of coping based on the investigators' work with caregivers (Cignac & Gottlieb, 1997), metropolitan adults (Menaghan, 1982; Menaghan & Merves, 1984), and multiple population sources from Asia, Europe, Scandinavia, Middle East, South America, and the United States (Folkman & Lazarus, 1988). In stressful situations, many experienced managers, in effect, attempted to break down the stressful events into a series of "small wins" as conceptualized by Karl Weick (1984), where a small win is "… a concrete, complete, implemented outcome of moderate importance" (p. 11). Stressful overwhelming problems then become reframed as a series of "mere" problems. This helps lower one's arousal, which then allows information to be processed more readily. In essence, individuals can gain a level of control over what can be controlled and can begin to understand what cannot be changed. As an illustration of this process, one author observed in a set of exploratory longitudinal interviews of midlevel and senior managers that they used on average over seven coping strategies for each defined stressful event. There were some instances where people even implemented over 20 coping tactics (Segovis, 1990). In essence, managers were working to find ways to transform the situation into something that could be controlled, managed, or changed. Even when

Table 4.3 Coping Approaches and Strategies

Menaghan and Merves (1984)	Folkman and Lazarus (1988)	Cignac and Gottlieb (1997)
Direct Action	Accepting responsibility	Avoidance/escape
Helpless Resignation	Confrontive coping	Behavioral symptom management
Negotiation	Distancing	Emotional expression
Optimistic Comparisons	Escape–avoidance	Emotional inhibition
Restricted Expectations	Planful problem solving	Help seeking
Selective Ignoring	Positive reappraisals	Humor
	Seeking social support	Making meaning
	Self-controlling	Optimistic future expectancies
		Pessimistic future expectancies
		Positive framing
		Verbal symptom management
		Vigilance
		Wishful thinking

something appeared to be irresolvable, people continued to find ways to conserve their energies and maintain their equilibrium for the future. For example, in another study, Folkman, Moskowitz, Ozer, and Park (1997) discovered that caregivers of patients dying of AIDS worked to manage their feelings of hope as a coping tool to handle their protracted and severe chronic stress experiences. Despite these conditions, individuals emphasized a future of possibility and positive results that, in effect, eventually created hope for positive events to happen rather than waiting for them to happen.

This transformative vision of stress and the coping process stands in contrast to the stress management intervention model that traditional Western research has emphasized. In primary interventions, the focus is on what the organization's management will do rather than what employees in conjunction and response to these initiatives will creatively do. Within the secondary and tertiary interventions, the focal point is on a person's responses in a reactive protective manner. The emphasis is on the management of symptoms. These types of interventions do not consider the employee as an actor or participant in the creation of coping story. Even in more complex integrated frameworks, such as portrayed by Griffin and Clarke (2011) in Chapter 3, the model reflects only simple approach–avoidance or active–passive themes without capturing the actual potential transformative nature of coping in subtly shaping one's environment. Even Hobfoll's (1989) Conservation of Resource Model only highlights one aspect of this process, but not the actual "small wins" aspect of the coping process, as well as the variety of coping strategies available to individuals. Lazarus and Folkman in their seminal works (Lazarus, 1999; Lazarus & Folkman, 1984) strongly argued for this type of approach in stress-coping research by capturing this rich, dynamic process through longitudinal investigations; however, Western stress management intervention studies have yet to make significant strides in this area.

Toward a Transformational Model of Stress Management

To broaden our perspective of traditional Western stress management interventions using a more holistic approach, a Transformative Model of Stress Management is presented highlighting the key elements suggested by Quick et al. (2007) in building a healthy organization; it also incorporates the work of Taylor (1983, 1989) in coping with threatening life events and the considerable research done on control, social support, and symptom management (Figure 4.2). For each stress management intervention, whether it is at a primary, secondary, or tertiary level in its focus, we must consider its ability to provide individuals with increased mastery, meaning, social–community connections, positive self-regard, and symptom management.

Mastery

In stressful situations, individuals need to have a sense of personal control in managing their daily lives (Lazarus & Folkman, 1984; Taylor, 1983). This sense of control can reflect primary attempts to shape the environment or secondary efforts to fit in with the flow of the environment (Lazarus & Folkman, 1984; Rothbaum et al., 1982). Secondary approaches would manifest internal cognitive endeavors, such as illusory control strategies (aligning with powerful forces of chance or fate), vicarious control (associating with powerful others, such as God), and predictive control (forecasting adverse consequences of events to avoid disappointment). Religious-based coping exhibits this form of control. Organizational and psychological research streams, as reviewed in Chapter 3, have found that perceived control provides a main or additive effect in dealing with the negative

Figure 4.2   A Transformative Model of Stress Management.

impact on a person's well-being (Cooper et al., 2001; Jones & Fletcher, 1996). Other than social support, it is considered one of the most powerful tools management practitioners can use to limit the negative consequences of experienced stressful life and workplace demands (Cooper et al., 2001; Shirom, 2007). The importance of having a sense of mastery of one's environment can be seen in the burnout literature (Cherniss, 1980; Hobfoll & Freedy, 1993; Leiter & Maslach, 1988). Chronic stressors that cannot be mastered or combated create emotional exhaustion that leads to depersonalization, physical fatigue, cognitive deterioration, depression, helplessness, numerous physical ailments, and decreased job performance (Lee & Ashforth, 1996; Maslach & Pines, 1979; Pines, 1993). Karasek's (1979) work based on epidemiological research studies of different occupational groups further reinforces these findings; there is a significant positive relationship between the actual decision latitude or authority a person has on a job versus the psychological demands the job places upon the person and the resulting amount of individual psychological strain, depression, pill consumption, and exhaustion.

Meaning

Ryff and Singer (1998) postulate that *leading a life of purpose* is a core cultural dimension of human life, a critical feature of our ultimate mental health and physical health. We have a spiritual center that needs nourishment. Frankl's (2006) philosophical reflections as a concentration camp prisoner, as well as his psychotherapy work with other former concentration camp prisoners and survivors, underscored the significance for survival by finding one's purpose and meaning in whatever circumstances one finds oneself. In her work with cancer patients, Taylor (1983) discovered that finding meaning in a highly traumatic life event helped cancer patients survive longer and thrive with a better quality of life. As mentioned earlier in this chapter, Folkman et al. (1997) found similar results with AIDS patients. People in these types of situations needed to make attributions that helped them understand, predict, and control their environment. This is why spirituality and religion play such a critical role in helping people manage difficult or even tragic life circumstances. Religious practices, such as prayer and meditation, become important coping devices whether at home or at work. They allow us to find meaning in the event, which fosters a sense of control over one's future. In terms of organizations, people need to find a connection to meaningful work. We cannot conveniently separate our spirit or soul from how we make our living. Organized religion has long argued this claim in such works as Pope John XXIII's 1963 encyclical *Pacem in Terris* and social philosopher E. F. Schumacher's (1979) *Good Work*. Terkel (1985) also illustrated this point through his extensive interviews of workers who felt diminished and "dying" from within by the effects of overly specialized, mechanized jobs. Organizational research has captured this theme, as well, from the early works of Mary Parker Follett from the 1920s (Follett, 1924/1951) and Kornhauser's (1965) investigation in *Mental Health and the Industrial Worker*. Hackman and Oldham (1980) further stress this line of thought through their Job Characteristics Model. The experience of meaningfulness by an individual is a critical component in their theory to obtain job satisfaction and productivity. Therefore, managers need to find ways to nourish workers' spirits through meaningful work conditions (Duchon & Plowman, 2005).

Social–Community Connections

Along with control as a core dimension of being, social support has been found to be one of the most powerful stress management and coping approaches. The importance of this variable has been highlighted in Chapter 3. In fact, social support has been argued by some researchers as the most important buffer to stress (Cohen & Wills, 1985; Ornish, 1998). In research studies, it has consistently been shown to have main effects as well as buffering effects (Cooper et al., 2001; Kahn & Byosiere, 1992) in terms of a number of physical illnesses, mental health, and job performance outcomes (Kahn & Byosiere, 1992; Quick, 1998; Russell, Altmaier, & van Velzen, 1987; Spielberger, Vagg, & Wasala, 2003).

People who have been shown to have few social connections with others are more likely to die prematurely from a variety of physical diseases, such as heart attacks, strokes, substance abuse, some cancers, and suicide (Denollet, Pedersen, Vrints, & Conraads, 2006; Lepore, Evans, & Schneider, 1991; Quillian-Wolever & Wolever, 2003; Williams et al., 2007). Ryff and Singer (1998) broadened the concept of social support to include the "quality" of a person's social connections to others. This is a much deeper conceptualization and understanding of social support beyond how it has been historically conceived by Western organizational science research. Social support in this context is viewed more as "interpersonal" support. This approach implies a narrow one-way relationship between the supporter and the job incumbent. It does not fully see the person as part of an interacting social network of relationships and connections in community with one another. In this sense, you are part of a social system in which you find your identity, continuity, meaning, nurturance, sustenance, and emotional release (Hooker, 2003; Triandis, 1995). This community gives you a sense of security and attachment that sustains you to have the confidence to act individually or seek assistance when needed (Nelson & Simmons, 2011; Simmons, Gooty, Nelson, & Little, 2009). As researchers, we should be analyzing social support more as a phenomenon of social networks, community connections, family ties, and friendship in-groups in addition to organizational workplace interpersonal relationships. We need to see if one's total social community is life-giving or life-depleting. Is it a place of quality connections that nourish individuals in their time of need? Is it a place where people express genuine concern with the other's welfare (Dutton & Heaphy, 2003)?

Positive Self-Regard

Positive self-regard is considered a critical overarching dimension in Ryff and Singer's (1998) framework for individual positive human health and Quick et al.'s (2007) design of a healthy organization. In these authors' approaches, they include "mastery" as part of their conceptualization, but for our transformational model we have conceived it as two distinct but interacting constructs. If one is to be healthy, there must be a sense that one is a worthwhile human being. Mentally healthy individuals exhibit a sense of self-love, self-esteem, and self-acceptance. The individual personality moderators found in the stress literature that were reviewed in Chapter 3, such as hardiness, hope, optimism, self-efficacy, and vigor, have all been shown to have a positive moderating effect on the relationship between stressors and individual strain (Chang, 1998; Cooper et al., 2001; Luthans, Youssef, & Avolio, 2007; Maddi, 1998; Quellette, 1993; Schaubroeck & Merritt, 1997; Scheier & Carver, 1992; Shirom, 2007). The role positive self-regard plays in stress and coping can be seen especially in the work of Taylor and her associates in understanding how individuals' positive illusions maintain their mental health (Taylor, 1983; Taylor & Brown, 1994). In combating stressful life events, people must engage in self-enhancement strategies that nourish or restore their levels of self-esteem through devastating chronic illnesses and tragedies. Otherwise, their long-term prospects for health quickly declined.

Symptom Management

The focus of much of stress literature has been on symptom management, whether psychological and physiological (Lazarus & Folkman, 1984). How we manage our somatic health is critical. Otherwise, we will enter a negative spiraling loop with our health symptoms compounding the various situational problems we need to solve. Our struggles with specific stress illnesses, such as stomach ulcers or depression, will become an added burden as we confront the daily source of the stressors. As we lose critical health resources, we will struggle even more with our depleted energy base or attempt to conserve what we have through passive strategies (Hobfoll, 1989; Hobfoll & Shirom, 1993). Within organizational research, there is a dominance of secondary and tertiary symptom management interventions. Fortunately, a number of these interventions gives us a wide body of effective strategies to reduce and treat any harmful somatic and psychological effects, if only in a reactive fashion. Organizational wellness programs, though, have evolved as a secondary stress management intervention to be a valuable tool in this process (Bennett, Cook, & Pelletier, 2011). Of course as discussed earlier in this chapter, this depends on how seriously companies intend to integrate these practices into the fabric of their management systems to create a healthy workplace to assist workers' symptom management.

This transformative model of stress management then offers a comprehensive and dynamic framework to explain why specific interventions are more successful than others. The more a stress management strategy addresses the issues of mastery, meaning, social–community connections, positive self-regard, and symptom management, the more likely it will promote psychological and physical well-being. In essence, as each component of the model increases in use, it then builds an overall sense of coherence for individuals where their lives can be seen as comprehensible, manageable, and meaningful (Antonovsky, 1987, 1993). There exists a pervasive feeling that your life is predictable and you have the necessary resources to engage your environments' demands as challenges. At a macrolevel, this model also explains why many of the primary and secondary interventions developed by organizations have achieved mixed results. In many situations, management's leadership has not fully enabled workers to have the ability to master their situations, create meaningful work, or build a sense of community. It is then left to the employees to cope with this process with the numerous barriers placed in their way. Tertiary interventions remain then the only option at this point to treat the dysfunctional consequences of the distress. Fortunately, this negative scenario does not necessarily have to occur as frequently as it does. *Fortune* magazine's *Top 100 Companies To Work For* issue each year clearly illustrates along with the winners of such awards as the *Corporate Health and Productivity Management Awards* from the Institute for Health and Productivity Management in the United States, that worker health and company performance can be achieved together (see Bennett et al., 2011, for a review of these awards). These types of companies build healthy organizational climates incorporating many of the fundamental aspects suggested by the transformative model.

SYMPTOM MANAGEMENT—THE OLD WAYS BECOME NEW AGAIN

German executives are now going back to something old to combat their distress. Instead of traveling to a luxurious spa, chief executive officers (CEOs) have returned to monasteries in the idyllic countryside to rediscover their inner rhythms away from their hectic lives. Bursfelde Monastery, a 900-year-old Benedictine facility, for example, has opened its doors as a "spiritual center" as part of the Lutheran Church of Hanover.

Middle- and upper-level managers from a variety of large corporations leave their cell phones off when they enter Bursfelde Monastery to respect the atmosphere of silence maintained for self-examination, reflection, and prayer. At other monasteries, monks and nuns actually take the cell phones at the door at the start of the retreat. At Bursfelde, executives attend seminars having such titles as "Remaining True to Yourself in Processes of Change." People feel that these spiritual retreats strengthen them in making effective decisions, especially in guiding their careers. They also gain a perspective as to how their working lives have changed their personalities. According to one participant, Dettke from DaimlerChrysler (now Daimler AG), "Someone who sees his coworkers as nothing but cost factors or evaluates them based purely on performance cannot create a positive working environment. In the end, he too loses some of his humanity and suffers as a result." This attitudinal shift has now led to a permanent change at Volkswagen, according to Dettke. Employees now get together to spend an hour and a half every Friday for meditation.

Adapted from Wensierski, P., *Spiegel/Online,* 2007, pp. 1–4.

Future Directions

As the previous sections of this chapter have shown, we need to create a more comprehensive, holistic approach to stress and coping that integrates positive psychology and religious and spiritual perspectives if it is to be effective. In addition, this model needs to have a broader view of health as suggested by Ryff and Singer (1998). The separation of medicine and psychology has been an artificial construct based on a false mind–body dichotomy. This distinction has been increasingly challenged over the years through practitioner, medical, psychological, philosophical, sociological, and more recently organizational stress research literatures (Contrada, 1998; Cousins, 1979; Illich, 2010; Ito & Cacioppo, 1998; Moyers, 1993; Quick et al., 2007; Ryff & Singer, 1998). Quick and his associates even argued that the concept of health should be broadened to encompass ethical, as well as emotional and spiritual dimensions. As one step in creating this more holistic approach to stress management, organizational stress researchers need to recognize the Western nations' reliance on modern medical technology (i.e., the use of medicinal drugs) as a major coping and stress management tool.

One of the most prevalent methods for coping with effects of stress is pharmaceutical drugs. Of the top 10 most frequently used prescription drugs dispensed in 2006, for example, all but two deal with heart disease, hypertension, insomnia, depression, acid reflux, or ulcers (Verispan, 2006). All of these physical symptoms have been linked as responses to the distress experience (Cooper & Marshall, 1976; Ivancevich & Matteson, 1988; Karasek & Theorell, 1990; Landsbergis, Schnall, Belkic, Baker, Schwartz, & Pickering, 2003; Quick et al., 1997; Sapolsky, 1998). The preponderance of these drug expenditures is primarily in the Western nations of North America and Western Europe as well as the Asian countries of Japan and Korea. These countries' drug expenditures represent a range of 9.5% to 38.5% of their total health-care costs (OECD, 2006). Apparently, the highly industrialized lifestyle of these nations has come at a great cost, despite leading the world in total health-care expenditures as a percentage of their gross domestic product (GDP). In many ways, this significant use of drugs reflects our Western science and technology value orientation as described by Hooker (2003). First, this focus centers on the treatment of individuals while overlooking the reality that this is essentially an institutionally created issue. Second, pharmaceutical medical solutions reflect our underlining Western faith and belief in science to solve our problems. We assume that modern medical technology can cure, mitigate, or control a considerable portion of a person's ill health. Third, pill use underscores our "quick fix" mentality in a fast paced, pressured society. We feel that no matter what type of problem arises, we can engineer a ready-made solution even if it is only to mitigate the problem. Drug pills, whether for valid or questionable medicinal purposes, allow us to feel that we have dealt with the issue, when in reality we have not even begun the hard work of changing the way we live in confronting directly our stressors in a meaningful way.

Whether this type of medical approach has value in promoting health and longevity remains a research question (Fine & Peters, 2007). From the view of some medical practitioners it allows persons respite from their ailments and the ability to regulate their anxiety and stress symptoms to be functional; for other medical professionals, these types of drugs are overprescribed and cause the avoidance of analyzing fundamental lifestyle choices that need to occur to prevent these issues. Despite this debate, it is clear that prescription drugs play a significant part in a person's daily coping regimen for managing or regulating their stress experiences and symptoms. Historically, though, pill use has been viewed in the work stress literature primarily as a dependent outcome variable to indicate strain or perceived stress (Cooper et al., 2001; Karasek & Theorell, 1990; Quillian-Wolever & Wolever, 2003). Little attention appears to have been paid to the use of pharmacology in itself as a significant coping device for some people. When used appropriately and managed in conjunction with other coping approaches, pharmaceutical medical drugs can offer a valuable tool to mitigate future damage to one's body psyche and to eventually regain one's health and well-being. Future organizational research should create strong links to the medical literature by integrating pharmacotherapy approaches in their studies of individual coping. With this type of research, we can analyze its overall effectiveness and prevalence in combination with other tertiary stress management approaches. For example, in the revised "Ways of Coping" 67-item questionnaire from Lazarus and Folkman (1984), there *is no*t a listing of this as a possible coping tool. We need to know a person's cognitive appraisal of its use as to whether it is viewed in a positive or negative manner and how it has helped persons reduce their experience of stress longitudinally. This may present issues of self-report bias due to the negative connotations our society places on publicly revealing one's medical history. However, based on the evidence of extensive pharmaceutical drug use in Western or affluent populations to combat stress symptoms, researchers need to find ways to solve this problem.

In building a more holistic model and expanding our perspective of organizational stress management beyond its traditional conceptual boundaries, researchers need to also consider other approaches to coping with occupational stress based on alternative therapeutic modalities. Recently, attention has been brought to the role of animal-assisted therapy (AAT) for returning soldiers from Afghanistan and Iraq with posttraumatic stress disorder (PTSD; Thompson, 2010). Service animals (i.e., trained dogs) have offered comfort and healing to veterans reducing their isolation, crowd anxiety, and depression along with improving their desire to communicate with others. These results are not surprising given the long history of AAT research with a number of different patient populations (Barker, Knisely, McCain, & Best, 2005). Patients have reported decreases in fear after spending 15 minutes with a therapy dog (Barker, Pandurangi, & Best, 2003), decreases in anxiety in the presence of a fish aquarium (Barker, Rasmussen, & Best, 2003), and decreases in depression for patients with a companion bird (Jessen, Cardiello, & Baun, 1996). The positive psychological effects of dog ownership have been found to lead to improved long-term cardiovascular health, especially in single adults and young women (Cline, 2010; Friedmann, 2000; Friedmann, Thomas, Stein, & Kleiger, 2003). Overall, the therapeutic stream of research can be summarized as supporting the use of companion animals as offering a strong potential to reduce the onset and severity of the long-term effects of stress-related disorders.

Companies such as Covington Associates LLC, a specialty investment bank in Boston, Massachusetts, and Burgess Advertising and Marketing in Portland, Maine, along with many other companies have recognized for some time these potential benefits in the workplace. One in five companies allows companion animals in the workplace, according to one nationwide 2006 survey by the American Pet Products Manufacturers Association (Noblett, 2008). In that survey, it was reported that 73% of respondents felt that pets created a more productive work environment; 100% reported that employees were more relaxed because of the presence of an animal; 73% reported that they felt it increased creativity of employees; and 96% felt that it created an overall positive workplace. Wells and Perrine (2001a) substantiated this finding in a survey of 131 employees from 31 companies allowing pets in the workplace. People perceived that pets made for a more pleasant work environment and even helped relax customers into being more interactive. However, though most people enjoyed the benefits of pets, it should be noted not all workers and customers shared the same positive feelings about the presence of pets. Despite these overall promising positive survey statistics about companion animals in the workplace, there exists only a small number of peer-reviewed academic investigations of this phenomenon in contrast to the large number of therapeutic studies of ATT (Wilson & Barker, 2003). What does exist about workplace companion animals is mainly suggestive about their potential as a stress management tool. Barker et al. (2005) found that stress was reduced in 20 health-care professionals with as little as 5 minutes of interaction with a therapy dog. Somervill, Kruglikova, Robertson, Hanson, and MacLin (2008) also discovered that college students holding animals for 5 minutes could significantly decrease their diastolic blood pressure. In another study by Wells and Perrine (2001b) about the presence of pets in faculty offices, students in general perceived the office as more comfortable and the faculty member friendlier even when they just looked at slides of animals with the faculty member. Given these exploratory research investigations, it would be fruitful to expand this line of stress research. In addition to companion- or pet-assisted activities, organizational stress researchers should consider exploring the use of music as another nontraditional stress management tool in the workplace for employees. Music therapy research has found positive results for reducing anger (Jackson, 2010), burnout (Brooks, Bradt, Eyre, Hunt, & Dileo, 2010), pain (Bailey, 1986), and especially the risk factors associated with heart disease (Bradt & Dileo, 2009). Each of these lines of thinking, whether it concerns companion animals, music, religion, or pharmaceutical drugs, builds our vision of a holistic model in creating a richer understanding of stress management and coping in organizations. Moreover, researchers will capture more in their stress management models what many lay people already practice in managing the daily effects of their stressors at work or at home.

Conclusion

As discussed in this chapter, it is necessary to view the process of stress management as part of a much larger complex physical, psychological, and social system. The Transformational Model of Stress Management provides us a road map to accomplish this objective, especially in building healthy organizations. Western stress management interventions, as found in the chapters of the *Handbook of Workplace Stress* (Barling et al., 2005) and the *Handbook of Occupational Health Psychology* (Quick & Tetrick, 2003, 2010), offer a number of positive ways organizations and individuals can reduce the impact of stressors at work and in one's personal life. However, we need to think in a more holistic manner about the range of these interventions if we are to be more successful in our management of stressors and our ability to cope more fruitfully. Our research and interventions need to reflect a more interdisciplinary approach of medicine (physical), psychology (mental health), and religious (spiritual). This model allows researchers to gauge the level of effect a primary, secondary, or tertiary intervention has at different levels of mastery, meaning, social–community connections, positive self-regard, and symptom management in a particular situation. It suggests a more flexible approach for practitioners to determine how to approach any workplace stressor but in a much more comprehensive manner looking at both eustress and distress. Quick et al.'s (2007) *healthy organization* and Antonovsky's (1987, 1996) *salutogenic* model of health suggest several interesting insights into these possibilities and how they may emerge in the future. The focus would become more on how we create structures that enable workers to "flourish" at work with a sense of engagement and growth-building positive employee-support practices (Dutton, Roberts, & Bednar, 2011).

The Transformational Model of Stress Management also permits us to evaluate the effectiveness of traditional Western stress management in terms of their applicability on a global stage. From this perspective, Western models limit our understanding of the totality of stress management approaches and highlight the need for a broad framework that fits a highly competitive international economy. We cannot assume its basic assumptions are etic in their applicability to other nations. As we will see in the succeeding chapters, the concepts of mastery, meaning, social–community connections, positive self-regard, and symptom management will be interpreted differently based on the values, expectations, and norms of one's culture. Unfortunately, Western stress management research reflects a highly individualistic perspective when 80% of the world's population is collectivistic (Triandis, 1995) and account for 75% of the world's labor force (Houtman, Jettinghoff, & Cedillo, 2007). These societies determine the meaning of stressful events very differently from Western cultures (Wong & Wong, 2006). Religion plays a far more significant role in coping with events. The balance of work and home are intertwined and are not considered as distinct, separate entities as in many Western nations. Moreover, one's very identity and resources to cope with events depend on one's community within a collectivistic culture. The group itself participates in the coping process. Based on these cultural–societal variables, the design and selection of organizational and individual stress management interventions will be significantly different. Fortunately, the proposed Transformational Model of Stress Management offers a robust theoretical framework that anticipates these cross-cultural influences and allows us to interpret the model's conceptual components within a global context in a more integrative fashion. Chapter 5 deals with issues of work stress and coping from a non-Western perspective. In Chapter 6, we develop this perspective further by analyzing the experiences of various ethnic, cultural, national, and religious groups.

References

Antonovsky, A. (1979). *Health, stress, and coping.* San Francisco, CA: Jossey-Bass.

Antonovsky, A. (1987). *How people manage stress and stay well.* San Fransico, CA: Jossey-Bass Inc. Publishers.

Antonovsky, A. (1993). The structure and properties of the sense of coherence scale. *Social Science and Medicine, 36,* 725–733.

Antonovsky, A. (1996). The salutogenic models a theory to guide health promotion. *Health Promotion International, 11*, 11–18.

Argyris, C. (1993). *Knowledge for action.* San Francisco: Jossey-Bass.

Ashmos, D. P., & Duchon, D. (2000). Spirituality at work: A conceptualization and measure. *Journal of Management Inquiry, 9*, 134–145.

Aust, B., & Ducki, A. (2004). Comprehensive health promotion interventions at the workplace: Experiences with health circles in Germany. *Journal of Occupational Health Psychology, 9*, 258–270.

Bailey, L. M. (1986). Music therapy in pain management. *Journal of Pain and Symptom Management, 1*, 25–28.

Barker, S. B., Knisely, J. S., McCain, N. L., & Best, A. M. (2005). Measuring stress and immune responses in healthcare professionals following interaction with a therapy dog: A pilot study. *Psychological Reports, 96*, 713–729.

Barker, S. B., Pandurangi, A. K., & Best, A. M. (2003). Effects of animal-assisted therapy on patients' anxiety, fear, and depression before ECT. *Journal of ECT, 19*, 38–44.

Barker, S. B., Rasmussen, K. G., & Best, A. M. (2003). Effects of aquariums on eletroconvulsive therapy patients. *Anthrozoos, 16*, 229–240.

Barling, J., Kelloway, E. K., & Frone, M. R. (Eds.). (2005). *Handbook of work stress.* Thousand Oaks, CA: Sage Publications.

Beck, A., Rush, J., Shaw, B., & Emery, G. (1979). *Cognitive therapy of depression.* New York: Guilford Press.

Bennett, J. B., Cook, R. F., & Pelletier, K. R. (2011). An integral framework for organizational wellness: Core technology, practice models, and case studies. In J. C. Quick & L. E. Tetrick (Eds.), *Handbook of occupational health psychology, 2nd ed.* (pp. 95–118). Washington, DC: American Psychological Association.

Berridge, J., & Cooper, C. (1993). Stress and coping in U.S. organizations: The role of the Employee Assistance Programme. *Work and Stress, 7*, 89–102.

Bhagat, R. S., Steverson, P. K., & Segovis, J. C. (2007). International and cultural variations in employee assistance programmes: Implications for managerial health and effectiveness. *Journal of Management Studies, 44*, 229–249.

Bhagat, R. S., Steverson, P. K., & Segovis, J. C. (2008). Cultural variations in employee assistance programs in an era of globalization. In D. L.-R. Stone, *The influence of culture on human resource management processes and practices* (pp. 207–233). New York: Taylor & Francis.

Bond, M. H. (2004). Culture-level dimensions of social axioms and their correlates across 41 cultures. *Journal of Cross-Cultural Psychology, 35*, 548–570.

Bradt, J., & Dileo, C. (2009). Music for stress and anxiety reduction in coronary heart disease patients. In T. C. (Eds.), *Cochrane database of systematic reviews 2009, Issue 2*, Retrieved November 21, 2010, from http://ww.thecochranelibrary.com

Briner, R., & Reynolds, S. (1999). The costs, benefits and limitations of organizational level stress interventions. *Journal of Organizational Behavior, 20*, 647–664.

Brooks, D. M., Bradt, J., Eyre, L., Hunt, A., & Dileo, C. (2010). Creative approaches for reducing burnout in medical personnel. *The Arts in Psychotherapy, 37*, 255–263.

Burke, R. (1993). Organizational-level interventions to reduce occupational stressors. *Work and Stress, 7*, 77–87.

Burns, D. D. (1989). *The feeling good handbook.* New York: Plume.

Burrell, G., & Morgan, G. (1979). *Sociological paradigms and organizational analysis: Elements of the sociology of corporate life.* Portsmouth, NH: Heinemann Educational Books, Inc.

Canfield, J., Hansen, M. V., & Bergman, B. (1993). *Chicken Soup for the Soul: 101 stories to open the heart and rekindle the spirit.* Deerfield, FL: Heal Communications, Inc.

Carballo, M. (1999). *Gallup International Millennium Survey.* Retrieved November 15, 2010, from http://www.gallup-internationa.com: http://www.gallup-international.com/ContentFiles/millennium15.asp

Cartwright, S., & Cooper, C. (2002). *ASSET: An organizational stress screening tool, The management guide.* Manchester: RCI Ltd.

Cartwright, S., & Cooper, C. (2005). Individually targeted interventions. In E. K. J. Barling (Ed.), *Handbook of work stress* (pp. 607–622). Thousand Oaks, CA: Sage Publications, Inc.

Cecil, M. A., & Foreman, S. G. (1990). Effects of stress inoculation training and coworker support groups on teachers' stress. *Journal of School Psychology, 28,* 105–118.

Chang, E. (1998). Dispositional optimism and primary and secondary appraisal of a stressor: Controlling for confounding influences and relations to coping and psychological and physical adjustment. *Journal of Personality and Social Psychology, 74,* 1109–1120.

Chen, Y. (2006). Coping with suffering: The Buddhist perspective. In P. T. Wong & L. C. Wong (Eds.), *Handbook of multicultural perspectives on stress and coping* (pp. 73–89). New York: Springer.

Cherniss, C. (1980). *Professional burnout in human service organizations.* New York: Praeger.

Chui, W.Y.-Y., & Chan, S.W.-C. (2007). Stress and coping of Hong Kong: Chinese family members during a critical illness. *Journal of Clinical Nursing, (16),* 372–381.

Cignac, M. A. M., & Gottlieb, B. H. (1997). Changes in coping with chronic stress: The role of caregivers' appraisals of coping efficacy. In B. H. Gottlieb (Ed.), *Coping with chronic stress* (pp. 245–267). New York: Plenum.

Cline, K. M. (2010). Psychological effects of dog ownership: Role strain, role enhancement, and depression. *Journal of Social Psychology, 150,* 117–131.

Cohen, S., & Wills, T. A. (1985). Stress, social support, and the buffering hypothesis. *Psychological Bulletin, 90,* 310–357.

Conti, R., Angelis, J., Cooper, C., Faragher, B., & Gill, C. (2006). The effects of lean production on worker job stress. *International Journal of Operations & Production Management, 26,* 1013–1038.

Contrada, R. J. (1998). It is easier to accentuate the positive in the absence of physical disease. *Psychological Inquiry, 9,* 29–33.

Cooper, C., & Cartwright, S. (1994). Healthy mind; healthy organization: A proactive approach to occupational stress. *Human Relations, 47,* 455–471.

Cooper, C. L., Dewe, P. J., & O'Driscoll, M. P. (2001). *Organizational stress: A review and critique of theory, research, and applications.* Thousand Oaks, CA: Sage Publications, Inc.

Cooper, C. L., Dewe, P., & O'Driscoll, M. P. (2003). Employee assistance programs. In J. C. Quick & L. E. Tetrick (Eds.), *Handbook of occupational health psychology* (pp. 289–304). Washington, DC: American Psychological Association.

Cooper, C. L., Dewe, P. D., O'Driscoll, M. P. (2011). Employee assistance programs: Strengths, challenges, and future roles. In J. C. Quick & L. E. Tetrick (Eds.), *Handbook of occupational health psychology* (2nd ed., pp. 337–356). Washington, DC: American Psychological Association.

Cooper, C. L., & Marshall, J. (1976). Occupational sources of stress: A review of the literature relating to coronary heart disease and mental ill health. *Journal Occupational Psychology, 49*, 11–28.

Cooper, C. L., & Payne, R. (1988). *Causes, coping and consequences of stress at work.* Chichester: John Wiley & Sons.

Coping with stress. (2006, December 12). *China Daily* (North American ed.). Retrieved February 4, 2012, from http://proquest.umi.com/pqdweb?did=1177962441&sid= 1&Fmt=3&clientId=5046&RQT=309&VName=PQD

Cotton, J. L., Vollrath, D. A., Froggatt, K. L., Lengnick-Hall, M. L., & Jennings, K. R. (1988). Employee participation: Diverse forms and different outcomes. *Academy of Management Review, 13*, 8–22.

Cotton, S. J., Dollard, M. F., & de Jorge, J. (2003). *The Salvation Army officer well-being study: Final report time 2.* Adelaide, Salvation Army Southern Territory (Internal Report): Work and Stress Research Group.

Cousins, N. (1979). *Anatomy of an illness as perceived by the patient: Reflections on healing and regeneration.* New York: W.W. Norton & Co.

Davidson, K. W., Mostofsky, E., & Whang, W. (2010). Don't worry, be happy: Positive affect and reduced 10-year incident coronary heart disease: The Canadian Nova Scotia health survey. *European Heart Journal, 31,*1065–1070.

Denollet, J., Pedersen, S., Vrints, C., & Conraads, V. (2006). Usefulness of Type D personality in predicting five-year cardiac events above and beyond concurrent symptoms of stress in patients with coronary heart disease. *The American Journal of Cardiology, 97*, 970–973.

Dewe, P. (1994). EAPs and stress management: From theory to practice to comprehensiveness. *Personnel Review, 23*, 21–32.

Dollard, M. F., Le Blanc, P. M., & Cotton, S. J. (2008). Participatory action research as work stress intervention. In J. H. K. Naswall (Ed.), *The individual in the changing working life* (pp. 353–402). Cambridge: Cambridge University Press.

Duchon, D., & Plowman, D. A. (2005). Nurturing the spirit at work: Impact on work unit performance. *Leadership Quarterly, 16*, 807–833.

Dunham, R. B. (1980). The design of jobs. In L. L. Cummings & R. B. Dunham (Eds.), *Introduction to organizational behavior* (pp. 387–404). Homewood, IL: Richard D. Irwin.

Dutton, J. E., & Heaphy, E. D. (2003). The power of high-quality connections. In K. S. Cameron, R. E. Dutton, & R. E. Quinn (Eds.), *Positive organizational scholarship* (pp. 263–278). San Francisco: Berrett-Koehler Publishers, Inc.

Dutton, J. E., Roberts, L. M., & Bednar, J. (2011). Prosocial practices, positive identity, and flourishing at work. In S. I. Donaldson, M. Csikszentmihalyi, & J. Nakamura (Eds.), *Applied positive psychology: Improving everyday life, health, schools, work, and society* (pp. 155–170). New York: Psychology Press, Taylor & Francis Group.

Edwards, J. R., & Cooper, C. L. (1988). The impacts of positive psychological states on physical health: A review and theoretical framework. *Social Science & Medicine, 27,* 1447–1459.

Egan, M., Bambra, C., Thomas, S., Petticrew, M., Whitehead, M., & Thomson, H. (2007). The psychosocial and health effects of workplace reorganisation. 1. A systematic review of organisation-level interventions that aim to increase employee control. *Journal of Epidemiology and Community Health, 61,* 945–954.

Elkin, A., & Rosch, P. (1990). Promoting mental health at the workplace: The prevention side of stress management. *Occupational Medicine: State of the Art Review, 5,* 739–754.

Ellis, A., & Harper, R. (1975). *A new guide to rational living.* Englewood Cliffs, NJ: Prentice-Hall.

Fine, M., & Peters, J. W. (2007). *The nature of health: How America lost, and can regain, a basic human value.* Oxford, UK: Radcliffe Publishing Ltd.

Folkman, S., & Lazarus, R. S. (1988). *Manual for the Ways of Coping Questionnaire.* Palo Alto, CA: Mind Garden.

Folkman, S., Moskowitz, J. T., Ozer, E. M., & Park, C. L. (1997). Positive meaningful events and coping in the context of HIV/AIDS. In B. H. Gottlieb (Ed.), *Coping with chronic stress* (pp. 293–314). New York: Plenum.

Follett, M. P. (1924/1951). *Creative experience.* New York: Peter Brown, Inc.

Francis, M. E., & Pennebaker, J. W. (1992). Putting stress into words: The impact of writing on psychological, absentee, and self-reported emotional well-being measures. *American Journal of Health Promotion, 6,* 280–287.

Frankl, V. (2006). *Man's search for meaning.* Boston, MA: Beacon Press.

Freeman, L. W. (2001). Meditation. In L. W. Freeman & G. F. Lawlis (Eds.), *Mosby's complementary and alternative medicine: A research-based approach* (pp. 166–195). Saint Louis, MO: Mosby.

Friedman, M., & Ulmer, D. (1984). *Treating type A behavior and your heart.* New York: Fawcett Crest.

Friedmann, E. (2000). The animal–human bond: Health and wellness. In A. H. Fine (Ed.), *Handbook on animal assisted therapy: Theoretical foundations and guidelines for practice* (pp. 41–58). San Francisco, CA: Academic Press.

Friedmann, E., Thomas, S. A., Stein, P. K., & Kleiger, R. E. (2003). Relation between pet ownership and heart rate variability in patients with healed myocardial infarcts. *American Journal of Cardiology, 91,* 718–721.

Gall, T. L., Charbonneau, C., Clarke, N. H., Grant, K., Joseph, A., & Shouldice, L. (2005). Understanding the nature and role of spirituality in relation to coping and health: A conceptual framework. *Canadian Psychology, 46,* 88–104.

Ganster, D., Mayes, B., Sime, W., & Tharp, G. (1982). Managing occupational stress: A field experiment. *Journal of Applied Psychology, 67,* 533–542.

Gentleman, A. (2005, June 10). *In India, spirituality is going commercial.* Retrieved June 15, 2010 from http:// www.nytimes.com/2005/06/10/world/asia/10iht-india.html

Giddens, A. (1979). *Central problems in social theory: Action, structure, and contradiction in social analysis.* Berkley: University of California.

Grant, D., O'Neil, K., & Stephens, L. (2004). Spirituality in the workplace: New empirical directions in the study of the sacred. *Sociology of Religion, 65*, 265–283.

Griffin, M. A., & Clarke, S. (2011). Stress and well-being at work. In S. Zedeck (Ed.), *APA handbook of industrial and organizational psychology* (Vol. 3, pp. 359–397). Washington, DC: American Psychological Association.

Hackman, J. R., & Oldham, G. R. (1980). *Work design.* Reading, MA: Addison-Wesley.

Hackman, J. R., Oldham, G., Janson, R., & Purdy, K. (1975). A new strategy for job enrichment. *California Management Review*, 57–71.

Hackman, J. R., & Wageman, R. (1995). Total quality management: Empirical, conceptual, and practical issues. *Administrative Science Quarterly, 40*, 309–342.

Harenstam, A. (2008). Organizational approach to studies of job demands, control, and health. *Scandinavian Journal of Work, Environment and Health, Supplement, 6*, 144–149.

Heaney, C. (2003). Worksite health interventions. In J. C. Quick & L. E. Tetrick (Eds.), *Handbook of occupational health psychology* (pp. 305–324). Washington, DC: American Psychologist Association.

Heaney, C. A. (2011). Worksite health interventions: Targets for change and strategies for attaining them. In J. C. Quick & L. E. Tetrick (Eds.), *Handbook of occupational health psychology* (2nd ed., pp. 319–336). Washington, DC: American Psychological Association.

Hobfoll, S. (1989). Conservation of resources: A new attempt at conceptualizing stress. *American Psychologist, 44*, 513–524.

Hobfoll, S., & Freedy, J. (1993). Conservation of resources: A general stress theory applied to burnout. In W. Schaufeli, C. Maslach, & T. Marek (Eds.), *Professional burnout: Recent developments in theory and research* (pp. 115–129). Washington, DC: Taylor & Francis.

Hobfoll, S., & Shirom, A. (1993). Stress and burnout in the workplace. In R. Golembiewski (Ed.), *Handbook of organizational behavior* (pp. 41–60). New York: Marcel Dekker.

Hofstede, G. (2001). *Culture's consequences: Comparing values, behaviors, institutions and organizations* (2nd ed.). Thousand Oaks, CA: Sage.

Hofstede, G., & Hofstede, G. J. (2005). *Cultures and organizations: Software of the mind.* New York: McGraw-Hill.

Hooi, J. (2009, May 13). Short on bonuses and high on stress; Local professional among worst hit by cost cutting and overwork: survey. *The Business Times Singapore.*

Hooker, J. (2003). *Working across cultures.* Stanford, CA: Stanford University Press.

Houtman, I., Jettinghoff, K., & Cedillo, L. (2007). *Raising awareness of stress at work in developing countries: A modern hazard in a traditional working environment: Advice to employers and worker representatives,* (Protecting Workers' Health Series No. 6). Geneva, Switzerland: World Health Organization Press.

Hsu, W., Chen, M., Wang, T., & Sun, S. (2008). Coping strategies in Chinese social context. *Asian Journal of Social Psychology, 11*, 150–162.

Hurrell, J. J. (2005). Organizational stress intervention. In E. K. J. Barling, *Handbook of work stress* (pp. 623–645). Thousand Oaks, CA: Sage Publications, Inc.

Illich, I. (2010). *Limits to medicine.* London: Marion Boyars Publishers LTD.

Ito, T. A., & Cacioppo, J. T. (1998). Representations of the contours of positive human health. *Psychological Inquiry, 9*, 43–48.

Ivancevich, J. M., & Matteson, M. T. (1988). Promoting the individual's health and well-being. In C. L. Cooper & R. Payne (Eds.), *Causes, coping and consequences of stress at work* (pp. 267–299). Chichester, UK: John Wiley & Sons.

Ivancevich, J. M., Matteson, M. T., Freedman, S. M., & Phillips, J. S. (1990). Worksite stress management interventions. *American Psychologist, 45*, 252–261.

Jackson, N. A. (2010). Models of response to client anger in music therapy. *The Arts in Psychotherapy, 37*, 46–55.

Jessen, J., Cardiello, F., & Baun, M. M. (1996). Avian companionship in alleviation of depression, loneliness, and low morale of older adults in skilled rehabilitation units. *Psychological Reports, 78*, 339–348.

Jex, S. M., & Crossley, C. D. (2005). Organizational consequences. In J. Barling, E. K. Kelloway, & M. R. Frone (Eds.), *Handbook of work stress* (pp. 575–599). Thousand Oaks, CA: Sage.

John XXXIII. (1963, April 11). *Pacem terris (Peace on Earth): On establishing universal peace in truth, justice, charity and liberty.* Vatican City: Vatican Publishing House.

Jones, F., & Fletcher, B. C. (1996). Job control and health. In M. Schabracq, J. Winnubst, & C. Cooper (Eds.), *Handbook of work and health psychology* (pp. 33–50). New York: John Wiley.

Kabat-Zinn, J. (1990). *Full catastrophe living: Using the wisdom of your body and mind in everyday life.* New York: Delacorte.

Kahn, R. L., & Byosiere, P. (1992). Stress in organizations. In M. D. Dunnette & L. M. Hough (Eds.), *Handbook of industrial and organizational psychology* (2nd ed., Vol. 3, pp. 57–650). Palo Alto, CA: Consulting Psychologists.

Karasek, R. A. (1979). Job demands, job decision latitude, and mental strain: Implications for job redesign. *Administrative Science Quarterly, 24*, 285–311.

Karasek, R., & Theorell, T. (1990). *Healthy work: Stress, productivity, and the reconstruction of working life.* New York: Basic Books.

Kelloway, E. K., Hurrell, J. J., & Day, A. (2008). Workplace interventions for occupational stress. In J. H. K. Naswall (Ed.), *The individual in changing working life* (pp. 419–441). Cambridge: Cambridge University Press.

Kess, J. F. (2001). Review of humor: The psychology of living buoyantly. *Canadian Psychology, 42*, 232–234.

Klaassen, D. W., McDonald, M. J., & James, S. (2006). Advance in the study of religious and spiritual coping. In P. T. Wong & L. C. Wong (Eds.), *Handbook of multicultural perspectives on stress and coping* (pp. 105–132). New York: Springer.

Klein, K. J., Ralls, R. S., Smith-Major, V., & Douglas, C. (2000). Power and participation in the workplace. In J. Raooaoirt & E. Seidman (Eds.), *Handbook of community psychology* (pp. 273–295). New York: Kluwer Academic/Plenum.

Kompier, M. A. J., & Kristensen, T. S. (2000). Organizational work stress interventions in a theoretical, methodological and practical context. In J. Dunham (Ed.), *Stress in the workplace: Past, present, and future* (pp. 164–190). London: Whurr.

Kornhauser, A. (1965). *Mental health and the industrial worker.* New York: Wiley & Sons.

Kuhn, T. S. (1996). *The structure of scientific revolution,* (3rd ed.). Chicago: University of Chicago Press.

Kuiper, N. A., Martin, R. A., & Olinger, L. J. (1993). Coping humor, stress, and cognitive appraisals. *Canadian Journal of Behavioural Science, 25,* 81–96.

Kushner, H. S. (1981). *When bad things happen to good people.* New York: Avon Books.

LaFargue, M. (1994). *Tao and method: A reasoned approach to the Tao Te Ching.* New York: SUNY Press.

Landsbergis, P. A., Schnall, P. L., Belkic, K. L., Baker, D., Schwartz, J. E., & Pickering, T. G. (2003). The workplace and cardiovascular disease: Relevance and potential role for occupational health psychology. In J. C. Quick & L. E. Tetrick (Eds.), *Handbook of occupational health psychology* (pp. 265–287). Washington, DC: American Psychological Association.

Landsbergis, P. A., & Vivona-Vaughan, E. (1995). Evaluation of an occupational stress intervention in a public agency. *Journal of Organizational Behavior, 16,* 29–48.

Lawler, E. E. (1992). *The ultimate advantage: Creating the high involvement organization.* San Francisco: Jossey-Bass.

Lawrence, D. (2008, October 21). As stress grows, modern Chinese turn to western psychotherapy. *New York Times,* Retrieved from http://www.nytimes.com/2008/10/21/world/asia/21iht-letter.1.17130599.html

Lazarus, R. S. (1991). Psychological stress in the workplace. *Journal of Social Behavior and Personality, 6,* 1–13.

Lazarus, R. S. (1999). *Stress and emotion: A new synthesis.* New York: Springer Publishing Company.

Lazarus, R. S., & Folkman, S. (1984). *Stress, appraisal, and coping.* New York: Springer.

Lee, R. (1995). Cultural tradition and stress management in modern society learning from Hong Kong expereince. In T. Y. Lin, W. S. Tseng, & E. K. Yeh (Eds.), *Chinese societies and mental health* (pp. 40–55). Hong Kong: Oxford.

Lee, R., & Ashforth, B. (1996). A meta-analytic examination of the correlates of the three dimensions of job burnout. *Journal of Applied Psychology, 81,* 123–133.

Lefcourt, H. M. (2001). The humor solution. In C. R. Synder (Ed.), *Coping with stress: Effective people and processes* (pp. 68–92). Oxford: Oxford University Press.

Leiter, M., & Maslach, C. (1988). The impact of interpersonal environment on burnout and organizational commitment. *Journal of Organizational Behavior, 9,* 297–308.

Lepore, S., Evans, G., & Schneider, M. (1991). Dynamic role of social support in the link between chronic stress and psychological distress. *Journal of Personality and Social Psychology, 61,* 899–909.

Lilienfeld, S., Lynn, S. J., Ruscio, J., & Beyerstein, B. (2010). *50 great myths of popular psychology.* Chichester: Wiley-Blackwell.

Lourijsen, E., Houtman, I., Kompier, M., & Grudemann, R. (1999). The Netherlands: A hospital, "Healthy working for health." In M. Kompier & C. Cooper (Eds.), *Preventing stress, improving productivity. European case studies in the workplace* (pp. 86–120). London: Routledge.

Luthans, F., Youssef, C. M., & Avolio, B. J. (2007). *Psychological capital: Developing the human competitive edge.* Oxford, UK: Oxford University.

MacDonald, S., Lothian, S., & Wells, S. (1997). Evaluation of an employee assistance program at a transportation company. *Evaluation and Program Planning, 20,* 495–505.

MacDonald, S., Wells, S., Lothian, S., & Shain, M. (2000). Absenteeism and other workplace indicators of employee assistance program clients and matched controls. *Employee Assistance Quarterly, 15*, 41–57.

Macik-Frey, M., Quick, J. C., & Nelson, D. L. (2007). Advances in occupational health: From a stressful beginning to a positive future. *Journal of Management, 33*, 809–840.

Maddi, S. (1998). Hardiness in health and effectiveness. In H. S. Friedman (Ed.), *Encyclopedia of mental health* (Vol. 2, pp. 323–335). San Diego, CA: Academic Press.

Malone, M. B. (1995, October 30). Killer results without killing yourself. *US News and World Report*, 1–6.

Mamberto, C. (2007, August 13). Theory & practice: Companies aim to combat job-related stress: At Glaxo, program uses teams as part of effort to improve workplace. *Wall Street Journal, Eastern Ed.*, p. B6.

Martin, R. A. (2001). Humor, laughter, and physical health: Methodological issues and research findings. *Psychological Bulletin, 127*, 504–519.

Maslach, C., & Pines, A. (1979). Burnout, the loss of human caring. In A. M. Pines & C. Maslach (Eds.), *Experiencing social psychology*. New York: Random House.

Mattimore, P. (2010, June 1). *A bad idea to combat stress*. Retrieved June 22, 2010, from http://www.chinadaily.com.cn: http://www.chinadaily.com.cn/opinion/2010-06/01/content_9916437.htm

Mehrotra, S., & Sukumar, P. (2007). Sources of strength perceived by females caring for relatives diagnosed with cancer: An exploratory study from India. *Supportive Care in Cancer, 15*, 1357–1366.

Menaghan, E. (1982). Measuring coping effectiveness: A panel analysis of marital problems and coping efforts. *Journal of Health and Social Behavior, 23*, 220–234.

Menaghan, E. G., & Merves, E. S. (1984). Coping with occupational problems: The limits of individual efforts. *Journal of Health and Social Behavior, 25*, 406–423.

Mikkelsen, A., Saksvik, P., O. & Landsbergis, P. (2000). The impact of a participatory organizational intervention on job stress in community health care institutions. *Work & Stress, 14*, 156–170.

Mitroff, I. I., & Denton, E. A. (1999). *A spiritual audit of corporate America: A hard look at spirituality, religion, and values in the workplace*. San Francisco, CA: Jossey-Bass.

Monat, A., & Lazarus, R. S. (1991). *Stress and coping: An anthology, (*3rd ed). New York: Columbia University Press.

Monat, A., Lazarus, R. S., & Reevy, G. (2007). *The Praeger handbook on stress and coping* (Vol. 1.). Westport, CT: Praeger.

Morgeson, F. P., & Champion, M. A. (2003). Work design. In W. C. Borman, D. R. Ilgen, & R. Klimoski (Eds.), *Handbook of psychology: Vol. 12. Industrial and organizational psychology* (pp. 423–452). Hoboken, NJ: Wiley.

Moyers, B. (1993). *Healing and the mind*. New York: Doubleday.

Munz, D. C., Kohler, J. M., & Greenberg, C. I. (2001). Effectiveness of a comprehensive worksite stress management program: Combining organizational and individual interventions. *International Journal of Stress Management, 8*, 49–62.

Murphy, L. R. (1996). Stress management in work settings: A critical review of the health effects. *American Journal Health Promotion, 11*, 112–135.

Nelson, D. L., & Simmons, B. L. (2003). Health psychology and work stress: A more positive approach. In J. C. Quick & L. E. Tetrick (Eds.), *Handbook of occupational health psychology* (pp. 97–119). Washington, DC: American Psychological Association.

Nelson, D. L., & Simmons, B. L. (2011). Savoring eustress while coping with distress: The holistic model of stress. In J. C. Quick & L. E. Tetrick (Eds.), *Handbook of occupational health psychology* (2nd ed., pp. 55–74). Washington, DC: American Psychological Association.

Newman, J. E., & Beehr, T. A. (1979). Personal and organizational strategies for handling job stress: A review of research and opinion. *Personnel Psychology, 32*, 1–43.

Newton, A. T., & McIntosh, D. N. (2010). Specific religious beliefs in a cognitive appraisal model of stress and coping. *International Journal for the Psychology of Religion, 20*, 39–58.

Nezu, A. M., Nezu, C. M., & Blissett, S. E. (1988). Sense of humor as a moderator of the relation between stressful events and psychological distress: A prospective analysis. *Journal of Personality and Social Psychology, 54*, 520–525.

Noblett, J. (2008, April 14). Going to the dogs: Pooch-friendly office can be big perk or big nuisance. *Boston Business Journal*, Retrieved November 20, 2010, from http://www.bizjournals.com/boston/stories/2008/04/14/story1.html

Organization for Economic Cooperation and Development (2006). *OECD Health Data 2006.* Paris, France: OECD.

Ornish, D. (1998). *Love and survival: The scientific basis for the healing power of intimacy.* New York: Harper Collins.

Pargament, K. I., Poloma, M. M., & Tarakeshwar, N. (2001). Methods of coping from the religions of the world: The bar mitzvah, karma, and spiritual healing. In C. R. Snyder, *Coping with stress: Effective people and processes* (pp. 259–284). New York: Oxford University Press.

Peck, M. S. (1978). *The road less traveled: A new psychology of love, traditional values and spiritual growth.* New York: Touchstone.

Pennebaker, J. W. (1993). Putting stress into works: Health, linguistic, and therapeutic implications. *Behaviour Research and Therapy, 31*, 539–548.

Pennebaker, J. W. (1997). *Opening up: The healing power of expressing emotions.* New York: Guilford Press.

Peterson, C. (2006). *A primer in positive psychology.* New York: Oxford University Press.

Peterson, C., Park, N., Hall, N., & Seligman, M. E. P. (2009). Zest and work. *Journal of Occupational Behavior, 30*, 161–172.

Pierce, J., & Newstron, J. (1983). The design of flexible work schedules and employee responses: Relationships and processes. *Journal of Occupational Behaviour, 4*, 247–262.

Pines, A. M. (1993). Burnout. In E. L. Goldberger & S. Breznitz, *Handbook of stress: Theoretical and clinical aspects* (2nd ed., pp. 386–402). New York: Free Press.

Plante, T. G., & Sherman, A. C. (2001). Research on faith and health: New approaches to old questions. In T. G. Plante & A. C. Sherman (Eds.), *Faith and health: Psychological perspectives* (pp. 1–12). New York: Guilford Press.

Popper, K. (2002). *The logic of scientific discovery* (2nd ed.). New York: Routledge.

Powell, T. (1995). Total quality management as competitive advantage: A review and empirical study. *Strategic Management Journal, 16*, 15–37.

Quellette, S. C. (1993). Inquiries into hardiness. In L. Goldberger & S. Breznitz. (Eds.), *Handbook of stress: Theoretical and clinical aspects* (pp. 77–100). New York: Free Press.

Quick, J. C. (1979). Dyadic goal setting and role stress: A field study. *Academy of Management Journal, 2,* 241–252.

Quick, J. C. (1998). Introduction to the measurement of stress at work. *Journal of Occupational Health Psychology, 3,* 291–292.

Quick, J. C., Macik-Frey, M., & Cooper, C. (2007). Guest editors introduction: Managerial dimensions of occupational health: The healthy leader at work. *Journal of Management Studies, 44,* 189–205.

Quick, J. D., Quick, J. C., & Nelson, D. (1998). The theory of preventive stress management in organizations. In C. L. Cooper, (Ed.). *Theories of organizational stress* (pp. 246–268). Oxford: Oxford University Press.

Quick, J. C., Quick, J. D., Nelson, D. L., & Hurrell, J. J., Jr. (1997). *Preventative stress management in organizations.* Washington, DC: American Psychological Association.

Quick, J. C., & Tetrick, L. E. (Eds.). (2010). *Handbook of occupational health psychology,* 2nd ed. Washington, DC: American Psychological Association.

Quillian-Wolever, R. E., & Wolever, M. E. (2003). Stress management at work. In J. C. Quick & L. E. Tetrick (Eds.), *Handbook of occupational health psychology* (pp. 355–375). Washington, DC: American Psychological Association.

Richardson, K. M., & Rothstein, H. R. (2008). Effects of occupational stress management intervention programs: A meta-analysis. *Journal of Occupational Health Psychology, 13,* 69–93.

Rothbaum, F., Weisz, J. R., & Snyder, S. S. (1982). Changing the world and changing the self: A two-process model of perceived control. *Journal of Personality and Social Psychology, 42,* 5–37.

Russell, D., Altmaier, E., & Van Velzen, D. (1987). Job-related stress, social support, and burnout among classroom teachers. *Journal of Applied Psychology, 72,* 269–274.

Ryff, C. D., & Singer, B. (1998). The contours of positive human health. *Psychological Inquiry, 9,* 1–28.

Salovey, P., Rothman, A. J., Detweiler, J. B., & Steward, W. T. (2000). Emotional states and physical health. *American Psychologist, 55,* 110–121.

Sapolsky, R. M. (1998). *Why zebras don't get ulcers: An updated guide to stress, stress-related diseases, and coping.* New York: W. H. Freemand and Company.

Schaubroeck, J., & Merritt, D. E. (1997). Divergent effects of job control on coping with work stressors: The key role of self-efficacy. *Academy of Management, 40,* 738–754.

Scheier, M., & Carver, C. (1992). Effects of optimism on psychological and physical well-being: Theoretical overview and empirical update. *Cognitive Therapy and Research, 16,* 201–228.

Schumacher, E. F. (1979). *Good work.* New York: Harper & Row.

Schweiger, D., & DeNisi, A. (1991). Communication with employees following a merger: A longitudinal field experiment. *Academy of Management Journal, 34,* 110–135.

Segerstrom, S. C., & Sephton, S. E. (2010). Optimistic expectancies and cell-mediated immunity: The role of positive affect. *Psychological Science, 21,* 448–455.

Segovis, J. C. (1990). An investigation into the structure of work related coping: A grounded theory approach. Unpublished doctoral dissertation, University of Texas at Dallas.

Seligman, M. (1991). *Learned optimism.* New York: Alfred A. Knopf.

Seligman, M. E. P., & Csikszentmihalyi, M. (2000). Positive psychology. *American Psychologist, 55,* 5–14.

Selye, H. (1976). *Stress in health and disease.* Reading, MA: Butterworths, Inc.

Semmer, N. K. (2003). Job stress interventions and organization of work. In J. C. Quick & L. E. Tetrick (Eds.), *Handbook of occupational health psychology (2nd ed.,* pp. 325–353). Washington, DC: American Psychological Association.

Semmer, N. K. (2011). Job stress interventions and organization at work. In J. C. Quick & L. E. Tetrick (Eds.), *Handbook of occupational health psychology* (2nd ed., pp. 299–318). Washington, DC: American Psychological Association.

Shi, C. T. (2007, April 7). Buddhist reawakening answers new realities, Younger generations see a path to inner peace while political leaders see its role in a harmonious society. *South China Morning Post, Hong Kong Edition,* p. 5.

Shirom, A. (2003). Feeling vigorous at work? The construct of vigor and the study of positive affect in organizations. In D. Ganster & P. L. Perrewé (Eds.), *Research in organizational stress and well-being* (Vol. 3, pp. 135–165). Greenwich, CT: JAI Press.

Shirom, A. (2007). Explaining vigor: on the antecedents and consequences of vigor as a positive affect at work. In D. L. Nelson & Cary L. Cooper (Eds.), *Positive organizational behavior: Accentuating the positive at work* (pp. 86–100). Thousand Oaks, CA: Sage Publications, Inc.

Shraga, O., & Shirom, A. (2009). A qualitative investigation into the construct validity of vigor and its antecedents. *Human Relations, 62,* 271–279.

Siegel, K., & Schrimshaw, E. W. (2002). The perceived benefits of religious and spiritual coping among older adults living with HIV/AIDS. *Journal of Scientific Study of Religion, 41,* 91–102.

Simmons, B. L. (2000). Eustress at work: Accentuating the positive. Unpublished doctoral dissertation, Oklahoma State University, Stillwater.

Simmons, B. L., Gooty, J., Nelson, D. L., & Little, L. M. (2009). Secure attachments: Implications for trust, hope, burnout, and performance. *Journal of Organizational Behavior, 30,* 233–247.

Simmons, B. L., & Nelson, D. L. (2001). Eustress at work: The relationship between hope and health in hospital nurses. *Health Care Management Review, 26,* 7–18.

Simmons, B. L., & Nelson, D. L. (2007). Eustress at work: The relationship between hope and health in hospital nurses. *Health Care Management Review, 26,* 7–18.

Snyder, C. R., Sympson, S. C., Ybasco, F. C., Borders, T. F., Babyak, M. A., & Higgins, R. L. (1996). Development and validation of the State Hope Scale. *Journal of Personality and Social Psychology, 70,* 321–335.

Somervill, J. W., Kruglikova, Y. A., Robertson, R. L., Hanson, L. M., & MacLin, O. H. (2008). Physiological responses by college students to a dog and a cat: Implications for pet therapy. *North American Journal of Psychology, 10,* 519–528.

Sonnentag, S., & Niessen, C. (2008). Staying vigorous until work is over: The role of trait vigour, day-specific work experiences and recovery. *Journal of Occupational and Organizational Psychology, 81,* 435–458.

Spector, P. E. (1997). *Job satisfaction: Application, assessment, causes and consequence.* London: Sage.

Spector, P. E., Cooper, C. L., Sanchez, J. I., Sparks, K., Bernin, P., Bussing, A., et al. (2002). A twenty-four nation/providence study of work study of work locus of control, well-being, and individualism: How generalizable are western work findings. *Academy of Management Review, 45*(2), 453–66.

Spielberger, C., Vagg, P. R., & Wasala, C. F. (2003). Occupational stress: Job pressures and lack of support. In J. C. Quick (Ed.), *Handbook of occupational health psychology* (pp. 185–200). Washington, DC: American Psychological Association.

Staw, B. M., & Barsade, S. G. (1993). Affect and managerial performance: A test of the sadder-but-wiser vs. happier-and-smarter hypothesis. *Administrative Science Quarterly, 38,* 304–331.

Taylor, S. E. (1983). Adjustment to threatening events: A theory of cognitive adaptation. *American Psychologist, 38,* 1161–1173.

Taylor, S. E. (1989). *Positive illusions: Creative self-deception and the healthy mind.* New York: Basic Books.

Taylor, S. E., & Brown, J. D. (1988). Illusion and well-being: A social psychological perspective on mental health. *Psychological Bulletin, 110,* 193–210.

Taylor, S. E., & Brown, J. D. (1994). Positive illusions and well-being revisited: Separating fact from fiction. *Psychological Bulletin, 116,* 21–27.

Taylor, S. E., Kemeny, M. E., Reed, G. M., Bower, J. E., & Gruenewald, T. L. (2000). Psychological resources, postive illusions, and health. *American Psychologist, 55,* 99–109.

Terkel, S. (1985). *Working.* New York: Ballantine.

Tetrick, L. E., & Quick, J. C. (2003). Prevention at work: Public health in occupational settings. In J. Quick & L. E. Tetrick (Eds.), *Handbook of occupational health psychology* (pp. 3–17). Washington, DC: American Psychological Assocation.

Thombre, A., Sherman, A. C., & Simonton, S. (2010). Religious coping and post-traumatic growth among family caregivers of cancer patients in India. *Journal of Psychosocial Oncology, 28,* 173–188.

Thompson, M. (2010, November 22). Bringing dogs to heal. *Time,* pp. 54–57.

Tolle, E. (2005). *A new earth: Awakening to your life's purpose.* New York: Penguin Group.

Tracey, D. (1995, April 21). *Japan's imported stress relief.* Retrieved June 21, 2010, from http://nytimes.com/1995/04/21/style/21iht-fmass.html?emc=eta1

Triandis, H. C. (1995). *Individualism and collectivism.* Boulder, CO: Westview Press.

Tweed, R. G., & Conway, L. G. (2006). Coping strategies and culturally influenced beliefs about the world. In P. T. Wong & L. C. Wong (Ed.), *Handbook of multicultural perspectives on stress and coping* (pp. 133–153). New York: Springer.

Ustey, S. O., Adams, E. P., & Bolden, M. (2000). Development and initial validation of the Africultural coping systems inventory. *Journal of Black Psychology, 26,* 194–215.

van der Klink, J. J. L., Blonk, R. W. B., Schene, A. H., & van Dijk, F. J. H. (2001). The benefits of interventions for work-related stress. *American Journal of Public Health, 91,* 270–276.

Verispan, V. (2006). *RxList—The Internet drug index.* Retrieved March 11, 2012 from Web MD LLC, http://www.rxlist.com/script/main/art.asp?articlekey=79437.

Wall, T., & Clegg, C. (1981). A longitudinal study of work group design. *Journal of Occupational Behaviour, 2,* 31–49.

Warr, P. (1987). *Work, unemployment and mental health.* New York: Oxford University Press.

Warr, P. (2007). *Work, happiness, and unhappiness.* Mahwah, NJ: Erlbaum.

Weick, K. E. (1984). Small wins: Redefining the scale of social problems. *American Psychologist, 39,* 40–49.

Wells, M., & Perrine, R. (2001a). Critters in the cube farm: Perceived psychological and organizational effects of pets in the workplace. *Journal of Occupational Health Psychology, 6,* 81–87.

Wells, M., & Perrine, R. (2001b). Pets go college: The influence of pets on students' perceptions of faculty and their offices. *Anthrozoos, 14,* 161–168.

Wensierski, P. (2007, August 16). In search of the quiet life: Stressed executives swap boardrooms for monastic cells. *Spiegel/Online,* pp. 1–4.

Whatmore, L., Cartwright, S., & Cooper, C. (1999). United Kingdom: Evaluation of a stress management programme in the public sector. In N. Kompier & C. Cooper (Eds.), *Preventing stress, improving productivity: European case studies in the workplace* (pp. 149–174). London: Routledge.

Williams, L., O'Connor, R., Howard, S., Hughes, B., Johnston, D., Hay, J., et al. (2007). Type-D personality mechanisms of effect: The role of health-related behavior and social support. *Journal of Psychosomatic Research, 64,* 63–69.

Wilson, C. C., & Barker, S. B. (2003). Challenges in designing human–animal interaction research. *American Behavioral Scientist, 47,* 16–28.

Wong, P. T. P., and Wong, L. C. J. (2006). *Handbook of multicultural perspectives on stress and coping.* New York: Springer.

Wright, T. A., & Bonett, D. G. (2007). Job satisfaction and psychological well-being as nonadditive predictors of workplace turnover. *Journal of Management, 33,* 141–160.

Yeh, C. J., Arora, A. K., & Wu, K. A. (2006). A new theoretical model of collectivistic coping. In P. T. Wong & L. C. Wong (Eds.). *Handbook of multicultural perspectives on stress and coping* (pp. 55–72). New York: Springer.

Chapter 5

Work Stress and Coping: Non-Western Perspectives

As discussed in earlier chapters, the human and financial costs of work stress and psychological strains can be substantial (DeFrank & Ivancevich, 1998; Macik-Frey, Quick, & Nelson, 2007; Murphy, 1999). The estimated cost due to work stress for U.S. businesses varied between $50 billion and $300 billion in lost productivity and health-care costs between 1990 and 2001 depending on the nature of the industry. These high costs are typically borne by organizations undergoing rapid economic changes due to continuous pressures from rapid technological advances and global competition.

Organizational stress also happens to be the second most reported reason for work-related health problems in the European Union (EU), affecting over 22%. A report published by European Agency for Health and Safety at Work (2009) notes that the number of people suffering from work stress–related situations is likely to increase. The changing world of work is making increased demands on workers; that is, downsizing, outsourcing, and greater need for flexibility in occupational skills and abilities are stressful for young and old workers alike. The situation in Australia is not much better. The latest data on workplace stress and the cost of work place stress in the Australian economy is over 14.81 billion (Australian) annually.

In this chapter, we discuss the relevance of non-Western perspectives in understanding the process of work stress and coping. This is not to say that Western models for examining processes of work stress and coping are not valid, but they have limitations in their applicability to non-Western contexts. National and cultural variations not only influence the appraisal of stress and how individuals and work groups might respond to stressful situations at work but also affect the acceptability of various treatment methods that are available in occupational health psychology and medicine. For example, overt expression of emotional distress is considered more unacceptable in some collectivistic countries such as Japan, Korea, and China than in more individualistic cultures such as the United States, Canada, the United Kingdom, and Australia (Mesquita, Frijda, & Scherer, 1997). This finding suggests that psychosomatic symptoms of distress need to be assessed more frequently in many Asian as opposed to Western cultures.

As discussed extensively in Chapter 2, the workplace of the twenty-first century is remarkably different from previous eras. This is true not only in the advanced globalized countries but also in the developing countries and the emerging economies (e.g., BRIC countries and others). Organizational researchers are beginning to pay attention to the issues associated with the emergence of a modern workplace (e.g., dual-career families, much larger participation of women in various globalizing countries, rapid technological changes, challenges of an aging workforce, and concerns regarding health worldwide). However, there has not been a great deal of systematic research into the nature and consequences of work stress on individually and organizational valued outcomes in countries that are largely non-Western and collectivistic in their orientation.

Cooper's (1998) *Theories of Organizational Stress* provided a balanced description of all the major theories of work stress and has indeed been a valuable resource. In the preface of the book, Cooper raises important issues concerning work and organizational stress and health in the EU. An examination of the theories presented in this book shows that although they are quite effective in understanding the theoretical underpinnings of the phenomena of work stress in Western (i.e., individualistic) countries such as the United States, Canada, Australia, New Zealand, the United Kingdom, Ireland, France, the Netherlands, and France, they do not fully capture the nature and complexity of work stresses in countries that are largely non-Western (i.e., collectivistic) in orientation. The current composition of the European Union of 27 countries includes nations of Eastern Europe (i.e., Czech Republic, Poland, Hungary), and Southern Europe (i.e., Greece, Portugal) that are largely collectivistic. Cross-national and cross-cultural research becomes important in probing the dynamics of work stress and coping in these countries since we cannot assume that the United States and Western Europe based theories of job stress apply to these countries (Hofstede,

2001; Wong & Wong, 2006). The nature of job stresses and strains are indeed experienced differently among employees with different national and cultural backgrounds (Liu & Spector, 2005; Liu, Spector, & Shi, 2008; Narayanan, Menon, & Spector, 1999). Therefore, a non-Western (including multicultural) perspective on work stress, coping, and social support becomes highly relevant for understanding the patterns of work stresses that are particularly salient in the current era of globalization. Knowledge of national and cultural variations in this area is going to be vital for multinational and global companies as they rapidly expand their operations in Asia, Latin America, and Africa. It must be noted that such knowledge will be useful for all types of global organizations regardless of their national origin. Before discussing theoretical issues and frameworks that are particularly suitable from a cross-cultural point of view, we provide some recent reports on work stress and its consequences from non-Western contexts.

Recent Reports from Business Periodicals

- ▪ A report titled "Busy Signals" (*The Economist*, 2005) reports that despite the boom in India's call center and business processing operations, the worry about shortage of well-trained personnel is becoming a major issue. These jobs were glamorous until recently but are losing their appeal. Staff often have to work late nights and tolerate undignified security checks and bullying from their supervisors. The stress levels continue to be higher than expected, and women employees in particular are resorting to religious rituals for coping with work stress and resulting distress.
- ▪ *Business World* (October 7, 2008), in an interesting report of the Watson Wyatt survey involving 8,000 employees from over 450 companies in Japan, India, Hong Kong, Malaysia, Philippines, South Korea, Taiwan, and Thailand, noted that even in the face of worsening global economy these companies would rather not resort to outright layoffs. Individuals leave their organizations due to their inability to handle work-related stresses and achieve work–life balance. There is not a great deal of effort made by these individuals to cope with additional pressures by restructuring their duties and responsibilities.
- ▪ A report published in the *Africa News* (August 5, 2010), notes that stress over work–life issues is increasing among women in South Africa as an increasing number are moving into senior positions in management while still carrying a majority of the responsibilities and duties at home. There is an increase in overtime work often without pay, which greatly interferes with their family responsibilities especially when they have young children at home. A majority of them are unable to relax easily and experience significant marital strains, and the use of antidepressant drugs is on the rise.

Historical Perspective on International and Cross-Cultural Stress Research

As noted in Chapter 3, research on work stress and coping developed primarily in the Western context. While some of the basic concepts and frameworks are valid across dissimilar nations and cultures (i.e., tend to be etic), one needs to consider the role of cultural variations in a detailed fashion. Many researchers have studied patterns of work stress and coping in cross-national contexts. We provide a selective description of some of the important studies.

- In a 21-nation study of middle managers, role conflict, role ambiguity, and role overload were related to national scores on power distance, individualism–collectivism, uncertainty avoidance, and masculinity (Peterson et al., 1995). It is important to note that various indicators of role stresses were related to national and cultural characteristics more than differences in person-specific and organization-specific variations.
- Spector et al. (2002) collected data on role conflict, role ambiguity, and role overload from middle managers in work organizations in 24 nations. The cultural variations of individualism–collectivism and power distance were closely related to these role stressors. Just like the Peterson et al. (1995) study, these three role stressors varied more strongly as a function of national and cultural variations compared with demographic, personal, and organizational characteristics. In an earlier study of 24 nations and territories, Spector, Cooper, Sanchez, and O'Driscoll (2001) found that there were significant differences on measures of job satisfaction, psychological strain, locus of control, and individualism–collectivism. Individuals with higher internal locus of control reported higher subjective well-being, but well-being was not associated with measures of individualism despite the fact that individualism and internal locus of control were correlated.
- Perrewé et al. (2002) conducted a nine-country study investigating the relationship among role stressors (i.e., role ambiguity, role conflict), general self-efficacy (GSE), and burnout. Generalized self-efficacy was associated with burnout in all of the countries; however, self-efficacy mediated the relationship between these two indicators of role stresses with the work-related outcome of burnout.
- In a study concerning differences in job stresses among working college students and university personnel from the United States, China, and Hong Kong, Spector, Cooper, Sanchez, Siu, Salgado, and Ma (2004) found significant differences in role ambiguity, role conflict, job autonomy, and interpersonal conflict. Role ambiguity was significantly higher in the

Hong Kong sample compared with samples from China and the United States. However, role ambiguity was significantly higher in the U.S. sample compared with the sample from Mainland China. Respondents from both Hong Kong and Mainland China were significantly higher than the United States in experiencing more role conflicts. It is interesting that the samples from Mainland China and the United States reported higher levels of autonomy compared with the Hong Kong respondents. Finally, the respondents from Hong Kong reported the highest level of interpersonal conflict among these three groups with the U.S. respondents reporting the lowest amount and the Chinese respondents somewhere in between.

■ In a qualitative study involving female clerical workers in India and the United States, Narayanan et al. (1999) explored the nature of work-related stressful events. Participants in both countries were asked to describe a specific stressful event that occurred while performing their job-related responsibilities and duties. Indian workers reported stressful work situations resulting from the lack of structure and clarity, lack of appropriate rewards and recognition, lack of time and support from coworkers, high incidences of interpersonal conflict, and equipment problems. In contrast, workers from the United States reported stressful work situations resulting from having too much work to do, a lack of adequate control and autonomy, and time wasted in dealing with bureaucratic roles and procedures.

■ Narayanan et al. (1999) also found that Indian and American employees tended to use different types of coping strategies to deal with work-related stresses and strains. For Indians, the preferred mode of coping was talking to family members, members of in-groups, and close friends. In contrast, Americans emphasized the importance of discussing the nature and possible resolution of stressful experiences with coworkers. Americans tended to engage in more direct action and dealt with the source of the problem as opposed to talking with members of their families and in-groups.

■ DeFrank, Ivancevich, and Schweiger (1988) investigated the nature of job stresses between Eastern and Western countries by measuring overall job stress (called global job stress, which assessed perceived amounts of job stress during the month prior to the data collection), specific facets of stress (e.g., role ambiguity, role conflict, quantitative and qualitative role overload), and job satisfaction among samples of lower-, middle-, and upper-level managers in the United States, Japan, and India. Japanese managers reported the highest level of job stresses in terms of both specific and overall aspects. It is interesting that U.S. managers reported the lowest level on both of these aspects and Indian managers were somewhere in the middle. Japanese managers were also less satisfied with their jobs compared with U.S. and Indian managers. In a related study, Bae and Chung (1997) found that perceived job insecurity is the most important job stressor for Korean workers compared with their U.S. and Japanese counterparts. It is interesting to note that while Korean employees reported higher levels of satisfaction with their jobs, they were not inclined to seek the same line of work if they could decide all over again. In addition, the Korean and Japanese workers were similar in terms of emphasizing virtues of teamwork and effective supervision. Apparently, teamwork was not as highly valued in the U.S. workers.

■ Harari, Jones, and Sek (1988) compared levels of experienced job stresses in the United States and Poland—a country from Eastern Europe that scores higher on the cultural value of collectivism and power distance. Polish employees reported higher levels of work stress compared with Americans. American employees reported higher levels of internal locus of control, whereas the Polish workers exhibited more external locus of control. Internal locus of control moderated the relationship between job stressors and job-related strains for the Americans, whereas for the Poles locus of control of either kind (internal or external) did not moderate such relationships.

■ Cooper and Hensman (1985) compared job stressors among; senior and chief executives from 10 countries including the United States; the United Kingdom, Sweden, and Germany from Europe; Singapore and Japan from East Asia; Brazil from Latin America; and Nigeria, Egypt, and South Africa from Africa. Time pressures, unreasonable deadlines, long working hours, and interpersonal problems with colleagues and members of one's close families were the primary sources of job stresses for executives from the developing countries of Latin American and Africa. The major stressors for the executives from the developed countries were concerned with a relative lack of decision latitude and autonomy. In a related vein, Liu, Spector, & Shi (2008) used the stress incident record (SIR) method (Keenan & Newton, 1985) to collect information on various types of job stresses in China and the United States in a qualitative design. For both countries, the most frequently reported experience with job stressors involved poor working conditions involving occasional failure of equipment, lack of adequate training, difficulties in working with work teams, and lack of structure. Interpersonal conflict, heavy workload, and time pressure were also cited as job stressors in both countries. However, the Chinese employees reported that being penalized and reprimanded for mistakes at work and unfair job evaluations to be more important as sources of stress on the job. In contrast, the Americans reported lack of adequate control as being the most important source of job stress. These two research studies provide important insights into the role of cross-national and cross-cultural differences in the perception and reporting of job stressors.

- Psychological strains, physical strains, and employee well-being have been of significant interest in the study of human stress and cognition in work organizations for the past 3 decades (Beehr, 1995; Beehr & Bhagat, 1985; Cooper, Dewe, & O'Driscoll, 2001; Cooper & Payne, 1988; Quick & Tetrick, 2003). An interesting question that arises in this context is the comparison of workers from socialist countries of East and Central Europe (e.g., Bulgaria, the Czech Republic, Hungary, Poland, Romania, Russia, and Transylvania)
- In a related vein, Bhagat and his colleagues (Bhagat et al., 1994, 2010) found that problem-focused coping and decision latitude served to lower the experience of psychological strain that results from work stress in six of the seven countries: the United States, New Zealand, Germany, Spain, South Africa, and Japan. Their finding underscores the importance of problem-focused coping in dealing with work stress in the United States and New Zealand, both individualistic countries. It is interesting to note that this pattern was found to be valid even in collectivistic contexts of India, Spain, and South Africa (three of the seven countries in their cross-national study). They interpreted the results by noting that problem-focused coping is likely to be more prevalent among professionals compared with nonprofessional and blue-collar employees. Their sample was predominately professional employees in financial and high technology–based organizations in these countries.

Toward a Theoretical Model Applicable to Both Western and Non-Western Contexts

International research involving cultural variations in work stress, coping, and social support related processes has increased in the past two decades (see Liu & Spector, 2005, for a detailed summary of the research findings). They noted that much of the research in this area tends to be exploratory in nature. In addition, they do not seem to have appropriate theoretical underpinnings. Theories developed in the United States and in Western European countries are often tested to determine their generalizability. While there is some merit in this line of research, much of the research could have been better framed by taking into account findings from established theoretical frameworks of cultural variations (e.g., Berry, 1997; Berry & Sam, 1997a; Hofstede, 1980, 1991, 1995, 2001; Schwartz, 1999; Triandis, 1989). Issues of measurement and related methodological issues are also of considerable importance in cross-national and cross-cultural research involving work and organizational stresses. (See Chapter 8 for a detailed discussion of this topic.)

It is well known that much of coping behaviors as well as the development of appropriate coping styles and resources takes place primarily in the cultural context of the employees. As Mechanic (1974, 1978) noted over four decades ago, the ability of individuals to acquire coping skills and applying them to resolve stressful situations is largely dependent on the beliefs and values of the cultural context in which they are socialized. More recently, Markus and Kitayama (1991), Sanchez-Burks (2007), and Aldwin (2007) argued that cultural guidelines and knowledge systems are enmeshed with individuals' emotional systems. The implication is that people feel good when they have successfully coped by employing techniques and methods that are sanctioned by their culture. Furthermore, they feel discomfort when they cope with a stressful situation by using techniques that are not culturally appropriate. Such situations may arise for members of ethnic and racial minorities when they experience acts of prejudice, bullying, harassment, and related stressful experiences at work. For immigrants, coping by making use of principles and techniques that are not culturally sanctioned may take place during the experience of acculturation and acculturative stress (Berry, 2006; Bhagat, McDevitt, & Segovis, 2011).

In Chapter 2, we noted that social and cultural environments of modern work organizations increase in complexity due to pressures to globalize. This happens in both developed and developing countries. New types of work stresses are generated. The effects of such stresses are often chronic and multilayered and tend to become more difficult to cope with as complexities of work environments increase. Let us consider one of the distinctive features of Western societies: the strong emphasis on structuring lives by the clock. Such situations do not necessarily exist in countries that are not yet globalized or are in the process of being globalized. Another distinctive feature of Western societies, especially in the United States in particular, the sense of belongingness to one's community is on the decline, as portrayed in *Bowling Alone* (Putnam, 2000), *Next Stop, Reloville* (Kilborn, 2009), and *Elsewhere, U.S.A.* (Conley, 2009). The loss of belongingness to one's community results in lack of social support networks that are important for coping with stressful experiences in work and nonwork situations. Individuals seek psychological counseling and other cognitive-behavioral methods for managing stress (Lehrer, Woolfolk, & Sime, 2007). However, non-Western societies have not yet experienced such losses of community and related social support networks even in this era of globalization. Despite the growing importance of examining work stress and coping from non-Western perspectives, there are no established models that provide insights into this area. The fact that cultural variations have substantial influence on employee psychological and stress-related processes underlying health related outcomes is recognized and cross-cultural issues in occupational health psychology are becoming important (Chang & Spector, 2011). We adapt Aldwin's (2007) sociocultural model of stress, coping, and adaptation to provide insights into the processes of work stress and coping in non-Western cultures. In our view, this model provides better guidance in understanding the underpinnings of work stress and coping across nations and cultures (Figure 5.1). It must be emphasized that the role of cultural beliefs, attitudes, and values were hardly incorporated in much of the Western theories on work stress and coping. (See Chapter 3 for a detailed review of the Western perspectives.)

As shown in Figure 5.1, culture-specific beliefs and values not only influence the beliefs and values that individuals bring to their work organizations but also shape the reactions of their coworkers, supervisors, and other managerial personnel in the organization. Cultural demands and resources also affect both work stresses and individual coping resources—both of which in their turn influence the appraisal of work stress and subsequent development of psychological strain. These in turn affect coping efforts that individuals may choose to engage in. Work stress is conceptualized as a multiplicative function of uncertainty, importance, and duration (i.e., $S = U_C \times I \times D$). This multiplicative function suggests that individuals experience work stress where (1) they have an important set of outcomes to obtain, (2) there are considerable uncertainties associated with obtaining these valued outcomes, and (3) the length of time associated with resolving the uncertainties (if they can be resolved) is significantly longer than they might have the capacity or patience to cope with (Beehr & Bhagat, 1985). Cultural differences (i.e., demands and resources that are available in the cultural context of the individual) strongly influence the perception of each of these three components (uncertainty, importance, and duration) and

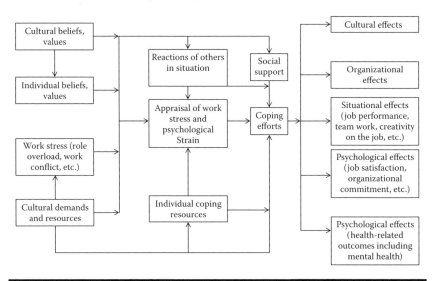

Figure 5.1 **A theoretical model of work stress, coping, and adaptation applicable to both Western and non-Western contexts. (Adapted from Aldwin, C. M., *Stress, Coping, and Development,* 2nd ed., Guilford Press, New York, 2007, p. 247. With permission.)**

their interplay in determining the nature of organizational stress that evolves. In cultures that are high in uncertainty avoidance (e.g., Greece, Japan), individuals are likely to have low tolerance for the ambiguities that are inherent in the situation and therefore experience considerable work stress. In a similar vein, persons from highly individualistic countries (e.g., the United States, the United Kingdom, Canada, Australia) are likely to be more accepting of situations that require higher job autonomy or decision latitude and experience lower stresses than individuals from collectivistic countries (e.g., China, India, Japan, Brazil, Mexico). Employees from work organizations in collectivistic countries expect their supervisors to have the necessary autonomy and decision-making power. They rarely expect to have much autonomy in their work roles. In a related vein, individuals from relationship-based countries (Hooker, 2003) are likely to experience considerable stress when the organization does not provide enough intangible rewards such as recognition from one's supervisor and peers, positive social relationships, and emotional support. In contrast, individuals from rule-based cultures are likely to be more concerned with tangible outcomes (e.g., pay, promotional opportunities, better health-care benefits) and are likely to experience job stress when the probability of obtaining these outcomes is rather uncertain.

Societal culture-based variations that influence the three components of stress are individualism–collectivism, uncertainty avoidance, power distance, masculinity–femininity, and short- versus long-term orientation (Hofstede, 1991, 1995, 2001). In addition, cultural variations described in Triandis (1998), the World Values Survey (Inglehart & Baker, 2000), the Chinese Culture Connection (1987), and Trompenaars (1993) are relevant. They exercise selective influences depending on their salience in a given context.

Organizational culture-based variations that influence work stress include process versus job orientation, employee versus results orientation, parochial versus professional orientation, loose versus tight control (Hofstede, 2001; Hofstede, Neuijen, Ohayv, & Sanders, 1990), and fragmented versus integrative focus in managing operations (Martin, 1993). These dimensions of organizational culture can influence the kind of demands (persistent vs. episodic) that may impinge on the individual. Figure 5.1 also shows that individuals' appraisal of the significance of the work stress and development of psychological strain depends on the nature of interactions among cultural beliefs and values, individual beliefs and values (which are largely determined by the cultural beliefs and values in the individual's immediate social context), and the nature of the work stress and its immediate and long-term significance for personal well-being. As we have discussed earlier, the nature of work stress that evolves in an organizational context is highly dependent on the cultural demands and resources.

Reactions of others (coworkers, supervisors, and significant others in the work context) also determine the nature and quality of the cognitive appraisal of the stressful situation. If coworkers and important others provide significant and valued information about the meaning of the stressful situation then the accuracy and the comprehensiveness of the appraisal is likely to increase. Individuals' coping styles and resources also play an important role in determining the appraisal of stress. Experienced individuals who have functioned in the organization for a long time and have encountered similar stressful situations are likely to be effective in engaging appropriate and accurate appraisals. The coping efforts that individuals will engage in after having appraised the stressful experience will depend on the quality social support that they receive from both the work and nonwork contexts. The importance and availability of all types of social support varies greatly across racial, ethnic, religious, and cultural groups. Ethnic groups that are strongly collectivistic in orientation are more inclined to provide significant amount of social support to individuals when they experience stressful situations in the workplace (Chun, Moos, & Cronkite, 2006). Similarly, women might receive higher levels social support from their female coworkers in deciphering and coping with the stressful situation.

The point is that since there are strong cultural variations among various groups in terms of their predispositions to provides various types of social support, the ability to cope with a stressful situation also varies. Consider the case of a Japanese manager who is confronted with a stressful situation at work in Japan. Compared with his U.S. or Western Europe–based colleague, he might have greater availability of social support both in work and nonwork situations. Both societal and work cultures of Japan are highly collectivistic and relationship-based in orientation. Therefore, Japanese coworkers are likely to provide greater social support than would be the case in either the United States or Western Europe.

The point is that employees of different ethnic, racial, religious, cultural, and age groups are viewed by organizations differently and are provided different kinds of opportunities and resources with which to perform their work-related tasks. In addition, gender-related differences also complicate the experience, appraisal, and coping with a stressful situation in no less a significant manner. Aldwin (2007) noted that patterns of stresses that individuals are likely to encounter is largely affected by the nature of demands and constraints that are inherent in their unique cultural context. She also noted that the sociocultural perspective on coping emphasizes that coping-related efforts and behaviors occur in a social context that in its turn is influenced by various cultural beliefs, attitudes, and values. Successful coping by members of various ethnic groups result in creation of new rules, principles, standards, guidelines, and policies in the organization. Outcomes of successful coping aid the new members of the work organization from the various ethnic and subcultural groups to appraise stressful encounters on their jobs accurately and therefore function more effectively.

In noting that cultural demands and resources directly influence the nature of work stress (e.g., role overload, role conflict, work–family conflicts), it must be mentioned that nonwork-related stresses and demands are also quite relevant in exacerbating the effects of work stress. In some cultural contexts, the demands and pressures from one's nonwork domain are regarded more important than those from the work domain (Wharton & Blair-Loy, 2006). Much of the non-Western world, which is largely collectivistic in orientation (e.g., China, India, Brazil, Russia, Mexico, South Africa), put much stronger emphases on the importance of one's commitment and effective functioning in the nonwork domain. Such is not the case in most of the individualistic countries (e.g., the United States, Canada, the United Kingdom, Australia, France). Stressful experiences from one's nonwork and family lives are likely to receive less attention and in fact are ignored when work-related pressures and expectations increase as is likely to be the case in this era of globalization. The experience of psychological and behavioral strains results after attempts to cope with the stressful situation at work with the aid of various types of social support has been largely unsuccessful. Individuals experience psychological and related strains after they have appraised their encounters with the stressful work. They consider the availability of relevant coping resources, social support at work and nonwork, and reaction of significant others. Figure 5.1 depicts that ongoing experience of psychological and behavioral strains result in decreased levels of job satisfaction, organizational commitment, job involvement, job performance, and other organizationally and personally valued outcomes. Employees experiencing significant types of work stresses (and resultant psychological and behavioral strains) are not likely to be much less effective as members of work teams. Propensities to remain creative and innovative are likely to decline over time as well. This situation becomes more complicated when employees work in cross-national and multicultural work teams and have to be flexible with their work hours, that is, work at their stations when there is need to communicate with members of work teams located in dissimilar nations and cultures (Stanko & Gibson, 2009).

To assist employees in dealing with dysfunctional consequences of work stress, some organizations create stress management training programs and evolve towards more effective human resources policies and practices (e.g., family-friendly work environment, flexible working hours, and employee assistant programs). Over time, the individuals learn techniques of better coordination of tasks with others in their work groups, and their work adjustment and job performance may not decline as much. They may also be able to identify better methods and techniques for coping with the demanding nature of work stress by actively seeking helpful guidance and assistance from their supervisors and coworkers and from members of their in-groups and families. In this respect, one's ethnic or cultural group may indeed facilitate the process of coping with work stress—more about this is discussed in Chapter 6.

However, there are many situations where one's coping efforts are not successful. The pressures on the job due to continuous changes in the workplace coupled with low job decision latitude increase both psychological and behavioral strains. This is when employees are likely to develop major mental and physical health-related consequences. Absenteeism and turnover tendencies increase and conflicts with supervisors and coworkers are likely to take place.

In the next section, we discuss the phenomenon of work stress and its management in non-Western countries such as China, India, Turkey, and Mexico. As noted in Chapter 1, these countries have become major participants in the global market place. They are also characterized by high levels of collectivism and power distance. Therefore, it is important to study the patterns of the evolution of work stress and coping in these countries.

Work Stress and Its Management in Selected Non-Western Countries

The factors that create stress in the workplace and the process associated with the experience of strains tend to be similar in Western and non-Western contexts. As discussed earlier in the context of the model adapted from Aldwin's (2007) sociocultural model of stress, coping, and adaptation, the basic process underlying the experience of work stress tends to be similar across Western and non-Western contexts. However, the interpretation of what kinds of work-related experiences and events are perceived as being stressful and what are not is largely dependent on the cultural background of the employees. As a general rule, one experiences stress when confronted with those situations (i.e., both chronic and episodic) that are demanding, cause uncertainties, and tend to be of long duration. For example, dealing with an unexpected increase in workload that often arises from the challenge of meeting unexpected demands from the global marketplace can be quite stressful—especially if this situation is going to last for a relatively long period of time. However, cultural variations come into play in the appraisal of the stressful experience. The type of coping skills and resources (including various types of social support) that one has tends to vary greatly across dissimilar nations and cultures. Members of collectivistic countries (including employees of work organizations) receive more social support from their coworkers and supervisor as well as from their in-groups and families. This may lead to an unexpected increase in work-related duties and responsibilities experienced not being as stressful in the context of a non-Western country (e.g., China, India, Turkey, or Mexico) than is likely to be the case in the Western countries (e.g., the United States, Canada, the United Kingdom, and Australia). The point is if a job-related experience event is fundamentally stressful or has the potential to cause a stress, it is perceived in the same fashion across dissimilar nations and cultures. However, cultural differences influence the degree to which a difficult situation at work becomes stressful and is likely to cause psychological and behavioral strains. There are considerable differences in the way individuals of non-Western countries approach the management of stress compared with Western countries. We present an analysis of stress management practices in four countries.

Stress management mechanisms that are prevalent in non-Western countries are focused on making the best use of resources in the family and social network, religion and religion and rituals, and culturally sanctioned use of diversions and holistic medicine. In China, India, Turkey, Mexico, Vietnam, Indonesia, and many countries of Latin America and Africa, seeing a professional counselor or therapist on a regular basis for managing work stress and symptoms of strains is not a culturally viable option. Not only would the cost of such services be rather high, but one would also risk losing one's reputation.

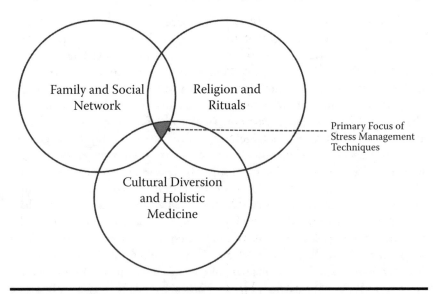

Figure 5.2   Primary focus of stress management in non-Western cultures.

Methods for managing stress that seem to work in non-Western contexts rely a great deal on implicit sources of support and coping techniques that are embedded in the social and religious contexts. In Figure 5.2, we depict the focus of stress management techniques in non-Western cultures as having their roots in three highly important and overlapping domains of life: family and social network, religion and rituals, and cultural diversion and holistic medicine.

First, let us consider the stress management mechanisms in China. The most important social resource that Chinese have been socialized to value (whether they are rural peasants in Chendu or executives of multinational and global companies located in Hong Kong, Shanghai, or Beijing) is one's family. The Chinese concept of family is rather different from the ones emphasized in the Western cultures. It is not merely the kind, warm, intimate, nuclear family that the Chinese have historically emphasized and still do, but it extends to a broad pattern of networks-based authority relations and mutual obligations established over a long period of time. Parents and grandparents often look after and take care of little children when both parents work. Even older brothers and sisters may help in dealing with the pressures of work by sharing family-related duties and responsibilities. When one experiences job-related stresses and pressures such as having more work to do, dealing with conflicts with the management, and pressure to learn new kinds of technologies, one can always depend on a social network developed in the context of guānxí. Guānxí relationships are unique to the Chinese culture and emphasizes a strong role of mutual obligations between two individuals or groups who are linked in some way—having the same family name, sharing of ancestors, attending the same school, or working together for a long time. Members in the guānxí network are expected to remember and reciprocate favors over a long period of time.

The role of religion is also quite important in managing work stress in the Chinese context particularly for hourly and blue-collar workers. The importance of religion and rituals has increased after the liberation of the Chinese economy in 1978. Various ritualistic practices associated with Confucianism, Buddhism, and Taoism are regarded as crucial for managing both work and nonwork stress. Exercise regiments including *chi gong, tai chi*, and *falun gong*, which according to the Chinese beliefs help control one's mood and emotions are becoming common. Reliance on traditional holistic medicine, which supposedly helps control one's fate through adoption of a healthy lifestyle, is also an important component in managing stress. Finally, culturally sanctioned diversions such as the use of humor, playing various games, and eating as a community are also regarded as important in managing difficult and stressful experience at both work and nonwork.

The persistence of loyalty among members of families of the Chinese expatriate community confirms the paramount importance of one's family not only for managing daily pressures and hassles of modern living but also during very stressful and traumatic situations. A Chinese worker or manager is aware of the presence of both implicit and explicit social support. Such strong social support is particularly helpful for Chinese executives who manage overseas operations in dissimilar cultural contexts such as the United States, the United Kingdom, and Australia. Next, we focus on the process of managing work stress in India, which is also an emergent economy with a high growth rate of around 8% for the past several years.

Just as the Chinese, Indians rely on the members of one's family and in groups in managing stressful situations at work. Family members are likely to provide much needed assistance, guidance, and help in stressful times. Compared with the Chinese though, there is more reliance on Western styles of cognitive therapies with the expectation that they will provide a greater sense of control. However, these techniques for managing work stress are available to only a selected segment of the affluent class, a majority of whom are employed by large Western multinationals and global companies, are self-employed, or are entrepreneurs. The role of religion is of paramount importance with followers of Hinduism, Jainism, Sikhism, Islam, Christianity, and Zoroastrianism. The practice of various forms of religious rituals is quite common all over India. A total of 80% of Indians practice Hinduism, which offers relative peace and salvation from difficult experiences of life by encouraging the practice of mental discipline. The basic Hindu ceremony is practiced by performing *puja* (organized religious events typically performed by a priest) at home or in the temple. These ceremonies are supposed to provide a spiritual means for relieving distress—both psychological and behavioral.

As with the Chinese, Indians have access to and make use of their social networks and support systems in managing stresses whether they are work or nonwork related. Indian expatriates are found in many globalized and globalizing countries of the world. They are comfortable with working for a Western or Indian multinational firm and do not experience as much stress when working in dissimilar cultures. They feel at home in many countries of the world because of the extensive social networks and support systems to which they have access. Probably due to their abilities to function effectively in dissimilar countries, including much of the Middle Eastern countries such as United Arab Emirates, Saudi Arabia, and Bahrain, they are often sought after as expatriates by multinational and global companies. Hooker (2003) provided a detailed analysis of how stress management works in the cultural context of India. There seems to be a greater emphasis on self-discipline and making necessary adjustments to changing demands in the workplace. Both implicit and explicit types of social support are present in most communities where Indians live and work. This is true in India as well as abroad. Indians manage stress primarily by employing their distinctive worldview, which is *pantheistic* in nature, meaning it emphasizes one's capacity to rise above the chaos and uncertainties of the materialistic world. One learns to be patient and exercise various kinds of mental discipline to cope with difficult situations and stressful events that occur in one's life. One essential philosophical doctrine that is highly relevant in the management of work stress is that one should not be excessively reliant on one's immediate physical and social surroundings. Hooker observed that it is not surprising that such a worldview is quite functional in the Indian context. Western businesses, which have long experienced the frustrations of dealing with bureaucratic and rigid rules and procedures of governmental agencies and public sectors, begin to appreciate the significance of a worldview that highlights the importance of rising above immediate chaos and concerns. Indians are used to getting things done by adopting a polychronic mode (Levine, 1997) of organizing time at both work and nonwork. Keeping one's commitments to one's family and members of in-groups even during working hours and in the process managing conflicting demands on one's time is regarded as more important than accomplishing stated goals and objectives. The importance of *connections* in getting things done is of vital importance. One who has a large number of connections with superiors and others at the higher ranks of the organization tends to experience much less stress in dealing with demanding situations at work. Many of these connections are often based on one's extended family networks, professional relationships, and the fact that one is a fellow school alumnus. In many ways, the Indian's use of social networks is similar to the guānxí in the Chinese context.

Dealing with Indian governmental bureaucracies can be a frustrating experience for Western multinational and global companies. Getting a project or business transaction approved by responsible officials can be problematic and time-consuming. Hooker (2003) used the analogy that it is like watching a tree grow slowly. An orderly environment is rare in the majority of Indian work organizations. Incidents of stressful encounters and daily hassles are commonplace. However, the Indian high-tech and information-processing organizations are notable exceptions. They are efficient only in their operations but do not tend to create many bureaucratic and procedural difficulties for their employees and clients. This is not to say that individuals working in these companies are immune to experiencing work stress. The workforce of these information technology (IT) industries is highly educated and has access to advanced types of recreational facilities and other opportunities for relieving pressures of working long hours. However, the importance of emphasizing the role of one's family and in-groups along with spiritual and religious practices are not forgotten. Next, we consider the management of stress in another non-Western country that is actively seeking to become a member of the European Union—Turkey.

Recently, Turkey has been emerging as an important economy in Southern Europe. The sense of nationalism is high in Turkey, and people believe it is easier to confront uncertainties of life if they maintain a sense of cohesion whether as a family, a group of friends, a village, an ethnic group, or a nation. Like the Chinese and Indian situations, the role of extended family is very important. Turkish style of developing and maintaining friendship especially at the level of male camaraderie is crucial for interpreting and coping with stressful experiences in the workplace. Unlike the friendships in the Western contexts where competition among friends and peers is commonplace and is encouraged, the primary function of friendship in the Turkish context is to provide social support for ongoing and episodic encounters with difficulties in life whether they are from the domain of work or nonwork. A competitive relationship works against developing this kind of mutual obligation, and it is not unlikely to see old friends working together hand in hand in many parts of Turkey.

Religion, just as in the Chinese and Indian contexts, also plays a significant role in Turkey. Turkey is a country whose dominant majority is composed of moderate Muslims. According to many Western observers of Turkey, this country has been successful in blending its Islamic background with the demands of industrialization and modernity rather well. The month of fasting (i.e., Ramadan) is recognized, but most citizens in urban areas of Turkey do not necessarily fast, close their shops or businesses, or stop going to work. The practice of Islam as a religion is less overt in Turkey compared with other countries in the Middle East. However, the importance of Islam and Islamic rituals in managing stresses and strains should not be deemphasized. Hooker's (2003) approach for understanding stress management mechanisms in Turkey is quite useful in this regard.

Finally, we take a closer look at the practice of stress management in Mexico. Despite numerous setbacks, including serious issues with drug cartels, Mexico has been emerging as one of the important economies in recent years. Religion and religious rituals are crucial in dealing with the harshness of daily hassles and stressful experiences that are present in the lower socioeconomic classes in Mexico. The regularity and predictability of the church calendar and the social solidarity that is built during elaborate preparations for various religious festivals seem to provide relief from stressful experiences at work and nonwork.

Mexican life is Dionysian in character, meaning that people like to escape from pressures and stresses of life by engaging in intense experiences—either spiritual or social. A pragmatic problem-solving approach is not as likely to be emphasized to deal with a stressful encounter whether it originates at work or nonwork. Personal and family relationships are intense and emotional. Displays of various types of emotions (e.g., joy, sorrow, disgust, frustration) are common among both men and women. Unlike North American men who need to show control over their emotions especially in their work organizations, Mexican men feel free to express their emotions to cope with difficult and stressful experiences. Work relations in Latin cultures including Mexico are guided by the relational script of *simpatia* (Diaz-Guerrero, 1967; Sanchez-Burks & Lee, 2007; Triandis, Marin, Lisansky, & Betancourt, 1984). Similar to the emphasis on guānxí and relatedness in East Asian cultures, *simpatia* emphasizes interpersonal and social harmony, and the importance of understanding, accepting, and respecting others. However, unlike the East Asian cultures *simpatia* also includes use of personal charm, graciousness, and hospitality to members of in-groups and out-groups (Hooker, 2003; Triandis, 1994; Sanchez-Burks & Lee, 2007). Experiences, of both work and nonwork stresses are better managed and coped with when one can depend on relationships forged by *simpatia*. Hooker (2003) noted that the Spanish language is pushed to its limits to find the various extreme expressions of emotions, both positive and negative, found in Latin America.

Strong extended family and friendships are frequently relied on for advice and action strategies during difficult times such as dealing with excessive workload and conflicts with coworkers. For men, *machismo* is a preferred mode of dealing with stresses whether the stresses are present in the current context or are expected to occur in the future. *Machismo* signifies a sense of control over one's life, providing some sense of security to one's family—both financial and emotional. The essence of *machismo* in the Mexican culture is that it is an essential function to reduce stress. Some forms of *machismo* are dysfunctional and may often be a source of violence and oppression, but to be sure, it has a constructive side in that it helps men in particular, and women in some specific situations, to deal with stresses associated with difficult economic times, hardships, and deprivations that often accompany the status of being unemployed. The culture of *machismo* signifies that women should play a role that is subordinate to men, but in exchange they can rely on men to protect them while they perform their maternal and nurturing roles. *Machismo* is supposed to protect one's self from stressful experiences by emphasizing the acts associated with taking control of one's self and others who are involved in the situation.

Recent Reports From Business Periodicals

The following recent business reports further illustrate the different ways individuals manage work stresses in non-Western countries as we have discussed in the previous section.

- In *Business Week*, Conlin and Roberts (2007) portray the picture of how work stress is affecting Chinese workers in "Go-Go-Going to Pieces in China." In the process of rapidly globalizing its economy, Chinese organizations have caused tremendous stresses for its workers. They show severe symptoms of distress typically associated with workers in the West. Moreover, since traditional Chinese culture considers psychological counseling and psychotherapy unacceptable (i.e., it may cause loss of face) many are turning to religion especially Buddhism. Chestnut Global Partners, which is affiliated with Minsheng Bank (one of China's largest publically traded banks), had offices in Beijing and found that stress management methods that worked in the United States did not seem to be suitable in China. Chinese workers are reluctant to undergo face-to-face therapy. This has led to the development of online group counseling sessions so that the identity of the workers is not necessarily revealed. Chestnut Global Partners reports that this adaptation has worked well with Chinese employees complaining about the same types of issues as U.S. employees: too much work, bad bosses, interpersonal conflicts, decreased job performance, and disappointed spouses and kids.
- In *Business Times–Singapore* (Hock, 2009), managing directors of several companies note that pro-family human resource management policies are ideally suited for the current economic difficulties. Flexible work arrangements, shorter work weeks, and family care leave are helpful in managing work stresses and lowering risks of burnout. The National Family Council of Singapore is also emphasizing establishment of centers for effective parenting and other issues that help manage challenges at both work and nonwork.
- In *Harvard Business Review*, Hewlett and Rashid (2010) document the growing need to locate professional female talent in emerging markets, including the BRIC countries and United Arab Emirates. They report that 80% of the female respondents were "willing to go the extra mile" for their companies if they have the opportunity to work on projects that provide a sense of personal growth and intellectual stimulation and have implications for reshaping their countries. Some issues that are important to these females are elder care, providing safety in job-related travels, and assistance in building professional networks. A considerably higher percentage of working women in the BRIC countries and United Arab Emirates live with parents than is the case in Western countries. Consequently, 40% to 68% are likely to provide

financial help to their parents since Social Security types of arrangements found in the West are not present in these emergent economies. Child care is also often mentioned as being important in managing work–family stresses. The point is that multinational companies that provide opportunities for managing family-related issues are likely to be more successful in recruiting female talent in these countries. Overall, family issues are more important in the BRIC countries, and the techniques that help manage stresses at the interface of work and family are more desirable.

A Conceptual Model

The model shown in Figure 5.3 depicts both work- and nonwork-related demands that are activated by unsettling events (economic, social, and cultural) experienced due to globalization. It highlights the demands and stressors that lead to the potential of experiencing decision-making or problem-solving circumstances characterized by different degrees of uncertainty, importance, and duration (Beehr, 1995, 1998; Beehr & Bhagat, 1985). These three components take on different perceptions when viewed in distinctive national and cultural contexts. For example, in Greece or Japan, which are high in uncertainty avoidance, individuals are prone to have limited tolerance for ambiguous and uncertain situations and are likely to experience higher levels of stresses—at both work and nonwork.

Constant changes in the global marketplace influence the development of uncertainties in various business units of multinational and global corporations. Especially, the boundary-spanning units (e.g., global marketing, research and development, product development, corporate finance) often encounter unpredictable and important demands from the global market place. Such unpredictable demands may also last for a considerable period of time. Rapid changes in science and technology require fast and appropriate responses in production, marketing, and other boundary-spanning units. These demands require employees to learn new types of skills, to adopt new ways of working, to accept more pressure for productivity, to supply better quality of work, to manage increased time pressure and hectic jobs, to adjust to the demands of more job competition, to reconcile themselves with increased job insecurities, to accept fewer benefits, and to be willing to have less free time with their friends and families (Houtman, Jettinghoff, & Cedillo, 2007). Some examples of unsettling events include implementation of Lean production methods, total quality management, and advanced Japanese-style *kaizen* teams or quality circles, and increased use of technology. Typically these kinds of changes are likely to increase cognitive demands on employees and their responsibilities and at the same time affect the sense of cohesiveness among employees (Charness, Czaja, & Sharit, 2007; Katz & Rice, 2002; Quick & Tetrick, 2003). Wall and Jackson (1995) indicate these types of demands can result in the

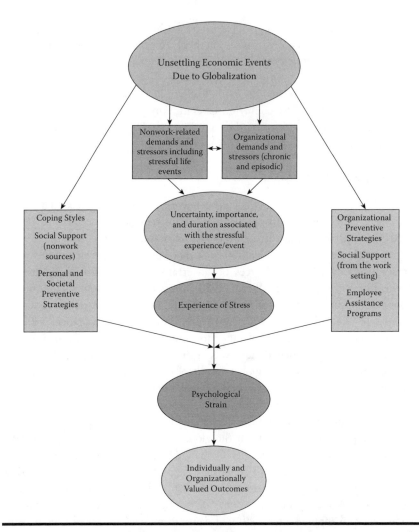

Figure 5.3   A conceptual model of work stress and coping in the era of globalization. (Adapted from Bhagat, R. S., Steverson, P. K., & Kuo, B. C. H., in R. S. Bhagat & R. M. Steers (Eds.), *Culture, Organizations, and Work* (pp. 418–441), Cambridge University Press, Cambridge, UK, 2009, p. 429.)

experience of stress and psychological strain known to lead to negative health effects such as:

1. Cognitive responses (e.g., reduction or narrowing of attention and perception, forgetfulness)
2. Emotional responses (e.g., feeling nervous, irritated)

3. Physiological responses (e.g., increased heart rate, blood pressure)

4. Behavioral reaction (e.g., aggressive, impulsive behavior, making mistakes)

The rapid changes that are associated with globalization are linked to adverse mental health outcomes. Global economic crises like the recession of 2008 exacerbate psychological strain and strongly affect both individually and organizationally valued outcomes. Sudden economic crises that create unemployment, job insecurity, and income inequality are major sources of depression and other mental disorders including thoughts of suicide (Marmot & Bobak, 2000). Long-lasting unemployment tends to diminish worker skills, cognitive abilities, and work motivation (Marmot & Bobak, 2000). A situation that is stressful becomes more intolerable due to increased uncertainties about future employment potential using one's current occupational skills and abilities. This kind of situation is a good example of Beehr and Bhagat's (1985) uncertainty theory of work stress.

Employees have to manage their work situation along with their nonwork-related circumstances such as interacting with family (and social) situations. Cultural and social factors can be pervasive influences on the occurrence and construal of life events, such as financial hardships, lack of employment, family-related stressors, physical and mental health problems, and discrimination (Chun et al., 2006). The interface between home and work can cause additional stress if a balance is not maintained (Greenhaus & Allen, 2011). This type of work-related stress is prone to affect working women in countries that are characterized by high levels of masculinity as discussed in Hofstede and Hofstede (2005), where gender roles are clearly differentiated and women are largely responsible for family duties such as child rearing and elder care. Such situations become even more difficult when risk of unemployment, poverty, and poor living conditions exist (Houtman, Jettinghoff, & Cedillo, 2007). Women's responsibilities at work often conflict with their family obligations such as housework, child care, care of an elderly relative, or commitments to family and friends. Spillover effects between work and home duties have been found to be one of the best predictors of psychological strains in women workers at all levels (Cedillo & Scarone, 2005).

The point is that demands from work and nonwork domains collectively lead to the worker experiencing stresses. Stresses in the work domain include extensive and inconsistent work hours, abusive supervisor behavior, conflict with coworkers, and inadequate resources such as equipment, supplies, and training required to carry out one's job duties.

Cops of the Global Village

It took rescue workers a week to dig out the bodies after a garment factory collapsed in Dhaka, Bangladesh. Approximately

80 people died, and about 100 were seriously injured. The factory supplied sweaters to Carrfour and Zara, European retailers. This is the nightmare of globalization: poor people working in poor and unsafe conditions to produce goods for consumers in Western countries. Corporate critics refer to this scenario as a "race to the bottom." Basically multinational companies seek out locations where labor is cheap and safety, health, and environmental laws are weak.

While this is part of globalization, there is a flip side to this scenario. There are U.S. companies that search for low-cost labor in developing countries, but some of them export health and safety standards when they open factories. In addition, multinational companies closely monitor their suppliers to avoid having the term *sweatshop* attached to their brand. For example, Nike employs over 90 people in 21 countries to enforce a code of conduct that covers safety, child labor, overtime pay, and human rights.

Over 90% of the world's computers, digital cameras, and mobile phones are produced in low-wage factories in Asia. Last year Walmart imported approximately $15 billion in goods just from China. The search for cheap labor creates opportunities for tragedies like the sweater factory in Bangladesh where workers told horror stories about being forced to work and the difficulty and sometimes the inability to collect their pay. The *Daily Star* (an English-language Bangladeshi newspaper) wrote the following after the accident, "It is the collusive arrangement of government agencies and factory owners who cut costs at the expense of the safety of the workers that is the cause of so many deaths and injuries in this [garment] sector."

Global companies are beginning to notice that if their world-wide suppliers treat their workers in their home countries fairly and provide decent working conditions, then the products they produce are reliable and of high quality.

Adapted from Gunther, M. Fortune, 151(13), 2005, pp. 158–166.

Nonwork stress can involve major life events such as death of a spouse or child, separation or divorce, terminal illness of a loved one, or transfer to an undesirable location. These types of life events are naturally stressful but even more so because they necessitate social readjustment and adaptation (Bhagat, 1983). Minor stresses including daily hassles (Cooper et al., 2001; Lazarus, 1993) from both the work and nonwork domains (e.g., renovating one's home, chauffeuring children from one event to another, performing extra household chores, running errands for a friend) can be just as taxing stressfully as a major life event requiring significant social and personal adjustments (Bhagat, McQuaid, Lindholm, & Segovis, 1985).

Individuals respond to the experience of psychological or mental strain in either an adaptational or dysfunctional mode. Dysfunctional responses are reactions to psychological strains that adversely affect workers' job satisfaction, commitment, motivation, and life satisfaction. It can also cause an increase in depression, alcoholism, and suicidal thoughts. Decreases in job performance, morale, and commitment to the organization occur, followed by increases in absenteeism and voluntary turnover.

The model also depicts how the relationship between the experience of stress and psychological strain is moderated by work and nonwork sources of social support, coping style and resources, availability of employee assistance programs (EAPs), and personal and societal strategies for managing stress. There are findings that demonstrate the critical role that social support from supervisors, coworkers, friends, or family—or a combination of—plays in decreasing incidences of burnout (Dignam, Barrera, & West, 1986; Leiter, 1990; Maslach, 1976). Another effective approach to diminishing or preventing stress is through EAPS (Bhagat, Steverson, & Segovis, 2007, 2008).

Conclusion

Globalization of trade has had significant effects on organizations and their work environments. While people usually think in terms of globalization as markets, trade, capital, and economies, the buttress of this process includes importing and exporting not only goods and services but also people, values, cultures, norms, and expectations across national borders. Non-Western perspectives in analyzing the underpinnings of stress experiences are necessary in the current era of globalization. As we have argued numerous times, globalization involves the expansion of economic activities across dissimilar nations and cultures. Stress of any kind, whether it originates from the domain of work or nonwork, is interpreted through one's own national and cultural perspective. In this chapter, we have illustrated how globalization-induced unsettling economic events create work stress and how these stresses and their consequences may be understood in non-Western contexts. In Chapter 6, we will expand this discussion to include multicultural perspectives of work stress in racial, ethnic, and cultural groups.

References

Aldwin, C. M. (2007). *Stress, coping and development* (2nd ed.). New York: Guilford Press.

Bae, K., & Chung, C. (1997). Cultural values and work attitudes of Korean industrial workers in comparison with those of the United States and Japan. *Work and Occupations, 24*(1), 80–96.

Beehr, T. A. (1995). *Psychological stress in the workplace.* London: Routledge.

Beehr, T. A. (1998). Research on occupational stress: An unfinished enterprise. *Personnel Psychology, 51*, 835–841.

Beehr, T. A., & Bhagat, R. S. (1985). Introduction to human stress and cognition in organizations. In T. A. Beehr & R. S. Bhagat (Eds.), *Human stress and cognition in organizations* (pp. 3–22). New York: John Wiley & Sons.

Berry, J. W. (1997). Immigration, acculturation, and adaptation. *Applied Psychology: An International Review, 46*, 5–68.

Berry, J. W. (2006). Stress perspectives on acculturation. In D. L. Sam & J. W. Berry (Eds.), *The Cambridge handbook of acculturation psychology* (pp. 43–57). Cambridge: Cambridge University Press.

Berry, J. W., & Sam, D. L. (1997a). Acculturation and adaptation. In J. W. Berry, M. H. Segall, & C. Kagitcibasi (Eds.), *Handbook of cross-cultural psychology: Vol. 2. Basic processes and human development* (2nd ed., pp. 291–326). Boston: Allyn & Bacon.

Berry, J. W., & Sam, D. L. (1997b). Acculturation and adaptation. In J. W. Berry, M. H. Segall, & C. Kagitcibasi (Eds.), *Handbook of cross-cultural psychology: Vol. 3. Social behavior and application.* Needham Heights, MA: Allyn and Bacon.

Bhagat, R. S. (1983). Effects of stressful life events on individual performance effectiveness and work adjustment processes within organizational settings: A research model. *Academy of Management Review, 8*(4), 660–671.

Bhagat, R. S., Krishnan, B., Nelson, T. A., Leonard Mustafa, K., Ford, Jr., D. L., & Billing, T. K. (2010). Organizational stress, psychological strain, and work outcomes in six national contexts: A closer look at the moderating influences of coping styles and decision latitude. *Cross Cultural Management: An International Journal of Cross Cultural Management, 17*(1), 10–29.

Bhagat, R. S., McDevitt, A. S., & Segovis, J. C. (2011). Immigration as an adaptive challenge: Implications for lifelong learning. In M.L. London (Ed.), *Handbook of lifelong learning* (pp. 402–421). New York: Oxford University Press.

Bhagat, R. S., McQuaid, S. J., Lindholm, H., & Segovis, J. (1985). Total life stress: A multi-method validation of the construct and its effects on organizationally valued outcomes and withdrawal behaviors. *Journal of Applied Psychology, 70*(1), 202–214.

Bhagat, R. S., O'Driscoll, M. P., Babakus, E., Frey, L. T., Chokkar, J., Ninokumar, B. H., et al. (1994). Organizational stress and coping in seven national contexts: A cross-cultural investigation. In G. P. Keita & J. J. Hurrell, Jr. (Eds.), *Job stress in a changing workforce* (pp. 93–105). Washington, DC: American Psychological Association.

Bhagat, R. S., Steverson, P. K., & Kuo, B. C. H. (2009). Cultural variations in work stress and coping in an era of globalization. In R.S. Bhagat & R.M. Steers (Eds.), *Culture, organizations, and work* (pp. 418–441). United Kingdom: Cambridge University Press.

Bhagat, R. S., Steverson, P. K., & Segovis, J. C. (2007). International and cultural variations in employee assistance programmes: Implications for managerial health and effectiveness. *Journal of Management Studies, 44*, 229–249.

Bhagat, R. S., Steverson, P. K., & Segovis, J. C. (2008). Cultural variations in employee assistance programs in an era of globalization. In D. L. Stone-Romero & E. F. Stone-Romero, *The influence of culture on human resource management processes and practices* (pp. 207–233). New York: Taylor & Francis.

Busy signals. (2005, September 10). *The Economist, 376*(8443), 60.

Cedillo, B. L., & Scarone, M. (2005). *Psychosocial risk factors for women workers and psychological strain.* Presented at the 2nd International Conference on Psychosocial Factors at Work sponsored by the International Conference of Occupational Health, Okayama, Japan.

Chang, C., & Spector, P. E. (2011). Cross-cultural occupational health psychology. In J. C. Quick & L. E. Tetrick (Eds.), *Handbook of occupational health psychology* (2nd ed., pp. 119–138). Washington, DC: American Psychological Association.

Charness, N., Czaja, S., & Sharit, J. (2007). Age and technology for work. In K. S. Schultz & G. A. Adams (Eds.), *Aging and work in the 21st century*. Mahwah, NJ: LEA Publishers.

Chinese Culture Connection. (1987). Chinese values and the search for culture-free dimensions of culture. *Journal of Cross-Cultural Psychology, 18*(2), 143–164.

Chun, C.-A. C., Moos, R. H., & Cronkite, R. C. (2006). Culture: A fundamental context for the stress and coping paradigm. In P. T. P. Wong & L. C. J. Wong (Eds.), *Handbook of multicultural perspectives on stress and coping*, New York: Springer Publishing.

Conlin, M., & Roberts, D. (2007, April 23). Go-go-going to pieces in China: Frazzled managers are displaying all the classic signs of Western-style stress. *Business week,* 4031, 88.

Conley, D. (2009). *Elsewhere, U.S.A.: How we got from the company man, family dinners, and the affluent society to the home office, BlackBerry moms, and economic anxiety.* New York: Pantheon Books.

Cooper, C. L. (1998). *Theories of organizational stress*. New York: Oxford University Press.

Cooper, C. L., Dewe, P. J., & O'Driscoll, M. P. (2001). *Organizational stress: A review and critique of theory, research and application*. Thousand Oaks, CA: Sage.

Cooper, C. L., & Hensman, R. (1985). A comparative investigation of executive stress: A ten-nation study. *Stress Medicine, 1*(4), 295–301.

Cooper, C. L., & Payne, R. (Eds.). (1988). *Causes, coping, and consequences of stress at work*. Chichester, UK: Wiley.

DeFrank, R. S., & Ivancevich, J. M. (1998). Stress on the job: An executive update. *Academy of Management Executive, 12*, 55–66.

DeFrank, R. S., Ivancevich, J. M., & Schweiger, D. M. (1988). Job stress and mental well-being: Similarities and differences among American, Japanese and Indian managers. *Behavioral Medicine, 14*, 160–170.

Diaz-Guerrero, R. (1967). *Estudios de psicologia del Mexicano.* Mexico: Trillas.

Dignam, J. T., Barrera, M. J., & West, S. G. (1986). Occupational stress, social support, and burnout among correctional officers. *American Journal of Community Psychology, 14*, 177–193.

European Agency for Safety and Health at Work. (2009). OSH in figures: Stress at work—facts and figures. Luxembourg: Office for Official Publications of the European Communities.

Gender roles and violence push women to mental illness. (2010, April 5). *Africa News.*

Greenhaus, G. H., & Allen, T. D. (2011). Work-family balance: A review and extension of the literature. In L. Tetrick & J. C. Quick (Eds.), *Handbook of occupational health psychology* (2nd ed., pp. 165–183). Washington, DC: American Psychological Association.

Gunther, M. (2005, June 27). Cops of the global village. *Fortune, 151*(13), 158–166.

Harari, H., Jones, C. A., & Sek, H. (1988). Stress syndrome and stress predictors in American and Polish college students. *Journal of Cross-Cultural Psychology, 19*, 243–255.

Hewlett, S. A., & Rashid, R. (2010). The battle for female talent in emerging markets. *Harvard Business Review, 88*(5), 1–5.

Hock, L.S. (2009, June 15). All in the family: How has the current economic situation affected your organisation's pro-family policies? What can employers do in the current circumstances to boost Singapore's family-friendly work practices? *The Business Times Singapore.*

Hofstede, G. (1980). *Culture's Consequences: International differences in work-related values.* Beverley Hills, CA: Sage.

Hofstede, G. (1991). *Cultures and organizations: Software of the mind.* London: McGraw-Hill.

Hofstede, G. (1995). Multilevel research of human systems: Flowers, bouquets and garden. *Human Systems Management, 14*(3), 207–218.

Hofstede, G. (2001). *Culture's consequences: Comparing values, behaviours, institutions, and organizations across nations* (2nd ed.). Thousand Oaks, CA: Sage.

Hofstede, G., & Hofstede, G. J. (2005). *Cultures and organizations: Software of the mind.* New York, NY: McGraw-Hill.

Hofstede, G., Neuijen, B., Ohayv, D. D., & Sanders, G. (1990). Measuring organizational cultures: A qualitative and quantitative study across twenty cases. *Administrative Science Quarterly, 35*(2), 286–316.

Hooker, J. (2003). *Working across cultures.* Stanford, CA: Stanford University Press.

Houtman, I., Jettinghoff, K., & Cedillo, L. (2007). *Raising awareness of stress at work in developing countries* (Protecting Workers' Health Series No. 6.) Geneva: World Health Organization.

Inglehart, R., & Baker, W. E. (2000). Modernization, cultural change and the persistence of traditional values. *American Sociological Review, 65,* 19–51.

Katz, J. E., & Rice, R. E. (2002). *Social consequences of internet use: Access, involvement, and interaction.* Cambridge, MA: MIT Press.

Keenan, A., & Newton, T. J. (1985). Coping with work-related stress. *Human Relations, 38*(2), 107–126.

Kilborn, P. T. (2009). *Next stop, Reloville: Life inside America's new rootless professional class.* New York: Henry Holt & Company.

Lazarus, R. S. (1993). From psychological stress to the emotions: A history of changing outlooks. *American Review of Psychology, 44*, 1–21.

Lehrer, P. M, Woolfolk, R. L., & Sime, W. E. (Eds.). (2007). *Principals and practice of stress management* (3rd ed.). New York: Guilford Press.

Leiter, M. P. (1990). The impact of family resources, coping control, and skill utilization on the development of burnout: A longitudinal study. *Human Relations, 41*(11), 1067–1083.

Levine, R. (1997). *A geography of time: The temporal misadventures of a social psychologist, or how every culture keeps time just a little bit differently.* New York: Basic Books.

Liu, C., & Spector, P. E. (2005). International and cross-cultural issues. In J. Barling, E. K. Kelloway, & M. R. Frone (Eds.), *Handbook of work stress* (pp. 487–515). Thousand Oaks, CA: Sage.

Liu, C., Spector, P. E., & Shi, L. (2008). Use of both qualitative and quantitative approaches to study job stress in different gender and occupational groups. *Journal of Occupational Health Psychology, 13*(4), 357–370.

Liu, K. J. R. (2008, October 7). Layoffs not the first choice for Asia-Pacific firms. *Business World*, S1.

Macik-Frey, M., Quick, J. C., & Nelson, D. L. (2007). Advances in occupational health: From a stressful beginning to a positive future. *Journal of Management, 33*(6), 809–840.

Markus, H. R., & Kitayama, S. (1991). Culture and the self: Implications for cognition, emotion, and motivation. *Psychological Review, 98*, 224–253.

Marmot, M., & Bobak, M. (2000). Psychosocial and biological mechanisms behind the recent mortality crisis in Central and Eastern Europe. In G. A. Cornia & R. Paniccia (Eds.), *The mortality crisis of transitional economies* (pp.127–148). Oxford: Oxford University Press.

Martin, J. (1993). *Cultures in organizations.* New York: Oxford University Press.

Maslach, C. (1976). Burned out. *Human Behavior, 5*, 16–22.

Mechanic, D. (1974). Social structure and personal adaptation: Some neglected dimensions. In G. V. Coelho, D. A. Hamburg, & J. E. Adams (Eds.), *Coping and adaptation* (pp. 32–44). New York: Basic Books.

Mechanic, D. (1978). *Students under stress: A study in the social psychology of adaptation.* London: University of Wisconsin Press.

Mesquita, B., Frijda, N. H., & Scherer, K. R. (1997). Culture and emotion. In P. Dasen & T. S. Saraswathi (Eds.), *Handbook of cross-cultural psychology: Basic processes and human development* (Vol. 2, pp. 255–297). Boston, MA: Allyn & Bacon.

Murphy, R. (1999). Organizational interventions to reduce stress in health care professionals. In J. Cozens & R. Payne (Eds.), *Stress in health professionals* (pp. 149–162). London: John Wiley & Sons.

Narayanan, L., Menon, S., & Spector, P. E. (1999). A cross-cultural comparison of job stressors and reactions among employees holding comparable jobs in two countries. *International Journal of Stress Management, 6*, 197–212.

Perrewé, P. L., Hochwarter, W. A., Rossi, A. M., Wallace, A., Maignan, I., Castro, S. L., et al. (2002). Are work stress relationships universal? A nine-region examination of role stressors, general self-efficacy, and burnout. *Journal of International Management, 8*(2), 163–187.

Peterson, M. F., Smith, P. B., Akande, A., Ayestaran, S., Bochner, S., Callan, V., et al. (1995). Role conflict, ambiguity and overload: A 21-nation study. *Academy of Management Journal, 38*, 429–542.

Putnam, R. D. (2000). *Bowling alone: The collapse and revival of American community.* New York: Simon & Schuster.

Quick, J. C., & Tetrick, L. E. (Eds.). (2003). *Handbook of occupational health psychology.* Washington, DC: American Psychological Association.

Sanchez-Burks, J. (2007). Cultural differences. In R. Baumeister & K. Vohs (Eds.), *Encyclopedia of social psychology* (pp.). Thousand Oaks, CA: Sage.

Sanchez-Burks, J., & Lee, F. (2007). Cultural psychology of workways. In S. Kitayama & D. Cohen (Eds.), *Handbook of cultural psychology* (pp. 346–369). New York: Guilford.

Schwartz, S. H. (1999). A theory of cultural values and some implications for work. *Applied Psychology: An International Review, 48*(1), 23-47.

Spector, P. E., Cooper, C. L., Sanchez, J. L., & O'Driscoll, M. (2001). Do national levels of individualism and internal locus of control relate to well-being: An ecological level international study. *Journal of Organizational Behavior,* (22), 815–832.

Spector, P. E., Cooper, C. L., Sanchez, J. I., Siu, O. L., Salgado, J., & Ma, J. (2004). Eastern versus Western control beliefs at work: An investigation of secondary control, socioinstrumental control, and work locus of control in China and the US. *Applied Psychology: An International Review, 141*(1–2), 70–113.

Spector, P. E., Cooper, C. L., Sanchez, J. I., Sparks, K., Bernin, P., Bussing, A., et al. (2002). A twenty-four nation/province study of work locus of control, well-being, and individualism: How generalizable are Western work findings? *Academy of Management Journal, 45*(2), 453–566.

Stanko, T., & Gibson, C. B. (2009). Virtuality here and now: A review of the concept of virtual work. In R. S. Bhagat & R. M. Steers (Eds.), *Handbook of culture, organizations, and work* (pp. 272–304). Cambridge: Cambridge University Press.

Triandis, H. C. (1989). The self and social behavior in differing cultural contexts. *Psychological Review, 96*, 269–289.

Triandis, H. C. (1995). *Individualism and collectivism.* Boulder, CO: Westview Press.

Triandis, H. C. (1998). Vertical and horizontal individualism and collectivism: Theory and research implications for international comparative management. In J. L. Cheng & R. B. Peterson (Eds.), *Advances in international and comparative management* (pp. 7–35). Greenwich, CT: JAI Press.

Triandis, H., Marin, G., Lisansky, J., & Betancourt, H. (1984). *Simpaffa* as a cultural script of Hispanics. *Journal of Personality and Social Psychology, 47*, 1363–1375.

Trompenaars, F. (1993). *Riding the waves of culture: Understanding cultural diversity in business.* London: Nicholas Brealey Publishing.

Wall, T. D., & Jackson, P. R. (1995). New manufacturing initiatives and shop floor design. In A. Howard (Ed.), *The changing nature of work* (pp. 139–174). San Francisco: Jossey-Bass.

Wharton, A. S., & Blair-Loy, M. (2006). Long work hours and family life: A cross-national study of employees' concerns. *Journal of Family Issues, 27*, 415–436.

Wong, P. T. P., & Wong, L. C. J. (Eds.). (2006). *Handbook of multicultural perspectives on stress and coping.* New York: Springer

Chapter 6

Multicultural Perspectives on Work Stress

In the previous chapter we discussed the relevance of examining work stress and coping in non-Western contexts. We presented various reports from business periodicals that show how coping with work stress is an inherently social process largely influenced by the social and cultural contexts of the individual and work organization. Anthropological studies on human adaptation and coping effectiveness reveal influences of culture-specific beliefs, practices, and values (Utsey et al., 2007). Strong evidence exists regarding influences of national and cultural variations on incidences of psychopathologies, organic and substance disorders, depression, and schizophrenia (see Berry, Poortinga, Segall, & Dasen, 2006). For example, culture-specific roots of mental illnesses such as *amok* in Indonesia, *susto* in South America, *espanto* in Spain, and *ataque* among Puerto Ricans in New York continue to be debated in the mental and public health literature (see Lincoln, 2001; McCormick & Wong, 2006; Tseng, 2001). *Amok* represents a sort of frenzied attack as if possessed by a demon in Indonesia. *Susto* and *espanto* are relatively similar concepts and represent progressive levels of "fright sickness" with strong psychological overtones with *espanto* being the near fatal version of *susto*. *Ataque* or *ataque de nervios* is also known as "Puerto Rican Syndrome" and is characterized by a variety of symptoms including temporary loss of consciousness, hyperactivity resulting in aggression, and impulsive suicidal and homicidal acts. Note that exact equivalences of these mental disorders are not easily found in Western psychological research.

While it is widely recognized that cultures influence the way emotion is experienced and expressed (see Mesquita & Leu, 2007), much less attention has been paid to how individuals may select specific types of coping strategies in dealing with stressful work situations. As noted earlier, individuals acquire coping skills and learn to be either effective or ineffective in dealing with stressful experiences depending largely on the social, institutional, and cultural contexts with which they are most familiar (Mechanic, 1974). Antonovsky (1979, pp. 117–118) noted:

> Culture gives us an extraordinarily wide range of answers to demands. The demands and answers are routinized: from the psychological point of view, they are internalized; from the sociological point of view, they are institutionalized .... A culture provides ... ready answers ... with keening for a death, an explanation for pain, a ceremony for crop failure, and a form for disposition and accession of leaders.

Work Stress and Coping: A Cultural Perspective

Approaches to coping with both stressful experiences at work and life can be studied across racial, ethnic, and cultural groups. The few studies that have examined cross-cultural differences in work stress have not been explicitly concerned with how cultural variations influence choice of coping styles or resources. Bhagat and his colleagues (1994, 2001, 2010) found that problem-focused coping is negatively related with work overload and psychological strain, and in the collectivistic context of South Africa emotion-focused coping is found to be a moderator of the relationship between work stress and psychological strain. They note that problem-focused coping is likely to be a moderator of the relationship between role stressors and psychological strain in countries that are largely individualistic. In addition, they report that emotion-focused coping is an effective moderator between work stress and psychological strains in the collectivistic context of Japan. With recent exceptions (see Bhagat, Steverson, and Kuo, 2009, for a review), most studies in this area have been largely atheoretical and anecdotal in nature. While news and special reports about how individuals, work groups, and work organizations experience stresses and cope with them are often found in business periodicals, one wishes for theoretical foundations that might provide integrative and meaningful interpretations of the phenomena.

Developing more theoretically grounded insights into the work stress and coping patterns of ethnic, racial, cultural, and religious groups is useful for the following reasons:

1. Knowledge in this area will improve human resources practices to enable these groups to appraise and manage various work stresses with unique cultural and ethnic roots. Their work effectiveness will also increase with a better adjustment to the demands of organizations and societies whose mores and norms might be less familiar.
2. From a practical point of view, both the globalized and the globalizing world have to learn to reinvent the meaning of the *melting pot* (Jacoby, 2004). The new world of work is composed not only of ethnic minorities but also of immigrants who are culturally dissimilar from the mainstream population. Lewin, Manning, and Massini (2008) discuss the growing significance of the global race for talent in sustaining innovation for multinational and global companies. Creative talent is distributed across dissimilar national contexts and cultures. To harness and effectively integrate the contribution of various groups, it is necessary to develop sophisticated insights in this area. Countries that do a poor job of integrating the contribution of various groups across racial, ethnic, cultural, and religious divides will experience conflicts, ethnic and racial strife, lower levels of productivity, and loss of international competitiveness.

To develop a theoretical foundation that will help us in analyzing the work stress and coping patterns from a multicultural perspective, we employ the construct of *cultural syndromes*. A cultural syndrome is a pattern of shared beliefs, attitudes, categorization, self definitions, norms, role definitions, and values that is organized around a theme that can be identified by those who speak a particular language and reside in a given geographical locale during a specific period of history. Thus, if a given operation in a geographical locale of the world is high on a given dimension of cultural variation, the theory will take one form; however, if the population is low on the dimension, then the theory might take a different form (Kitayama, Duffy, & Uchida, 2007; Kitayama, Markus, & Lieberman, 1995; Kitayama, Markus, & Matsumoto, 1995). Various dimensions of cultural syndromes are

■ *Tightness:* In some cultures, there are many norms and expected patterns of behavior that apply across many social and organizational situations; minor deviations from these norms are often criticized and punished. In other cultures, there are few norms and only minor deviations from norms are criticized and may often be tolerated. The United States, for example, at this time is a rather loose culture, whereas Japan is a much tighter culture. There are many rules governing social and organizational behaviors in the Japanese context, and people are extremely concerned about not breaking them (Iwao, 1998; Triandis, 1996).

■ *Cultural complexity:* The number of different social and cultural elements that are present in a society can be either large or small. Cultural complexity is higher when the number of elements that people of a given region have to deal with on regular basis is rather large. For example, New York City is much more complex than a rural village in Brazil. The complexity and multiplicity of religious, economic, political, social, and other forms of institutions in a large city like New York in the United States directly contributes to increases in its cultural complexity.

■ *Active–passive:* This dimension of cultural syndrome was first described by Diaz-Guerrero (1967) and includes a number of active as opposed to passive elements. A society that is high on this dimension encourages ongoing competition among its members, action, and self-fulfillment. On the other hand, societies that are passive encourage engagement in reflective thoughts, leaving the initiative to others and fostering cooperation among its members.

■ *Individualism–collectivism:* Individualism is defined as a social pattern that consists of loosely linked individuals who view themselves as largely independent of collectives (e.g., family, work groups, community, and related social networks) and are motivated by their own preferences, needs, rights, and contracts. Collectivism, on the other hand, is a social pattern that consists of closely linked individuals that see themselves as belonging to one or more collectives (e.g., family, tribes or clans, coworkers, in-groups, and work organizations) and are largely motivated by the expectations, norms, duties, and obligations associated with these groups. While individualists think of self reliance as "being free and able to do my own thing," collectivists think of self reliance as "not being an unnecessary burden to my family or in-groups." The four defining attributes of individualism and collectivism that are essential to understanding how these individuals and groups appraise work stresses and cope with them are as follows:

  – *Definition of the self:* Individualists view their "selves" as independent and autonomous from the groups to which they belong. They construe themselves in an independent mode (Markus & Kitayama, 1991; Reykowski, 1994) and largely rely on their own efforts for coping with difficult situations that occur in both work and nonwork contexts. Collectivists, on the other hand, view themselves as interdependent with the members of their collectives and appraise and cope with stressful events in a manner that is highly isomorphic with the views of their in-groups. They feel much less constrained in sharing stories of their stressful experiences with members of their family, in-groups, and other important collectives.

- *Structure of goals:* Individualists pursue those goals in work and life that reflect their personal desires and objectives. These goals need not necessarily be compatible with those of their collectives. Collectivists, on the other hand, are socialized to pursue goals that are usually compatible with the goals of their in-groups (Schwartz, 1992, 1994; Triandis, 1994b, 1995, 1998). In case of conflict between individual and collective goals, collectivists are more comfortable giving priority to in-group goals. However, individualists are not likely to abandon the pursuit of personal goals in favor of goals of the collectives to which they might belong.

- *Emphasis on norms versus attitudes:* The drivers of social and organizational behaviors for individualists are primarily their own attitudes, personal needs, perceived rights, and contracts (Bhawuk, 2001; Bontempo & Rivero, 1992; Davidson, Jaccard, Triandis, Morales, & Diaz-Guerrero, 1976; Miller, 1984; Triandis, 1998), whereas for collectivists they are norms, duties, and obligations. Social norms and expectations regarding how one ought to deal with a stressful experience are more important for collectivists, whereas personal attitudes, preferences and inclinations are more important for individualists. The link among personal attitudes, behavioral intention, and behavior is more ambiguous in describing the collectivists than individualists. In other words, collectivists may behave in accordance with the expected norms and mores that are preferred by members of the in-group, even in situations where their personal attitudes may be reflective of a divergent point of view.

- *Emphasis on relatedness versus rationality:* The collectivists emphasize almost unconditional relatedness whereas individualists emphasize rationality and rational calculations in dealing with members of their collectives. Relatedness means that one gives priority to relationships and is diligent about taking in the account the needs of one's in-group even when such relationships are not necessarily advantageous and may even be costly in the long term. Rationality, on the other hand, emphasizes careful calculation of the cost and benefits of engaging in a relationship (whether within the individual, work groups, or organizations).

Vertical and Horizontal Relationships

In some societies, hierarchy is very important, and in-group authorities determine most of the preferred patterns of social and organizational behavior; however, in other societies, social and organizational behavior is more egalitarian and much less concerned with hierarchical relationships. Vertical societies assume that people are different from each other and that a social hierarchy is essential for effective functioning and coordination of human action. Vertical relations are common in societies that are high in Hofstede's (1980, 2001) power distance. Horizontal relations are found in societies that are low in power distance. The cultures of China, Japan, India, South Korea, and much of Latin America and Africa reflect vertical patterns of relationships. In contrast, horizontal cultures strongly emphasize a tradition of equality as is found in the Israeli kibbutz. The cultures of Australia, New Zealand, Sweden, and other Scandinavian countries are largely horizontal in nature. Integrating horizontal (i.e., same self) and vertical (i.e., different self) dimensions of self with interdependent and independent self results in four distinct types of individualism and collectivism:

- *Horizontal collectivism* (e.g., found in Israeli kibbutz)
- *Horizontal individualism* (e.g., Sweden, Denmark, Australia, New Zealand)
- *Vertical collectivism* (e.g., much of traditional India, China, Japan, South Korea, Greece, and Brazil)
- *Vertical individualism* (e.g., France, the United States, the United Kingdom)

Cultural Syndromes and the Management of Work Stress

Cultural syndromes are integral for developing insights into the management of work stress in dissimilar countries. Perhaps the two most important dimensions of cultural syndrome that are relevant for understanding the process of coping with work stress and seeking social support are individualism–collectivism and cultural complexity. As shown in Figure 6.1, which is derived from the theoretical framework presented in Bhawuk (2001), individualists are more interested in pursuing their own personal goals and objectives. They emphasize rational and calculative exchanges in their relationships with supervisors, coworkers, and other significant members of their work group and organizations. In addition, they are strongly driven by their attitudinal (i.e., affective) preferences, their personal ideas about what can be accomplished, and meaningful actions that are consistent with their self-concept. Collectivists, on the other hand, are largely motivated by the expectations and norms of their in-groups and are more likely to abandon their own personal goals and objectives in favor of collective goals—which often include members of their work groups and organizations.

Another major distinction between individualists and collectivists that can be linked to facets of cultural syndrome is concerned how individuals sample or

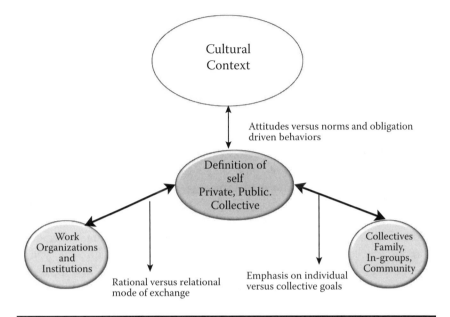

Figure 6.1 Defining attributes of individualism and collectivism. Emphasis on attitude, individual goals, and rational mode of exchange is more important for individualists. Emphasis on norms and obligations, collective goals, and relational mode of exchange is more important for collectivists.

collect information from their interpersonal and social world in defining their *self* (Baumeister, 1986; Greenwald & Pratkanis, 1984; Triandis, 1989, 1994b, 1995). Three aspects of *selves* are presented in Triandis (1989): the *private, public,* and *collective*. *Private self* involves sampling of cognitions regarding one's traits, mental states, and behaviors concerning one's self (e.g., I am honest; I like working under pressure; I am likely to quickly learn new techniques). *Public self* involves sampling of cognitions regarding the generalized view of one's self (e.g., people think I am honest; people think I am able to work under pressure). *Collective self* concerns sampling of cognitions regarding a view of the self that are embedded in one's collectives such as family, coworkers, community, or members of a scientific society (e.g., my close friends think I am a honest person; my co-workers think I am an accomplished engineer). The significance of these three kinds of selves is that the likelihood that individuals will sample cognitions from any of these three domains is largely determined by one's cultural background (Triandis, 1989). The private self is an assessment of the self by the self, whereas public self is an assessment that corresponds to the views of the person held by important others, that is, generalized and socially significant others in one's social context. The collective self is an assessment of the self by members of a particular reference group (which may be an in-group composed of co-workers and who are therefore likely to be intimately familiar with characteristics and preferences of the person). The notion of collective self corresponds to the notion of *social identity*, that is, that part of an individual self-concept that derives from their membership in a social group to which one is emotionally attached. In addition, these groups provide much of the foundation, or underpinnings, for the structure of one's values. It follows that all of the facets of self (private, public, and collective) have unique consequences for appraising social and work behavior including appraisal of and coping with work stresses. In other words, the relevance of sampling information from the domain of private self may be more important in appraising some types of stressful situations (such as coping with role overload—an important aspect of work stress that characterizes much of the globalized world) that occur in our lives whereas sampling information from one's collective self may be important in appraising a different type of stressful situation (such as having to take the responsibility of letting go of a beloved subordinate due to economic decline). It should be clear that sampling cognitions from the collective domain is going to be more important in the case of "letting go" or "firing" a subordinate. In contrast, sampling and monitoring cognitions from the private self is clearly more important in having to cope with role overloads which are experienced on an individual basis more often than not in the Western context.

We suggest that individualists are much more likely to sample their private selves to appraise, manage, and cope with stressful experiences at work (and at nonwork contexts as well). On the other hand, collectivists are likely to be more inclined to appraise stressful experiences at work by sampling relevant cognitions and beliefs from their public and collective selves. Coping with such stresses also tends to be different along the individualism and collectivism divide. It must be noted that while collectivists tend to emphasize relevant cognitions from their public or collective selves (such as seeking counsel and guidance from those who are members of their family or in-groups), they do not totally abandon the relevant and useful cognitions regarding their personal self (making use of personal insights and efforts to appraise and deal with the stressful situation). The point is that collectivists are more inclined to make use of information, knowledge, and techniques that are culturally sanctioned or applicable to the situation. Individualists, in contrast, are likely to make use of their personal efforts and resources and act in a manner largely consistent with their personal attitudes toward the stressful situation. Since individualists sample cognitions largely from the domain of their private selves they might act in a fashion that does not conform to the standard operating norms and expectations of the work and societal contexts. This is the essence of individualism—individuals may choose to stand out and act in a fashion that is consistent with their beliefs regardless of consequences. However, for collectivists, such scenarios are less likely—the style of coping and coping-related resources is largely determined by the work and societal contexts.

Coping refers to the cognitive and behavioral efforts that people use to manage internal and external demands of a chronic or episodic stressful situation. It can be classified as being either problem-focused or emotion-focused. *Problem-focused* coping involves activities that are primarily directed at changing the stressful situation, whereas *emotion-focused* coping involves activities that are directed toward ameliorating negative emotions caused by the experience of psychological strains or distress (Folkman & Moskowitz, 2004; Lazarus & Folkman, 1984). According to this definition, coping is a dynamic process involving transactions between individuals and their stressful environment. Assessment of coping necessarily involves asking individuals to indicate the extent to which they use either problem-focused, emotion-focused, or a combination of both strategies.

The central propositions of the Lazarus and Folkman model (see Folkman & Moskowitz, 2004, for a recent review) are supported, and there is some evidence for the cross-national generalizability of their coping checklist (Bhagat et al., 1994, 2010). There is an intuitive appeal of this approach to work stress researchers worldwide. However, given the wide array of phenomena that are affected by rapid advances in globalization, there is a clear need for additional research on the applicability of this model in countries characterized by vertical collectivism (over 70% of the world's population are vertical collectivists.) As discussed earlier, collectivists and individualists are guided by two different views of self (interdependent versus independent), and therefore they will engage in different types of coping strategies in identical stressful work situations. Chang, Tugade, and Asakawa (2006) found that East Asians (who are largely collectivistic) report a higher propensity to avoid or confront problems directly and choose to withdraw from the situation more than their American colleagues.

In collectivistic cultures, individuals tend to have fewer in-groups; however, they exercise profound influence. One is much more dependent on the in-group not only for routine interactions but also for their roles in providing supportive and caring functions (Yeh & Wang, 2000). Collectivists seek help from their family members in dealing with work-related stresses much more readily than members of individualistic cultures. In certain Asian cultures, disclosing personal problems outside one's family or in-groups (even if it concerns one's ongoing difficulty with a work situation) is believed to bring shame to the entire family (Sue, 1994). In the highly collectivist Japanese culture, for example, engaging in family activities aids in the process of coping with work-related stress (Homma-True, 1997; Yeh, Arora, & Wu, 2006). It is important to distinguish between *collective coping strategies* (i.e., mobilizing group resources) from *collectivistic coping style* (i.e., preferred method of coping of members of collectivistic cultures). Collectivistic individuals are more prone to use collective coping strategies such as seeking social support and counsel from their in-groups because of the nature of solidarity they have with their in-groups. But it is always important for them to protect harmony in the group and not become a burden. In a major research project involving Asians and Asian Americans, Taylor, Sherman, Kim, Jarcho, Takagi, and Dunagan (2004) find that despite their collectivistic orientations more often than not there is less reliance on sharing of stressful experiences with the members of one's in-groups. This happens because the member undergoing the stressful situation does not like to upset in-group harmony. The underlying rationale is that when one shares one's personal difficulties and stressful encounters (whether from the domain of work or nonwork) with the members of one's in-groups, one may cause the in-group members to experience anxieties and feelings of being overwhelmed.

Taylor et al. (2004) also found that collectivists are less likely to use social support compared to European Americans because of their desire to not disturb group harmony, to save face, and to avoid possible embarrassment. This happens in dealing with stressful events that are likely to result in major consequences and can indeed be demanding for the members of one's family and in-groups. Next, we present an analysis of the role cultural syndrome in problem-focused and emotion-focused styles of coping with stress.

Cultural Syndromes and Problem-Focused Coping

Problem-focused coping is understood as an attempt (i.e., an act) or a series of attempts to exercise control and manage a stressful situation. Since Rotter's (1966) classic work on the importance of locus of control, there have been literally thousands of studies examining the role of personal control and psychological adaptation to difficult and stressful situations. Therefore, it is not surprising that organizational stress researchers have been interested in exploring the generalizability of a problem-focused mode of coping in dealing with various types of role stresses. Western conceptions of control generally fall into the categories of internal versus external, active versus passive, and primary (i.e., environmental) versus secondary (i.e., emotional). Using a theoretical perspective of life span, Heckhausen and Schulz (1995) suggested that primary control is the preferred mode of action in coping with stressful experiences. Secondary control is to be used as a fallback option when attempts at exercising primary control do not work. It has generally been assumed that individualists are more likely to engage in actions that assist them in exercising primary control over stressful work situations than collectivists are (Bhagat et al., 2001; Bhagat et al., 1994;

Bhagat et al., 2010). In a study involving Thai and American youths, McCarty et al. (1999) found that primary control (i.e., over the environment) is preferred by Thai youths more than American youths. However, American youths are five times more likely than Thai youths to use secondary control (i.e., over oneself) for dealing with physical injuries. There seems to be a complex interaction between one's cultural background and the type of stressful situation with which one is confronted. A three-way interaction involving personality characteristics ultimately determines the nature of coping. Ethnic groups tend to differ in their preferences for direct action (i.e., problem-focused coping) versus indirect strategies (i.e., emotion-focused coping). Caplovitz (1979) studied preference for coping with inflationary pressures among Anglo Americans, African Americans, and Hispanic Americans. Anglo Americans were most likely to curtail expenditures by decreasing their standards of living; African Americans were most likely to spend time hunting for bargains; and Hispanic Americans were most likely to share the cost of various purchases with members of their families, in-groups, and neighbors.

When taking direct action tends to violate the cultural norms in situation, collectivists may choose to focus attention on a preferred activity that will eventually help them gain control over the stressful situation. Shifting the locus of preferred activity is not the same as being less internal in one's locus of control. It simply refers to the belief that when individuals cannot directly affect the external environment, it is better to adopt an indirect mode of action that controls one's emotional reactions.

It has been suggested that in coping with stressful situations, it is useful to distinguish between taking responsibility for the occurrence of an event and taking responsibility for engaging in appropriate actions for its solution. This is particularly important as we seek to develop insights into management of work stress and help individuals from both individualistic and collectivistic cultures to develop appropriate styles of coping in the current era of globalization. Many stressful situations that occur at work due to the continuous pressure of competition are not under direct control. However, by accepting the situation as it really is and then taking whatever appropriate actions might be possible (as opposed to optimal) in that situation. (See the discussion of the role of cultural variations on stress and coping in the context of the theoretical model presented in Figure 5.2.)

The various facets of cultural syndromes are helpful in understanding the relative prevalence and efficacies of problem-focused, emotion-focused, and other types of coping strategies. For example, we suggest that individuals working in large multinational and global types of firms located in culturally complex cities (e.g., New York, London, Berlin, Tokyo) are likely to prefer problem-focused more than emotion-focused strategies. A variety of unrelated cognitions is required for effective functioning in the multinational contexts of today's global organizations. One needs to sample from all three aspects of selves (private, public, and collective) and be more cognitively complex to appraise the types of work stresses that one encounters. Another set of propositions along this line of reasoning may be derived by applying the cultural syndromes framework to emotion-focused strategies.

Cultural Syndromes and Emotion-Focused Coping

Emotion-focused coping is more likely to occur when individuals appraise that relatively little can be done to modify the harmful, threatening, and challenging aspects of the work environment. Distinct types of strategies under the rubric of emotion-focused coping are found in the literature (see Aldwin, 2007; Folkman & Moskowitz, 2004; Kuo, 2010). A majority of strategies are directed at lowering emotional distress and include such actions as a selective attention to the stressful situation, distancing oneself from the situation, minimizing possible harmful effects on oneself or important members of in-group and family, positive comparisons, and thinking of "a silver lining in the dark clouds." Another group of cognitive strategies is, however, used to increase emotional arousal associated with experiencing the stressful situation. It seems as though some individuals need to feel worse before they can feel better. It is as if some individuals need to experience psychological distress more acutely than to engage in self-blame and other forms of emotional strategies (Folkman & Moskowitz, 2004; Lazarus & Folkman, 1984). Recall that in Chapter 5 we discussed the significance of intense emotional involvement in coping with stressful experiences in Indonesian and Latino cultures.

Current theories of work stress and coping are rooted in the individualistic context of Western cultures, which emphasize the value of strict emotional control (see Sanchez-Burks & Lee, 2007). In other cultures, however, a strong emphasis on emotional control may not be important and may in fact be counterproductive. These cultures socialize individuals from an early age to display their emotions in an appropriate fashion in various stressful situations. Puerto Ricans in New York, for example, call their colleagues cold or hard-hearted when they fail to display emotional warmth and caring in dealing with painful or culturally complex situations. Indeed, in some cultures emotional expression is instrumental for gaining social support and other resources for dealing with the stressful situation (Kuo, 2010). In a study with Egyptian women, Saunders (1977) found that an emotional expression called *zar*—dissociative episodes of shouting, laughing, weeping, or singing—is more effective in influencing husbands in situations where direct influence is either discouraged or prohibited.

Knight, Silverstein, McCallum, and Fox (2000) found that African Americans are more likely to use emotion-focused coping in care-giving situations such as health clinics and hospitals compared with non-African Americans. Qualitative studies also reveal that African Americans are more apt to use religious-based strategies such as engaging in prayer (Loukissa, Farran, & Revenson, 1999). In a study on sociocultural determinants, Wasti and Cortina (2002) investigated responses to sexual harassments in four samples of working women from three cultures and two occupational classes. They found that Turkish and Hispanic American women tend to engage in more avoidance coping compared with Anglo American women. In addition, Hispanic women use more denial-focused coping strategies and are less interested in advocacy-focused coping strategies in dealing with the initiator of the harassment. Their findings clearly suggest that there are significant differences in both proactive (e.g., problem-focused and action-oriented) coping and reactive (e.g., avoidance and denial) coping across cultures and occupational classes. Professional women tend to seek social support more than simply engaging in emotion-focused coping in dealing with harassment-related situations. Research shows that ethnic groups in the United States use more emotional expression as well as engage in various forms of religion-based coping (see Chapter 4 for details). However, additional research is needed involving work and organizational behaviors. Recent findings on ethnic and cross-cultural variations on emotion and emotional experience (Mesquita & Leu, 2007) should be of considerable value in future research on work stress and coping.

Work Stress Across Ethnic, Racial, Cultural, and Religious Divides

As discussed in Chapter 2, numerous countries in the current era of globalization are going through significant economic, social, and organizational restructuring. The need for integrating substantial minority populations, including people who differ in terms of their ethnic, cultural, racial, and religious backgrounds, has been increasing since the 1970s. Much has been written on the growing role of these groups in sustaining the productivity and competitiveness of all types of organizations in the United States and Europe: domestic, public, private, multinational, and global (see Pfeffer, 1996).

The percentage of foreign-born workers in the United States, Western Europe, Australia, and New Zealand has continued to grow since the 1970s. In addition, there has been a significant growth of Islamic populations in Western countries such as France, the United Kingdom, Germany, and the Netherlands causing significant cultural tensions and public debates. These demographic developments make it necessary to develop theories that are uniquely sensitive

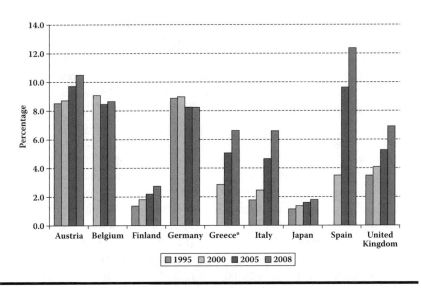

Figure 6.2 The percentage of foreign-born workers by country from 1995 to 2008. (From Migration Policy Institute Data Hub, 2011. Retrieved from http://www.migrationpolicy.org/datahub. With permission.)

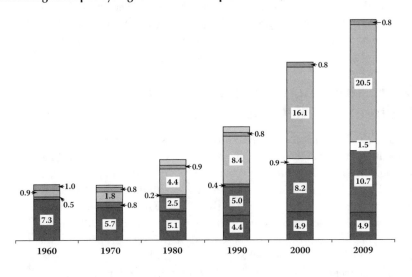

Figure 6.3 Foreign-born population by region of birth: 1960 to 2009 (in millions). (From Migration Policy Institute Data Hub, 2011. Retrieved from http://www.migrationinformation.org/datahub/comparative.cfm. With permission.)

in capturing the nuances of work stress and coping across ethnic, racial, cultural, and religious divides (Figures 6.2 and 6.3).

As Figures 6.4 and 6.5 depict, the percentages of minority workers have continued to increase in the United States since 1966. It was about 10% in 1966 and increased to 33% in 2007. The percentages of African Americans, Hispanic Americans, Asian Americans and Pacific Islanders, and Native Americans have continued to increase in the U.S. workforce (see Figure 6.5). In the 1990 census, the population of Hispanics was 22.4 million (U.S. Census Bureau, 2001). In 2010, there were 50.5 million Hispanics in the United States, composing 16% of the total population (U.S. Census Bureau, 2010). According to the 2006 U.S. Census Bureau data, racial and ethnic minorities in the United States made up over 33% of the total population—phenomenal growth since the early twentieth century. It is projected that in the next three decades racial and ethnic minority groups will constitute about 40% of the total population and that the current majority of White Americans will drop below 50%. In June 2009, the Hispanic population in the United States surpassed the African American population and became the largest ethnic group. The next largest ethnic group is composed of African Americans and currently

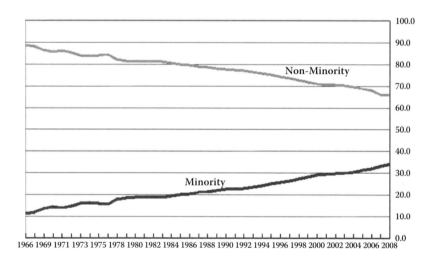

Figure 6.4 **T2 private-sector employment of minority versus nonminority (1966–2007) U.S. summary. (From Equal Employment Opportunity Commission, Employer Information Reports [EEO-1 Single and Consolidated Reports]. Figures prior to 2005, 2008 from Indicators of Equal Employment Opportunity, EEOC, 2009.)**

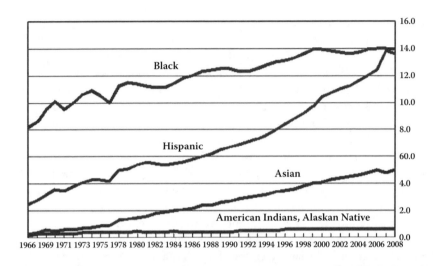

Figure 6.5 T3 private sector employment by minority groups (1966–2007) U.S. Summary. (From Equal Employment Opportunity Commission, Employer Information Reports [EEO-1 Single and Consolidated Reports]. Figures prior to 2005 from Indicators of Equal Employment Opportunity, EEOC, 2009.)

constitutes about 11% of the total population, followed by Asian Americans, Pacific Islanders, and Native Americans.

The various ethnic groups in the United States may function in the context of dominant Eurocentric U.S. culture, but they do not easily abandon their unique cultural patterns that reflect their historical, religious, and other important traditions. It is safe to note that minorities have culture-specific responses to work and organizational stresses and cope with stresses in ways that are different from the mainstream (i.e., White Americans) population (Aldwin, 2007; Wong & Wong, 2006). The issues of managing workforce diversity that became important for U.S. organizations (both domestic and multinationals) in the 1990s recognized the significance of cultural differences across ethnic, racial, national, and religious divides.

Issues of Religious Diversities

The United States is a predominantly secular nation and employees may belong to any religion and practice their religious faith and rituals freely. Most nations of Europe, Asia, Latin America, and Africa recognize the freedom of individuals to belong to any religion. However, in many countries of the Middle East, the freedom to practice one's own religion is not a fundamental right. The primacy of Islam is regarded as being supreme in the design and conduct of organizational practices. Immigrants from these countries are likely to encounter significant difficulties in acculturating and adapting to Western societies and work organizations. The controversy surrounding the building of mosques and places of worship for the Islamic communities in the United States, France, Switzerland, and other Nordic European countries have increased during the past decade. The proposed construction of a mosque and Islamic community center in Murfreesboro, Tennessee, generated considerable controversies and national media attention since 2010. Muslim women in France are beginning to protest the banning of the burqa, a headdress that shields a woman's face from public view. A female protestor recently noted:

> This is an attack on my freedom of conscience, my freedom of religion, my freedom of simply being a woman, so this is a really big attack on my own life. (Hurd, 2011)

Another woman wearing a veil said:

> God willing, I am going to continue to wear this. We are free to practice our religion because it is our democratic right. (Hurd, 2011)

However, views to the contrary also exist. French economist Laurent Berrebe claimed that the law was not racist and that one has to:

> Understand the history of France to accept this kind of law.... It's not something racist. It's not a racist law. It's just a law that is coming from the history of France and so you need to accept it, if you want to integrate into France and to the French people. (Hurd, 2011)

Controversies surrounding religious identities do not necessarily involve the Islamic community in the Western countries; issues of religious conflicts involving violence have been reported in secular India, China, Nigeria, and many parts of sub-Saharan Africa. Such conflicts, while originating largely in the immigrant communities, quickly spill over into the world of work and create serious consequences for work stresses involving interpersonal conflict, problems with performance appraisal, upward mobility, and a sense of belonging or commitment.

In 2008, 74.6% of the U.S. population identified themselves as Christians with other religious groups comprising 5.2%. Muslim and Jewish populations were roughly about 0.6% and 1.2%, respectively. Agnostics and those with no religion identification made up about 15.0% of the U.S. population (Kosmin & Keysar, 2009). In Western Europe, 72% of the population is Christian, with the Islamic population being the next largest religious group (about 6%) and agnostics about 18%. Freedom to practice one's religion has always been an important right for the United States and much of Western and Nordic Europe. However, as discussed earlier, incidents of religious conflicts and clashes in the globalized and globalizing parts of the world not only are drawing the attention of the global media but also have consequences for work stress and well-being of individuals. Some corporations encourage the practice of some types of religious rituals in the workplace. However, except for anecdotal and newspaper reports, it is not clear to what extent such programs might cause work-related interpersonal and group conflict leading to work stresses. Clearly this is an area where both qualitative and quantitative inquiries including large-scale surveys of immigrant enclaves and communities are needed. Findings from this area will not only enrich the paradigms of work stress and coping but also act as guidelines for enlightened practices that can be successfully implemented. Right now the policies and programs are based on traditional notions of tolerance and coexistence. However, research findings from the social sciences are likely to be more useful in the design and implementation of best practices.

Work Stress: The Hispanic American Experience

Hispanic Americans are the largest ethnic group in the United States and accounted for one-half of the nation's population growth between 2000 and 2006. The Hispanic population growth rate (28.9%) between 2000 and 2009 was over 248% larger than the overall U.S. growth rate (8.3%). In Western and Southwestern states, Hispanics constituted 33.1% of the total population and about 10% in the South. As of 2009, the 10 states with the largest Hispanic population were California (13.7 million), Texas (9.1 million), Florida (4.0 million), New York (3.2 million), Arizona (2.0 million), Illinois (2.0 million), New Jersey (1.5 million), Colorado (1.0 million), New Mexico (0.9 million), and Georgia (0.8 million). The latest census data show that while 44% of all Hispanics are concentrated in the two largest states in the United States— California and Texas—Hispanic population levels are growing rapidly in all regions of the country with exceptional growth rates in the Great Lakes region, the Upper Midwest, and the South. While Hispanics are settling in different states, census data indicate that majority of the Cubans live in the South, Puerto Ricans in the Northeast, and Mexicans in the West and Southwest (U.S. Census Bureau, 2010).

Understanding work stress and coping processes among the Hispanics must take into account their experiences of acculturation and acculturative stress. Inevitably, the inconsistencies and conflicts between the cultural patterns of Hispanics and the dominant U.S. culture result in the experience of both acculturative and work-related stresses. Hispanic Americans who have adopted the beliefs, norms, and values of the mainstream U.S. culture have been found to adapt with the challenges of the host society relatively easily. A study conducted in the 1960s (Tharp, Meadow, Lennhoff, & Satterfield, 1968) found that Mexican American women who were acculturated into the dominant U.S. culture were more egalitarian and comfortable with the male not necessarily being the primary bread earner and decision maker in the family. In a later study conducted during the 1980s, Vega, Kolody, and Valle (1988) found support for the hypothesis that less acculturated Mexican American women experienced increased marital conflicts, feelings of self-denigration, and loss of the ability to negotiate with their spouse.

In the prevailing literature, there is hardly any mention that acculturation-related processes have significant implications for work stress and coping among immigrants and ethnic minorities. Processes of acculturation, cultural adaptation, and acculturative stresses of the immigrants and their families occur following migration to a new country and culture (Berry, 1994; Cervantes, Padilla, & Salgado de Snyder, 1991; Flores, Tschann, Marin, & Pantoja, 2004). Cervantes et al. (1991) found that the Mexican Americans indicated the following situations as being particularly stressful:

■ Having poor English language skills
■ Believing that the immigrant would never again regain the status and respect that he or she had had in his or her country of origin (i.e., home country)
■ Not feeling accepted by Americans because they belong to Latino culture
■ Feeling discrimination because of Hispanic background and ethnicity

Stressful experiences for Hispanic Americans are also related to the differential rates of acculturation between males and females—with females enjoying greater autonomy and decision-making power in the United States compared with their counterparts in the traditional Hispanic-dominated countries. The specific stressful situations identified by Cervantes et al. (1991) are

■ Personal goals conflicting with goals of the family, tension with family members during various stages of acculturation.
■ Women becoming more individualistic in the United States as they acculturate and learn the values of mainstream U.S. In traditional Hispanic families, women are supposed to play subordinate roles.

■ Organized religion being not as important as institutionalized practices for managing stressful experiences at work.

Work Stress: The African American Experience

African Americans (Black Americans) constitute 12.8% of the U.S. population—as of July 2008, 39.1 million. African Americans accounted for 14.8% of the change in the U.S. population between 2000 and 2008. The change in the African American population (9.1%) was higher than the change in the U.S. population (7.8%) between 2000 and 2008 (U.S. Census Bureau, 2008). A large percentage of African Americans live in the Southern part of the United States, followed by the Midwest, Northeast, and then the West. The top five states with significant percentages of African American population in 2008 were New York, Florida, Georgia, Texas, and California.

The social and cultural experience of African Americans is quite different from that of Hispanic Americans. Stressful experiences involving race is an unavoidable reality for a large percentage of African Americans regardless of the positions they hold in their work organizations. African Americans, in addition to experiencing the generic job and organizational stresses (e.g., role overload, role ambiguity, role conflict, interpersonal conflict) are also confronted with a set of social strains or stigmas rooted in the context of the historical experience of their ethnic group. African American managers are known to experience certain job-related strains that are known as the *Black tax* (Harper, 1975). The Black tax refers to the subtle aspects of racism that are reflected in a sense of power-lessness and alienation largely resulting from mutual distrust between African Americans and their peers. The conflicting pressures of being labeled as an *Uncle Tom* or *sellout* by the African Americans and being regarded as a *nonconformist* by Whites lead to job-related stresses and strains for African Americans. The typical sources of stresses that are unique to the African Americans regardless of the type of organizations that they work for and where the organizations may be located in the United States are as follows:

■ A majority of the African Americans believe that the system of upward mobility and career development is often biased against them.
■ Whites are less likely to believe that African American managers are hired based on competence and experience as opposed to being hired to fill affirmative action–based quotas or as "tokens" for enhancing cultural and racial diversity.
■ There exists the strong attribution error in the perception of the causes of work-related failures. A majority of African Americans believe that if any

of them fail or does not succeed as well as their White or Asian American counterparts, then all African Americans in the organization are likely to be stereotyped as being incompetent.

■ Over two-thirds of African American managers report that they are not fairly evaluated in their performance appraisals. A majority feel that they are largely excluded from the informal social networks, the organizational "grapevine," regarding new career opportunities, job transfers, and lucrative assignments. In other words, they feel that they remain less knowledgeable concerning "ropes to know and the ropes to skip" in their companies.

Racial discrimination elevates the experience of work stress and negatively affects mental health. Landrine and Klonoff (1996) found that African Americans reported higher incidences of stressful experiences associated with racism and discrimination compared with other ethnic and minority groups—98% report experiencing some form of discrimination in the past year. The most common event was the experience of being discriminated against by strangers (e.g., customers) and coworkers in service professions (83%). Discrimination by institutions was reported by 64% of African Americans, whereas 55% of African Americans reported discrimination (e.g., being subjected to racial slurs) in the context of care-giving professions.

As a general rule, African Americans experiencing discrimination on the job report less life satisfaction (Broman, 1997). According to Landrine and Klonoff (1996), more than a third of the respondents indicated that they had to take extreme measures to deal with race-related stressful experiences. Dysfunctional consequences such as quitting a job or filing a lawsuit were not uncommon; however, these experiences exacerbated feelings of stress. It is interesting to note that there were no gender differences in the frequencies of occurrence of stressful experiences at work. However, African Americans who are more acculturated into the Eurocentric aspects of the mainstream culture tended to experience less discrimination and learned to balance negative reactions from members of their own racial group who were less acculturated.

Jones (1988), a distinguished African American psychologist, developed a contrast between African American and European American personalities and work styles. In his view, contemporary African Americans are trying to find a balance between the two tendencies: One is rooted in the mainstream values of African culture, whereas the other is found in the cultures of Europe and European American. The contrast between the contemporary African American and European American values that are relevant for the experience of work stress is presented in Table 6.1.

For African Americans who have largely been socialized outside the mainstream U.S. culture, it is not surprising that a large majority of them feel that

Table 6.1   Contrasting Patterns of Cultural Attributes (of Relevance for the Study of Work, Stress, and Coping)

European Americans	African Americans
Predominately individualistic in orientation	Primarily individualistic but collectivistic tendencies are also found in dealings with family and in-groups
Rationality and rational calculations are more important	Relational considerations are almost as important as rational considerations
Self-identity defined by record of accomplishments and experience	Self-identity defined by expression, style, and engagement in spontaneous activities
Strong emphasis on planning, predictability, and routine in work activities	Less emphasis on routine
More future oriented	More present oriented
More task oriented	More gregarious
Materialistic and mechanistic	More spiritual and religious

Source: Adapted from Triandis, H. C., *Cultural and Social Behavior*, McGraw-Hill, New York, 2004, p. 243. With permission.

they are not sufficiently included in the decision-making processes in organizations. Majors and Mancini-Billson (1992) argued that African American professionals have largely internalized the mainstream values of self-reliance and economic independence, but structural barriers have prevented and continue to prevent them from being as successful as other minority or ethnic groups. Job characteristics play an important role in maintaining harmony. Broman (1997) reports that jobs with higher decision latitude or autonomy, are associated with marital harmony and personal life satisfaction. As discussed in Chapter 3, a sense of control over one's job is critical to maintaining low levels of stress whether it is professional or blue collar in nature. It is interesting that feelings of empowerment and strength are common among those African Americans who practice religion while confronting unpredictable and uncontrollable events at work (Siegel & Schrimshaw, 2002). Additional research looking into the interactions of racial and religious factors in the area of work stress and coping for African Americans will be useful in the future.

Work Stress: The Asian American Experience

As the third largest ethnic and cultural group in the United States, Asian Americans constitute 16.3 million, or 3.4% of the U.S. population of 304 million (U.S. Census Bureau, 2008). Asian Americans accounted for 13.1% of the change in the U.S. population between 2000 and 2008. Coupled with immigration of Asians during the past decade, the population of Asian Americans is projected to be about 40 million by 2050 (U.S. Census Bureau, 2008).

Despite considerable research showing the adverse effects of stress in the workplace and the high rate of employment of professional Asians in various professional roles, it is surprising that both theoretical and empirical research on work stress and coping among Asian Americans is relatively rare. Leong and Tolliver (2006) provide some theoretical insights that aid the process of understanding occupational stress among Asian Americans. It is widely recognized that there are unique pressures (i.e., of the financial, cultural, and social variety) associated with ethnic minority status in the United States and other globalized countries. The vulnerability to experience psychosocial and work stresses tends to be considerably higher in Asian Americans. Asian Americans have distinct notions about who they are as members of an ethnic group, "what is the right or appropriate" thing to do for them as members of their ethnic group, and how members of the mainstream culture are likely to perceive and relate to them because of their distinct ethnic group identities. Abe and Zane (1990), for example, found higher levels of psychological distress among foreign-born Asian American students than among Caucasian American students even after controlling for demographics, personality, and response-style effects. Earlier research by Sue and Frank (1973) and Sue and Kirk (1973) found incidences of greater nervousness, anxiety, and loneliness among Chinese American and Japanese American students—largely due to stresses associated with psychosocial adaptation to the new cultural environment.

Among the ethnic groups, the case of Asian Americans is particularly interesting because even though they are the third largest minority in the United States and are growing as a percentage of the total population in the European Union (EU), there is a surprising scarcity of research on work, occupational, and organizational stress involving this ethnic group. The major stress experienced by Asian Americans is the stress associated with the pressures maintaining bicultural identities (Roysircar & Maestas, 2002). Bicultural stress occurs when members of an ethnic group have to negotiate between the pressures and expectations of two contrasting cultural orientations. Bicultural socialization (de Anda, 1984) is not an easy process (it often involves a series of conflicts and painful encounters with both cultures), and ethnic identity slowly evolves at the intersection of the two cultures. The experience of bicultural stresses involves stages characterized by the processes of cultural alienation, cultural confusion, and cultural conflicts with their unique demands on all three aspects of self (i.e., private, public, and collective). The generational status, physical appearance, and conflicts with immigrant parents over values, behaviors, and family roles moderate the evolution of bicultural stresses in ethnic groups, and Asians are no exception to this rule. Padilla, Wagatsuma, & Lindholm (1985) found that second- and third-generation Asian Americans reported less stress and higher self-esteem than the first generation; however, the second generation reported lower self-esteem than the third generation. Stresses involving bicultural identities decline over the generations, and it seems that its primary role is to act as a mediator between work stress and valued outcomes—both at the personal and organizational levels.

More often than not, Asian Americans do not view themselves as members of a minority group per se because they are not underrepresented in corporate, academic, health care, and other advanced occupations both in the United States and in Europe (see Takaki, 2007). In addition, Asian Americans are likely to be more culturally integrated than Hispanic and African Americans—their rate of intermarriage with the members of the dominant mainstream culture is higher than other ethnic groups (Chang et al., 2006). The label *model minority* is often used to describe Asian Americans, which suggests there is much overlap between Asian and American values of achievement and economic success. Some Asian Americans may view themselves as examples of a model minority, whereas others may experience difficulties in establishing their occupational identities because of such characterization. The model minorities are expected to perform better in their work roles, have children who are highly successful in schools and universities, and have higher incomes. Many Asian Americans complain that being regarded as members of a model minority can be stressful because pressures to conform to the expected roles of model minority can conflict with the various family and in-group related obligations of their ethnic cultures. Considerable evidence suggests that Asian Americans attempt to separate the pressures and expectations of work from the duties and responsibilities of their family lives. However, this process results in conflicts between professional accomplishments and self-reliance versus loyalty to family and members of in-groups. Leong and Chou (1994) examined an integrated model of racial and ethnic identity in a sample of Asian Americans to test the hypothesis that more acculturated Asian Americans perceived more opportunities in the U.S. occupational structure and developed their careers faster. Asian Americans who pursued assimilation and integration strategies found it easier to move upward in their chosen careers and experienced higher levels of job satisfaction. Leong (2001) found that less acculturated individuals tended to experience higher levels of occupational stresses and lower job satisfaction. Leong suggested that the experience of stress and strain result from an interaction among the level of acculturation and the type of organization. Asian American executives from a Fortune 500 company who were not sufficiently acculturated experienced higher levels of work stress when compared with Asian American managers of an engineering company.

The experience of Asian American women as they participate in increasing numbers in the globalized economies should receive increased research attention. Gender differences have long been an organizing principle of work family research and women's experiences are central to this line of research (particularly women from predominantly collectivistic cultures of Asia). Work stresses are higher in both dual-career and multiple-earner families (Wharton, 2006). With women taking on nontraditional work roles in a 24/7 economy, the pressures on Asian American families seem to be growing. This has been debated in the popular press, but systematic research-based insights into the consequences of increased participation of Asian women in the advanced economies of the world are yet to be developed.

A large number of Asian American women feel a sense of embarrassment and shame when they experience pressures of modern life affecting the traditional emphasis on family harmony. For women in dual-career families, the experience of the work–family conflict is likely to lead to a sense of guilt, especially if they are raised to believe that women should be dutiful and self-sacrificial in their spousal and maternal roles (Doi, 1973; Weibe, 1985). In Asian families, a great deal of family stress, whether the root causes are from the domain of work or nonwork, tends to cause a "loss of face," meaning losing the respect and status of the family in their community. Next, we discuss the nature of work stresses that are likely to affect immigrants who are becoming increasingly important as employees in various multinational and global corporations.

Immigrants: Acculturation and Acculturative Stress

Since the 1960s, the liberation of U.S. immigration laws as well as the immigration laws of other countries has created a significant growth of immigrants in G-8 countries. The number of immigrants has doubled since 1975 due to the spread of globalization, and by year 2010 over 214 million people lived and worked outside their countries of origin. While the majority of the immigrants move from their country of origin to the host country in search of better occupational opportunities, professional growth, and improved quality of living, there has also been a corresponding growth of large number of illegal immigrants. U.S. Census data collected in 2010 reveal that currently over 10.8 million immigrants living in the United States are illegal (i.e., they have no legal permission to work or live in the United States; U.S. Department of Homeland Security, 2011).

In addition to the native born minority population, the influx of immigrants from culturally dissimilar countries also increased the complexity of issues that need to be analyzed in understanding the phenomenon of stress and coping. As of 2002, 23% of the U.S. population comprised first- and second-generation immigrants (Bean, Van Hook, Bloemraad, & Brown, 2004). In U.S. cities, the population of foreign born is much higher. Census figures from 2000 show that over 40% of people living in the five boroughs of New York city were born in countries other than the United States (i.e., first-generation immigrants) compared with just 28% in 1990 (U.S. Census Bureau, 2000). In Los Angeles in 2000, 30% of the population was foreign born.

There is clearly an uneven distribution of immigrants living in the various regions in the United States, with the metropolitan areas and large cities accounting for the largest increases in immigrants since the 1970s. The situation of the illegal immigrants is quite dire, but organizational research on this group has been almost nonexistent except for some economic analyses pertaining to their contributions to the regions of the United States where they tend to settle. For example, labor economists have claimed that the cost of agricultural products would rise if illegal immigrants were barred from working on farms in California, Texas, and Florida. Regardless of the economic role of illegal immigrants in the United States, the United Kingdom, and other advanced globalized economies, we are concerned with acculturation and acculturative stress of immigrant professionals who have attained professional status and intend to and are able to continue their chosen profession in the host country. In the globalized economies, a significant percentage of engineers, managers, nurses, doctors, and professors are immigrants from various collectivistic countries of the world (e.g., China, India, Philippines, South Korea, Vietnam, Greece) and have considerable professional training and hold higher expectations to succeed in their professional work roles and achieve economic success.

Immigration is typically accompanied by unresolved stresses and anxieties, and immigrants experience work stresses in the new culture context of the host country with a dissimilar perspective. *Acculturative stress* (Antoniou & Dalla, 2009; Berry, 1994; Berry & Sam, 1997; Bhagat, Davis, & London, 2009) is an unsettling experience that occurs during the process of acculturation and is largely responsible for generating adverse psychological, psychosomatic, and behavioral reactions. Both positive (e.g., better career opportunities in their new environments) and negative (e.g., adverse encounters with abrasive and culturally insensitive supervisors or coworkers) stressful experiences occur during the process of acculturation. Acculturative stress has been studied as a phenomenon that evolves at the intersection of two cultures. Bhagat and London (1999) and Bhagat, McDevitt, and Segovis (2011) provide a typology of the kind of stresses that immigrants are likely to encounter in the process of acculturation. As with any other type of work stress, acculturative stresses tend to accompany those situations where the demands associated with culture specific changes accompanying the process of acculturation (both in the context of work and nonwork) exceed the capacity of the immigrant to cope with them (Berry, 2006; Berry & Ataca, 2000; Wong & Wong, 2006).

Immigrants, whether they work in the United States, Canada, or countries in the European Union, Australia, New Zealand, Israel, and Middle Eastern countries (e.g., United Arab Emirates), must learn to function by slowly acculturating into the mainstream culture. As discussed earlier, acculturative stress (stress resulting from the ongoing demands of adjustments to the culture of the country of settlement) can be difficult. Successful adjustment and adaptation with the cultural values of the host society is often necessary for performing well in work roles. However, the degree to which immigrants can learn and appreciate the fundamental beliefs, norms, and values of the host society depends on their cultural background prior to migration. Immigrants who remain on the periphery of U.S. culture or the culture of other host societies report increases in work stress, marital stress, and self-denigration and loss of self-esteem and ability to negotiate the various issues that arise in intercultural adjustments (Antoniou & Dalla, 2009; Bhagat et al., 2009). Berry and his colleagues (Berry, 2006; Berry & Sam, 1997) have found that most behavioral changes result when immigrants make deliberate attempts to learn and absorb the values and practices of the mainstream culture. This is the strategy of *assimilation*. Minimal changes occur when they pursue the strategy of *separation* (i.e., remain largely isolated from the influences of mainstream culture). The third is the strategy of *integration,* which involves selected adoption of some of the new norms and behaviors of the host society and retention of some of the valued practices of the culture of one's home country of origin.

As immigrants acquire knowledge regarding the values and practices of the host culture, they displace the values and practices of their heritage culture. The ability to navigate bicultural and sometimes multicultural identities is crucial in developing accurate appraisals of work related stressful experiences (Hong, Wan, No, & Chiu, 2007). According to research summarized in Hong et al., several cultural identities may coexist without adverse psychological consequences.

Rapid demographic changes due to the increased flow of immigrants in the globalized world are creating ethnic enclaves that must be analyzed in a multicultural perspective. Some research exists on entrepreneurship among immigrants (Ndofor & Priem, 2011); however, as noted earlier there is a relative scarcity of theoretical models and research findings dealing with work stress and coping. While research on processes of acculturation and acculturative stresses have grown in the past four decades (Bhagat et al., 2009; Kirkcaldy, Furnham, & Siefen, 2009), there seems to be little integration of this line of research with mainstream research on work and organizational stress in the West. Given the growth and importance of immigrant professionals in this era of globalization, it is crucial to develop a systematic body of research that is both theoretically robust and practically useful.

Coping With Work Stress: Experience of Hispanics, African Americans, and Asian Americans

Hispanic Americans

A number of multicultural studies investigating the effectiveness of coping styles on psychological well-being in ethnic minorities have been conducted in the United States (Wong & Wong, 2006). In a study examining coping and health-seeking patterns for personal, interpersonal, and academic stressors among African American and Latino American college students, Chiang, Hunter, and Yeh (2004) found that both groups were similar in emphasizing the role of family and religion in coping with stressful events. However, on a closer inspection, Latino students were significantly more likely to seek help from parents than were African American students. For Hispanic Americans, the importance of family support and togetherness is reflected in the notion of *familismo* (Castillo, Conoley, & Brossart, 2004; Kobus & Reyes, 2000). Kobus and Reyes (2000) found that seeking support from one's family is a common method for dealing with stressful situations whether in the work or nonwork domain. Chiang et al. (2004) also found that although both African American and Hispanic American college students tended to seek support from their family while dealing with mental health-related problems, the Hispanic Americans expected a lot more from their older family members. The value of saving face across generations and the establishment of lifelong relationships among grandparents, parents, and children are highly revered practices in the Hispanic culture. Collectivistic values are promoted in developing resilience against daily stressors and incidences of violence in urban areas of the United States. Culturally congruent forms of counseling such as seeking help and counsel from indigenous healers, an elder, or an authoritative figure who is respected in the community and strong adherence to collectivistic norms and values of the community are also important forms of coping. It is safe to conclude that the thoughts, emotions, motivations, and behaviors of Hispanic Americans are largely rooted in their collective and interdependent selves.

While dealing with stressful encounters at work, Hispanic Americans tend to avoid speaking about or formally reporting problems of difficulties to their supervisors and managers. They instead prefer to deal with them by sharing their concerns with close members and associates of their community. The Western tradition of seeking help from a professional counselor or from the employment assistance programs (EAPs) seems to be culturally inappropriate for a large segment of the Hispanic Americans regardless of their occupational ranks (Yeh et al., 2006; Yeh & Wang, 2000).

Catholicism plays a dominant role in the lives of people throughout Latin America and among the Hispanics in the United States. Religion and spirituality play strong protective roles in moderating the effects of stress in their work and nonwork lives. For Hispanic women in particular, religiosity is very important in coping with adverse experiences in life. The collectivistic orientation of Hispanics contributes to a holistic worldview and a strong tendency to believe that control of difficult situations may lie in the hands of external forces (Morling & Fiske, 1999). This holistic view encourages a connection among mind, body, spirit, nature, and a strong belief in Catholicism and fate. Some of the coping methods involving religion are seeking spiritual support and connection, seeking forgiveness from God, religious purification, caring and compassion, and religious reappraisal (Pargament et al., 1998).

African Americans

Research with African Americans also finds that religious activities are important in coping with the ambiguous and discriminatory events and acts that they often experience in the workplace. The African American worldview places the role of spirituality and religion in high regard (Sheu & Sedlacek, 2004). In a related vein, Plummer and Slane (1996) report that African Americans engage less in proactive and problem-focused coping styles and strategies in dealing with stressful experiences related to racism. In an earlier study, Feagin (1991) found that a significant percentage of African Americans considered that avoiding stressful experiences is less strenuous and more manageable in terms of both time and energy. This strategy of avoidance coping is frequently practiced in dealing with the stressful experiences associated with subtle as opposed to blatant or overt acts of racism and discrimination. Not only is it difficult to prove to others that a subtle act of racism has occurred, but one also has to be convinced in one's own mind that such an event can indeed be proven or validated. Most organizations do not have appropriate methods of addressing subtle acts of racism and often choose to "look the other way." Given the significant difficulties in dealing with subtle acts of racism, most African American managers choose to avoid and do not actively cope with such situations.

The point is that spirituality and religion are of central importance in coping with work-related stresses and stressful life events. For example, Utsey and his associates (Utsey, Brown, & Bolden, 2004) found that community-based as well as spiritually oriented methods in coping with stresses are more common among African Americans. As do Hispanic Americans, African Americans tend to promote collectivistic values that seem to provide the community with resilience against daily stressors, hassles, and incidences of violence. Historically, family and family-based resources have been vital sources of social support in coping with stressful situations at work and nonwork (Daly, Jennings, Beckett, & Leashore, 1995). However, there has been a significant decline of the importance of family and family values in dealing with difficult situations—dysfunctional families are on the rise in inner cities of large metropolitan areas.

In addition to emphasizing spirituality, expressive communication, temporal rhythms, and harmony with nature are some of the other values that are of significance in construing acts of coping in this ethnic group. Belgrave, Townsend, Cherry, and Cunningham (1997) found that sensitive interpersonal orientation and perception and predisposition toward emphasizing the optimistic as opposed to pessimistic mode of thinking are also emphasized among the African Americans. Other culture-specific or emic styles of coping are concerned with *cognitive/emotional debriefing* style, which represents an adaptive reaction to environmentally complex stressors by detaching oneself from the situation and focusing on the positive cues and signals. The researchers note that this type of coping has its roots in centuries of racial oppression that have characterized the experience of African Americans in the U.S. society. The second coping style, termed the *spiritual-centered strategy,* represents mechanisms for maintaining one's sense of harmony with the immediate environment even in the face of difficult and often unchangeable events. The third coping style, called the *collective strategy,* is concerned with the efforts to seek resolution and comfort by marshalling social support from members of one's in-group and significant others in the community. The fourth coping style, termed the *ritual-centered* strategy, emphasizes the importance of spiritual rituals (e.g., attending important religious events, lighting candles, burning incense). Another study involving a culturally sensitive scale for measuring coping patterns (Afro-cultural coping systems inventory; ACSI) further supports the existence of these four coping styles for African Americans (Utsey et al., 2004). Collectively, these studies revealed the importance of in-group norms, community values, spiritual rituals, and practices in the evolution of coping styles and strategies of African Americans.

Asian Americans

Issues of acculturation and acculturative stress are important to consider in understanding the work stress and coping patterns among this ethnic and cultural group in the United States. Despite being the third largest ethnic group in the United States, the number of studies on stress and coping that are conducted with this group compared with other ethnic groups seems to be high. We provide a series of examples of research conducted with Asian Americans. Mena, Padilla, and Maldonado's (1987) study of coping mechanisms among four generation groups of immigrant college students in the United States showed that the generation status had a significant effect on the preference of coping strategies in dealing with acculturative stress. First-generation immigrant groups reported greater use of active coping methods than individuals from later generations. The second- and third-generation respondents relied more on social networks as a coping mechanism than did the first-generation immigrant groups. These results may be interpreted by noting that second- and third-generation immigrants are more acculturated with the values and norms of the mainstream society and develop appropriate and culture-specific resources and mechanisms for coping and adaptation.

In a study involving immigrants to Canada, Zheng and Berry (1991) found that Chinese sojourners who were recent arrivals and the least acculturated to the Canadian culture reported more stresses and problems (e.g., homesickness, loneliness) than either Chinese Canadians or European Canadians. However, this group relied more on positive coping strategies (e.g., more tension reduction and information seeking) and less on passive coping (e.g., wishful thinking and self-blame) than did European Canadians. Kuo, Kwantes, Towson, and Nanson (2006) were interested in testing the structure of coping among Asians by using the Cross Cultural Coping Scale (CCCS). Collective coping (i.e., the use of counsel and guidance from one's in-group and members of collectives) is strongly emphasized. For example, when Chinese American or Indian American employees seek counsel and guidance from their immigrant colleagues (from same country of origin) in dealing with a difficult situation with their supervisor, it would be considered an act of collective coping. It is different from problem-focused and emotion-focused coping strategies that have been significant in the research on work stress and coping. Collective coping strategies along with avoidance-focused and engagement-focused modes of coping were more important among Asians compared with Caucasians in both the United States and Canada. Yeh, Arora, & Wu (2006) developed and validated the Collectivistic Coping Scale (CCS) to capture the collectivistic aspect of stress and coping among U.S. ethnic minorities (Yeh, Chang, Arora, Kim, & Xin, 2003). A seven-factor model of collectivistic coping consisting of (1) family support, (2) respect for authority figures, (3) intercultural resources, (4) importance of relational resource, (5) forbearance, (6) participation in meaningful social activities, and (7) fatalism emerged. This scale was correlated with measures of collectivism, which is a predominant value among U.S. minorities—particularly among Asian Americans and Hispanic Americans. Zhang and Long (2006) examined collective coping strategies in the context of work-related stresses among Chinese expatriates in Canada. They developed and validated an occupational collective coping scale. *Collective coping* was defined as coping activities that one engages in by focusing attention on the relationship and the resources that are present in the context of in-group members as well as members of other important and close social networks. Collective coping was found to be related strongly with a tendency to seek help from family for coping with stresses experienced in the Canadian work context. In a related vein, Yeh, Inose, Kobori, and Change (2001) found that individuals who emphasized their personal identities as being highly rooted in the collective identity of their in-groups tended to cope better in dealing with stresses in culturally dissimilar situations.

Collective coping strategies play critical roles in helping individuals cope with serious and dramatic life events. In a qualitative study, Yeh, Inman, Kim, and Okubo (2006) found that collective coping was more effective among 8 of 11 Asian Americans who had lost close family members in the World Trade Center terrorist attack on September 11, 2001.

Issues that are particularly useful in understanding the responses of Asian Americans to work stress and stressful events are as follows:

- The tendency is to rely on supportive in-group networks composed of culturally similar individuals such as one's family network- or community-based social groups. While this tendency may be a valid strategy in dealing with many stressful situations, it can also be ineffective. Supervisors, coworkers, and significant members of one's work group or organization can often provide better counsel and guidance even though they may not be members of the in-groups or collectives.
- Most Asians emphasize the importance of "saving face" while coping with stressful situations whether they are work or nonwork related. Disclosing personal problems or the inability to deal with difficult situations to an other than family members is suppose to bring *shame* to the entire family (Sue, 1994; Triandis, 1994a). Triandis noted that the loss of face and honor is a serious matter in Asian American cultures, particularly among East Asians. Asian Americans may spend considerable time and effort in finding out about their adversaries at work, satisfy as many of them as possible, and go to great lengths to avoid situations that may result in loss of face or honor. Their tendency to not seek counseling from professional counselors and EAPs can be problematic in many instances because while family members may act as sympathetic listeners they are often unable to provide the right kind of guidance or assistance one may truly need.

A vast majority of the Asian Americans are members of cultures that emphasize the norms and values of *vertical collectivism*. Vertical collectivists are more willing to sacrifice personal desires and goals for the sake or benefit of in-group members and are more willing to undertake important tasks and responsibilities on behalf of the members of the in-group or the collective (Triandis, 1995). In Asian cultures, an elder or authority figure who is known in the community and strongly adheres to collectivistic norms (Sue & Sue, 2003) may command respect from the community. However, it is also true that these elderly individuals despite their status often may provide inappropriate guidance for coping with work stress encountered in Western work organizations. More research into the culture-specific ways of coping with work stress among Asians is needed in the context of the European Union, Australia, and New Zealand. Research in these countries has been relatively rare compared with research on Asian Americans and Asian Canadians.

Immigrants

A majority, but not all, of immigrants experience difficulties with acculturation soon after migration. Many, but not all, learn to cope and adapt successfully. Factors that facilitate successful coping and adaptation include educational accomplishments, positive work orientations, existence of social support networks at work and nonwork, economic and welfare policies of the host country, and last but not least, the nature of cultural differences between the country of origin and country of settlement. Loneliness can be a major difficulty for single immigrants entering a new community, and it is a strong predictor of dissatisfaction with life (Neto, 1995). Social support is very helpful in this regard, and it plays the most significant role in facilitating the process of transition between the two cultures and in psychological adaptation (Kirkcaldy, Siefen, Wittig, Schuller, Brahler, & Merbach, 2005). Social support from family members, friends, acquaintances, and work organization is strongly associated with subjective well-being (See, e.g., Kirkcaldy & Furnham, 1995). In a study of Korean immigrants in the United States (average length of residence being over 12 years), Noh and Avison (1996) found that social resources that are available in one's immediate social network tends to facilitate development of coping skills and resources. The more self-esteem individuals have prior to migration, the better able they are to gain mastery and establish much needed social support from their ethnic group. Social support buffers the adverse effects of stress (see Chapter 3) and reduces the possibility of depression later in life. Kirkcaldy et al.'s (2005) study of Russian immigrants to Germany found that those who actively attempted to establish and maintain favorable and warm relationships with members of the host country were healthier than those who avoided or tended to have low interest in maintaining social contacts. Aroian, Spitzer, and Bell (1996) found that support from family has both instrumental and emotional significance for Russian immigrants.

The process of immigration to a culturally dissimilar country (i.e., from a vertical collectivistic country such as China to a vertical individualistic country such as the United States or Canada) can indeed be quite stressful. Support from family from both the home country and the country of settlement lowers the adverse effects of acculturative stresses and also aids in communicating effectively with members of the host country.

Rigid cultural expectations regarding one's role in the family and ethnic community can often be a potential source of stress in both work and nonwork contexts—Turkish immigrants to Germany reflect this pattern. The immigrants who are able to focus on transformative learning (i.e., open to new experiences and learning new techniques as prompted by the needs of a changing environment; Sessa & London, 2006) have a much easier time in adjusting and creating an experience of renewal for themselves and their families. Bhagat et al. (2009) suggest that career motivation (i.e., having resilience, developing insights and professional identities) is crucial for predicting successful acculturation and helps deal with acculturative stresses.

Multicultural Perspectives on Work Stress: An Appraisal

How individuals construe their self (i.e., either in an independent or interdependent mode) is crucial in influencing personal beliefs, emotions, and motivations (Markus & Kitayama, 1991). Research reported by Bailey and Dua (1999), Cross (1995), Lam and Zane (2004), Schaubroeck, Lam, and Xie (2000), and Zaff, Blount, Phillips, and Cohen (2002) clearly depicts that how one copes with stressful situation at work or nonwork is influenced by self-construal processes and cultural background. For example, Asian American emphasize coping strategies that focus on changing one's thoughts and feelings in dealing with interpersonal problems and accept the notion that they may sometimes be unable to assert control over the environment. Mainstream Americans, on the other hand, are more interested in changing the existing environment to fit with their needs and beliefs.

Individuals who operate in an independent mode use active coping styles compared with those who function in an interdependent mode (Cross, 1995). However, the choice of self-construal (independent or interdependent mode) may change over one's life span in response to changing contingencies in the external environment. The longer one stays in the context of a culture that strongly emphasizes functioning in an independent mode of self construal, the more one tends to use an active and problem-focused coping style. In exploring the relevance of ethnic differences in coping, it is more important to focus on ethnic identity and mode of self-construal. Schaubroeck et al. (2000) found that personal attributes of idiocentrism (putting interest of self over the interest of one's group) and allocentrism (putting group interest ahead of one's self-interest) influenced coping effectiveness of individuals from the United States and Hong Kong.

Research on coping, whether directed toward dealing with stressful experiences from the domain of work or nonwork, has been criticized for grounding the concepts and theories in an individualistic perspective—one that focuses primarily on mainstream Americans (Bjorck, Cuthbertson, Thurman, & Lee, 2001; Hobfoll, 2001). One of the major findings is that action-oriented, problem-focused coping styles and strategies are strongly related to positive psychological outcomes in individualistic contexts, which in turn influence organizationally valued outcomes in a positive fashion. Research in this tradition also finds that individuals who engage in avoidance and emotion-focused coping styles and strategies are less likely to be successful in experiencing positive psychological outcomes and will continue to have poor mental health and strain (Endler & Parker, 1990; Folkman, Lazarus, Dunkel-Schetter, DeLongis, & Gruen, 1986; Lazarus & Folkman, 1984).

Coping is a process "embedded in context," and therefore a comprehensive understanding of how individuals cope requires insights into the role of both the person and the context and their interactions (Zeidner & Saklofske, 1996). Contextual issues involve the cultural contexts in which coping behaviors must occur—in that what is considered effective coping in one setting might be regarded as an inappropriate strategy in another setting. Depending on the cultural tradition that one must adhere to, the appropriate prescription for dealing with work stress and other stressful experiences may be to adapt to the situation, achieve a sense of control by engaging in continuous problem-focused approaches, eliminate personal desire and submit to a religious deity, or seek self-improvement (Tweed & Conway, 2006). These strategies are not necessarily mutually exclusive, and depending on what the cultural context requires, one particular strategy might be emphasized more than others. The Euro-American approaches to work stress and coping are based on the notion that coping is overt, constructive, and adaptive, whereas tendencies to avoid coping in a covert manner are passive and maladaptive because they clearly signify lack of motivation and effort. In other words, the Western approach to *functional coping* involves taking concrete actions whereas *dysfunctional coping* includes withdrawal behaviors, controlling one's emotions and feelings, and having a fatalistic orientation. However, a significant number of Asian collectivistic cultures emphasize approaches that seem to be congruent with the Western ideas of dysfunctional coping. Some of the differences that are inherent in the way individuals from the Eastern collectivistic cultures cope with work stress (both of the chronic and episodic variety) are as follows:

- The collective, not the individual, as the unit for obtaining coping resources: One of the major conclusions of research involving multicultural perspectives on stress and coping is that coping patterns of individuals in Eastern cultures are based on obtaining coping resources from the collective (Wong & Wong, 2006). The concept of *collective self* is strongest in the East Asian cultures including Japan, China, South Korea, Vietnam, Malaysia, and also parts of Southern Asia including India and Thailand. Given the history of human survival in these cultures, the centrality of collective coping is of paramount importance in these nations. One is socialized from childhood to emphasize the importance of functioning in an interdependent mode and copes by sampling relevant cognitions from the collective self.
- From cognitive to existential mode of coping: Despite the growing importance of *meaning-based coping* (Affleck & Tennen, 1996; Folkman & Moskowitz, 2004; Taylor, 1983; Tweed & Conway, 2006), which focuses on the nature of causal attributions and finding positive dimensions of a stressful experience or event, this perspective has not been sufficiently used to develop insights into the coping processes of non-Western cultures. *Existential coping,* which includes acceptance of what cannot be changed and discovering meaning and purpose of individual existence, is crucial to many of the Eastern cultures. The worldview prevailing in much of India reflects a strong emphasis on the existential mode of coping. Dealing with sluggish bureaucracies and persistent bottlenecks in organizational decision making requires an *existential* and *pantheistic* worldview. Hooker (2003) defines the pantheistic worldview that prevails in Indian context as one's ability to rise above the chaos and uncertainties of the external world. Cultivation of patience, self-control, and much less reliance on an active mode of coping are the essence of this perspective.
- From dichotomic to dualistic thinking: Another major point of departure that can greatly enrich future studies on how members of Eastern and Western cultures cope with work and life stresses is to focus on dichotomous versus dualistic thinking. In Western cultures, there is an emphasis on dichotomous thinking where absolutism is important. Eastern cultures, on the other hand, socialize their members in dualistic thinking where one can accept both internal and external control (Wong & Sproule, 1984) and be simultaneously optimistic and pessimistic (Wong & McDonald, 2002).

Spector et al.'s (2004) research involving Chinese and American employees found no relationship between work locus of control and job stress and strains among the Chinese. Findings such as these may be explained by adopting the perspective of dualistic thinking. In other words, one can be simultaneously internal and external in locus of control but not necessarily use internal locus of control in dealing with work-related stresses. Acceptance of an external locus of control in dealing with a stressful event can indeed be more effective in some contexts (e.g., when faced with an utterly futile situation). Recall the situation of entrapment experienced by the members of the U.S. Embassy in Tehran, Iran, during the Iranian Revolution of 1979. Members of the embassy staff were held captive for over 444 days, and there was nothing that could be done by the staff by adopting a strict internal mode of control. A dualistic mode of thinking where one could simultaneously accept this unfortunate situation with some hope would have been more helpful as in the recent case of the entrapped Chilean miners in 2010. Our analysis of the coping strategies of these miners suggests that they adopted a dualistic mode of thinking. A straightforward application of this notion in dealing with work stress is that individuals can be simultaneously high and low in their desire to control stressful situations. Dualistic thinking is more helpful in explaining work-related coping behaviors in cultures that are more holistic in orientation (e.g., East and South Asia, most of sub-Saharan Africa, and a majority of Latin America).

Social Support Across Ethnic, Racial, and Cultural Divides

Seeking social support to deal with stressful encounters in the domain of work or nonwork is commonplace regardless of national and cultural differences. Individuals talk about their needs for support from family and close friends when they experience distress and other dysfunctional outcomes. Social support, when readily accessible, provides one of the best mechanisms for adjusting to and coping with stressful experiences at work and in personal lives. Social support has been defined as validation from others that individuals are loved, valued, and cared for and that they are regarded as important members of their collective (Beehr, 1995; Cobb, 1976; Cohen & Wills, 1985; Payne, 1980).

Research with Asian Americans in the United States finds that they are more sensitive to potential negative relationship–related consequences from seeking social support compared with European Americans. It is safe to note that a majority of collectivistic cultures of East Asia, Latin America, and other parts of the world emphasizes a mode of seeking social support that is different from the individualistic cultures of the West. The Western approach is to seek social support by getting valuable advice, instrumental aid, and emotional comfort—all of these being *explicit* in nature. In contrast, Asians seem to prefer *implicit* social support, which is typically obtained from in-group members and collectives without necessarily disclosing or discussing the exact nature of the stressful encounters or situations. In using implicit social support, individuals get the benefit of information that one is cared for without necessarily worrying about relational implications (e.g., losing face, experiencing shame, or worrying about others). Recent findings regarding the role of cultural differences in seeking social support are reported in Kim, Sherman, and Taylor (2008) and clearly depict distinctive ways of seeking social support to lower experiences of distress or psychological strain.

Recent research involving multicultural perspectives (including racial and religious differences) provides us with better insight into human experience in coping with work stress. A positive and transformational orientation coupled with these new insights should open up new avenues for managing dysfunctional consequences of work stress in the era of globalization. Implications of these findings for the development of EAPs are discussed in the next chapter.

Conclusion

The central theme of this chapter has been that cultural variations shape the process of experiencing work stress and construing approaches to coping. In addition, use of social support greatly varies across ethnic, racial, cultural, and national groups. Culture shapes the meaning of work stress and coping styles in ways that are not easy to decipher. However, it is crucial that we adopt a multicultural perspective in the study of work stress and coping in this era of globalization. There has been significant growth of ethnic minorities in the United States, which is the largest economy in the world. A similar pattern characterizes the growth of population in Western Europe where religious minorities including members of the Islamic countries have been increasing rapidly. Ethnic, cultural, and religious minorities experience and cope with stress rather differently from the members of the mainstream population whether in the United States, European Union, or Australia.

The adoption of a multicultural perspective becomes necessary in grasping the true realities of how work stress affects all segments of the workforce in different countries. Theoretical perspectives discussed in this chapter should act as a guide in further research inquiries and have relevance for developing culture-specific methods for managing work stress. In the next chapter, we take the next logical step by discussing the institutional and culture-specific approaches for managing work stress in the context of managing EAPs.

References

Abe, J. S., & Zane, N. W. (1990). Psychological maladjustment among Asian and White American college students: Controlling for confounds. *Journal of Counseling Psychology, 37*, 437–444.

Affleck, G., & Tennen, H. (1996). Construing benefits from adversity: Adaptational significance and dispositional underpinning. *Journal of Personality, 64*, 899–922.

Aldwin, C. (2007). *Stress, coping and development* (2nd ed.). New York: Guilford.

Antonovsky, A. (1979). *Health, stress, and coping*. San Francisco: Jossey-Bass.

Antoniou, A.-S. G., & Dalla, M. (2009). Immigration, unemployment, and career counseling: A multicultural perspective. In A.-S. G. Antoniou, C. L. Cooper, G. P. Chrousos, C. D. Spielberger, & M. W. Eysenck (Eds.), *Handbook of managerial behavior and occupational health* (pp. 311–327). Cheltenham, UK: Edward Elgar Publishing.

Aroian, K., Spitzer, A., & Bell, M. (1996). Family stress and support among former Soviet immigrants. *Western Journal of Nursing Research, 18*, 655–674.

Bailey, F. J., & Dua, J. (1999). Individualism-collectivism, coping styles, and stress in international and Anglo-Australian students: A comparative study. *Australian Psychologist, 34*, 177–182.

Baumeister, R. E. (1986). *Public self and private self*. New York: Springer.

Bean, F. D., Van Hook, J., Bloemraad, I., & Brown, S. K. (2004). *Minimizing risk versus maximizing gain: The welfare reform contexts of immigration reception, naturalization, and second-generation incorporation*. Paper presented at Radcliffe Institute for Advanced Study, Harvard University, Cambridge, MA.

Beehr, T. A. (1995). *Psychological stress in the workplace*. London: Routledge.

Belgrave, F. Z., Townsend, T. G., Cherry, V. R., & Cunningham, D. M. (1997). The influence of an Africentric worldview and demographic variables on drug knowledge, attitudes, and use among African American youth. *Journal of Community Psychology, 25*(5), 421–433.

Berry, J. W. (1994). Acculturative stress. In W. J. Lonner & R. S. Malpass (Eds.), *Psychology and culture* (pp. 211–215). Boston: Allyn & Bacon.

Berry, J. W. (2006). Stress perspectives on acculturation. In D. L. Sam & J. W. Berry (Eds.), *The Cambridge Handbook of Acculturation Psychology* (pp. 43–57). Cambridge, UK: Cambridge University Press.

Berry, J. W., & Ataca, B. (2000). Cultural factors. In G. Fink (Ed.), *Encyclopedia of stress* (pp. 604–610). San Diego: Academic Press.

Berry, J. W., & Sam, D. L. (1997). Acculturation and adaptation. In J. W. Berry, M. H. Segall, & C. Kagitcibasi (Eds.), *Handbook of cross-cultural psychology: Vol. 2. Basic processes and human development* (2nd ed., pp. 291–326). Boston: Allyn & Bacon.

Berry, J. W., Poortinga, Y. H., Segall, M. H., & Dasen, P. R. (2006). *Cross-cultural psychology: Research and applications*. Cambridge, UK: Cambridge University Press.

Bhagat, R. S., Davis, C., & London, M. L. (2009). Acculturative stress in professional immigrants: Towards a cultural theory of stress. In G. Alexander-Stamatios, G. Antoniou, C. L. Cooper, & G. P. Chrousos (Eds.), *Handbook of managerial behavior and occupational health* (pp. 345–361). Cheltenham, UK: Edward Elgar Publishing.

Bhagat, R. S., Ford, D. L., O'Driscoll, M. P., Frey, L., Babakus, E., & Mahanyele, M. (2001). Do South African managers cope differently from American managers? A cross-cultural investigation. *International Journal of Intercultural Relations, 25,* 301–313.

Bhagat, R. S., Krishnan, B., Nelson, T. A., Leonard Mustafa, K., Ford, Jr., D. L., & Billing, T. K. (2010). Organizational stress, psychological strain, and work outcomes in six national contexts: A closer look at the moderating influences of coping styles and decision latitude. *Cross Cultural Management: An International Journal of Cross Cultural Management, 17*(1), 10–29.

Bhagat, R. S., & London, M. L. (1999). Getting started and getting ahead: Career dynamics of immigrants. *Human Resource Management Review, 9,* 349–365.

Bhagat, R. S., McDevitt, A. S., & Segovis, J. C. (2011). Immigration as an adaptive challenge: Implications for lifelong learning. In M. L. London (Ed.), *The Oxford handbook of lifelong learning* (pp. 402–421). New York: Oxford.

Bhagat, R. S., O'Driscoll, M. P., Babakus, E., Frey, L. T., Chokkar, J., Ninokumar, B. H., et al. (1994). Organizational stress and coping in seven national contexts: A cross-cultural investigation. In G. P. Keita & J. J. Hurrell, Jr. (Eds.), *Job stress in a changing workforce* (pp. 93–105). Washington, DC: American Psychological Association.

Bhagat, R. S., Steverson, P., & Kuo, B. C. (2009). Cultural variations in work stress and coping in an era of globalization. In R. S. Bhagat & R. M. Steers (Eds.), *Handbook of culture, organizations, & work* (pp. 418–441). Cambridge: Cambridge University Press.

Bhawuk, D. P. (2001). Evolution of culture assimilators: Toward theory-based assimilators. *International Journal of Intercultural Relations, 25*(2), 141–163.

Bjorck, J. P., Cuthbertson, W., Thurman, J. W., & Lee, Y. S. (2001). Ethnicity, coping, and distress among Korean-, Filipino-, and Caucasian-Americans. *Journal of Social Psychology, 14*(4), 421–442.

Bontempo, R., & Rivero, J. C. (1992). *Cultural variation in cognition: The role of self-concept in the attitude–behavior link.* Paper presented at the Academy of Management Annual Conference, Las Vegas, NV.

Broman, C. L. (1997). Race-related factors and life satisfaction among African-Americans. *Journal of Black Psychology, 23,* 36–49.

Caplovitz, D. (1979). *Making ends meet: How families cope with inflation and recession.* Beverly Hills, CA: Sage Publications.

Castillo, L. G., Conoley, C. W., & Brossart, D. F. (2004). Acculturation, white marginalization, and family support as predictors of perceived distress in Mexican American female college students. *Journal of Counseling Psychology, 51,* 151–157.

Cervantes, R. C., Padilla, A. M., & Salgado de Snyder, N. (1991). The Hispanic Stress Inventory: A culturally relevant approach toward psychosocial assessment. *Psychological Assessment, 3,* 438–447.

Chang, E. C., Tugade, M. M., & Asakawa, K. (2006). Stress, appraisals, and coping among Asian Americans: Lazarus and Folkman's model and beyond. In C. Scott & P. T. Wong (Eds.), *Handbook of multicultural perspectives on stress and coping. International and cultural psychology series* (pp. 439–455). Dallas, TX: Spring Publications.

Chiang, L., Hunter, C. D., & Yeh, C. J. (2004). Coping attitudes, sources, and practices among Black and Latino college students. *Adolescence, 39,* 793–815.

Cobb, S. (1976). Social support as a moderator of life stress. *Psychosomatic Medicine, 38,* 300–314.

Cohen, S., & Wills, T. A. (1985). *Psychological Bulletin, 98,* 310–357.

Cross, S. E. (1995). Self-construals, coping, and stress in cross-cultural adaptation. *Journal of Cross-Cultural Psychology, 26,* 673–697.

Daly, A., Jennings, J., Beckett, J. O., & Leashore, B. R. (1995). Effective coping strategies of African Americans. *Social Work, 40,* 240–248.

Davidson, A. R., Jaccard, J. J., Triandis, H. C., Morales, M. L., & Diaz-Guerrero, R. (1976). Cross-cultural model testing: Toward a solution of the etic-emic dilemma. *International Journal of Psychology, 11,* 1–13.

de Anda, D. (1984). Bicultural socialization: Factors affecting the minority experience. *Social Work, 29*(2), 101–107.

Diaz-Guerrero, R. (1967). *Estudios de psicologia del Mexicano.* Mexico: Trillas.

Doi, T. (1973). *The Anatomy of Dependence.* Tokyo: Kodansha.

EEOC. (2009). Job patterns for minorities and women in private industry, 2008 indicators over time. Retrieved March 2010 from http://www.eeoc.gov/eeoc/statistics/employment/jobpat-eeo1/docs/indicators.html

Endler, N. S., & Parker, J. D. A. (1990). Multidimensional assessment of coping: A critical evaluation. *Journal of Personality and Social Psychology, 58,* 844–854.

Feagin, J. R. (1991). The continuing significance of racism: Discrimination against Black students in White colleges. *Journal of Black Studies, 22*(4), 546–578.

Flores, E., Tschann, J., Marin, B., & Pantoja, P. (2004). Marital conflict and acculturation among Mexican American husbands and wives. *Cultural Diversity and Ethnic Minority Psychology, 10*(1), 39–52.

Folkman, S., Lazarus, R. S., Dunkel-Schetter, C., DeLongis, A., & Gruen, R. J. (1986). Dynamics of a stressful encounter: Cognitive appraisal, coping, and encounter outcomes. *Journal of Personality and Social Psychology, 50*(5), 992–1003.

Folkman, R. S., & Moskowitz, J. T. (2004). Coping: Pitfalls and promise. *Annual Review of Psychology, 55,* 745–774.

Greenwald, A. G., & Pratkanis, A. R. (1984). The self. In R. S. Wyer & T. K. Srull (Eds.), *Handbook of social cognition* (Vol. 3, pp. 129–178). Hillsdale, NJ: Erlbaum.

Harper, R. (1975). The Black tax: Stresses confronting Black federal executives. *Journal of Afro-American Issues, 3*(2), 207–218.

Heckhausen, J., & Schultz, R. (1995). A life-span theory of control. *Psychological Review, 102,* 284–304.

Hobfoll, S. E. (2001). The influence of culture, community, and the nested-self in the stress process: Advancing conservation of resources theory. *Applied Psychology: An International Review,* 337–421.

Hofstede, G. (1980). *Culture's consequences: International differences in work-related values.* Beverley Hills, CA: Sage.

Hofstede, G. (2001). *Culture's consequences: Comparing values, behaviours, institutions, and organizations across nations* (2nd ed.). Thousand Oaks, CA: Sage.

Homma-True, R. (1997). Japanese American families. In E. Lee (Ed.), *Working with Asian Americans: A guide for clinicians* (pp. 114–124). New York: Guilford.

Hong, Y. Y., Wan, C., No, S., & Chiu, C. Y. (2007). Multicultural identities. In S. Kitayama & D. Cohen (Eds.), *Handbook of cultural psychology.* New York: Guilford.

Hooker, J. (2003). *Working across cultures.* Stanford, CA: Stanford University Press.

Hurd, D. (2011, April 12). Muslim women protest French burqa ban. Retrieved from http://www.cbn.com/cbnnews/world/2011/April/Muslim-Women-Protest-French-Burqa-Ban

Iwao, S. (1998). *Social psychology's models of man: Isn't it time for East to meet West?* Invited address to the International Congress of Scientific Psychology, Sydney, Australia.

Jacoby, T. (2004). *Reinventing the melting pot: The new immigrants and what it means to be American.* New York: Basic Books.

Jones, J. M. (1988). Racism in Black and White. In P. A. Katz & D. A. Taylor (Eds.), *Eliminating racism: Profiles in Controversy* (pp. 117–135). New York: Plenum Press.

Kim, H. S., Sherman, D. K., & Taylor, S. E. (2008). Culture and social support. *American Psychologist, 63,* 518–526.

Kirkcaldy, B., & Furnham, A.F. (1995), Coping, seeking social support and stress among German police officers. *European Review of Applied Psychology, 45*(2), 121–125.

Kirkcaldy, B. D., Furnham, A. F., & Siefen, R. G. (2009). The effects of gender and migrant status on physical and psychological well-being. *International Journal of Adolescent Medicine and Health, 21*(1), 61–72.

Kirkcaldy, B. D., Siefen, R. G., Wittig, U., Schuller, A., Brahler, E., & Merbach, M. (2005). Health and emigration: Subjective evaluation of health status and physical symptoms in Russian-speaking migrants. *Stress Health, 21*(5), 295–309.

Kitayama, S., Duffy, S., & Uchida, Y. (2007). Self as cultural mode of being. In S. Kitayama & D. Cohen (Eds.), *Handbook of cultural psychology* (pp. 136–174). New York: Guilford Press.

Kitayama, S., Markus, H. R., & Lieberman, C. (1995). The collective construction of self-esteem: Implications for culture, self, and emotion. In J. Russell, J. Femandez-Dols, T. Manstead, & J. Wellenkamp (Eds.), *Everyday conceptions of emotion: An introduction to the psychology, anthropology, and linguistics of emotion* (pp. 523–550). Dordrecht, The Netherlands: Kluwer Academic.

Kitayama, S., Markus, H. R., & Matsumoto, H. (1995). A cultural perspective on self-conscious emotions. In J. P. Tangney & K. W. Fisher (Eds.), *Self-conscious emotions: The psychology of shame, guilt, embarrassment, and pride* (pp. 439–464). New York: Guilford.

Knight, B.G., Silverstein, M., McCallum, T.J., & Fox, L. S. (2000). A sociocultural stress and coping model for mental health outcomes among African American caregivers in Southern California. *Journal of Gerontology: Psychological Sciences, 55*(B), 142–150.

Kobus, K., & Reyes, O. (2000). A descriptive study of urban Mexican American adolescents' perceived stress and coping. *Hispanic Journal of Behavioral Sciences, 22*(2), 163–178.

Kosmin, B. A., & Keysar, A. (2009). *American Religious Identification Survey (ARIS 2008): Summary report.* Hartford, CT: Trinity College.

Kuo, B. C. (2010). Culture's consequences on coping: Theories, evidences, and dimensionalities. *Journal of Cross-Cultural Psychology,* 1–17.

Kuo, B. C. H., Kwantes, C. T., Towson, S., & Nanson, K. M. (2006). Social beliefs as determinants of attitudes toward seeking professional psychological help among ethnically diverse university students. *Canadian Journal of Counseling, 40,* 224–241.

Lam, A. G., & Zane, N. W. (2004). Ethnic differences in coping with interpersonal stressors: A test of self-construals as cultural mediators. *Journal of Cross-Cultural Psychology, 35,* 446–459.

Landrine, H., & Klonoff, E. A. (1996). The schedule of racist events: A measure of racial discrimination and a study of its negative physical and mental health consequences. *Journal of Black Psychology, 22,* 144–168.

Lazarus, R. S., & Folkman, S. (1984). *Stress, appraisal, and coping.* New York: Springer.

Leong, F. T. (2001). The role of acculturation in the career adjustment of Asian American workers: A test of Leong and Chou's (1944) formulations. *Cultural Diversity and Ethnic Minority Psychology, 7*(3), 262–273.

Leong, F. T., & Chou, E. L. (1994). The role of ethnic identity and acculturation in the vocational behavior of Asian-Americans: An integrative review. *Journal of Vocational Behavior, 44,* 155–172.

Leong, F. T., & Tolliver, D. (2006). Towards an understanding of occupational stress among Asian Americans. In P. T. Wong & L. C. Wong (Eds.), *Handbook of multicultural perspectives on stress and coping* (pp. 535–553). New York: Springer-Verlag.

Lewin, A.Y., Manning, S., & Massini, S. (2008). A dynamic perspective on next-generation offshoring: The global sourcing of science and engineering talent. *Academy of Management Perspectives, 22,* 35–54.

Lincoln, B. (2001). Revisiting "magical fright." *American Ethnologist,* 28(4), 778–802.

Loukissa, D., Farran, C., & Graham, K. (1999). Caring for a relative with Alzheimer's disease: The experience of African American and Caucasian caregivers. *American Journal of Alzheimer's Disease, 14*(4), 207–216.

Majors, R. G., & Mancini-Billson, J. (1992). *Cool pose: The dilemmas of Black manhood in America.* New York: Lexington.

Markus, H., & Kitayama, S. (1991). Culture and the self: Implications for cognition, emotion, and motivation. *Psychological Review, 98,* 224–253.

McCarty, C. A., Weisz, J. R., Wanitromanee, K., Eastman, K. L., Suwanlert, S., Chaiyasit, W., et al. (1999). Culture, coping, and context : Primary and secondary control among Thai and American youth. *Journal of Child Psychology and Psychiatry, 40*(5), 809–818.

McCormick, R., & Wong, P. T. P. (2006). Adjustment and coping in aboriginal people. In P. T. P. Wong & L. C. J. Wong (Eds.), *Handbook of multicultural perspectives of stress and coping* (pp. 515–534). New York: Springer.

Mechanic, D. (1974). Personal adaptation: Some neglected dimensions. In G. V. Coelho, D. A. Hamburg, & J. E. Adams (Eds.), *Coping and adaptation.* New York: Basic Books.

Mena, F. J., Padilla, A. M., & Maldonado, M. (1987). Acculturative stress and specific coping strategies among immigrant and later generation college students. *Hispanic Journal of Behavioral Sciences, 9*(2), 207–225.

Mesquita, B., & Leu, J. (2007). The cultural psychology of emotions. In S. Kitayama, & D. Cohen (Eds.), *Handbook for cultural psychology.* New York: Guilford Press.

Migration Policy Institute Data Hub (MPI Data Hub). (2011). Accessed April 16, 2011, from http://www.migrationinformation.org/datahub/comparative.cfm

Miller, J. G. (1984). Culture and the development of everyday social explanation. *Cross-Cultural Research, 28,* 961–978.

Morling, B., & Fiske, S. T. (1999). Defining and measuring harmony control. *Journal of Research in Personality, 33*(4), 379–414.

Ndofor, H. A., & Priem, R. L. (2011). Immigrant entrepreneurs, the ethnic enclave strategy, and venture performance. *Journal of Management, 37*(3), 790–818.

Neto, F. (1995). Predictors of satisfaction with life among second generation migrants. *Social Indicators Research, 35*, 93–116.

Noh, S., & Avison, W. R. (1996). Asian immigrants and the stress process: A study of Koreans in Canada. *Journal of Health and Social Behavior, 37*, 192–206.

Padilla, A. M., Wagatsuma, Y., & Lindholm, K. (1985). Generational differences in acculturative stress and personality among Mexican and Japanese Americans. (Original papers No. 20). Los Angeles: Spanish Speaking Mental Health Research Center.

Pargament, K. I., Zinnbauer, B. J., Scott, A. B., Butter, E. M., Zerowin, J., & Stanik, P. (1998). Red flags and religious coping: Identifying some religious warning signs among people in crisis. *Journal of Clinical Psychology, 54*, 77–89.

Payne, R. (1980). Organizational stress and social support. In C. Cooper & R. Payne (Eds.), *Current concerns in occupational stress* (pp. 269–298). Chichester, UK: John Wiley & Sons.

Pfeffer, J. (1996). *Competitive advantage through people: unleashing the power of the work force.* New York: Harvard Business Press.

Plummer, D. L., & Slane, S. (1996). Patterns of coping in racially stressful situations. *Journal of Black Psychology, 22*, 302–315.

Reykowski, J. (1994). Collectivism and individualism as dimensions of social change. In U. Kim, H. C. Triandis, C. Kagitcibasi, S. Choi, & G. Yoon (Eds.), *Individualism and collectivism: Theory, method and applications* (pp. 276–292). Thousand Oaks, CA: Sage.

Rotter, J. B. (1966). Generalized expectancies for internal versus external control of reinforcement. In *Psychological Monographs* (pp. 1–28). Storrs: University of Connecticut Press.

Roysircar, G., & Maestas, M. L. (2002). Assessing acculturation and cultural variables. In K. S. Kurasaki & S. Okazaki (Eds.), *Asian American mental health: Assessment theories and methods* (pp. 77–94). Moscow: Kluwer Academic/Plenum.

Sanchez-Burks, J., & Lee, F. (2007). Cultural psychology of workways. In S. Kitayama & D. Cohen (Eds.), *Handbook of cultural psychology* (pp. 346–369). New York: Guilford.

Saunders, L. W. (1977). Variants in Zar experience in an Egyptian village. In V. Crapanzano & V. Garrison (Eds.), *Case studies of spirit possession* (pp. 177–191). New York: John Wiley.

Schaubroeck, J., Lam, S. S., & Xie, J. L. (2000). Collective efficacy versus self-efficacy in coping responses to stressors and control: A cross-cultural study. *Journal of Applied Psychology, 85*(4), 512–525.

Schwartz, S. H. (1992). Universals in the content and structure of values: Theory and empirical tests in 20 countries. In M. Zanna (Ed.), *Advances in experimental social psychology* (pp. 1–65). New York: Academic Press.

Schwartz, S. H. (1994). Are there universal aspects in the content and structure of values? *Journal of Social Issues, 50*, 19–45.

Sessa, V. I., & London, M. L. (2006). *Continuous learning.* Mahwah, NJ: Erlbaum.

Sheu, H. B., & Sedlacek, W. E. (2004). An exploratory study of help-seeking attitudes and coping strategies among college students by race and gender. *Measurement and Evaluation in Counseling and Development, 37,* 130–143.

Siegel, K., & Schrimshaw, E. W. (2002). The perceived benefits of religious and spiritual coping among older adults living with HIV/AIDS. *Journal for the Scientific Study of Religion, 41*(1), 91–102.

Spector, P. E., Cooper, C. L., Poelmans, S., Allen, T. D., O'Driscoll, M., Sanchez, J. I., et al. (2004). A cross-national comparative study of work–family stressors, working hours, and well-being: China and Latin America vs. the Anglo world. *Personnel Psychology, 57,* 119–142.

Sue, D. W., & Frank, A. C. (1973). A typological approach to the study of Chinese and Japanese-American college males. *Journal of Social Issues, 29,* 129–148.

Sue, D. W., & Kirk, B. A. (1973). Differential characteristics of Chinese and Japanese American students. *Journal of Counseling Psychology, 20,* 142–148.

Sue, D. W., & Sue, D. (2003). *Counseling the culturally diverse: Theory and practice.* New York: John Wiley & Sons.

Sue, S. (1994). Mental health. In N. Zane, D. T. Takeuchi, & K. Young (Eds.), *Confronting critical health issues of Asian and Pacific Islander Americans* (pp. 266–288). Newbury Park, CA: Sage.

Takaki, R. (2007). The success of Asian Americans has been exaggerated, in part, to criticize other minority groups. In J. F. Healey & E. O' Brien (Eds.), *Race, ethnicity, and gender.* Los Angeles: Pine Forge Press.

Taylor, S. E. (1983). Adjustment to threatening events: A theory of cognitive adaptation. *American Psychologist, 38,* 1161–1173.

Taylor, S. E., Sherman, D. K., Kim, H. S., Jarcho, J., Takagi, K., & Dunagan, M. S. (2004). Culture and social support: Who seeks it and why? *Journal of Personality and Social Psychology, 87,* 354–362.

Tharp, R. G., Meadow, A., Lennhoff, S., & Satterfield, D. (1968). Changes in marriage roles accompanying the acculturation of the Mexican-American wife. *Journal of Marriage & the Family, 30,* 404–412.

Triandis, H. C. (1989). The self and social behavior in differing cultural contexts. *Psychological Review, 96,* 269–289.

Triandis, H. C. (1994). Cross-cultural industrial and organizational psychology. In H. C. Triandis, M. D. Dunnette, & L. M. Hough (Eds.), *Handbook of industrial and organizational psychology* (2nd ed., Vol. 4, pp. 103–172). Palo Alto, CA: Consulting Psychologists Press, Inc.

Triandis, H. C. (1994). *Culture and social behavior.* New York: McGraw-Hill.

Triandis, H. C. (1995). *Individualism and collectivism.* Boulder, CO: Westview Press.

Triandis, H. C. (1996). The psychological measurement of cultural syndromes. *American Psychologist, 51,* 407–415.

Triandis, H. C. (1998). Vertical and horizontal individualism and collectivism: Theory and research implications for international comparative management. In J. L. Cheng & R. B. Peterson (Eds.), *Advances in international and comparative management* (pp. 7–35). Greenwich, CT: JAI Press.

Triandis, H. C. (2004). *Culture and social behavior.* New York: McGraw Hill.

Tseng, W. S. (2001). Amok: Indiscriminate mass homicide attacks. In W. S. Teng (Ed.), *Handbook of cultural psychiatry* (pp. 230–233). San Diego, CA: Academic Press.

Tweed, R. G., & Conway III, L. G. (2006). Coping strategies and culturally influenced beliefs about the world. In P. T. Wong & L. C. Wong (Eds.), *Handbook of multicultural perspectives on stress and coping* (pp. 133–153). New York: Springer.

U.S. Census Bureau. (2000). *Foreign-born immigrants in New York City*. Washington, DC.

U.S. Census Bureau. (2001, March). *Overview of race and Hispanic origin*. Retrieved March 15, 2011, from www.census.gov/population/www/socdemo/race.html

U.S. Census Bureau. (2008). *National population estimates, July 1 and April 1, 2000 to July 1, 2008*. Retrieved April 16, 2011, from http://www.census.gov/population/www/socdemo/race/race.html

U.S. Census Bureau. (2010). *Data for 2000 to 2009: Annual state resident population estimates for 6 race groups (5 race alone groups and one group with two or more race groups by age, sex, and Hispanic origin: April 1, 2000 to July 1, 2009*. Retrieved April 16, 2001, from http://www.census.gov/compendia/statab/cats/population.html

U.S. Department of Homeland Security. (2011). *Illegal alien resident population*. Washington, DC.

Utsey, S. O., Bolden, M. A., Williams III, O., Lee, A., Lanier, Y., & Newsome, C. (2007). Spiritual well-being as a mediator of the relation between culture-specific coping and quality of life in a community sample of African Americans. *Journal of Cross-Cultural Psychology, 38*(2), 123.

Utsey, S. O., Brown, C., & Bolden, M. A. (2004). Testing the structural and invariance of the Africultural Coping Systems Inventory across three samples of African descent populations. *Educational and Psychological Measurement, 64*(1), 185–195.

Vega, W. A., Kolody, B., & Valle, R. (1988). Marital strain, coping, and depression among Mexican-American women. *Journal of Marriage and Family, 50*, 391–530.

Wasti, S. A., & Cortina, L. M. (2002). Coping in context: Sociocultural determinants of responses to sexual harassment. *Journal of Personality and Social Psychology, 83*, 394–405.

Weibe, K. (1985). *Violence against immigrant women and children: An overview for community workers*. Vancouver: Women Against Violence Against Women/Rape Crisis Centre.

Wharton, A. (2006). Understanding diversity of work in the 21st century and its impact on work family area of study. In M. Pitt-Catsouphes, E. E. Kossek, & S. Sweet (Eds.), *The work and family handbook* (pp. 17–40). Mahwah, NJ: LEA Publishing.

Wong, P. T., & McDonald, M. (2002). Tragic optimism and personal meaning in counselling victims of abuse. *Pastoral Sciences, 20*, 231–249.

Wong, P. T., & Sproule, C. F. (1984). Attributional analysis of locus of control and the Trent Attribution Profile (TAP). In H. M. Lefcourt (Ed.), *Research with locus of control construct: Vol. 3. Limitations and extension* (pp. 309–360). New York: Academic Press.

Wong, P. T. P., & Wong, L. C. J. (Eds.). (2006). *Handbook of multicultural perspectives on stress and coping*. New York: Springer.

Yeh, C. J., Arora, A. K., & Wu, K. A. (2006). Culture: A fundamental context for the stress and coping paradigm. In P. T. P. Wong & L. C. J. Wong (Eds.), *Handbook of multicultural perspectives on stress and coping* (pp. 29–53). New York: Springer.

Yeh, C. J., Chang, T., Arora, A. K., Kim, A. B., & Xin, T. (2003). *Reliability, validity, and factor analysis of the Collectivistic Coping Scale.* Paper presented at the American Psychological Association.

Yeh, C. J., Inman, A. G., Kim, A. B., & Okubo, Y. (2006). Asian American families collectivistic coping strategies in response to 9/11. *Cultural Diversity and Ethnic Minority Psychology, 12,* 134–148.

Yeh, C. J., Inose, M., Kobori, A., & Change, T. (2001). Self and coping among college students in Japan. *Journal of College Student Development, 42,* 242–256.

Yeh, C. J., & Wang, Y. W. (2000). Asian American coping attitudes, sources, and practices: Implications for indigenous counseling strategies. *Journal of College Student Development, 41,* 94–103.

Zaff, J. F., Blount, R. L., Phillips, L., & Cohen, L. (2002). The role of ethnic identity and self-construal in coping among African American and Caucasian American seventh graders: an exploratory analysis of within-group variance. *Adolescence, 37*(148), 751–773.

Zeidner, M., & Saklofske, D.H. (1996). Adaptive and maladaptive coping. In M. Zeidner (Eds.), *Handbook of coping: Theory, research and applications* (pp. 505–531). New York: John Wiley.

Zhang, D., & Long, B. C. (2006). A multicultural perspective on work-related stress: Development of a collective coping scale. In P. T. P. Wong & L. C. J. Wong (Eds.), *Handbook of multicultural perspective on stress and coping* (pp. 555–576). New York: Springer.

Zheng, X., & Berry, J. W. (1991). Psychological adaptation of Chinese sojourners in Canada. *International Journal of Psychology, 26,* 451–470.

Chapter 7

Employee Assistance Programs: An International Perspective

One institutional response to assist workers in their ability to manage the emotional and physical toll placed on them in a rapidly changing, highly competitive economy is an employee assistance program (EAP). The climate of the modern workforce is to do more with less. With layoffs, downsizing, and outsourcing, many employees face unique challenges that appear unrelenting. Even for those who remain afterward, many suffer from "survivor guilt" along with a form of "white-collar blues" from the increased workload, longer hours, and fewer resources (Brockner, 1992; Brockner, Grover, Reed, DeWitt, & O'Malley, 1987; Heckscher, 1995). According to one Fisher Vista Survey (2001), 96% of Fortune 500 companies find it necessary to have an EAP to confront and mitigate these workplace dysfunctions as well as the emotional toil this places on workers' personal lives. In fact, EAPs along with workplace counseling have emerged as the most common forms of stress management (Cooper, Dewe, & O'Driscoll, 2011).

The purpose of an EAP is to "improve and/or maintain the productivity and healthy functioning of the workplace and to address a work organization's particular business needs through the application of specialized knowledge and expertise about human behavior and human health" (EAPA, 2007). The primary objectives of EAPs are to assist organizations in

1. Addressing work organization productivity issues
2. Assisting "employee clients" in identifying and resolving personal concerns

The personal concerns of employees may be health, marital, family, financial, alcohol, chemical dependency, abuse, legal, emotional stress, or other personal problems that may affect job performance. Potential work issues affecting employees may include work demands, fairness issues, work relationships, harassment, bullying, interpersonal skills, work–life balance, and work-related stress (EAPA, 2007). Overall, EAPs are intended to provide a comprehensive array of services to help employees become more productive by increasing their mental health and well-being with the results of decreased accidents, reduced turnover, decreased health-care costs, and increased organizational productivity. As an illustration of the potential positive impact of these types of EAP services, McDonnell Douglas's EAP (Smith & Mahoney, 1989) reported that over a 5-year period it had 29% fewer absences from those individuals with a chemical dependency, 25% fewer missed days for those with psychiatric conditions, 42% fewer job terminations for chemical dependency, and 28% fewer terminations with employees suffering psychiatric issues. In addition, the company experienced significantly lower medical costs for individuals and families (Smith & Mahoney, 1989; Attridge, 2010a). These gains represented a return on investment (ROI) in excess of 4:1 for McDonnell Douglas.

In offering EAP services, there are four delivery models: internal, external, combination, and consortium (Berridge, Cooper, & Highley, 1997; Cooper, Dewe, & O'Driscoll, 2001; Cooper et al., 2011; Irish Employee Assistance Professionals Association, 2007). In the internal EAP model, the services are offered solely by an organization's employees. The nature of services offered by a company's internal EAP will vary with the size of the organization and the historic practices of the industry. Larger organizations possess the resources to offer a variety of services with several full-time trained staff to cope with chronic and episodic stressful encounters in one's work and personal life domains. However, smaller organizations with fewer resources still have the ability to mitigate their employees' difficulties on a smaller scale through alternative means whether they be contracting for part-time help or partnering with other companies to gain economies of scale. As a second approach, if an organization employs an external model, it will outsource the EAP services to an outside service vendor on a contractual basis. At the beginning, there will be an education and promotion period to encourage employees to use the EAP services from the vendor. However, the services are usually held off-site, and the confidentiality of who uses these services is strictly enforced. Workers can reach the EAP service provider by direct telephone and online contact. Newsletters with advice and information on its training and counseling programs are sent to the organization's workforce in cooperation with the organization's human resource department. In the third approach, the internal/external combination model, there may be an internally trained staff member assigned to perform some of these services with external professionals handling some contractually designated activities. The fourth model, a consortium approach, consists of several smaller employers joining together to create a shared EAP or jointly contracting with an outside provider. With all these models, their central core services remain similar depending on the organization's financial resources and human resource objectives. EAPs usually offer a number of services, such as some form of confidential individual assessments and counseling services; referral support, tracking, and follow-up; information services about how to handle problems; emergency intervention and critical incident stress management (CISM); substance abuse expertise; a 24-hour crisis telephone response line; access to qualified employee assistance clinical providers; and selected continuing mental health and physical health programs. Along with these initiatives, EAPs can provide the organization with needs assessments, management consultations, supervisory leadership training, EAP policy development, and EAP program evaluation (EAPA, 2007). Within the United States, the internal, on-site model dominates, where as in Britain and Europe the external contract mode of delivery appears more frequently. The reasons for the preponderance of this model's practices in this part of the world stems from the later development of the EAPs in this region and a stricter economic climate constraining their growth, as well as organizations possessing alternative governmental services that act as substitutes for what EAPs offer (Cooper, Dewe, & O'Driscoll, 2003). The existence of the other two models (internal/external combination and consortium) has been a more recent development to provide more flexibility in an organization's choice of an EAP that fits its needs. These two models also favor small to medium businesses, which dominate the U.S. workplace, and it appears that this trend will continue. Starting in the 1980s, businesses began to dramatically downsize and outsource their work in Western nations to meet their strategic global challenges. Within the United Kingdom, large-scale businesses now account for less than one-third of the nation's total workforce (Cooper et al., 2011). In the United States, 52% of the workers are employed by enterprises with fewer than 500 workers, according to the U.S. Small Business Administration. (Conte & Karr, 2001). More significantly, small businesses have created approximately 65% of new jobs over the past seventeen years (Conte & Karr, 2001; U.S. Small Business Administration, 2011).

Since 2000, EAP associations have emerged beyond the North American and European borders to Africa, Asia, Central America, and South America. In South Africa, as an illustration, companies using EAPs have increased from 42% in 1996 to 70% by 2009 (Davies & Terblanche, 2005; Terblanche, 2009). Given this growth, it is important to learn how EAPs can operate within different countries given the pressing dynamics of a global economy. Unfortunately, the research on the effectiveness of these programs has occurred primarily with EAPs within the United States, the United Kingdom, and some parts of Western Europe (Bhagat, Steverson, & Segovis, 2008). Little information exists regarding how EAPs operate and whether these programs are effective in the globalizing and emerging economies of China, India, Brazil, Ireland, Turkey, and Egypt. As competition within the global economy intensifies, the human resource practices of subsidiaries of multinational and global organizations, as well as those of indigenous companies will become a greater concern as an important strategic tool (Stewart, 1997). The mental health and well-being of workers becomes paramount, especially since in many emerging countries there is a shortage of highly qualified knowledge workers in technology industries. The attraction and retention of these types of workers are critical to being an innovative, competitive company in a rapidly changing globalized economy ("Special Report," 2010). Our survey of the academic and practitioner-oriented literature indicates that the transfer of the EAP core technologies to other countries may not be a straightforward process. The evolution, maintenance, and growth of EAPs may depend on a number of factors within a global context: the level of affluence in a given country as a function of globalization, the culture-based variations in societal and organizational contexts, and the predispositions of employees to seek and use EAP services.

In this chapter, we (1) discuss the historical evolution of EPAs with a focus on discerning their central tenets and concerns, (2) present a conceptual model for understanding cross-cultural variations of human stress and cognition in organizations with understanding different emphases of EAPs as a function of societal and organizational culture-based variations, (3) advance a theoretical framework for examining the determinants of EAP effectiveness from a global perspective, and (4) explore an emerging model for EAP adaptation in different societal and cultural contexts. This examination of EAPs will offer guidance for researchers and professionals who wish to understand the cultural variations of EAPs and the implications for their evolution, sustenance, and growth.

Historical Evolution of EAPs

Forms of employee assistance type programs appear to have emerged during the industrial social reform movements of the late nineteenth century (Kelloway, Francis, & Montgomery, 2005; Kelloway, Hurrell, & Day, 2008). Popple (1981) reported that during the 1920s a third of the largest U.S. companies had a full-time welfare secretary who counseled employees with personal problems. The present day roots of EAPs, though, appear to have come primarily from many companies' efforts to combat alcoholism in the workplace (Masi, 2003;

Matteson & Ivancevich, 1988). With the success of Alcoholics Anonymous (AA) in the 1940s, complete abstinence became the driving objective in the treatment of employees. Workers were terminated then rehired if they maintained sobriety with the help of AA. This type of approach spread since individuals who went through this program had excellent records of increased work productivity. The purpose of these alcoholic treatment programs was to identify alcoholic employees and get them help before they would be terminated due to excessive absences, tardiness, or poor performance. Fellow workers who were recovering alcoholics themselves served as the point people in running these programs. An important finding from these initiatives was that the threat of job loss may have been the driving force for getting alcoholics to change and transform their lives (Masi, 2003).

This treatment of alcoholics by companies reflected a long history of positive corporate actions to provide occupational programs for their workers (Sonnenstuhl & Trice, 1986, 1990). These types of programs were centered on a philosophy of integrating the dual concerns of economic performance and humanitarian values. By helping employees with their problems, organizations would gain commensurate benefits in increased productivity. Unfortunately, though, these innovative beginning programs failed to progress beyond their initial design stages due to a number of obstacles. Alcoholism still possessed a social stigma in addition to programs' receiving few company resources to manage the problem. Supervisors would choose to cover up the problem to protect the worker, but paradoxically they would wait until it was too late to help the worker from being fired. To compound the problem, alcoholism was still seen as only a "lower echelon" rather than a company-wide issue (Masi, 1984). Over time, despite these difficulties, due to the success of programs of several major corporations, such as Caterpillar, Consolidation Edison, DuPont, Eastman Kodak, New England Electric, and North American Aviation, the concept slowly widened its adherents through the 1950s and 1960s. Governmental agencies and health-care providers also began to adopt these types of alcohol treatment–related programs. In addition, organizations also began using outside external contractors for services as an alternative delivery mode. In the 1970s, the focus of EAPs started to transform beyond alcoholism to other sources that impaired job accomplishment (Spicer, 1987). Substance abuse and chemical dependency became the new focus. Employee assistance programs slowly developed into today's *broad-brush* approach of comprehensive services to help employees with all types of work and life difficulties. This expansion of services was further stimulated by a cultural shift in the destigmatization of alcoholism as less of a character defect and more as a disease to be treated (Masi, 1984). This fundamental change of perspective was furthered by the passing of the Hughes Act–Comprehensive Alcohol Abuse and Alcoholism Prevention, Treatment, and Rehabilitation Act of 1970 where alcoholism was decriminalized and rehabilitation became the objective. During the 1980s, EAPs grew further with a change to private-sector providers and alcohol and drug treatment centers. Their services greatly expanded to include a vast array of activities. The programs evolved to include stress management, health wellness, and addiction treatment services (smoking and overeating). The focus became prevention through controlling stress and fostering healthier lifestyles. As an illustration, Lifewatch, a major employee assistance program provider, has information on its website for alcoholism but also on aged care, email etiquette, pet loss, the flu, smoking cessation, identify theft, and financial debt (Lifewatch, 2010). By the 1990s, EAPs grew to become a main feature of many organizations to manage the complex pressures from downsizing, mergers, outsourcing, and international competition. They were viewed as a source for social support for employees managing the intricate demands of life and work (Kramer & Rickert, 2006).

Today's EAPs should be seen as the result of an evolutionary process to accommodate the changing socioeconomic trends facing Western society over a number of years. Now they face a new set of challenges. Health-care costs continue to rise with significant increased insurance rates to companies (The Street, 2010); this is a trend that goes back to the 1970s (Luthans & Davis, 1990). These costs began to be shifted in increasing amounts to employees, along with the advent of more managed care programs. EAPs confront a difficult challenge in maintaining their role in improving worker productivity and well-being while fighting cost containment concerns. Fortunately, EAPs have produced a number of studies that have shown their effectiveness at a bottom-line level. Within U.S., U.K., and European companies, EAPs have become an essential human resource component for strategic performance for competitive advantage (Stewart, 1997). Campbell Soup Company, when it used mental health treatment and counseling as part of its EAP, saw medical costs from visits to psychiatrists drop 28% in one year (Spicer, 1987). In a Hartford Financials Services Group's 4-year study, the insurance firm saw improvements in worker productivity through the treatment of depression in 11 companies with 94,000 combined employees. EAPs in these companies shortened the duration of short-term disability (STD) claims, increased the number of employees returning to work at the end of the STDs, and decreased the overall incidence of STD claims (The Hartford, 2007). Attridge (2010c) reported three studies with sample sizes of over 26,000, 59,000, and 3,500, which revealed outstanding gains (50% average) in the average amount of improvement in work productivity per clinical case. Two of the studies also found dramatic absenteeism reductions from a 2.4 days average to a 0.9 days average (62.5%) and a 7.2 days average to a 4.8 days average (33.3%), respectively, for 30 days before versus 30 days after EAP use concluded. Goplerud and McPherson's (2010) review of several studies of alcohol-related programs incorporating the program components of screening, a brief intervention, treatment referral, and follow-up shows a similar set of results with productivity gains measuring from 50% to 64%. However, these types of gains have to be carefully weighed in the light of a number of historical measurement and methodological design issues related to EAP studies (Berridge & Cooper, 1994; Cooper et al., 2003, 2011; Highley & Cooper, 1994; Kelloway et al., 2008). Although some studies show positive gains, others show none. Some research studies show no systematic advantages of this approach versus other treatment or counseling modalities. In general, research conducted on the outcomes of EAPs is mixed (Arthur, 2000; Cooper et al., 2003, 2011). However, it appears that EAPs do yield positive results in an individual's stress reduction; in terms of its affect on work productivity and other organizational outcomes, the results remain uncertain (Cooper et al., 2011). A lot of the problems of inconsistent or unclear results centers on how program evaluation effectiveness studies have failed to address a number of evaluation criteria to attain more reliable and valid research results. Cooper et al.'s (2011) excellent review of this literature points to a number of issues: a lack of defined program evaluation outcomes, failure to incorporate both qualitative and quantitative effectiveness criteria, weak rigorous comparative experimental research designs, and no 3-year pre- and 3-year post data collections following the EAP intervention. These criteria create a high standard to meet, especially considering their costs of time, resources, and opportunities. They become even more challenging when one considers the cross-cultural implications these assessment intervention designs entail. Despite these challenges, a number of efforts have been made recently to address these methods and measurement issues with EAPs in practitioner journals, such as the *Journal of Employee Assistance*. Professionals have realized the need to have a reliable and valid set of studies to substantiate their claims of a significant return on investment for their organizations (Attridge, 2010a, 2010b, 2010c; Goplerud & McPherson, 2010). Nevertheless, despite these methodological issues, comprehensive EAPs have been shown to play a positive institutional role in selectively managing the dysfunctional consequences of stress from work- and nonwork-related demands. They are especially valuable when employing combined treatment program approaches (Arthur, 2000). These accumulated results about EAP effectiveness appear to have stimulated corporate and governmental decision makers to expand their use beyond their home borders to other countries.

Due to their success, EAPs have evolved over the years to be a global phenomenon. The International EAP Association consists mainly of 6,200 members in the United States but also has 800 members from other countries. As part of the International EAP Association, the Washington, D.C.–based Employee Assistance Professionals Association (EAPA) alone has a membership in 39 countries. Other EAP professional organizations include the U.K. EAPA, EAPA Ireland,

Hellenic Chapter–International EAP Association, Employed Assistance Society of North America (EASNA), Asia Pacific Employee Roundtable (APEAR), and the European Network for Workplace Health Promotion (ENWHIP). Overall, eight EAP organizations exist worldwide (Masi, 2003).

This worldwide presence of EAPs underscores their success as an institutional stress management intervention mechanism. For many companies, EPAs have become a valuable tool to assist workers in handling their stressful life experiences at work and in their personal lives, given the ever increasing pressures of global competition. The Hong Kong and Shanghai Banking Corporation (HSBC) Group, one of the world's largest banking and financial services organizations offers a model of a traditionally designed EAP for managing these issues for their workers. HSBC Group's services include a nursery school (for ages 2–6) to provide its workers more flexibility to handle their demanding schedules, along with a company sports club to promote a healthy lifestyle. In addition, the HSBC Group offers a 24-hour professional counseling service through the Christian Family Service Centre to help employees cope with their personal difficulties. These services include stress management, interpersonal and family relationships counseling, marriage counseling, parenting counseling, and retirement planning as well as medical, legal, and financial advice (Tsui & Lui, 2009).

As EAPs have grown globally, so has their network of providers as an emerging industry. Private consulting agencies, such as Stuecker & Associates, a Kentucky-based company, provide EAP services in the United States, the United Kingdom, Mexico, and Puerto Rico. Their clients are employees of public-sector organizations from all levels of local, state, and federal government agencies as well as private corporations from the fields of transportation, manufacturing, and health care. Stuecker & Associates offers a comprehensive set of services to these organizations, including employee counseling, family counseling, conflict resolution skills, substance abuse programs, coping with traumatic stress, life transitions programs, financial counseling, work–life balance seminars, and online counseling services. EAP International, part of Horizon Behavioral Services of Texas, has targeted a strategic niche as a global EAP provider by offering customized services to companies' human resource departments and divisions. EAP International typically focuses on risk management procedures for medical, safety, and legal issues, along with providing child-care and elder-care counseling and referral services. Besides the United States, the company offers its services in Australia, Canada, New Zealand, Switzerland, the United Kingdom, Singapore, Mexico, Hong Kong, Russia, and Japan. Another global EAP provider, ComPsych Corporation in Chicago, Illinois, services 23 million people in over 6,000 organizations in 92 countries. They are especially recognized for their online and customized programs using a 24-hour/7 days-a-week model (Bhagat et al., 2008). Most of these types of organizations, provide assistance to expatriates of global corporations attempting to cope with the dislocation of moving to foreign countries with one's family members. Besides these U.S.-based global EAP providers, international EAP consulting companies can be found in Tokyo, Japan (the K2 Corporation); Dublin, Ireland (EAP Solutions); and London, England (Dovedale Counseling Ltd.) (Burgess, 2001).

Given the global recognition and adoption of EAP services, the question now arises as to how long this growth will continue. What are the limits of a "one-size-fits-all model"? At this point in their evolution, EAP services have followed the rise of large scale global businesses. These companies have especially used the EAP approach in supporting their expatriate workers along with their families on foreign assignments, or they have decided to continue their home-based country services to the locale of their subsidiaries. The challenge now is to learn where this type of adoption will be most effective and whether EAPs will be limited in their application due to cross-cultural and societal norms.

EAPs: Cross-Cultural Variations

Culture is to society what memory is to an individual (Triandis, 1994a, 1994b, 1995, 2002). One should not assume that a person from China would view the world the same as someone from Europe. One's culture shapes one's values, lifestyles, locus of causation, and sense of time. Even within one's ethnic group there exist clear cultural differences. Within Hispanic communities, EAP professionals cannot assume that Hispanics raised in the United States have similarities when compared to Hispanic immigrants; or a professional of Argentinean descent who is born and raised in Chicago does not share the same culture experiences as a factory worker of African descent who comes from Cuba and speaks Spanish (Esquilin, 2008). Each of these cultural differences presents a challenge when examining the usefulness of EAPs for stress management. As the previous chapters have clearly documented, these cultures' sanctioned ways of thinking and acting affect a work group's coping responses and ultimately the individual's transactional adaptation to stressful life events (Bhagat, Krishnan, Harnisch, & Moustafa, 2004; Bhagat et al., 1994; Lazarus & Folkman, 1984; Spector et al., 2001). The variations stemming from these different cultures significantly influence the types of coping that may occur and the kinds of social support systems that are likely to be available to contend with episodic or chronic stressors. EAPs, just like these other social support mechanisms, exist in this rich social, cultural, and organizational milieus with their design and effectiveness shaped by them.

Table 7.1   Prevalence of Employee Assistance Programs in Four Different Grids of Societal Cultural Variations

VERTICAL	**Cell 2:** **In Vertical Individualistic Countries** (e.g., Canada, United States, United Kingdom) EAPs are mostly institutional, company driven	**Cell 3:** **In Vertical Collectivistic Countries** (e.g., Egypt, India, Japan) Less frequent in number and are generally a function of the state of globalization and economic well-being of the population in the country
HORIZONTAL	**Cell 1:** **In Horizontal Individualistic Countries** (e.g., Australia, Denmark, Sweden) Strongly embedded in social, legal, and political framework	**Cell 4:** **In Horizontal Collectivistic Countries** (e.g., Costa Rica, Mongolia, Israeli Kibbutzim) Existence of EAPs largely unknown; if known, are highly dependent on the nature of social relations found in the country
	Individualism	**Collectivism**

Source: Adapted from Bhagat, R. S., Steverson, P. K., & Segovis, J. C., *Journal of Managerial Studies, 44,* 2007, pp. 229–249.

To understand how culture affects the prevalence of EAPs around the globe, Table 7.1 offers a four-grid model based on two dimensions: *individualist–collectivist* and *vertical–horizontal.* Four cultural grids emerge from this model that are salient for our investigation: vertical–individualism, vertical–collectivism, horizontal–individualism, and horizontal–collectivism (see Table 7.1).

From our perspective, one critical cultural dimension that strongly influences the variations in the prevalence of EAPs centers on the roles of individualism and collectivism. Individualism and collectivism act as social patterns that explain cultural syndromes (Hofstede, 2001; Triandis, 1994a, 1995, 1998, 2002). *Individualism* consists of a social pattern of loosely linked individuals who view themselves as independent of their social groups and are motivated by their distinct set of preferences, needs, rights, and contracts. *Collectivism,* in contrast, is defined by a pattern of closely linked individuals who see themselves and their identity as part of one or more collectives (e.g., family, coworkers, in-groups, or organizations). These types of individuals become motivated by the norms, duties, and obligations demanded by their particular work or home community. Collectivistic workplaces by definition would be highly unlikely to encourage the kind of contractual, formal EAPs found throughout the West (Bhagat, Steverson, & Segovis, 2007; Bhagat et al., 2008). They would be more likely to provide the appropriate mechanisms for evoking social support from one's immediate workplace members as well as community ties built through a history of interrelationships and trust rather than through EAP services.

Verticalness represents the propensity of members in a culture to stand out or be different from others, whether it is their friends, associates, or neighbors. Verticals view the world as consisting of people differing in social status. In fact, they view standing out from others in the crowd as desirable and appropriate. *Horizontals,* on the other hand, view themselves as having the same status, more or less, as others in their circle of friends, family, and associates. Horizontals do not desire or see it as appropriate to stand out from others. This cultural perspective emerges when individuals see themselves in terms of their self-concept being integrally part of an in-group, family, and community. When one's self-identity merges with those of one's valued groups, then individuals tend to reflect similar tastes and preferences as well as strategies on how to cope with their personal and work environments. A traditional Israeli kibbutz can be characterized as this type of horizontal relationship.

In *vertical–individualistic* countries such as the United States, the United Kingdom, and Canada. EAPs offer a standardized system of services that are typically found in U.S. human resource departments. There exists in the companies a strong focus on maintaining the privacy of individuals and families. This desired value can also be seen as a legal right reflected in the recent legislation in the United States, such as the Health Insurance Portability and Accountability Act (HIPAA). Since the outward expression of emotions and distress is strongly discouraged in vertical–individualistic workplace environments, EAPs in this context focus on role performance and production concerns along with employee issues (Sanchez-Burks, 2002, 2004). However, EAPs located in vertical–individualistic countries primarily will still focus on worker productivity despite their services to help employees. Employers in the vertical–individualistic grid leave it up to their employees to solve their distress and problems with the help of EAPs through the institution's management-sanctioned EAP programs. As a contrast, within *horizontal–individualistic* cultural contexts, such as in Denmark, Norway, Finland, Sweden, and Australia, the main thrust for the evolution, support, and development of EAPs stems from the countries' governmental and public agencies. There exists a strong inherent belief that the community's well-being can be achieved through the political, social, and legal frameworks of these countries. This stands in contrast to the vertical–individualistic countries where the push for EAPs remains toward a private-sector approach. Even though there exists a number of governmental and quasi-governmental health agencies in the U.S. context, such as the National Institute Mental Health (NIMH), National Institute for Occupational Safety and Health (NIOSH), and the Occupational Health and Safety Administration (OSHA), who may play some role in assisting company sponsored EAPs, the fact remains that this type of EAP originates from human resource management departments, not government organizations.

Vertical–collectivistic countries (e.g., China, India, Egypt, Brazil, Argentina, Mexico, and Turkey) will emphasize social support practices that pervade both work and nonwork domains, much more than horizontal–individualistic countries (e.g., such as Australia, Sweden, and Denmark; Bhagat et al., 2008). EAPs in this section of the grid will occur less frequently. Their pervasiveness is more of a function of the state of globalization and the economic well-being of the population in the country. Also, the societal–cultural mechanisms of social support will be determined more by one's community rather than any company's EAP mechanisms or practices. Within the *horizontal–collectivistic* section of the grid, EAPs are largely unknown. It should be noted, though, that these societies usually are relatively poor in economic resources and often are not significant actors in global, transnational commerce. Mongolia, parts of rural China and Africa, as well as Israeli kibbutz, are all representative of these types of societies. Organizations in these countries would most likely not be affluent enough to offer EAPs since they lack the necessary institutional resources. Also, in horizontal–collectivistic societies, help is always around as one's community and in-group would provide most of the support in one's time of need.

Influence of Organizational Culture on EAPs

In addition to the influence of societal–cultural factors upon EAPs, there exists the potential for organizational culture-based interventions. These differences influence social support practices and the existence of EAPs as well as directly affecting the management of individual and organizational distress. In Table 7.2, a second grid outlines a cultural matrix of coping styles and social support mechanisms, along with the effects of distinctive organizational cultural milieu on the type of EAPs created. Two dimensions of cultural variations that can be used to classify organizational cultures are *employee-oriented* versus *job-oriented* organizations (Hofstede, 2001) and *rule-based* versus *relationship-based* organizations (Hooker, 2003). This classification will give us several additional insights into how different types of EAPs can emerge and grow beyond the societal–cultural norms of the countries. In *employee-oriented* cultures according to Hofstede (2001), the organization's attention focuses on the problems of

Table 7.2   An Organizational Culture-Based Matrix of the Prevalence of Styles of Coping, Social Support Mechanisms, and Differential Emphasis of Employee Assistance Programs

Rule Based		
	Cell 2 Moderate emphasis on social support and emotion-focused and problem-focused coping EAPs are likely to be not as prevalent	**Cell 3** Strong emphasis on problem-focused coping Less emphasis on emotion-focused coping, social support EAPs are likely to be most prevalent and well organized
	Cell 1 Strong emphasis on social support especially from one's coworkers and in-group Strong emphasis on emotion-focused as opposed to problem-focused coping Virtually no EAPs	**Cell 4** Moderate emphasis on social support from one's work group Moderate emphasis on emotion-focused and problem-focused coping EAPs are likely to be infrequent except in organizations in rapidly globalizing regions
Relationship Based		

Employee Oriented ◄──────────► Job Oriented

Source: Bhagat, R. S., Steverson, P. K., & Segovis, J. C., in D. L. Stone & E. F. Stone-Romero, *The Influence of Culture on Human Resource Management Processes and Practices* (pp. 207–233). New York: Lawrence Erlbaum Associates, 2008. Copyright 2008. Reproduced by permission of Taylor & Francis Group, LCC, a division of Informa plc.

people and takes responsibility for their welfare. In *job-oriented* cultures, as a contrast, there is a strong demand on employees to get the job done; organizations of this type seem more interested in worker productivity than employee well-being. Extending the concepts of Hooker (2003) for the second dimension, we advance the idea that relationship-based organizations focus primarily on the maintenance of harmonious relationships despite the costs to organizational productivity. Conflicts among workers are smoothed over and discouraged. Behavior is largely regulated by one's clan, peers, and authority figures, such as parents, older siblings, senior relatives, or bosses. It is expected that the entire community has the responsibility to watch and socialize its children. These types of cultures are most likely to be discovered in nonindustrialized or highly collectivistic countries or regions. The majority of countries of Africa, Asia, and Latin America are good examples of relationship-based countries. In contrast, rule-based organizational cultures appear to be impersonal with a strong focus of "doing things by the book." There is a bureaucratic flavor with formalized modes of communication, a stress on procedures, and a focus on contractual arrangements. Unless something has been formally sanctioned or exists as a formal policy, an individual would not receive special consideration for requests. Rule-based cultures exist in countries such as Austria, Germany, Sweden, Switzerland, United Kingdom, and the United States.

Within this *Organizational Culture-Based Matrix* in Table 7.2, Cell 1 with its *employee-orientation* and its *relationship-based* culture would stress a harmonious workplace. These types of organizations can be found in countries unaffected by the process of industrialized globalization, especially in rural areas. Small family-owned businesses found in horizontal– or vertical–collectivistic parts of the world (e.g., rural China, India, Brazil, Mexico, rural Latin America, the Middle East, Africa, and Israeli kibbutz) are likely to exhibit strong social support and strong emotion-focused coping. In Mexico, as an illustration, work relationships become strongly guided by the traditional social norms of *simpatico* (Diaz-Guerrero, 1967; Triandis, Marin, Lisansky, & Betancourt, 1984). People value this relational style and seek social harmony as well as being actively concerned for their immediate in-group network. This type of culture reflects many East Asian societies. Within Cell 1 organizational cultures, EAPs rarely exist.

Organizations with a Cell 2 organizational cultural prototype (*rule-based and employee-oriented*) would most likely exhibit a moderate emphasis on social support mechanisms, problem-focused coping, and emotion-focused coping. EAPs with this profile would not occur frequently unless they were in the urban regions of the global economy, such as in South Korea, China, Taiwan, and India. Cell 3 type organizations (rule-based and job-oriented) can be found in the highly industrialized and knowledge economies of the world. In this cell, one would find organizations within the United States, most of Western Europe, Australia, and Canada. This cell would have a high incidence of EAPs. The cultural messages here are to deal with one's challenges and difficulties with problem-focused coping while suppressing emotions. In these organizational cultures the expectation would be that it would be strongly preferred for workers to handle their affective and relational concerns away from the workplace (Sanchez-Burks, 2002, 2004). EAPs in this cultural context would be highly institutionalized and offered frequently by organizations. Finally, Cell 4 organizational cultures (job-oriented and relationship-based) emphasized social support from ones' in-group community and a moderate emphasis on both problem-focused and emotion-focused styles of coping. These types of organizations would reflect the Chinese principle of *guānxí* and Andean countries' concept of *anyi*, that is, a strong sense of interconnectedness and caring among one's in-group members (Gose, 1994; Hooker, 2003; Leung & White, 2004). The existence of EAPs would be primarily in rapidly growing regions of the world; otherwise, their occurrence would be infrequent. Examples of Cell 4 organizations can be found in South Korea, Taiwan, and Thailand; also they would be found in the globalized urban regions of China (e.g., Shanghai, Guangzhou, and Beijing) and India (e.g., Bangalore, Bombay, and Chennai).

Effectiveness of EAPs for Global Organizations

Researchers and practitioners have recognized that EAPs offer not only potential economic benefits but also the possibility of employee productivity, health, and well-being. They are being seen by executives as tools for assisting them in dealing with unfamiliar issues of managing the challenges of subsidiaries of multinational and global corporations. Part of their willingness to use EAPs in non-U.S.-based corporations is based on their success in helping U.S. multinationals' expatriates and families adjust to life in different parts of the world. However, as our previous section on EAPs' cross-cultural variations demonstrated, the diffusion of these types of programs continues to face a number of challenges to their growth.

Of the 3,246 members reported by the EAPA, 3,047 are in the United States. Membership in Asia, though growing in China and Japan, stands at 1.5% in 2010. In addition, published reports indicate that traditionally designed EAPs have very low use rates in many countries, such as 3% to 10% in Argentina to 3.6% in Japan (Ichikawa, 2000; Iwasaki, 2000; Lambardi & Lardani, 2002; Pensel & Lambardi, 2001). This is in contrast to the 15 to 20% coverage of all employees in the United Kingdom and Ireland, the most developed EAP markets in Europe (Barth & Hopkins, 2007). Research also shows that the majority of supervisors in non-English-speaking countries have little awareness of EAPs (Buon, 2006). In fact, our research indicates that EAPs are rooted mainly in countries with Anglo-Saxon, individualistic–vertical traditions. In other words, the spread of EAPs has been slow to countries that have a collectivistic orientation or have non-Western national, economic, political, legal, and cultural expectations (Bhagat et al., 2007). The reasons for these low nonuse rates stem are rooted in their fundamental beliefs, practices, and values.

EAPs reflect primarily the humanistic paradigms of Western organizational behavior. Organizations should aid their workers when they are experiencing difficulties. This paradigm stresses that companies must meet the needs of their workforce for them to remain productive and satisfied while facing stressful work and nonwork experiences. However, the values of this humanistic approach may not necessarily reflect the societal norms of non-Western contexts. In Latin America, for example, Pagani-Tousignat (2000) discovered that companies feel that just offering their workers a job is sufficient enough as a responsibility. They owe their workers nothing beyond a day's pay. In Latin American countries, as well as other countries, there is a clear expectation between the employer and employee to keep one's personal issues separate from work (Pensel & Lambardi, 2001). If one has a drinking or drug problem, it is the individual's own private affair (Bennett, 2000). This type of attitude is often seen in areas with high unemployment rates, such as Argentina, Brazil, Mexico, Indonesia, Singapore, Nigeria, or countries of the former Soviet Union. For companies within these countries, it is often easier and preferred to replace an employee suffering from stressful situations. This approach would be the opposite in countries, such as the Netherlands, United Kingdom, United States, or Sweden, with societal norms that provide a social safety net of programs to support the employees through stressful situations.

In addition to the challenges of adopting the humanistic underpinnings of EAPs, there exists a social stigma against using counseling or psychiatric programs. The propensity to find mental health counseling through EAPs varies throughout the world (Kossek, Meece, Barratt, & Prince, 2005: Reynolds & Lehman, 2003; U.S. Department of Health & Human Services, 1999). This can be readily seen in Cell 3 of Table 7.1; in vertical–collectivistic cultures, the demographic and cultural predispositions are to seek out social support mechanisms and rely more on personal emotion-focused coping and rituals of these countries. In collectivistic countries, individuals are concerned with their ingroup or collective to which they belong rather than their own personal goals. Problems, such as caring for the elderly and intimate domestic violence, are seen as problems to be solved by one's family and close friends rather than by professional counselors, social workers, or psychiatrists referred by their employing organizations' EAPs, which is more typical of a U.S. company (Pollack et al., 2010). In India, for example, the family would handle a member's alcoholism, not a company's EAP. This would be the same for traditional Chinese communities as well. Families in China, living with members who have contracted HIV/AIDS, would see this as a stigma bringing shame to the family while losing face in their home community (Li et al., 2008). A company's employee assistance program would not be seen as an option for help. In countries following socialistic and communistic ideological principles, it would be expected that governmental agencies and labor organizations would intervene when stressful incidents pervade the workforce and start to affect worker morale and production. Even in Germany, which has a humanistic tradition, EAPs have had a difficult time being accepted (Barth, 2006). Germany possesses a well-established welfare system with universal access to counseling and psychiatric services along with health care. In addition, where EAPs have been used, they must gain the support of their worker councils who want to be the primary resource for employees.

EAP EXPANSION IN CHINA—CHINESE MANAGERS GOING TO PIECES IN CHINA

The symptoms of the fast-paced competitive workplace have started to visit many Chinese managers. Complaints have occurred of burnout, depression, substance abuse, and eating disorders. The shift from a planned to market economy has come at a price. As Russ Hagen, chief executive officer (CEO) of the employee assistance firm Chestnut Global Partners has observed, "For China, it's as if the world has completely flipped on its axis." Where harmony dominated, now a worker has to compete. It's about results not relationships. The fabric of worker relationships is being strained. Family ties mean less in the workplace. The lure of large financial payoffs is driving people's concerns on a daily basis.

The tragedy is that in China one cannot conveniently seek counseling to find solace from one's stressors. There is a strong distrust of psychotherapy, but the major hurdle is the loss of face in admitting you need help. This stigma has contributed to the increasing acceptance of Buddhism. Temples have again become places to visit for the general population, especially from "frazzled" managers; there they can find spiritual support and sustenance. Despite these challenges, Western multinationals continue to extend counseling, along with other services, such as child-care assistance and credit card counseling, that traditionally have been available only to expatriate Western managers.

Mirroring this expansion of multinational services, U.S. employee assistance programs have begun to solicit Chinese clients. As one example of this trend, Chestnut Global Partners now works with Minsheng Bank, one of the largest Chinese banks. However, as soon as it started it hit a major bump in the road. Behavioral counseling was not acceptable. Now Chestnut's programs emphasize "personal well-being services" and "workplace harmony" programs rather than conflict management sessions. Also, to overcome the stigma of being seen using psychotherapy, online sessions or group problem-solving sessions have become more prevalent. The methods and labels have changed, but not the focus. Chinese workers complain about the same issues as American employees: job performance difficulties, bad supervisors, and home life marital issues. As a result, the Chinese clients use Chestnut's service twice as much as Americans.

Adapted from Conlin, M., & Roberts, D., *Businessweek*, 4031, 2007, p. 88.

Another challenge is the norms of confidentiality and privacy. Though it is seen as acceptable to use EAPs in Western cultures, individual confidentiality and privacy are paramount when individuals seek help and guidance within an EAP system. People in Western societies find it difficult to admit to others their lack of control over their environment. People's social image must reflect a sense of mastery and competence; otherwise it would have adverse effects on their self-esteem and perceived social status. However, within a majority of Eastern cultures, issues of confidentiality and privacy are not as significant (Bhagat et al., 2007). Offering aid to a friend and colleague who is undergoing difficult times or experiencing distress is considered a social obligation and moral duty; this would most likely happen in China, India, and much of South America and Africa. The Buddhist, Hindu, and Confucian world views are prevalent throughout much of India and Southeast Asia strongly stress the need to offer empathy and compassion to those in difficulty, especially toward the members of one's in-group (Hooker, 2003). In the majority of these countries, there exists an attitude that occasionally losing one's sense of control over one's environment should not be seen as inherently shameful. Within these societies, fatalism is a key component of their culture, especially in India, parts of Southeast Asia, and the Middle East (Triandis, 1994a). Individuals within these countries are more likely to accept the role of fate in determining their destinies or affecting the conduct of their daily lives.

In addition to these societal challenges to the diffusion of EAPs on a global basis to non-Western cultures, it appears that EAPs are found primarily in affluent, as well as Anglo-Saxon, individualistic countries. This reflects the reality that affluent countries usually appear to have an Anglo-Saxon and individualistic cultural background (Triandis, 1989, 1995). Organizations in these nations (i.e., the United States, the United Kingdom, Canada, and Australia) are able to afford EAPs on a scale that cannot be matched in emerging economies. Developing countries, such as Venezuela, Mexico, Egypt, Nigeria, China, India, and Brazil, are typical illustrations of this problem. Two collectivistic countries that do not fit this pattern are Japan and South Korea. Both are highly industrialized and affluent; both offer some type of EAP. However, there exists little evidence of EAP provider networks in these two nations (Bhagat et al., 2007). Trade-related publications and EAP research rarely mention specific company-related activities in global corporations within these countries, such as the Toyota Corporation, Mitsubishi, Sony-Japan, Samsung, Lucky and Goldstar, Inc., and Hyundai. Overall, it appears that the scientific research on the benefits of EAPs and the best practices for their implementation occurs primarily in Western countries and stands in sharp contrast to non-Western countries, despite their level of development or affluence (Cooper et al., 2003; Masi, 2003).

Emerging Model for EAP Adaptation

It is clear from our research that a "one-size-fits-all" model does not work in understanding the role and application of EAPs in the emerging global economy. Different societal and cultural variations operate at unique and often subtle levels that have not been easily discerned by the research and practitioner literature. In fact, no systematic investigations have been conducted on the interplay of societal culture and organizational cultural factors in the evolution, maintenance, and growth of EAPs within the global economy. Figure 7.1 presents an organizing framework for investigating the effectiveness of EAPs in different countries from a cross-cultural lens. As the figure shows, the effectiveness of EAPs from a global perspective is a function of four components: (1) the extent of globalization that exists in the given locale; (2) societal cultural-based variations in terms of prevalence of EAPs (shown in Table 7.1); (3) organizational culture-based variations in terms of prevalence of EAPs versus the emphasis on styles of coping and social support mechanisms (shown in Table 7.2); and (4) the role of demographic and cultural predispositions inherent in the population to seek EAPs (Bhagat et al., 2008). This model can help researchers investigate the complex coping and adaptational processes that are uniquely interpreted in the cultural context of one's society. It also provides guidance to practitioners as to the design of EAPs for

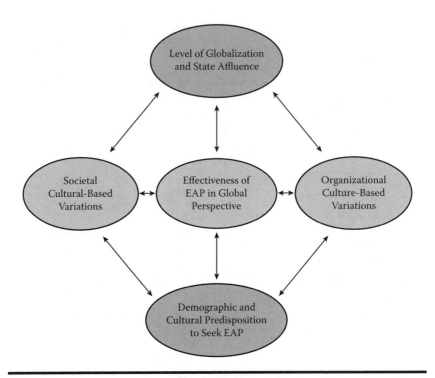

Figure 7.1 **Effectiveness of employee assistance programs in an era of globalization. (From Bhagat, R. S., Steverson, P. K., & Segovis, J. C., in D. L. Stone & E. F. Stone-Romero, *The Influence of Culture on Human Resource Management Processes and Practices*, Lawrence Erlbaum Associates, New York, 2008, p. 227. Copyright 2008. Reproduced by permission of Taylor & Francis Group, LLC, a division of Informa plc.)**

global organizations. EAPs, by their definition, are meant to be devised to enable employees to function more effectively so that their psychological and physical health is not unfavorably affected by stressful life and work experiences, as well as to assist them to consistently contribute to an organization's effectiveness (Cooper et al., 2003). Global organizations then need to learn how to create employee assistance programs that accomplish these goals within their cultural milieu.

Several examples currently exist that illustrate how managers could make this adaptation of EAPs from a Western-focused model to one fitting other non-Western forms. In Japan, for example, one company discovered that if it renamed one EAP initiative from psychological counseling to "Personal Consulting Services," it had significantly more participation (Iwasaki, 2000). This mitigated the social stigma about counseling as an approach. It has also been suggested that the type of counseling offered needs to be changed in Southeast

Asia to a "solutions-oriented" rather than an emotion-focused model to be seen as less threatening, as well as better fitting the Chinese culture of the area (Ho, Tsui, Chu, & Chan, 2003). When counseling was introduced in Argentina, it was found that the short-term five-session approach typically employed by EAPs needed to be modified to a more long-term model given individual expectations stemming from the strong psychoanalytic tradition of the country (Pensel & Lambardi, 2001). Also, one EAP in Argentina shifted its emphasis to a more problem-solving approach around more culturally acceptable issues. This avoided the limitations of psychological coping strategies and dealt directly with the immediate crisis everyone was facing. Due to the threats of rapid inflation and the confiscation of personal bank accounts in this country, companies started to offer legal and financial counseling to assist their employees. Programs began to deal with money movement in bank accounts, property, and auto sales to elude withdrawal restrictions, breach of contract issues, loan risk exposure, currency exchange strategies, as well as counseling for traumatic events, such as kidnapping and robberies that were occurring (Lambardi & Lardini, 2002). Since everyone was facing an overwhelming set of events, they were appreciative of any assistance that could directly manage their issues. The psychological interventions were also changed to supplement the legal and financial help. Workshops were held on preserving the family amid the crisis, along with sessions on optimism and stress management, programs more fitting the culture's norms.

One example of an attempt to apply a Western style member assistance program (MAP; similar to an EAP) in Israel highlights the key challenges of adapting a stress management intervention to another culture, but it also suggests its potential opportunities for a reshaped form (Golan & Bamberger, 2009). A MAP uses a voluntary, peer-based design to support employees seeking assistance for substance abuse and other personal problems. When an Israel manufacturing company of 350 employees attempted to use a typical American MAP to combat the strong prevalence of substance abuse among Israeli workers, several key differences emerged. First in an American MAP, employees can contact the EAP directly or the supervisor can refer them. In the Israeli program, individuals did refer themselves for financial problems, but supervisory referrals were not used at all. The managers began to act as peer counselors to aid the employees, even to the point of helping one person handle his or her mortgage payments. At the request of the Israeli employees, peer counselors focused on aiding family members. In fact, 33% requested this type of assistance, which was higher than the family service requests of an American EAP. The Israeli peer counselors took a much more active role than their American counterparts. They sought creative solutions to the point of depositing the check of an addicted employee in the counselor's checking account for the employee's family; another time they personally replaced the lock on the door of an abused employee to prevent her husband from entering; and another peer counselor arranged temporary shelter for family members threatened by Hezbollah missile attacks. Overall the Israeli peer counselors were much more employee focused and became more advocates than counselors. They bypassed union structures and company rules to find solutions for their fellow workers in resolving conflicts or solving nonwork-related problems. This included taking food from the company kitchen illegally to help employees with financial difficulties. These types of interventions strongly underscore a general Israeli cultural perspective. It is collectivistic in nature where the family or the feeling of a workplace "family" dominates one's thinking. This humanistic, community mind-set became reflected in the number of family requests by workers as well as the intensity of the peer counselor's actions. Also, the Israeli culture can be characterized by a lower *power distance* in contrast to the American culture (Golan & Bamberger, 2009; Hofstede, 1984, 2001). In this case, it explains why bureaucratic managerial tools such as supervisory referrals or union procedures were not readily accepted or instructions were not followed as a primary concern. Therefore, as this Israeli study indicates, along with the reports from Japan, Latin America, and Argentina, EAPS can be successfully implemented in different cultures, but not as a Western prototype with its implicit individualistic and higher power distance cultural norms. As these case studies suggest, though they are few in number, there is a need for carefully adapting traditional EAP tactics into a much more flexible and robust model of offerings than what currently exist in EAPs, if they are to be successful globally beyond Western values-oriented countries.

KOREAN COMPANIES STRESS MANAGEMENT APPROACHES: CALMING THE DISTRESSED WORKER

When Korea's economy faltered in 2009 due to the global financial crisis, its leading corporations started to become concerned about its affect on workers. Managers observed anxiousness and tension as people learned to adjust to less resources but increased demands to remain competitive. Instead of ignoring these signs, these firms took a creative proactive approach reflecting their strong humanistic values. Their fear was that a distressed worker would become an unhealthy and ultimately unproductive employee. Shinhan Bank, the number two lender in Korea, and Samsung Electronics, the largest Korean company, put on stress reduction education programs. However, they were a bit different from Western traditional approaches. In one session, a "forest education and therapy program," Koo Do-hyun, a 30-year-old employee of Shinhan Bank walked and laid down among the trees giving him a chance to reflect. "It really helped me release tension," reported Do-hyun.

The SK Group in Seoul conducts *simgisn sureyeon* training classes during lunch and after work to strengthen their mind, body, and spirit. The company reported that it had to add classes at its headquarters as the program gained in popularity. Within LG CNS, the information technology (IT) service arm of the LG Group, the company created a stress management room with aroma lamps and music as employees relaxed on comfortable couches. As employees decompressed, they also used a health-care monitoring system—"Touch Doctor"—to measure their blood pressure and level of stress, as well as other health conditions. Whether it was walking in the woods, relaxing with music and aromas, or attending tension reducing training, all the company officials felt these stress relieving strategies worked and in the long-term helped the company benefit financially from better employee productivity.

Adapted from Hyun-joo, J., *The Korea Herald*, 2009.

As each of the previous EAP examples illustrates, organizations can modify or adapt their existing programs to deal with the stressful demands of a turbulent economy. In fact, as competition in the global economy intensifies, organizations' human resource practices may provide the critical edge to survive and thrive versus other less adaptive companies. As one example, Singapore's *Financial Times* reported in 2009 that the job satisfaction rate of Singaporean workers to be the second lowest in the world (Japan being the worst). Only 53% of its finance professionals were satisfied with their jobs based on the worldwide survey conducted by the Robert Half consulting firm (Hooi, 2009). Among the critical factors causing this, according to the survey participants, were the long working hours, poor work–life balance, as well as threatened job security (Lian, 2009). In responding to the problem, DHL Express Singapore attempted to address this ongoing societal issue by employing pro-family practices to help keep the employees engaged to prevent costly turnover of their workforce. Company staff members were able to leave an hour earlier every Wednesday. Besides the annual Family Day event, DHL regularly organized workplace-health programs, such as sporting activities, health screenings, and health talks. A special program was created for employees' children to visit the DHL facilities during school holidays. The goal was to help children to understand their parents' jobs by going behind the scenes and participating in selected work activities ("Views from the Top," 2008). Moreover, countries such as China that have historically enjoyed ample, cheap labor pools may not be able to depend on this competitive advantage anymore. Now companies in the manufacturing centers of Southeast Asia face labor shortages. They have to compete for workers with more attractive working conditions as well as salary increases. In addition, a number of worker strikes at large employers, such as Honda and Foxconn Technology, may force companies in developing countries to rethink their employment practices (Barboza & Tabuchi, 2010). Otherwise, they will lose foreign investment and ultimately production contracts. Given these circumstances, culturally sensitive designed EAPs that fit these cultures' norms, values, and expectations may be an additional institutional response beyond the usual promises of salary raises and promotions to attract and keep the best-trained workforce.

THE CHANGING RULES OF THE CHINESE WORKPLACE

"If Wang Jinyan, an unemployed factory worker with a middle school education in Zhongshan, China, had a resume, it might start out like this: 'Objective: seeking slow-paced assembly-line work in air conditioned plant with Sundays off, free wireless Internet, and washing machines in dormitory. Friendly boss a plus.'"

Job hunting has changed in the Pearl River Delta of the Guangdong Province. Now the onus is on the factory owner to attract the employee due to the shortage of workers. Manufacturers must compete by offering higher salaries, better conditions, and attractive benefits. The job shortages have emboldened workers to strike. In Zhongshan, Honda's Chinese operations were crippled temporarily from stoppages. Toyota suffered the same fate in Tianjin, along with a Japanese-owned electronics factory. Usually, the company capitulates by offering higher wages and improved conditions to get them back to work.

The labor shortages stem from the fact that the supply of 16–24-year-old workers has peaked and will fall to about a third of its total by 2022. China's family-planning policies may have controlled its population to prevent famine, but it may have also hindered its future growth. In addition, many migrants who left their homes to come to the region are now finding work closer to home. In places like

Zhongshan, the heart of the manufacturing capital of the world, there are 15 to 20% vacancies available in its factories. In addition, today's young Chinese factory worker was stimulated to have greater expectations. They do not want to toil for long hours and low wages as their parents did on their farms or the previous cohort of workers more than a decade ago. The modern youth refuses to taste *chi ku* or "eat bitterness," a cultural trait worn with pride by past generations. Moreover, current experienced workers have demanded that they should receive a higher salary since they have gained more job knowledge and skills along with a proven track record. These types of workers can leverage their skills to a position that fits their vision of the lifestyle they see in the sophisticated urban areas of Hong Kong, Beijing, and Shanghai.

So now factory owners, managers, and recruiters rush around in their BMWs, Mercedes, and Lexuses to recruit workers. One company, an electric heater producer, offers a 7.5-hour workday; an underwear company promises meal subsidies along with factory fashion shows by the employees. Where one worker used to consider taking a job making shoes, now she refuses due to the smell of noxious smelling glues. And to make matters worse, as owners and managers try to recruit new workers, they must also fight off other competitors stealing their current workforce with more attractive packages. All in all, it is a new world for Chinese employers and workers.

Adapted from Jacobs, A., *The New York Times*, 2010, p. A1.

New Directions for the Future of EAPs

Though Tables 7.1 and 7.2 demonstrate that certain societal and organizational cultures are more amenable to the traditional Western EAP model, this does not compromise the ability to use this institutional form of stress management in some countries that are different in terms of their cultural orientations from Western countries. It is just a reality that the pace of implementation of EAPs in these countries will continue to be constrained until managers learn the intricate complexities of culture-specific modes that are implicit within different national contexts. As designers of EAPs become more aware of culture-specific differences in organized rites and rituals and social support systems, they will begin to create more appropriate institutional processes and mechanisms that will facilitate peer group support. Over time, new forms of EAPs may emerge that have been modified to function harmoniously with the dominant cultural-specific modes of coping and social support mechanisms. In an edited book by Zeitlin and Herrigel (2000), different authors investigated the theme of "Americanization and Its Limits" in dealing with applications of U.S. technology and various knowledge management-based systems in postwar Europe and Japan. The authors concluded that although the major patterns mainly apply, there were also unique country-based variations in their evolution to the various countries of postwar Europe. The Italian steel and German rubber industries did not fully adopt, if at all in some cases, the U.S. model to be competitive. Within the Japanese context, U.S. manufacturing and process technologies needed to be reinvented and selectively adapted. Taking these case studies as a template, though it cannot be guaranteed, EAPs will be more effective in dealing with the adverse impact of rising levels of work and nonwork stressors, whether the EAP is sponsored by the organization itself or offered in the institutional context of a given society (Bhagat et al., 2007). As one example of this adaptation, South African EAPs tend to be more comprehensive in their services than historic European and North American models to reflect the evolutionary changes by an economy and society in transition (Terblanche, 2009). In many non-Western companies, critical stress debriefings (CIDs), workplace antiviolence training, and HIV/AIDS assistance are some of the major issues that need to be addressed and customized for a corporation more than an organization may do in traditional Anglo-Saxon EAPs. However, as these new adaptive forms of EAPs are discovered, EAP designers will have to be careful of their stereotypical assumptions about how a particular ethnic group might draw on social support resources from others in dealing with stressful experiences. As an illustration of this issue, some Asians may not enlist the help of friends and relatives despite the prevalent view that the majority of Asians would do so (Taylor et al., 2004). Researchers have learned that some Asian groups, however collectivistic in background, often are reluctant to seek social support from their friends, families, or members of their in-group because it might lead to a disruption of the harmonious relationships with others (Taylor et al., 2004). This tendency is compounded by the high verticalness of certain Asian collectivistic cultures. Shame and embarrassment become an issue for the person needing help.

One of the key steps in facilitating the effectiveness of EAPs in their implementation is an increase in systematic, rigorous research investigations. Such research will be helpful in determining the validity of the theoretical schemas that have been advanced in this chapter. Also, there needs to be a significant increase in attention to country-specific EAP implementation programs in practitioner journals. As one illustration of this issue within one particular practitioner journal of the EAPA, the *Journal of Employee Assistance,* for a recent 5-year period, only 8 of the 148 articles published during this time covered international-related topics in countries such as the United Kingdom, Australia, Greece, Germany, and Argentina or the cross-cultural issues of Hispanic clients. Finally, professional and academic associations, such as the International Association of Applied Psychology and International Congress of Psychology, can provide significant leadership in the dissemination of information as to the benefits of EAPs along with other culture-specific methods in addressing the various types of stressful experiences that affect employee effectiveness (Bhagat et al., 2007). Unfortunately, EAP materials are usually written only in English, which limits their use worldwide and reflects only the concerns of the countries the material comes from—North America, United Kingdom, and Australia (Buon, 2006). As of 2003, the Council on Accreditation, which includes EAPs from the United Kingdom, Puerto Rico, and Japan, started to play a greater role in establishing international accreditation programs for EAPs not necessarily based on U.S. standards (Masi, 2003). With these three steps, it is hoped that the effectiveness of EAPs, as well as other preventive stress management programs (Cooper et al., 2003; Quick, Bhagat, Dalton, & Quick, 1987; Quick, Cooper, Nelson, Quick, & Gavin, 2003), in improving health and well-being at work will be expanded beyond their current individualist, job-oriented contexts to include more collectivistic, employee-oriented work settings.

Conclusion

EAPs are programmatic efforts predominately undertaken by work organizations in Western individualistic countries. We discussed the evolution of EAPs in the worldwide context and reported that they are culturally embedded. Some cultures have large numbers of prominent global organizations (e.g., Japan, South Korea) but do not spend adequate institutional resources to develop EAPs to assist employees in coping with difficult situations experienced at both work and personal life. We provided a cultural matrix for classifying EAPs in the worldwide context and noted that rule-based and individualistic countries are likely to be more vigilant in emphasizing EAPs and their vital importance in the lives of individuals than EAPs in relationship-based and collectivistic countries.

   In the next chapter, we discuss the role of research methodology in the conduct of sophisticated research on work stress and coping in the era of globalization.

References

Arthur, A. R. (2000). Employee assistance programmes: The emperor's new clothes of stress management? *British Journal of Guidance and Counseling, 28,* 549–559.

Attridge, M. (2010a). EAP cost-benefit research: 20 years after McDonnell Douglas. *Journal of Employee Assistance, 2,* 12–15.

Attridge, M. (2010b). Taking the Pareto path to ROI. *Journal of Employee Assistance, 3,* 8–11.

Attridge, M. (2010c). 20 years of EAP cost research: Taking the productivity path to ROI. *Journal of Employee Assistance, 4,* 8–11.

Barboza, D., & Tabuchi, H. (2010, June 8). Power grows for striking Chinese workers. *New York Times,* B1.

Barth, J. (2006). Germany: A difficult market for EAPs. *Journal of Employee Assistance, 1,* 26.

Barth, J., & Hopkins, R. (2007). Europe: Shocked, but little impact. *Journal of Employee Assistance, 1,* 34.

Bennett, A. (2000). One company, many countries: The challenges of providing EAP services within multinational firms. *EAPA Exchange, March–April,* 40.

Berridge, J. R., & Cooper, C. L. (1994). The Employee Assistance Programme: Its role in organizational coping and excellence. *Personnel Review, 23,* 4–20.

Berridge, J., Cooper, C., & Highley, C. (1997). *Employee assistance programmes and workplace counseling.* Chichester, UK: Wiley.

Bhagat, R. S., Krishnan, B. C., Harnisch, D. L., & Moustafa, K. S. (2004, April). Organizational stress and coping in twelve countries: Implications for a cultural theory of stress. Paper presented at the annual meeting of the Society for Industrial and Organizational Psychology. Chicago, IL.

Bhagat, R. S., O'Driscoll, M. P., Babakus, E., Frey, L. T, Chokkar, J. S., Ninokumar, B. H., Pate, L. E., Ryder, P. A., Fernandez, M. J. G., Ford Jr., D. L., & Mahanyele, M. (1994). Organizational stress coping in seven national contexts: A cross-cultural investigation. In G. Keita & J. J. Hurrell (Eds.), *Job stress in a changing workforce* (pp. 93–105). Washington, DC: American Psychological Association.

Bhagat, R. S., Steverson, P. K., & Segovis, J. C. (2007). International and cultural variations in employee assistance programmes: Implications for managerial health and effectiveness. *Journal of Managerial Studies, 44,* 229–249.

Bhagat, R. S., Steverson, P. K., & Segovis, J. C. (2008). Cultural variations in employee assistance programs in an era of globalization. In D. L. Stone & E. F. Stone-Romero, *The influence of culture on human resource management processes and practices* (pp. 207–233). New York: Lawrence Erlbaum Associates.

Brockner, J. (1992). Managing the effects of layoffs on survivors. *California Management Review, 34,* 9–28.

Brockner, J., Grover, S., Reed, T., DeWitt, R., & O'Malley, M. (1987). "Survivors" reactions to layoffs: We get by with a little help from our friends. *Administrative Science Quarterly, 32,* 526–41.

Buon, T. (2006). Non-English speaking countries: Adjusting for cultural differences. *Journal of Employee Assistance, 36*(3), 27–28.

Burgess, K. M. (2001, December). *The employee assistance program: An inappropriate model for supporting expatriates and families overseas.* Paper presented at the 8th annual Counseling in Asia Conference, Taipei, Taiwan.

Conlin, M., & Roberts, D. (2007, April 23). Go-go-going to pieces in China: Frazzled managers are displaying all the classic signs of Western-style stress. *Business Week*, Issue 4031, 88, Retrieved from http://web.ebsco-host.com.ezproxy.memphis.edu/ehost/delivery?vid=16&hid=8&sid=68ae0 d3d-15c5-4a08-9eac-848aa7a9466f%40sessionmgr111

Conte, C., & Karr, A. R. (2001). Chapter 4: Small business and the corporation, an outline of the U. S. economy. Washington, DC: U. S. Department of State, International Programs, 2001. Retrieved September 21, 2011 from http://usa.usembassy.de/etexts/oecon/index.htm

Cooper, C. L., Dewe, P. J., & O'Driscoll, M. P. (2001). *Organizational stress: A review and critique of theory, research, and applications.* Thousand Oaks, CA: Sage Publications.

Cooper, C. L., Dewe, P. J., & O'Driscoll, M. P. (2003). Employee assistance programs. In J. C. Quick & L. E. Tetrick (Eds.), *Handbook of occupational health psychology* (pp. 289–304). Washington, DC: American Psychological Association.

Cooper, C. L., Dewe, P. J., & O'Driscoll, M. P. (2011). Employee assistance programs: Strengths, challenges, and future roles. In J. C. Quick & L. E. Tetrick (Eds.), *Handbook of occupational health psychology* (2nd ed., pp. 337–356). Washington, DC: American Psychological Association.

Conte, C., & Karr, A. R. Chapter 4: Small business and the corporation, an outline of the U.S. economy. Washington, D.C.: U.S. Department of State, International Programs, 2001. Retrieved September 21, 2001 from http://usa.usembassy.de/etexts/oecon/index.htm

Davies, A., & Terblanche, L. (2005). Employee assistance programs in South Africa. In D. Masi (Ed.), *The international employee assistance compendium* (3rd ed., pp. 178–182). Bloomington, IL: Chestnut Global Partners.

Diaz-Guerrero, R. (1967). *Psychology of the Mexican: Culture and personality.* Austin: University of Texas Press.

Employee Assistance Professionals Association. (EAPA). (2007). Guide to employee assistance programs and services. Retrieved July 24, 2007 from http://www.eapassn.org/public/providers

Esquilin, P. (2008). Working with Hispanics. *Journal of Employee Assistance, 38*(2). Retrieved from http://www.eapassn.org/i4a/pages/index.cfm?pageid=1029

Fisher Vista. (2001). Fisher Vista's survey of Fortune 500 decision-makers reveals untapped market opportunities for work-life service providers. Retrieved November 11, 2011 from http://www.fishervista.com/news_100123.htm

Frequently asked questions: Advocacy small business research and statistics. U.S. Small Business Administration, 2011. Retrieved September 21, 2011 from http://web.sba.gov/faqs/faqsIndexAll.cfm?areaid=24

Golan, M., & Bamberger, P. (2009). The cross-cultural transferability of a peer-based employee assistance program (EAP): A case study. *Journal of Workplace Behavioral Health, 24,* 399–418.

Goplerud, E., & McPherson, T. L. (2010). SBIRT at work: The big initiative. *Journal of Employee Assistance, 4,* 16–19.

Gose, P. (1994). *Deathly waters and hungry mountains: Agrarian ritual and class formation in an Andean town.* Toronto: University of Toronto Press.

Heckscher, C. (1995). *White-collar blues: Management loyalties in an age of corporate restructuring.* New York: Basic Books.

Highley, C., & Cooper, C. L. (1994). Evaluating EAPs. *Personnel Review, 23*(7), 46–59.

Ho, W-S., Tsui, M-S., Chu, C-K., & Chan, C. C. (2003). Towards culturally sensitive EAP counseling for Chinese in Hong Kong. *Employee Assistance Quarterly, 18,* 73–83.

Hofstede, G. (1984). *Culture's consequences: International differences in work-related values.* Abridged edition. Beverly Hills, CA: Sage.

Hofstede, G. (2001). *Culture's consequences: Comparing values, behaviors, institutions, and organizations across nations* (2nd ed.). Thousand Oaks, CA: Sage.

Hooi, J. (2009). S'pore ranks second-lowest for job satisfaction. *The Business Times.* Singapore Press Holdings Ltd. Co. Retrieved September 25, 2011, from http://www.asiaone.com/Business/News/Office/Story/A1Story20090417-135879.html

Hooker, J. (2003). *Working across cultures.* Stanford, CA: Stanford University Press.

Hyun-joo, J. (2009, May 19). Firms out to soothe stressed workers. *The Korea Herald.*

Irish Employee Assistance Professionals Association. (2007). Models of employee Assistance programs. Retrieved November 1, 2010, from http://www.eapaireland.ie/what_is.htm

Iwasaki, R. (2000, September–October). Adapting EAPs to Japanese culture: A case study. *EAPA Exchange,* 31–32.

Jacobs, A. (2010, July 13). In a shift, Chinese workers set their terms. *The New York Times,* A1.

Kelloway, E. K., Francis, L., & Montgomery, J. (2005). *Management of occupational health and safety* (3rd ed.). Toronto: Nelson.

Kelloway, E. K., Hurrell, Jr., J. J., & Day, A. (2008). Workplace interventions for occupational stress. In K. Naswall, J. Hellgren, & M. Sverke, *The individual in the changing working life* (pp. 419–441). Cambridge: Cambridge University Press.

Kossek, E. E., Meece, D., Barratt, M. E., & Prince, B. E. (2005). U.S. Latino migrant farm workers: Managing acculturative stress and conserving work-family resources. In S. A. Y. Poelmans (Ed.), *Work and family: An international research perspective.* (pp. 38–56) Mahwah, NJ: Lawrence Erlbaum Associates.

Kramer, R. M., & Rickert, S. (2006). Health and productivity management: market opportunities for EAPs: By integrating with health and wellness and disease management programs, EAPs can offer employers a powerful workforce productivity tool. *Journal of Employee Assistance, 36*(1), 23–25.

Lambardi, E., & Lardani, A. (2002, September–October, 8–9). The crisis in Argentina: EAPs in Argentina are adopting new tactics to help employees and workers survive financial and political problems of tragic proportions. *EAPA Exchange.*

Lazarus, R. S., & Folkman, S. (1984). *Stress, appraisal, and coping.* New York: Springer.

Leung, K., & White, S. (2004). Taking stock and charting a path for Asian management. In K. Leung & S. White (Eds.), *Handbook of Asian management* (pp. 3–18). Norwell, MA: Kluwer Academic.

Li, L., Wu, Z., Wu, S., Jia, M., Lieber, E., & Lu, Y. (2008). Impacts of HIV/AIDS stigma on family identity and interactions in China. *Families, Systems, & Health, 26,* 431–442.

Lian, T. K. (2009, May 7). Job satisfaction–inadequate measures to protect workers. Retrieved from http://theonlinecitizen.com/2009/05/job-satisfaction- inadequate-measures-to-protect-workers/

Lifewatch, Inc. (2010). Employee assistance program. Retrieved August 21, 2010, from http://www.lifewatch-eap.com/

Luthans, F., & Davis, E. (1990, February). The healthcare cost crisis: Causes and containment. *Personnel, 24*–30.

Masi, D. A. (1984). *Designing employee assistance programs.* New York: American Management Association.

Masi, D. A. (2003). Issues in international employee assistance program accreditation. *Employee Assistance Quarterly, 19,* 73–85.

Matteson, M. T., & Ivancevich, J. M. (1988). Health promotion at work. In C. L. Cooper & I. Robertson (Eds.), *International review of industrial organizational psychology.* Chichester, England: Wiley.

Pagani-Tousignat, C. (2000, May–June, 22). Managed care and EAPs in Latin America. *EAPA Exchange.*

Pensel, S. S., & Lambardi, E. (2001, May–June). Challenges for employee assistance programs in Argentina, *EAPA Exchange,* 37.

Pollack, K., Cummskey, C., Krotki, K., Salomon, M., Dickin, A., Gray, W. A., et al. (2010). Reasons women experiencing intimate partner violence seek assistance from employee assistance programs. *Journal of Workplace Behavioral Health, 25,* 181–194.

Popple, P. R. (1981). Social work in business and industry, *Social Services Review, 6,* 257–269.

Quick, J. C., Bhagat, R. S., Dalton, J. E., & Quick, J. E. (1987). *Work stress: Health care systems in the workplace.* New York: Praeger.

Quick, J. C., Cooper, C. L., Nelson, D. L., Quick, J. D., & Gavin, J. H. (2003). Stress, health, and well-being at work. In J. Greenberg (Ed.), *Organizational behavior: The state of the science* (2nd ed., pp. 53–89). Mahwah, NJ: Erlbaum.

Reynolds, G. S., & Lehman, W. E. K. (2003). Levels of substance abuse and willingness to use the Employee Assistance Program. *Journal of Behavioral Health Services & Research, 30*(2), 238–248.

Sanchez-Burks, J. (2002). Protestant relational ideology and (in) attention to relational cues in work settings. *Journal of Personality and Social Psychology, 79*(2), 919–929.

Sanchez-Burks, J. (2004). Protestant relational ideology: The cognitive underpinnings and organizational implications of an American anomaly. *Research in Organizational Behavior, 26,* 265–306.

Smith, D. C., & Mahoney, J. J. (1989). *McDonnell Douglas Corporation Employee Assistance Program financial offset study.* Paper presented at the annual meeting of the Employee Assistance Professionals Association, Baltimore, MD.

Sonnenstuhl, W. J., & Trice, H. M. (1986). *Strategies for employee assistance programs: The crucial balance.* Ithaca, NY: ILR Press.

Sonnenstuhl, W. J., & Trice, H. M. (1990). *Strategies for employee assistance programs: The crucial balance.* 2nd edition, revised. Ithaca, NY: Cornell University.

Special report: Innovation in emerging markets—The world turned upside down (2010, April 17). *Economist, 395,* 1–18.

Spector, P. E., Cooper, C. L., Sanchez, J. J., O'Driscoll, M., Sparks, K., Bernin, P., et al. (2001). Do national levels of individualism and internal locus of control relate to well-being: An ecological level international study, *Journal of Organizational Behavior, 22*, 815–832.

Spicer, J. (1987). EAP program models and philosophies. In J. Spicer (Ed.), *The EAP solution: Current trends and solutions.* Center City, MN: Hazeldon Foundation.

Stewart, T. A. (1997). *Intellectual capitals: the new wealth of organizations.* New York: Doubleday.

The Hartford. (2007). *Healthier, more productive employees: A report on the real potential of employee assistance programs (EAP).* Hartford, CT: Author.

The Street (2010, September 29). Health costs seen hitting five-year high. *Newsweek.* Retrieved November 5, 2010, from http://www.newsweek.com/2010/09/health-costs-seen hitting-five-year-high.html

Taylor, S. E., Sherman, D. K., Kim, H. S., Jarcho, J., Tsakagi, K., & Dunagan, M. S. (2004). Culture and social support: Who seeks it and why? *Journal of Personality and Social Psychology, 87*, 354–362.

Terblanche, L. S. (2009). Labour welfare in South Africa. *Journal of Workplace Behavioral Health, 24*, 205–220.

Triandis, H. C. (1989). Cross-cultural studies of individualism and collectivism. In L. Berman (Ed.), *Nebraska Symposium* (pp. 41–130). Lincoln: University of Nebraska Press.

Triandis, H. C. (1994a). Cross-cultural industrial and organizational psychology. In H. C. Triandis, M. D. Dunnette, & L. M. Hough (Eds.), *Handbook of industrial and organizational psychology* (2nd ed., Vol. 4, pp. 103–172).

Triandis, H. C. (1994b). *Culture and social behavior.* New York: McGraw-Hill.

Triandis, H. C. (1995). *Individualism and collectivism.* Boulder, CO: Westview Press.

Triandis, H. C. (1998). Vertical and horizontal individualism and collectivism: Theory and research implications for international comparative management. *Advances in International Comparative Management, 12*, 7–35.

Triandis, H. C. (2002). Generic individualism and collectivism. In M. L. Gannon & K. L. Newman (Eds.), *The Blackwell handbook of cross-cultural management* (pp. 16–45). Oxford, UK: Blackwell Business.

Triandis, H. C., Marin, G., Lisansky, J., & Betancourt, H. (1984). Simpatia as a cultural script of Hispanics. *Journal of Personality and Social Psychology, 47*, 1363–1375.

Tsui, M.-S., & Lui, J. K. W. (2009). Labor welfare in Hong Kong: Its context and content. *Journal of Workplace Behavioral Health, 24*, 274–280.

U.S. Department of Health and Human Services. (1999). *Mental health: A report of the Surgeon General.* Rockville, MD: U.S. Department of Health and Human Services, Substance Abuse and Mental Health Services Administration, Center for Mental Health Services, National Institutes of Health, National Institute of Mental Health.

Views from the top: Work-life balance; Are businesses doing enough to be family friendly? (2008, May 19). *The Business Times Online.* Singapore Press Holdings Ltd. Co. Retrieved September 25, 2011 from http://www.dso.org.sg/news_details.aspx?news_sid=20090320800091247835

Zeitlin, J., & Herrigel, G. (2000). *What more needs to be done? The Americanization and its limits.* Oxford: Oxford University Press.

Chapter 8

Methodological Issues for Research on Work Stress and Coping

As discussed in earlier chapters, research on work stress and its consequences has become a major topic of interest among organizational researchers. A large percentage of these studies have been conducted in a transactional perspective to discover the general principles relating to how individuals respond to stressful experiences and events at work especially in the Western contexts. However, there is a growing trend of research that focuses on generalizability of theories and concepts of work stress to cultures that are non-Western and largely collectivistic in their orientation. The reports from business periodicals published in different countries clearly reveal the need for better insights into the role of international and cultural variations in this area—especially with the growing importance of globalization in connecting dissimilar countries. Researchers recognize that individuals in non-Western cultures experience work stresses and strains in ways that are likely to be both similar as well as dissimilar to the patterns of such experiences observed in the West. As discussed in Chapters 1 and 2, globalization of businesses has created some new types of organizations, work experiences, and arrangements that did not exist about two decades ago. Therefore, it becomes important to consider the roles of new types of contextual factors in the creation of work stresses in different countries and cultures.

In this chapter, we discuss strategies for conducting research on work stress and coping in the current of era of globalization, which involve innovative techniques. Kasl (1978) recommended over three decades ago that research on work stress needs to include measures of stressors and strains that are based on self-report as well as those independent of self-reports. The logic of introducing such measures (i.e., both subjective or self-report and objective or assessments derived from other sources in the person's immediate work environment) was to get a better grasp of the reality of work stress beyond the perceptions of the individual. This approach has been adopted in many U.S. studies on work stress. However, it is rare to see the use of multimethod approaches as well as longitudinal designs in international and cross-cultural research on work stress and coping. In addition to sharing the same kinds of problems and limitations that are present in organizational stress studies conducted within a country, research involving multiple countries and cultures introduces unique sources of methodological challenges and opportunities.

We discuss the nature of eight challenges that characterize research on work stress and coping in the era of globalization. These issues have to be dealt with in sequential order, with the first challenge listed getting the most priority, followed by the second challenge and so forth.

Establishing Equivalence of Constructs

A basic problem that has to be addressed first is the establishment of equivalence of independent, moderator, mediator, and dependent variables of a theoretical framework across ethnic, racial, and cultural groups. Construct equivalence is established when the construct being measured has identical meanings in cultures being investigated. Cross-cultural findings are difficult to interpret when a measure does not have construct equivalence. We have discussed how cultural variations greatly influence what individuals appraise as being stressful. So a work situation that might be perceived as being stressful in one culture may not be stressful in another culture. Similarly, research showing a greater adherence to self-reliance among Chinese compared with European American undergraduates (Triandis, McCusker, & Hui, 1990) might suggest that the Chinese culture is more individualist. However, this conclusion is valid only if self-reliance means the same thing or has identical connotations in both Chinese and European American cultures. For European Americans, the preference for self-reliance is rooted in people's strong desire to assert their independence from their in-group or collective. In contrast, for the Chinese self-reliance is motivated by a desire not to be a burden or too dependent on their in-group or collective. Unless the concept of *reliance* has similar connotations in both cultures, the measure of self-reliance is likely to lack construct validity. Take another example concerning "loss of face," which is a stressful experience in East Asian cultures regardless of whether it occurs in work or nonwork situations. While loss of face is properly understood in Western cultures to be a troublesome experience, it may not be as stressful as it is in the Eastern cultures. Careful attention to establishing equivalence of constructs (e.g., self-reliance, loss of face, problem-focused and emotion-focused coping) is more important than establishing measurement equivalence (Van de Vijver & Leung, 1997; Van de Vijver & Tanzer, 2004).

Cultural variations affect what individuals perceive to be stressful. An experience or event that might be considered a stressor for people in a sub-culture of a nation (e.g., among the African Americans in the U.S. South) might not be perceived in the same manner by another subculture, either in the same country (among mainstream White Americans in the Northeast United States) or in another subculture of a different country (among the Indian immigrants in the United Kingdom). We discussed that direct dis-agreements and conflicts are considered major sources of interpersonal con-flicts among the Chinese, among whom the idea of group harmony is more important than advancing career goals. Cong Liu, in a study of stressful work incidents among Americans and Chinese, found that whereas Americans felt comfortable reporting the experience of direct confrontations and conflicts as a source of stress in their work situation, the Chinese were much more reluctant to do so (Shi, Feng, Lin, Liu, & Spector, 2003). In a related vein, Narayanan, Menon, and Spector (1999) found that lack of decision latitude and work overload were significant sources of stress for American employees, whereas for Indians having more decision latitude was a source of stress—just the opposite of what the Americans reported. These studies, some of which are discussed in Chapters 3, 5, and 6, raise questions about construct equivalence in cross-national and cross-cultural research. Construct nonequivalence has received much less attention from work stress researchers than measurement equivalence. In their rush to find the role of the cultural differences in some select dependent organizational phenomena, researchers start collecting data across nations and cultures without subjecting their entire theoretical frame-work to a nomological network analysis.

Some types of methodological techniques may be employed to establish both construct and measurement equivalence. However, establishment of con-struct validity of theoretical measures across various ethnic, racial, and cultural groups is a more difficult challenge. For establishing construct validity of a scale, researchers need to accumulate evidence for its relationship with similar con-structs. In cross-national and cross-cultural research, the nomological networks are influenced by national and cultural differences. Therefore, adequate theoretical experiences must be constructed to predict how a given construct might relate to other similar constructs across cultures. The question here is whether research instruments or questionnaires reflect the same underlying concept or construct across cultures. In research on work stress and coping, there are concepts that are not quite the same in their meaning and significance across cultures, and therefore there cannot be meaningful comparative measurement. Incomplete coverage of the definitions of the construct being employed across cultures and nations is often the source of nonequivalence. In addition, poor sampling of all relevant behaviors to tap the construct is also a problem. Cohen's (2007) comprehensive review and analysis of methods in cultural psychology is a valuable reference in resolving some of the persistent problems in establishing construct equivalence.

Level of Analysis

Confusion regarding level of analysis is another problem that needs to be adequately addressed. The need to distinguish between country- or national-level differences and individual differences has been recognized for over three decades (Hofstede, 1980; Leung & Bond, 1989; Berry, Poortinga, Segall, & Dasen, 2006). Data collected at the culture level to explain group or individual phenomenon lead to errors and fallacies of interpretation. A distinction is made between aggregation errors (applying individual data to make inferences at the population, country, or culture level) and disaggregation errors (applying population level data to make inferences about individual-level characteristics). An example of the inappropriate use of disaggregation is when population-level information such as rate of burnout among health-care professionals in a country is applied at the individual level to explain exhaustion. Aggregation errors are present when inferences about population- or country-level differences are made based on the information collected at the individual level. For example, how globalization affects job security at the country level cannot be explained in terms of how it affects the population at the individual level. More precision is needed regarding what to expect in terms of relationships among various constructs across different levels of analysis. Our knowledge of how globalization and cultural differences interact to produce work stress and how individuals cope with such stresses will improve by employing appropriate constructs at different levels of analysis. What may be true at the individual level in a subsidiary of a large multinational and global corporation may not be applicable at the level of a family–owned firm employing a few individuals. Compositional models (statistical analyses showing how to detect interactions and inferences across various levels) should be employed whenever possible to explain the role of national and cultural differences. For further information regarding level of analysis issues, see Berry, Poortinga, Segall, and Dasen (2006) and Gelfand, Nishii, Holcombe,

Dyer, Ohbuchi, and Fukono (2008). This issue is a complicated one and must be addressed both at the beginning and end of the investigation.

Establishing Measurement Equivalence

Along with construct equivalence, measurement equivalence is another requirement for valid and meaningful comparison across nations and cultures. More often than not, work stress researchers are faced with a situation where it is unclear whether a concept is the same and whether the instruments employed tap the construct in the same fashion across nations and cultures. Techniques of translation and back-translation are used to establish an item or a number of items in a given questionnaire or research instrument. Consider research on work stress in which Germans and South Koreans are compared on their predisposition to employ problem-focused coping at work. Most psychometrically valid measures of problem-focused coping are developed by U.S.-based researchers and written in English. To establish measurement equivalence, a multilingual speaker of English, German, and Korean can translate the English measure into German and Korean. Then another multilingual speaker back-translates the German and Korean into English, and discrepancies in the translations are identified and corrected by comparing the original English language version with the back-translated versions in German and Korean. Although the back-translation has been recommended for over 50 years as a useful technique to ensure that a measure has been properly translated, it still does not capture the subtle differences in the nuances of the languages or cultures of a given item. Take the case of problem focused coping as an example. Being highly problem focused has a positive connotation in U.S. and German cultures, but being highly problem focused is not necessarily considered to be a socially desirable coping style in South Korean cultures.

Systemic differences in response styles across culture are also a problematic issue in establishing measurement equivalence. For example, compared with Americans the Chinese are less likely to give extreme responses (using extreme end points on a rating or Likert-type scale) whereas members of Middle Eastern Arabic cultures are more likely to give extreme responses. Other cross-cultural studies show that members in different cultures may use different reference groups as standards when responding to a rating scale (Heine, Lehman, Peng, & Greenholtz, 2002). The Japanese, for example, rate themselves as individualists when they perceived themselves to be more individualistic compared with other Japanese. Similarly, Americans rate themselves as more individualist compared with other Americans. Because Japanese strongly identify with their reference groups (i.e., community and work organization) which vary according to the context in which they find themselves, their responses cannot be directly compared with the responses from a comparable U.S. sample. In the strictest sense, responses can be compared only if the reference groups used by both cultural groups are identical. See Chiu and Hong (2006) for more details on the issues of measurement equivalence.

Correlational techniques are used to examine the relationship of the items of the instruments to establish measurement equivalence whether the study is being conducted across ethnic, racial, or cultural divides. An exploratory factor analysis is conducted for each cultural sample to determine a common factor structure. In research on work stress and coping, it is well established that subjective interpretation of the work environment is more important than the environment itself. Therefore, nonequivalent items representing distinct facets of a job stress construct are likely to cause inaccurate interpretations across cultures. The point is that nonequivalence of items results in incorrect inferences regarding observed differences of the role of national and cultural variations on dependent variables of interest. As discussed earlier, it is also quite important to establish equivalence of translated and back-translated instruments across ethnic, national, and cultural groups. This may be accomplished by employing bilingual individuals who are able to provide culture-specific (i.e., emic) information pertaining to the significance and meaning of the items in their cultures. Details regarding establishment of measurement equivalence and cultural biases in response patterns and acquisitions tendencies are dealt with in detail in Van De Vijver and Fischer (2009) and Berry et al. (2006).

Applying Appropriate Methodological Strategies

A great deal has been written on this topic, and we wish to reiterate the following points.

More Emphasis Should Be Placed on Longitudinal Research Designs That Have Been Carefully Designed in Advance

Even within a country context, conducting longitudinal research is both expensive and time-consuming. In addition, it is likely that since the results from longitudinal research studies take a long time to interpret and report, it may well have adverse career consequences for junior researchers. However, longitudinal designs are most appropriate to employ in studies pertaining to cultural changes that occur as a result of both direct and indirect consequences of economic globalization and participation of non-Western cultures and emerging markets in the global economy. Not only do cultures change in some of their basic orientations, but so do work organizations and individuals within the cultures.

Comparative studies of the effectiveness of different kinds of coping styles are best undertaken in the context of longitudinal designs since the individuals learn new types of coping techniques as they appraise and reappraise the stressful encounters by accessing new information from their environment. It has been noted repeatedly by well-known researchers (see Aldwin, 2007, for a detailed analysis) that patterns of effective coping unfold over time and that a static picture involving checklists or even a psychometrically valid scale such as the ones used by Lazarus and Folkman (1984) is not likely to capture the dynamics of coping that evolve in distinctive national and cultural contexts. As discussed in Chapter 2, economic globalization precipitates adverse organizational and human consequences. In some situations, an individual or a work group may take sole responsibility for coping with the stressful experience, and in other situations the individual or the workgroup may combine their resources and coping strategies with their employing organization to cope more vigorously. As we develop more robust theoretical frameworks, we will also have the opportunity of employing longitudinal techniques to capture the various types of bidirectional interactions that characterize the evolution of coping. It is only through long-term commitments to longitudinal research designs that we can begin to grasp the complex interactions between various facets of globalization and culture changes that have important implications for work stress and coping.

Qualitative Research Methods Should Be Employed Whenever Feasible

Qualitative research methods have been common in cultural anthropology and cross-cultural psychology for over 50 years. However, we do not see much qualitative research in the area of work stress and coping. It is somewhat surprising, given the complexities of psychological processes that have been inherent in how individuals appraise and cope with stress in this era of globalization, that qualitative techniques that can provide highly context dependent interpretations have not been used much. Qualitative methods are employed when there is genuine interest in understanding the emic (or culture-specific) roots of a phenomenon.

Consider the process of loss of face as a stressful experience for Chinese managers whether they work for Western multinationals in Hong Kong or for Chinese multinationals in Western and other globalizing countries. To gain a richer perspective of how one experiences stress due to possible loss of face in a work group, it becomes necessary to interview the colleagues of the focal person and get a detailed understanding of the culture-specific causes and consequences over the loss of face. Research information obtained by questionnaires simply cannot capture the complexities that are involved in a phenomenon like loss of face, which is idiosyncratic and highly significant in the

Chinese context. A qualitative researcher is interested in exploring the socially constructed nature of realities with unique situational constraints that might shape or alter the nature of research inquiry. Participant observation is a highly creative method for collecting qualitative data over a period of time. Robert Cole's (1971) study on the Japanese blue-collar worker is an extremely good example. Abegglen's (1958) work on the social organizations of the Japanese factory is another fine example.

The ethnographic literature is full of examples such as these that show that the subjective meaning of behavior patterns is largely dependent on the rules, customs, and norms of societies. Measurement by use of questionnaires and instruments is not likely to be as helpful as participant observation methods, ethnographic techniques, and trace analyses. Behavior is described in terms of observations in social and organizational settings, and reference is often made to historical precedents to provide a rich contextual and chronological background.

Greenfield (1997) noted the importance of momentary events in context, allowing for observation of changes. She emphasized that in choosing a qualitative mode of inquiry the researcher stresses the importance of the analysis of culture as an ongoing process gathering information from the members of the cultural group. She emphasized two forms of validity as being particularly relevant in qualitative investigations involving cross-national and cross-cultural differences. The first is interpretive validity (Maxwell, 1992), which is concerned with the fact that the researcher has communicated successfully with the respondents using an appropriate mode. Interpretive validity implies an understanding of the communicational and epistemological assumptions of the respondents and making sure that the data collection procedures are designed in accordance with these assumptions. The second form is ecological validity, which is concerned with the issue of generalizability of the research procedure outside the research context. Ecological validity tends to be present when the data collection takes place in naturally occurring cultural contexts. Data collected in experimental studies have little to no ecological validity. Validity remains an important challenge for the qualitatively inclined researcher.

We feel that this method can address many of the interesting questions and issues in the area of work stress and coping in the current era of globalization. Qualitative researchers have to be conceptually bold, to remain convinced of their technique in collecting the valid data, and to interpret the cues and signals that are sometime confusing and ambiguous. While qualitative methodologies have their limitations and are not particularly suitable in ruling out rival or alternative explanations, they are nevertheless quite appropriate to adopt in the early stages of a cross-national investigation.

Use of Multimethod Approaches to Improve Methodological Robustness Should Be Emphasized as Much as Possible

Job stress research using a multimethod approach to measurement will add considerable validity to the findings whether obtained within a culture or across cultures. The use of physiological and unobtrusive measures along with self-report measures should be incorporated as much as possible. In collecting data on stressful experiences at work, members of some cultural groups are likely to be sensitive to providing important information and data relating to their stressful experiences at work—especially if such experiences involve incidences of sexual harassment, workplace bullying, and other types of culturally sensitive stressors. In these instances, the use of information from a confidant such as the employee's spouse, coworkers, friends, and socially significant others is strongly recommended. See Bhagat, McQuaid, Lindholm, and Segovis (1985) for details on the use of confidants for obtaining information on stressful experiences of focal respondents.

Use of unobtrusive measures to validate self-report data from respondents is also recommended. Creative methods of collecting unobtrusive data from participants in situations where self-report data are not likely to be valid and reliable (as is likely to be the case when strong cultural bias and acquisitions tendencies characterize responses) is recommended. See Folger and Belew (1985) for details. The use of physiology indicators as measures of job stress (e.g., monitoring of blood pressure, visits to one's doctor and health clinics) are not as convenient or straightforward as self-report data. They are also expensive to adopt, and problems of reactivity are common. For example, anxious persons are likely to recover more slowly in their physiology to stressful situations at work than individuals who are not anxiety prone. At any rate, a triangulation of different types of measures to collect data on work stress, coping styles, and various moderator variables is recommended.

Understandably, there are costs in terms of time and money associated with the adoption of multimethod approaches for collecting data and they are particularly difficult to implement across racial, ethnic and cultural divides. There have not been very many studies conducted by adopting a multimethod design despite many benefits. However, the results of adopting a multimethod approach for collection of data will enhance the quality of research findings that will emerge in the future.

Ruling Out Alternative Explanations

The goal of much cross-national and cross-cultural research is to explain individual-level differences across racial, ethnic, and cultural groups on some dependent variables (e.g., psychological distress, lower job performance, increased work–family conflict) in terms of contextual variables that are conceptualized at the population level. A cross-cultural study on work stress is viewed as successful when all differences on dependent variables are explained in terms of context-specific cultural variations. The goal of the analysis should be to split the total effect of cultural variations on dependent variables into meaningful components that are purely contextual in nature. At this stage, it is important to distinguish between effects due to other factors (e.g., economic, technological, task related, and situational) that may also be responsible for explaining the variation in the dependent variable. While it is theoretically more interesting to contribute observed differences in dependent variables of interest in terms of cultural variations that are present across the groups, it is advisable to examine the role of other relevant contextual variables as well. Rival or alternative explanations that are possible should be carefully ruled out before the role of culture-specific variations is established in explaining the findings.

Establishing Sampling Equivalence

The validity of cross-cultural comparison is based on the assumption that comparable samples are drawn from target cultures. Three issues are important to consider in establishing equivalence of samples drawn from dissimilar nations and cultures. First, a choice has to be made regarding which types of cultural groups or populations are to be included in the investigation. Second, the question arises as to whether selection should be restricted to certain subgroups from large-, medium-, or small-scale work organizations. Third, the investigators have to decide how individuals will be selected from these subgroups or occupational groups. The common practice is to select only a few cultures that clearly differ on some variables of interest that provide a contrast of interest to work, stress, and coping researchers. For example, one could select countries of Western Europe that are individualistic and compare the incidences of work–family conflicts in these cultures with those in more collectivistic cultures of East Asia or Latin America. Research by Gelfand and her colleagues (2008) is an excellent example.

It is also important to consider the role of subcultures within a nation in collecting cross-national data from cross-cultural comparisons. Subcultures are distinct cultural groups that may share a few major cultural values with other subcultures of a society but still have their own distinctive orientations based on their historical experiences. For example, African Americans as a subcultural group may be individualistic in their orientation just like the mainstream Eurocentric Americans, but they are likely to put much stronger emphasis on collectivistic and family-focused patterns of coping. Similarly, members of subcultures of North African Arabs in France are likely to appraise stressful encounters quite differently from mainstream members of the French culture. Subcultures are important to sample to demonstrate that the differences among these distinct groups within a national context are lower than what is observed across two distinct national groups. Consider the case of four distinct subcultural groups: African Americans, Hispanic Americans, Asian Americans, and mainstream White Americans. All four subcultures are largely comfortable in reporting experiences of interpersonal conflicts at work. However, such is not the case with cultural subgroups in the People's Republic of China. If an investigator establishes that the average level of comfort in reporting interpersonal conflict at work is much lower in the Chinese subcultures compared with the American subcultures, then the issue of cultural differences across these two nations is firmly established.

A rigorous way to conduct international research on work stress and coping is to collect information from a variety of subcultures from a sample of major national cultures of the world. Admittedly, this strategy is more complex and more expensive to execute. However, the best example of this kind of research exists in the area of cross-cultural variations in leadership effectiveness (Chhokar, Brodbeck, & House, 2007; House, Hanges, Javidan, Dorfman, & Gupta, 2004). We do not recommend selecting a few countries on the basis of personal connections or according to the travel schedule of the principal investigators (see Bhagat & McQuaid, 1982, for a detailed discussion of this issue). The selection of countries, work organizations, and individuals should be largely driven by rigorous theoretical considerations and their practical implications.

Using Multicultural Research Teams

To capture non-Western and indigenous concepts, it is necessary to seek inputs from researchers interested in exploring the same issues in other cultures and countries. For example, the respective roles of *guānxí*, *amae*, and *simpatico* in Chinese, Japanese, and Hispanic cultures are best understood by indigenous members of these three cultures. A multicultural research team composed of members of all the cultures from which data are being collected is most insightful in expanding the emic content of both the questionnaires and instruments. Their interpretations for generalizing the results are also of crucial significance. Multicultural teams are also very useful for the kind of insights that they can generate in conducting research with ethnic and racial groups in diverse countries such as the United States, Canada, France, and Australia. Indigenous perspectives from non-Western workers and others are becoming, increasingly becoming, important as globalization spreads to dissimilar cultures and countries of the world. We need to know more about how work organizations might inadvertently create stressful work situations for their employees as they globalize their operations. Knowledge regarding how individuals cope with both routine and nonroutine types of stressful situations at work is also likely to improve by incorporating indigenous and culture-specific views. We are aware of the problems that can exist in coordinating research efforts across various countries. Three decades ago, research cooperation was often hindered by physical distance and lack of proper communication among the members of the multinational research team. The situation is quite different today with the increasing use of email, Internet, and other computer-mediated communication. It is no longer difficult to maintain a high level of effective communication regarding the various phases of theory development, data collection, and data analyses among the members. A multicultural research team would eliminate many of the Western (sometimes ethnocentric) value-laden biases and assumptions that might be inherent in some of the studies on work stress and coping effectiveness—particularly relating to culture-specific styles of coping. For the past two decades, there has been a growing emphasis on research conducted by multinational research teams. This is a positive development, and we feel confident that accuracy and validity of knowledge in this area are also going to increase with insights from members of international research teams.

Integration of Research Findings

For research findings to be of value for future theory-building efforts as well as for guiding practices of multinational and global organizations, it is necessary for the results to be integrated into the mainstream theoretical frameworks in the areas of management and organizational behavior. Practically, insightful research in this area can guide multinational corporations in their formulations of organizational policies that reflect the nature of contextual and cultural variations that might be responsible for generating stressful experiences at work at various geographical locations. By helping to explain some of the variations observed in the responses and coping patterns of employees in different cultural contexts, the research findings will contribute to the growing trend of the internationalization of human resources practices.

A Typology of Cross-Cultural Research on Work Stress and Coping

In proposing the following scheme for improved cross-cultural research on work stress and coping in the era of globalization, we adopt a typology advanced by Sechrest (1977) and later adapted by Bhagat and McQuaid (1982) and others. See Chiu and Hong (2006) for details.

Type I: The Investigation of Specific Work Stress and Coping-Related Phenomena

The emphasis in type I studies is on understanding the nature of the phenomenon in a detailed fashion rather than demonstrating ethnic, racial, and cultural variations in it. A large majority of phenomena are best understood if the appropriate antecedents, moderators, and consequences are identified and interpreted in a monocultural context at the beginning. Bringing in the complexities of cultural influences can make development of theoretical frameworks difficult at best. While information of a qualitative nature can be sought at this stage from both monocultural and multicultural sources, it is not wise to let cultural variations come into play in developing the basic frameworks of the phenomenon. This means that the phenomenon perhaps has generalizability across cultures and that it is sufficiently etic or pancultural in nature. It is just that information on national, ethnic, racial, and cultural variations that will be obtained at a later stage of the investigation.

Type II: The Study of Specific Cultural Variations in Organizational Phenomena

Type II studies are focused on understanding the role of cultural variations by observing the phenomena in dissimilar cultures context. For example, if two ethnic or cultural groups value the utility of problem-focused versus emotion-focused coping differently, an investigator may choose to hypothesize that the prevalence of problem-focused coping will be higher in the ethnic or cultural group that values this coping style more than emotion-focused coping. Such studies are quite common in current international research on work stress and coping and contribute to our growing knowledge on the role of cultural differences in the prediction of a work stress–related phenomenon.

Type III: Ethnographically Motivated Studies

In type III studies, the focus is on understanding a specific culture or cultural group per se or some aspect of it in depth rather than seeking to make cross-cultural comparisons. Qualitative studies on work stress and coping conducted in a work organization in a developing country such as Mexico or Bolivia would be a good example of such studies. Although these studies do not directly contribute to our understanding of cultural variations in a given work stress and coping phenomenon across various societies, they have the strong potential for enriching indigenous content of cross-cultural research to be conducted at a later stage. As noted in the earlier section, ethnographically motivated studies have the limitation of not being able to address the issues of rival and alternative explanations because of their sole dependence on culture-specific or emic concepts.

A Recommended Sequence for the Research Scheme

Based on our review of the work stress and coping literature conducted during the past 50 years, we recommend that future research studies should involve the following three phases.

Phase I

To begin with conduct Type I studies, it is essential to get a robust understanding of the work stress and coping phenomenon under investigation. Unless a clear understanding into the nature of antecedents, moderators, mediators, and consequences of work stress is developed in a monocultural context, one will not grasp the nature of culture-specific variations that are likely to be present in the constructs of the framework. Bhagat and McQuaid (1982), Chiu and Hong (2006), and others note that in conducting phase I studies researchers develop a clearer understanding into the nature of the culture-specific (i.e., emic) concepts that need to be employed at a later stage.

Phase II

At this stage, conduct Type III to probe into specific dimensions of the culture that are potentially related to the dependent variables of interest. Conducting ethnographic and qualitative studies are useful. It helps in delineating the specific features of the culture relating to the dependent variable of interest. Existing findings from various ethnographic studies of cultures are likely to be useful in a deeper understanding of the nature of variations in the dependent variable. Admittedly, the information at this stage is quite qualitative and needs to be quantified at a later stage for establishing rigorous, scientific foundations for developing theory and guiding practical applications. However, the insights developed during this phase will be immensely helpful.

Phase III

At this stage, conducting Type II studies is necessary. They demonstrate the importance of specific cultural variations on the nature and variability of the dependent variables. The issue of alternative and rival hypotheses can be dealt with at this stage by controlling for various confounding factors.

The proposed scheme is designed to facilitate the creation of knowledge that would be scientifically valid and also useful for multinational and global corporations. It may appear complex, but the process enables us to eliminate rival explanations, which accompany many research studies in this area.

Conclusion

Many organizational studies have revealed important cultural differences in a wide range of phenomena of interest to researchers in the area of work stress and coping. As discussed in this chapter, methodological issues are important to deal with in the process of obtaining valid scientific information and data that may guide the development of effective human resources management as well as employee assistance programs for multinational and global corporations. We have noted that researchers should exercise care and interpret data by using multiple perspectives before drawing inferences regarding the presence of ethnic, racial, national, and cultural differences. When comparing cultures of nations, it is important to remember that dominant cultural traditions also differ in terms of their political orientations, level of affluence and globalization, technological sophistication typically found in the work organizations, and other contextual factors that also influence the attitudes and behaviors of employees at work. Confidence in the validity of international and cross-cultural comparisons can greatly improved if findings are replicated by other researchers using different methodological techniques and dissimilar cultures.

References

Abegglen, J. C. (1958). *The Japanese factory, aspects of its social organization.* Glencoe, IL: Free Press.

Aldwin, C. M. (2007). *Stress, coping, and development* (2nd ed.). New York: Guilford Press.

Berry, J. W., Poortinga, Y. H., Segall, M. H., & Dasen, P. R. (2006). *Cross-cultural psychology: Research and applications.* Cambridge, UK: Cambridge University Press.

Bhagat, R. S., & McQuaid, S. J. (1982). Role of subjective culture in organizations: A review and directions for future research. *Journal of Applied Psychology, 67*(5), 653–685.

Bhagat, R. S., McQuaid, S. J., Lindholm, H., & Segovis, J. (1985). Total life stress: A multimethod validation of the construct and its effect on organizationally valued outcomes and withdrawal behaviors. *Journal of Applied Psychology, 70,* 202–214.

Chhokar, J. S., Brodbeck, F. C., & House, R. J. (Eds.). (2007). *Culture and leadership across the world: The GLOBE book of in-depth studies of 25 societies.* New York: Routledge.

Chiu, C. Y., & Hong, Y. Y. (2006). *Social psychology of culture.* New York: Psychology Press.

Cohen, D. (2007). Methods in cultural psychology. In S. Kitayama & D. Cohen (Eds.), *Handbook of cultural psychology* (pp. 196–236). New York: Guilford.

Cole, R. E. (1971). *Japanese blue-collar: The changing tradition.* Berkeley: University of California Press.

Folger, R., & Belew, J. (1985). Non-reactive measurement: A focus for research on absenteeism and occupational stress. In L. L. Cummings & B. M. Staw (Eds.), *Research in organizational behavior* (pp. 129–170). Greenwich, CT: JAI Press.

Gelfand, M. J., Nishii, L. H., Holcombe, K. M., Dyer, N., Ohbuchi, K.-I., & Fukono, M. (2008). Cultural influences on cognitive representations of conflict: Interpretations of conflict episodes in the United States and Japan. In M. F. Peterson & M. Sondergaard (Eds.), *Foundations of cross-cultural management* (Vol. 4, pp. 118–145). Thousand Oaks, CA: Sage.

Greenfield, P. M. (1997). Culture as process: Empirical methods for cultural psychology. In J. W. Berry, Y. H. Poortinga, & J. Pandel (Eds.), *Handbook of cross-cultural psychology: Vol. 1. Theory and Method* (pp. 301–346). Boston, MA: Allyn and Bacon.

Heine, S. J., Lehman, D. R., Peng, K., & Greenholtz, J. (2002). What's wrong with cross-cultural comparisons of subjective Likert scales: The reference-group problem. *Journal of Personality and Social Psychology, 82*, 903–918.

Hofstede, G. (1980). *Culture's consequences: International differences in work-related values.* Beverley Hills, CA: Sage.

House, R. J., Hanges, P. J., Javidan, M., Dorfman, P. W., & Gupta, V. (2004). *Culture, leadership, and organizations: The GLOBE study of 62 societies.* New York: Sage.

Kasl, S. V. (1978). Epidemiological contributions to the study of work stress. In C. L. Cooper & R. Payne (Eds.), *Stress at work* (pp. 3–48). New York: John Wiley & Sons.

Lazarus, R. S., & Folkman, S. (1984). *Stress, appraisal, and coping.* New York: Springer.

Leung, K., & Bond, M. H. (1989). On the empirical identification of dimensions for cross-cultural comparisons. *Journal of Cross-Cultural Psychology, 20*, 133–151.

Maxwell, J. (1992). Understanding validity in qualitative research. *Harvard Educational Review, 62*, 279–300.

Narayanan, L., Menon, S., & Spector, P. E. (1999). Stress in the workplace: A comparison of gender and occupations. *Journal of Organizational Behavior, 20*(1), 63–73.

Sechrest, L. (1977). On the death of theory in cross-cultural psychology: There is madness in our method. In Y. H. Poortinga (Ed.), *Basic problems in cross-cultural psychology* (pp. 73–82). Amsterdam: Swets and Zeitlinger.

Shi, L., Feng, B., Lin, C., Liu, C., & Spector, P. E. (2003). Job stress study of university faculties and staffs in China. *Journal of Beijing Normal University, 177*, 65–71.

Triandis, H. C., McCusker, C., & Hui, C. H. (1990). Multimethod probes of individualism and collectivism. *Journal of Personality and Social Psychology, 59*, 1006–1020.

Van de Vijver, F. J., & Fischer, R. (2009). Improving methodological robustness in cross-cultural organizational research. In R. S. Bhagat & R. M. Steers (Eds.), (pp. 491–517) *Cambridge handbook of culture, organization, and work.* Cambridge: Cambridge University Press.

Van de Vijver, F. J., & Leung, K. (1997). *Methods and data analysis for cross-cultural research.* Newbury Park, CA: Sage.

Van de Vijver, F. J., & Tanzer, N. K. (2004). Bias and equivalence in cross-cultural assessment: An overview. *European Review of Applied Psychology, 54*, 119–135.

Chapter 9

Concluding Thoughts and Future Directions

At the dawn of the twenty-first century, it is widely known that we live in the era of globalization. Employees, work teams, and organizations of all types operate in dissimilar multinational and multicultural contexts. Cross-border transactions of goods, services, information, and people have become commonplace. Innovative technologies and organizational knowledge management systems create new patterns of work arrangements. Rapid and discontinuous changes characterize employees and their work organizations on a daily basis. Increased competition in both domestic and international markets, higher demands in productivity, coupled with the introduction of innovative technologies have created a world of highly interconnected economies. *The World Is Flat* (Friedman, 2005) and a *global village* (Ger, 1999) provide ample descriptions of the new realities of globalization. Many observers of globalization suggest that the spread of investment, trade production, technology, and democracy is making the economic systems of different countries converge. Greider's (1997) central argument as reflected in *One World Ready or Not* suggests that globalization affects people and organizations in similar ways and creates a more homogeneous, integrated, and smaller world. However, observers disagree as to whether greater integration, uniformity, and homogeneity reflect a positive or negative development. Concerns have been expressed about the limits of the convergence argument (Guillén, 2001).

In this book, we take the view that globalization does *not* have uniform consequences for individuals and work organizations regardless of the countries in which they are located. However, the rate of change that individuals, work groups, and organizations confront on a routine basis is much higher than was the case at any other time in the twentieth century. The acceleration of business activities around the globe has created a great deal of interest in management research on work organizations across nations and cultures. Research on work and organizational stress and how people cope with it is a topic that has a long tradition for more than half a century. During the past two decades, there has been a resurgence of research that takes into account the role of contextual factors (see Antoniou, Cooper, Chrousos, Spielberger, & Eysenck, 2009; Macik-Frey, Quick, & Nelson, 2007; Wong & Wong, 2006).

We have discussed the major theoretical frameworks that have guided and still continue to guide current research in this area. Much of the research has been conducted by researchers in Western countries (e.g., the United States, Canada, the United Kingdom, Australia, Sweden, and Germany). While a great deal of theoretical progress has been made since the early days of Selye's (1956) distinction between positive stress (eustress) and negative stress (distress), much of the work is grounded in the individualistic tradition of the Western cultures. The need to incorporate the significance of cultural variations of non-Western cultures (e.g., China, Japan, India, Brazil, and Russia) has grown rapidly as these countries have globalized over the past two decades. We provided a framework for incorporating the role of cultural syndromes in Chapter 6. It is hoped that this approach along with future research developments will generate useful information in terms theory and applications.

It is well established that how an individual or a work group appraises the nature of stressful work experiences determines the effectiveness of coping. Variables, such as working conditions, style of leadership, and the nature of work–family conflicts, have all been found to play important roles as either antecedents or moderators of experienced stress–psychological strain (or eustress) relationships. The findings in this tradition have also contributed to advances in occupational health psychology, which fulfills a void and reflects a necessary development in the era of globalization. Advances in occupational health psychology and medicine have been helpful in combating deleterious effects of work and organization stress on productivity at various levels of the organization. In addition, this line of research has been largely instrumental in the design of preventive stress management (Quick, Quick, & Nelson, 1998) and employee assistance programs (EAPs) (Cooper, Dewe, & O'Driscoll, 2003).

As noted earlier, labor markets, work organizations, and the nature of work itself have been experiencing major transformations caused by social, economic, market, and technological changes that accompany globalization. Collectively, these developments have significant implications on the nature and quality of working and work stress in both developed and developing countries.

In Chapters 3 and 4, we presented theoretical frameworks that provide guidelines for understanding work stress and coping in much of the Western countries including Australia and New Zealand. In writing this book, one of the major issues with which we have been concerned is to what extent are the findings of U.S. and Western European studies on work stress and coping applicable to non-Western context (e.g., BRIC countries, Mexico, South Africa). Most of the countries that are currently undergoing rapid economic, technological, and social changes due to globalization are collectivistic in orientation. In addition, the cultural significance of power distance (reflecting greater acceptance of the inequality of status and distribution of valued resources in the society) also has a major role. Research findings from Western individualist work organizations that are typically low in power distance do not apply in the work context of the countries that are currently globalizing rapidly (e.g., BRIC countries, Mexico, South Africa).

As discussed in Chapters 5 and 6, there are important limitations to theories developed in the individualistic traditions of the West. In many of the globalizing countries, there are important societal-, organizational-, and task-related limitations on individuals in the way they may appraise the nature of work stress and cope with it. In fact, in many countries employees have virtually no control over the work activities that are potentially stressful (e.g., working women in call center and outsourcing operations in the Philippines, India, and Malaysia). Work interconnectedness in the context of today's multinational and global corporations governs much of the working lives and requires one to learn to cope with increasing workloads and stay connected to one's work 24/7. Meece (2011) provides an insightful analysis of how current electronic systems of communication and networking (e.g., smart phones, text messaging, video calling, and social media) are controlling a large part one's life. It does not matter how successfully one has climbed up the corporate ladder, the need to stay connected to one's work has greatly increased. These work-related developments have adverse implications for one's personal and family lives resulting in work–family conflicts. Such conflicts are difficult to manage in the Western contexts and are highly unsettling in many other parts of the world that are in the process of globalizing. We suggest Poelmans and Caligiuri's (2008) research volume on *Harmonizing Work, Family, and Personal Life* for additional details. The point is that individuals need culture-specific guidance from members of their family and in-groups to cope with these new work arrangements, which make their work lives intrude into their personal lives with these electronic forms of communication. Clearly, more research needs to be conducted in this decade. We are hopeful that findings from this research conducted in both the Western and non-Western contexts will be helpful in managing negative effects of work stress.

In this chapter, we

1. Describe future directions of research that explicitly take into account the dynamic changes in work arrangements along with cultural variations
2. Discuss the nature of new directions in the management of work stress including innovation in occupational health
3. Discuss the role of positive organizational scholarship in the management of work stress and the evolution of new patterns of coping

Future Research and Directions

Much has been accomplished in our understanding of how new work arrangements influence work stress and coping. However, much more remains to be done by incorporating the roles of national and cultural differences. Harry Triandis, a highly noted scholar, 17 years ago assessed the accomplishments of cross-cultural research in organizational behavior and concluded that many of the ideas guiding research were somewhat imprecise in character and that additional theoretical rigor was necessary (Triandis, Dunnette, & Hough, 1994). We have come a long way since then. Gelfand, Erez, and Aycan (2007) note that cultural perspectives have begun to assert major influences in mainstream organizational research. Research on human consequences of various facets of globalization and culture change is making this area of inquiry more global in scope and less ethnocentric. We find the same to be true in our assessment of research on work stress and coping during the past three decades. However, important gaps remain. Antecedents and consequences of work stress and coping that are culture-specific to Hispanic Americans, African Americans, Asian Americans, and immigrants in the United States need to be emphasized more. These ethnic groups have been experiencing considerable growth in population during the past two decades. A similar demographic trend is noticed in Canada and in major countries of the European Union, Australia, and New Zealand. Research that takes into account the roles of ethnic and cultural variations in these countries will result in much needed insights into the processes of how these groups experience work stress and cope with it.

We have discussed the significance of migration as a major facet of globalization. As people move away from their home countries for better economic and career opportunities, they acquire new cultural values and identities. The issue of managing multiple cultural identities (Hong, Wan, No, & Chiu, 2007) along with one's work role is going to be an important area of research. However, it has not received much attention. Job-related stressful experiences of religious minorities in the United States and Europe also deserve research attention. Some of the themes that should be incorporated in future research are as follows.

The Changing Workplace of Tomorrow

As discussed in Chapter 1, global competition is creating major shifts in the way work is organized in organizations across nations and cultures. The current phase of major work-related transitions that began in the 1970s as innovations in technology—particularly computer-mediated innovations—started to affect work organizations in the United States and other Western countries. Globalization-related pressures were equally important in transforming the nature of work organizations regardless of their national location. To see this process at work, let us look at China. In its march to prosperity, the country has encouraged millions of its young people to move from farms to cities—some like Beijing, which remain ancient in character and others that are sprawling new cities like Shenzen and Zhuhai that were built from scratch in the 1980s. It is in these new cities and special economic regions that modern China has its factories. Foxconn Technology Group, the giant electronics manufacturer that builds components for Dell computers, Hewlett-Packard, and Apple in Shenzen and elsewhere in urban China, will soon employ enough Chinese workers to equal 60% of the jobs in Manhattan (Culpan, 2010). Foxconn has close to 920,000 workers, nearly all of whom are under 25. Foxconn announced plans to add another 400,000 workers—a large percentage of which are likely to be older than 25. A situation of age-related discrimination exists in the future. Aging of the work force in the United States, China, and Japan coupled with increased cultural diversity in the workplace creates interesting scenarios for research on work stress and coping. Some useful insights into the role of aging and work in the twenty-first century exist (Shultz & Adams, 2007); however, more work in this area is needed. The demographic transformations taking place in the United States, China, Japan, India, Brazil, and Russia have important implications for competitiveness in these economies. The nature of workplaces will also evolve in accordance with these demographic developments (see Fishman, 2010, for the consequences of aging in the world population).

Globalization and Culture Change

An evolving area of research related to the aforementioned topic is concerned with the role of globalization in precipitating cultural changes at the level of the individual, work organizations, and societies. Does increasing economic interdependence produce selective patterns of cultural changes in various countries of the world regardless of their level of affluence?

It has been suggested that countries that are globalizing aspire to be like the affluent countries of the Western world. They begin to transform their cultural orientations to make them consistent with these countries. Essentially, this reflects the essence of the convergence hypothesis, which was a major concern of comparative research on work organizations in the 1960s and 1970s (Haire, Ghiselli, & Porter, 1966). While this may be true in some countries, the point is that globalization does not necessarily lead to homogenization of cultures at the level of either the society or work organizations. In fact, it has diverse and unanticipated consequences in some countries. A careful analysis of the effects of globalization reveals that individuals and work organizations in dissimilar cultures often emphasize distinctive cultural values, practices, and guidelines (Hofstede, 2001; Leung, Bhagat, Buchan, Erez, & Gibson, 2005; Triandis, 1994, 2002). Cultural beliefs, attitudes, norms, and values of people in countries that are dissimilar from the West are not being ignored in favor of homogenizing forces that accompany the process of globalization.

Hofstede (2001) and Triandis (2002) have argued that cultural differences in organizational processes will persist because of the fundamental differences in which humans sample, emphasize, and process information from their environments. Members of ethnic or cultural groups who are socialized to sample more social information from the members of their families and in-groups and by emphasizing the functioning of their *collective selves* are likely to cope with work stresses by seeking guidance from these groups. On the other hand, members of individualistic cultures who are socialized to sample more task-related information and by emphasizing the functioning of their *private selves* are likely to emphasize problem-focused coping. As discussed in Chapter 6, such coping strategies are largely individualistic in orientation.

In contrast to the convergent hypothesis, the *divergence hypothesis* as reflected in the work of Hofstede (2001) argues that individuals retain their ethnic and national cultures and heritages. They do not necessarily gravitate toward the cultural patterns of the West even though the major economic incentives are clearly Western in nature. Leung et al. (2005) suggested that cultural changes that accompany the process of globalization are indeed bidirectional. Members of Western individualistic cultures are being exposed to values and practices of the Eastern collectivistic cultures (e.g., Japan, China, and India). Distinct changes are taking place at the level of the individual, work groups, and organizations. The growth rates of some of the collectivistic countries (e.g., BRIC economies) are increasing faster than the United States, Canada, and some of the countries of the European Union. Management practices that have developed in the unique cultural contexts of these collectivistic countries have implications for the management of Western multinational and global corporations (Leung et al., 2005). The point is that the relationship between globalization and the cultural changes that occur at the level of the individual, work group, and work organizations is not unidirectional. The management of work organizations in the era of globalization reflects a reality that is an amalgam of major cultural practices and traditions. Therefore, researchers interested in the phenomena of work stress and coping should be willing to combine Western perspectives with those of the Eastern cultures. A better approach would be to adopt a multicultural perspective to analyze the changing workplace of today.

When and How Culture and Cultural Variations Matter

This issue is of significant importance in future studies as globalization-related experiences create heterogeneous practices in the context of multinational and global organizations. It is quite likely that a subsidiary of a global corporation such as Toyota Inc. of Japan may have a hybrid management style reflecting the cultural traditions of Japan and the United States. In a similar vein, another subsidiary of the same corporation in India may develop a different hybrid style of management reflecting the cultural values of Japan and India. In these cases, it becomes important to know how cultural values of the headquarters matter and in which subsidiaries. As long as individuals and groups do not feel easily threatened that their unique cultural identities are going to be either lost or overwhelmed by the cultural practices of the global headquarters, they are less likely to be resistant to minor changes in organizational practices and cultures. Organizational practices that are strongly rooted in cultural traditions clearly matter more in some contexts than in others (Leung et al., 2005). Cultural variations can come into play in the way of independent, moderator, mediator, or dependent variables and at different stages of the development and unfolding of the organizational phenomenon. Proper identification of the types of context in which cultural variations are likely to display their effects and at what times is an important need for future research investigations in this area. See Gibson, Maznevski, and Kirkman (2009) for details regarding the role of when culture matters.

Moving Beyond Cultural Values

Gelfand et al. (2007) have recommended that researchers should move beyond the constructs of individualism–collectivism to explain relevant differences in organizational processes and outcomes across nations and cultures. We believe that the cultural variation of individualism–collectivism is the "deep structure" of cultural differences among societies (Greenfield, 2000; Hofstede, 2001; Triandis, 1995, 1998) and has provided much of the thrust behind work stress and coping research in the past two decades. However, in our efforts to unpackage ethnic, racial, national, and cultural differences, it is wise to consider other types of cultural variations. Strength of social norms (Gelfand, Nishii, & Raver, 2006), the nature of roles (McAuley, Bond, & Kashima, 2002; Peterson & Smith, 2000), beliefs about the physical and social world (Leung et al., 2002), and implicit, domain-specific theories that humans have (Chiu, Morris, Hong, & Menon, 2000) are all important sources of cultural and individual differences and should be incorporated in future research. Cultural differences that have important implications for understanding the evolution of unique patterns of work stresses and coping can also be tapped outside of the conscious awareness of humans. This suggests that efforts to detect the role of cultural differences on various patterns of work stress that evolve in different countries and how people cope with them can be measured by using unobtrusive and trace measures. Research findings on national differences in social axioms that people use to search for universal dimensions for general beliefs about how the world functions (Leung et al., 2002) are particularly promising in this regard. Social axioms are defined as generalized beliefs about one's self and the nature of physical and social environment including the spiritual world and reflect the nature of relationships that people hold about the relationship between two entities or concepts (see Chapters 2 and 5). A typical social axiom has the structure: A is related to B with A and B being any two entities or concepts and the relationship can be either correlational or causal. The perceived strength of the relationship varies across individuals, ethnic, racial, and cultural subgroups. For example, "good things will naturally happen to good people" is a typical example of an axiom. People may endorse this belief to differing degrees depending on their personalities, structure of self, and membership in a cultural group. These axioms can be extended to appraise the onset of stressful events at both work and non-work and when properly incorporated in research designs can yield culture-specific information and knowledge regarding how people appraise, cope with, and deal with stressful experiences at work and elsewhere. We recommend that future research endeavors should make use of this new framework of social axioms as pioneered by Leung et al. (2002).

Incorporating the Significance of Multilevel Theorizing

Cross-cultural research on work and organizations has been making important use of various contextual factors when examining cross-cultural differences. Regardless of whether the topic is work motivation, international work teams, negotiation, justice, leadership, or work stress and coping, the review of Gelfand et al. (2007) showed that situational factors are indeed important in the way they exacerbate and radically change the central effects of cultural variations. While main effects of cultural dimensions or variations are indeed important and theoretically interesting, it is necessary to take into account the role of contextual and situational factors at different levels of analysis for their main, mediating, and moderating effects. In other words, research in the area of work stress and coping can greatly benefit by developing theoretical frameworks that include contextual factors at the level of the society, work organizations, work groups, and individuals.

At the cultural level, contextual factors that are intertwined with the cultural variations include economic, political, legal, educational system, physical ecology, level of technological development, demographic composition of the population, and last but not least, the rate of economic globalization. At the organizational level, contextual factors include the industry type, size, ownership, life cycle, strategic processes, rate of technological and knowledge-management-related innovations, and workforce characteristics. At the level of the work group or team, contextual factors include team structure, team member composition, and task characteristics. At the individual level, it is important to include information on relevant facets of personality and demographics, cognitive styles including such variables as tolerance for ambiguity, and measures of horizontal and vertical individualism and collectivism. Finally, at the global level one could include the rate of globalization, level of economic interdependencies and uncertainties characterizing the global economy, and fluctuating interest rates should also be considered as deemed theoretically relevant.

The interplay between cultural variations (whether assessed by a value survey or the use of social axioms) and different levels of the context where the phenomena manifest is the most important theoretical frontier in international and cross-cultural research on work stress and coping. The methodological developments in multilevel theorizing and cross-level analyses are opening up new avenues for the study of work stress and coping across ethnic, racial, and cultural groups. In recent years, researchers have begun to focus on the experience of collective stress in work units and organizations (Peiró, 2001, 2008). A more systematic approach is still needed to understand the complex relationships among work stress phenomena that manifest at different levels. Assessing the level of work stress that individuals experience in the context of a given organization is valid to measure the nature of misfit between the demands of the job and the resources available to cope with the situation. However, this experience of stress that is often shared among members of the same department or work unit is not necessarily taken into an account. In many collectivistic cultures, the experience of stress and its outcomes in terms of psychological strains and reduced work effectiveness are shared by the members of the same department or work unit. Such joint sharing of the stress experience may motivate collective actions to cope with it. In these situations, a cross-level analysis of work stress and coping is needed to develop better insights into the nature interpersonal and social systems that work in these types of collectivistically oriented work organizations.

Given the innovations in multilevel theorizing and research methodologies, it is now possible to analyze and detect the respective contributions of various factors at the global, organizational, work group, and individual levels in the creations of stressful experiences whether perceived at the level of the individual or at any other levels. Similarly, coping strategies that originate at the level of the individual, the work group, and the work organization including influences from members of one's family and in-groups in the larger societal context can be analyzed for their respective contributions in managing work stress. Not only that but one can now assess the range of coping styles and social support mechanisms that are likely to be present in multinational and global corporations that are composed of workforces from various ethnic, racial, and cultural groups.

In future research endeavors, the research team should be able to move away from a purely individualistic, self-focused, and ahistorical approach to one that is more collectivistic, group focused, and contextual in nature. That is not to say that one should ignore the valuable contributions of research findings obtained in the individualistic tradition. Understanding the evolution of different types of work-specific stresses and strains (including eustress-related outcomes) by adopting a multilevel approach will go a long way toward helping us develop a body of knowledge that is more valid and useful in the current era of globalization. See Jex and Bliese (1999), Bliese and Jex (2002), Klein and Kozlowski (2000), and Gelfand et al. (2007) for details on multilevel issues in theory construction and analyses. The changes that have been occurring are vast, complex, and not sufficiently understood.

The information age with its ongoing emphases on the introduction of digital technologies in nearly all aspects of work life has been creating a very different workplace in the twenty-first century. There is no doubt that changes have made the prototypical late twentieth century bureaucratic organizations largely obsolete in favor of flat, network-based organizations where computer-mediated technologies are playing important roles. Globalization, as we noted in Chapter 2, introduces changes in three important areas of our lives: (1) the economy and the labor market in which we participate, (2) the structure of our families, and (3) the nature of technologies that we have to deal with in our work and nonwork lives. In global cities of the world such as New York, London, Tokyo, Frankfurt, Paris, Chicago, Mumbai, Beijing, Shanghai, and San Paulo, the distinctions between work and nonwork are beginning to blur due to rapid changes in technology particularly digital technology, (Bhagat, 2009). From the high levels of management echelons to the lower-level employees, there is a growing expectation that individuals should be accessible on most days of the year including holidays. The Internet, various forms of computer-mediated communication (e.g., emails, text messaging, and instant messaging), and smart phones (phones with additional features such as email, web access, and an operating system) keep the communication interface between work and nonwork life open every day and hour of the year.

A new breed of workers from different levels of the organization is beginning to evolve. Referred to as *intravidual* by Conley (2009), these individuals have multiple selves that compete for attention within their minds. In addition, they are also being bombarded by multiple pressures from a variety of roles and social/cultural identities that they have. The demands associated with managing these multiple identities can be quite high. We predict that new patterns of coping and social support mechanisms will evolve as individuals either experience considerable difficulties in managing or fail to manage the demands of these new roles on an ongoing basis. The workplace of tomorrow will be more complex than it is today, and it is likely that the scenarios portrayed by Conley (2009) in *Elsewhere, U.S.A.* will characterize a large percentage of workers and professionals in the global economy regardless of their national and cultural origins. As recently as 1990, lights out (in the workplaces) meant that work was finished for the day, but today as we enter the second decade of the twenty-first century, individuals can use their Blackberries, smart phones, and laptops to continue working on projects long after their spouses have fallen asleep. It is expected that these demands are likely to transform the workplace of tomorrow even more as radical changes take place in the nature of tasks that one needs to perform along with pressures of globalization.

Integrating Findings From Positive Organizational Scholarship Research Traditions

Along with incorporating the previously provided themes in future research that seek to be more generalizable as well as applicable, it is important to integrate findings from emerging research in the area of positive organizational scholarship. In addition to assessing effects of work and organizational stress on psychological strain and employee health, recognition of positive work behaviors (PWB) and finding ways of rewarding and reinforcing them will greatly aid the growing body of knowledge in terms of both its basic scientific findings and applied applications. Ryff and Singer (1998, 2002) note that while absence of negative outcomes like psychological strain is an important indicator of the effects of stressful experiences on the job, defining health as a presence of positive emotional states is important as well. Work behaviors that sustain positive emotional states include experiencing of autonomy, tendencies to facilitate personal as well as organizational growth, seeking mastery over difficult situations, emphasizing positive and rewarding relationships with others, sustaining meaningful purpose in life, and acceptance of self (Ryff & Singer, 2001; Ryff, Singer, & Love, 2004). There has been a major shift in mainstream psychology toward emphasizing the science of positive subjective experience (Seligman & Csikszentmihalyi, 2000). Its mission is to focus on broadening the scope of findings dealing with positive experiences that occur in work and nonwork domains of life. The work of Seligman and Csikszentmihalyi is reflected in the development of positive organizational scholarship (POS), which was pioneered by Kim Cameron and his colleagues (Cameron, Dutton, & Quinn 2004). Findings from POS research groups are likely to be useful in developing robust research findings regarding the role of work and organizational stress in different occupational, organizational, and cultural contexts. In a similar vein, Luthans (2002a, 2002b) also emphasized the need for shifting our attention to positive aspects of work behavior and psychological strains that individuals display while experiencing stressful events at work. He makes a strong case for identifying those aspects of PWB that can be improved by appropriate interventions in organizations. Nelson and Cooper (2007) also called for integrating positive organizational behaviors to include personal traits and styles in future research on work stress. Consider the case of U.S. Airlines pilot Chesley Sullenberger, who successfully navigated a plane with 155 people safely into the Hudson River near New York City on January 15, 2009, avoiding a major disaster (Baram, 2009). Incidences like this reflect the kind of positive organizational behaviors that should increasingly be included in future research on work stress and coping in both Western and non-Western countries.

Conclusion

As the workplace of tomorrow becomes increasingly multicultural in orientation, issues of work stress and coping across various racial, ethnic, and national cultures arise more frequently. In addition, the issues of occupational health and well-being that are not necessarily related to cultural and ethnic variation are a rising concern in the globalizing countries and emergent economies. Fortunately, there is a growing interest to protect the safety, health, and welfare of the workforce in the majority of the countries that are globalizing rapidly (Cassitto, Fattorini, Gilioli, & Rengo, 2003; Griffiths & Cox, 2004; Houtman, Jettinghoff, & Cedillo, 2007). In Chapters 5 and 6, we discussed the role of cultural differences in the appraisal of work stress and stressful work events. In a rapidly globalizing world, people and organizations from Asia, Latin America, and Africa are beginning to experience new forms of work arrangements and rewards of both the monetary and nonmonetary kind with which they were not familiar in the nineteenth and during the first part of the twentieth century. Research on quality of work life and work stress has been a central concern in the field of organizational behavior since the 1960s. However, as we have noted in this book, there was not a great deal of need to probe into work stress–, coping-, and social support–related processes until globalization began to expand at a rapid pace during the 1980s. Now, issues like whether the growth rate of India will outpace that of China are receiving attention from multinational and global organizations (see the *Economist*, September 2010). As a consequence the issue of managing dissimilar employees in these non-Western countries also becomes important. The experience of stress, whether from persistent sources in the work environment or from the stressful organizational events that occur as a result of the increased pressures of globalization, then becomes more significant for both its deleterious human and organizational consequences. It is critical for researchers to engage the role of cultural differences in a creative fashion as we pursue to expand the frontiers of knowledge in this area in addition to incorporating advanced issues in the construction of better theory and research. It is hoped that the ideas and frameworks presented in this book will be helpful for more innovative research that will aid the process of more effective interventions in the workplace.

References

Antoniou, A.S.G., Cooper, C.L., Chrousos, G.P., Spielberger, C.D., & Eysenck, M.W. (Eds.) (2009). *Handbook of managerial behaviour and occupational health.* Cheltenham: Edward Elgar Publishing Limited.

Baram, M. (2009, January 15). Chesley B. "Sully" Sullenberger, US airways pilot, hero of plane crash. *Huffington Post.* Retrieved from http://www.huffingtonpost.com/2009/01/15/chelsey-sullenberger-us-a_n_158331.html

Bhagat, R. S. (2009). Culture, work and organizations: A future research agenda. In R. S. Bhagat & R. M. Steers (Eds.), *Cambridge Handbook of Culture, Organizations, and Work* (pp. 518–525). Cambridge: Cambridge University Press.

Bliese, P.D. & Jex, S.M. (2002). Incorporating a multilevel perspective into occupational stress research: Theoretical, methodological, and practical implications. Journal of *Occupational Health Psychology,* 7, 265–276

Cameron, K. S., Dutton, J. E. & Quinn, R.E. (Eds.). (2004). *Positive organizational scholarship: Foundations of a new discipline.* San Francisco: Barrett–Koehler.

Cassitto, M. G., Fattorini, E., Gilioli, R., & Rengo, C. (2003). *Raising awareness of psychological harassment at work* (Protecting Workers' Health Series No. 4). Geneva: World Health Organization.

Chiu, C., Morris, M. W., Hong, Y., & Menon, T. (2000). Motivated cultural cognition: The impact of implicit cultural theories on dispositional attribution varies as a function of need for closure. *Journal of Personality and Social Psychology, 78,* 247–259.

Conley, D. (2009). *Elsewhere U.S.A.* New York: Pantheon.

Cooper, C. L., Dewe, P., & O'Driscoll, M. (2003). Employee assistance programs. In J. C. Quick & L. E. Tetrick (Eds.), *Handbook of Occupational Health and Psychology* (pp. 289–304). Washington, DC: American Psychological Association.

Culpan, T. (2010, August 18). *Foxconn to hire 400,000 China workers within a year.* Retrieved April 14, 2011, from Bloomberg News: http://www.bloomberg.com/news/2010-08-18/foxconn-to-increase-workforce-40-move-factories-after-spate-of-suicides.html

Fishman, T.C. (2010). *Shock of gray: The aging of the world's population and how it pits young against old, child against parent, worker against boss, company against rival, and nation against nation.* New York: Scribner.

Friedman, T. L. F. (2005). *The world is flat: A brief history of the twenty-first century.* New York: Farrar, Straus and Giroux.

Gelfand, M., Erez, M., & Aycan, Z. (2007). Culture in organizational behavior. *Annual Review of Psychology, 58,* 479–514.

Gelfand, M., Nishii, L. H., & Raver, J. L. (2006). On the nature and importance of cultural tightness-looseness. *Journal of Applied Psychology, 91*(6), 1225–1244.

Ger, G. (1999). Localizing in the global village: Local firms competing in global markets. *California Management Review, 41*(4), 64–83.

Gibson, C. B., Maznevski, M. L., & Kirkman, B. L. (2009). When does culture matter? In R. S. Bhagat & R. M. Steers (Eds.), *Cambridge Handbook of Culture, Organizations, and Work* (pp. 46–70). Cambridge: Cambridge University Press.

Greenfield, P. M. (2000). Three approaches to the psychology of culture: Where do they come from? Where can they go? *Asian Journal of Social Psychology, 3,* 223–240.

Greider, W. (1997). *One world ready or not.* New York: Simon and Schuster.

Griffiths, A., & Cox, T. (2004). *Organisation and stress: Systematic approach for employers, managers and trade union representatives* (Protecting Workers' Health Series No. 3). Geneva: World Health Organization.

Guillén, M. F. (2001a). Is globalization civilizing, destructive, or feeble? A critique of five key debates in the social science literature. *Annual Review Sociology, 27,* 235–260.

Guillén, M. F. (2001b). *The limits of convergence: Globalization & organizational change in Argentina, South Korea, and Spain.* Princeton, NJ: Princeton University Press.

Haire, M., Ghiselli, E., & Porter, L.W. (1966). *Managerial thinking: An international study.* New York, NY: Wiley.

Hofstede, G. (2001). *Culture's consequences: Comparing values, behaviors, institutions and organizations across nations* (2nd ed.). Thousand Oaks, CA: Sage.

Hong, Y., Wan, C., No., S., & Chiu, C. (2007). Multicultural identities. In S. Kitayama & D. Cohen (Eds.), *Handbook of Cultural Psychology.* (pp. 323–345). New York: Guilford Press.

Houtman, I., Jettinghoff, K., & Cedillo, L. (2007). *Raising awareness of stress at work in developing countries* (Protecting Workers' Health Series No. 6). Geneva: World Health Organization.

Jex, S. M., & Bliese, P. D. (1999). Efficacy beliefs as a moderator of the impact of work-related stressors: A multilevel study. *Journal of Applied Psychology, 84*(3), 349–361.

Klein, K. J., & Kozlowski, S. W. J. (2000). *Multilevel theory, research, and methods in organizations: Foundations, extensions and new directions.* San Francisco: Jossey-Bass.

Leung, K., Bhagat, R. S., Buchan, N. R., Erez, M., & Gibson, C. B. (2005). Culture and international business: Recent advances and their implications for future research. *Journal of International Business Studies, 36*(4), 357–378.

Leung, K., Bond, M. H., de Carrasquel, S., Munoz, C., Hernandez, M., Murakami, F., et al. (2002). Social axioms: The search for universal dimensions of general beliefs about how the world functions. *Journal of Cross-Cultural Psychology, 33,* 286–302.

Luthans, F. (2002a). The need for and meaning of positive organizational behavior. *Journal of Organizational Behavior, 23,* 695–706.

Luthans, F. (2002b). Positive organizational behavior: Developing and managing psychological strengths. *Academy of Management Executive, 16*(1), 57–72.

Macik-Frey, M., Quick, J., & Nelson, D. (2007). Advances in occupational health: From a stressful beginning to a positive future, *Journal of Management*, 33, 809–840.

McAuley, P. C., Bond, M. H., & Kashima, E. S. (2002). Toward defining situations objectively: A culture-level analysis of role dyads in Hong Kong and Australia. *Journal of Cross-Cultural Psychology, 33*, 363–379.

Meece, M. (2011, February 6). Who's the boss, you or your gadget? *The New York Times.* p. BU 1.

Nelson, D. L., & Cooper, C. L. (Eds.). (2007). *Positive organizational behavior: Accentuating the positive at work.* Thousand Oaks: Sage.

Peiró, J. M. (2001). Stressed teams in organizations. A multilevel approach to the study of stress in work units. In J. Pryce, C. Weilkert, & E. Torkelson (Eds.), *Occupational Health Psychology Europe 2001* (pp. 9–13). Nottingham: European Academy of Occupational Health.

Peiró, J. M. (2008). Stress and coping at work: New research trends and their implications for practice. In K. Naswall (Ed.), *The individual in the changing working life* (pp.284–310). Cambridge:Cambridge University Press.

Peterson, M. F., & Smith, P. B. (2000). Sources of meaning, organizations, and culture. In N. Ashkanasay, C. Wilderom, & M. F. Peterson (Eds.), *Handbook of organizational culture and climate* (pp. 101–115). Thousand Oaks, CA: Sage.

Poelmans, S.A.Y., & Caligiuri, P. (Eds.). (2008). Harmonizing work, family, and personal life. Cambridge, UK: Cambridge University Press.

Quick, J.D., Quick, J.C., & Nelson, D.L. (1998).The theory of preventive stress management in organizations. In C.L. Cooper (Ed.), Theories of organizational stress (pp. 246–268). Oxford: Oxford University Press.

Ryff, C. D., & Singer, B. (1998). The contours of positive human health. *Psychology Inquiry, 9*, 1–28.

Ryff, C. D., & Singer, B. (2001). Integrating emotion into the study of social relationships and health. In C. D. Ryff & B. Singer (Eds.), *Emotion, social relationships, and health* (pp. 3–22). New York: Oxford University Health.

Ryff, C. D., & Singer, B. (2002). From social structure to biology: Integrative science in pursuit of human health and well-being. In C. R. Snyder & S. J. Lopez (Eds.), *Handbook of positive psychology* (pp. 541–555). New York: Oxford University Press.

Ryff, C. D., Singer, B., & Love, G. D. (2004). Positive health: Connecting well-being with biology. *Philosophical Transactions of the Royal Society of London B, 359*, 1383–1394.

Seligman, M., & Csikszentmihalyi, M. (2000). Positive psychology: An introduction. *American Psychologist, 55*, 5–14.

Selye, H. (1956). *The stress of life.* New York: McGraw-Hill Book Company.

Shultz, K.S., & Adams, G.A. (Eds.). (2007). *Aging and work in the 21st century.* Mahwah, NJ: Lawrence Erlbaum Associates.

Triandis, H. C. (1994). *Culture and social behavior.* New York: McGraw Hill.

Triandis, H. C. (1995). *Individualism and collectivism.* Boulder, CO: Westview Press.

Triandis, H. C. (1998). Vertical and horizontal individualism and collectivism: Theory and research implications for international comparative management. *Advances in International Comparative Management, 12*, 7–35.

Triandis, H. C. (2002). Generic individualism and collectivism. In M. Gannon & K. Newman (Eds.), *The Blackwell handbook of cross-cultural management* (pp. 16–45). Oxford: Blackwell Business Publishing.

Triandis, H. C., Dunette, M. D., & Hough, L. M. (Eds.). (1994). *Handbook of industrial and organizational psychology* (2nd ed., Vol. 4). Palo Alto, CA: Consulting Psychologists Press.

Wong, P. T., & Wong, L.C., (Eds.). (2006). *Handbook of multicultural perspectives on stress and coping.* New York: Springer.

Author Index

Subject Index

A

Accepting responsibility coping strategy, 176
Acculturative stress, 197–200
Acquisitions, 21–22
Active-passive cultural activity, 176
Activity orientation, 39
African Americans, 192–194, 200–206
    cognitive/emotional debriefing style, 202
    ritual-centered strategy, 202
AIDS, 115, 118, 181, 206, 236, 246
Akasuri treatment, 114
Alcohol abuse, 77, 99, 222, 225–226
Alliance Card, 13
American Express, 13, 35, 56
Amok, 173
Anatomy of an Illness, 106
Animals in workplace, 124
Anxiety, 42, 51, 63, 68, 123–124, 195, 261
APEAR. *See* Asia Pacific Employee
        Roundtable
Appraisal
    approval process, 61, 62
    cognitive appraisal, 53, 62, 64, 123, 150
    primary, 59, 64, 70
    secondary, 64
    support, 72
    work stress, 142, 149, 150, 151, 153, 180,
        199, 280
ASEAN. *See* Association of Southeast Asian
        Nations
Asia Pacific Employee Roundtable, 228
Asian Americans, 38, 186, 195–197,
        202–205, 209
    Cross Cultural Coping Scale, 203
Assimilation strategy, 196, 199

Association of Southeast Asian Nations, 9
Ataque de nervios, 173
Attitudes of employees, 28–29
Australia, 5, 8, 11, 25, 35, 37, 41–42,
        141–142, 150, 152, 154, 156, 178,
        185, 199, 205, 228, 230–232, 234,
        239, 263, 270–272
Autogenic training, 93
Avoidance as coping strategy, 115–116

B

Balance between, life, work, 29–30
Behavioral plasticity, 67–68
Behavioral symptom management, 115
Behaviors, cultural differences in, 36
Brazil, 2, 4, 6–8, 29, 31, 42, 146, 150, 152,
        176, 178, 224, 232, 234, 236, 239,
        270, 273
Breath, 94, 98
Buddhism, 111–113, 155, 160, 237
Burnout, 21, 61, 72, 75–77, 97, 105, 108, 117,
        144, 160, 237, 256
Business periodical reports, 143, 160–165

C

Canada, 5, 8–9, 23, 31, 37, 39, 41–42, 142,
        150, 152, 154, 199, 203, 206, 228,
        230–231, 234, 239, 263, 270,
        272, 274
Cardiovascular disease, 54–55, 77, 108
CCCS. *See* Cross Cultural Coping Scale
Challenge, 59, 62, 99, 107, 109, 226, 229,
        238, 254–255, 260
    life as, 69